MARGINALITY IN SPACE – PAST, PRESENT AND FUTURE

Marginality in Space – Past, Present and Future

Theoretical and methodological aspects of cultural, social and economic parameters of marginal and critical regions

Edited by
HEIKKI JUSSILA
University of Oulu, Finland
ROSER MAJORAL
Universitat de Barcelona, Spain
CHRIS C. MUTAMBIRWA
University of Zimbabwe, Zimbabwe

Routledge
Taylor & Francis Group
LONDON AND NEW YORK

First published 1999 by Ashgate Publishing

Reissued 2018 by Routledge
2 Park Square, Milton Park, Abingdon, Oxon OX14 4RN
711 Third Avenue, New York, NY 10017, USA

Routledge is an imprint of the Taylor & Francis Group, an informa business

A Library of Congress record exists under LC control number: 98074504

ISBN 13: 978-1-138-32544-9 (hbk)
ISBN 13: 978-1-138-32546-3 (pbk)
ISBN 13: 978-0-429-45038-9 (ebk)

Contents

PART TWO: CULTURAL AND SOCIOECONOMIC VIEWS

PART THREE: POLICIES FOR REGIONAL DEVELOPMENT

List of Figures

List of Tables

List of Contributors

AJAEGBU, HYACINTH, I.	PEDA Jos, Nigeria
ANDERSSON, LENNART	University of Karlstad, Karlstad, Sweden
ANDREOLI, MARIA	Università degli Studi di Pisa, Pisa, Italy
ARCHER, J. CLARK	University of Nebraska, Lincoln, Nebraska, USA
BARRIO DE VILLANUEVA, PATRICIA	Univesidad Nacional de Cuyo, Mendoza, Argentina
BERG, VAN DEN, LEO M.	Staring Centrum, Wageningen, The Netherlands
CAPELLA-MITERNIQUE, HUGO	Universitat de Barcelona, Barcelona, Spain
COLPAERT, ALFRED	University of Oulu, Oulu, Finland
DAHL, JOHAN	University of Gothenburg, Gothenburg, Sweden
DELGADO CRAVIDÃO, FERNANDA	University of Coimbra, Coimbra, Portugal
FERNANDES, JOÃO LUÍS	University of Coimbra, Coimbra, Portugal
FONT-GAROLERA JAUME	Universitat de Barcelona, Barcelona , Spain
FURLANI DE CIVIT, MARIA ESTELA	Univeridad Nacional de Cuyo, Mendoza, Argentina
GROSSMAN, DAVID	Bar-Ilan University, Ramat-Gan, Israel,
GUTIÉRREZ DE MANCHON, JOSEFINA	Univeridad Nacional de Cuyo, Mendoza, Argentina
JUSSILA, HEIKKI	University of Oulu, Oulu, Finland
LEJONHUD, KRISTINA	University of Karlstad, Karlstad, Sweden
LONSDALE, RICHARD E.	University of Nebraska, Lincoln, Nebraska, USA
LUNDBERG, BERTIL	University of Karlstad, Karlstad, Sweden
MAJORAL, ROSER	University of Barcelona, Barcelona, Spain
MEHRETU, ASSEFA	Michigan State University, East Lansing, Michigan, USA
MEIR, AVINOAM	Negev Center, Israel

MUILU, TOIVO	University of Oulu, Oulu, Finland
MUTAMBIRWA, CHRIS, C.	University of Zimbabwe, Harare, Zimbabwe
NAUKKARINEN, ARVO	University of Oulu, Oulu, Finland
PELC, STANKO	University of Ljubljana, Slovenia
PERSSON, LARS OLOF	Royal Technical Institute, Stockholm, Sweden
PETAGNA DE DEL RIO, ANA MARIA	Universidad Nacional del Sur, Bahia Blanca, Argentina
PIGOZZI, BRUCE WM.	Michigan State University East Lansing, Michigan, USA
POTTS, DEBORAH	Geography Department, School of Oriental and African Studies, London, U.K.
RUSANEN, JARMO	University of Oulu, Oulu, Finland
SÁNCHEZ-AGUILERA, DOLORES	University of Barcelona, Barcelona, Spain
SCOTT, PETER	University of Tasmania, Hobart, Tasmania, Australia
SOMMERS, LAWRENCE M.	Michigan State University, East Lansing, Michigan, USA
TEVERA, DANIEL	University of Zimbabwe, Harare, Zimbabwe
TYKKYLÄINEN, MARKKU	Academy of Finland at the University of Joensuu, Joensuu, Finland
ZANAMWE, LAZARUS	University of Zimbabwe, Harare, Zimbabwe

Preface

This book discusses the role that marginality has had, has today and is going to have in the future. The Commission on Dynamics of Marginal and Critical Regions held its annual conference in Harare, Zimbabwe in July 1997. During that conference a series of papers were presented and this volume includes those that have been chosen after rewriting and reviewing.

The different articles of this volume reflect the various aspects of marginality currently existing in the world. It is the intention of the Commission to pursue research that would eventually result into a more coherent approach towards the issue of marginality in space.

The articles in this volume are grouped under three main parts. The first part discusses the role of theory and also methodological aspects and approaches towards the question of marginality. The second part gives a 'time-space' perspective by examining the past, present and future aspects of marginality. The third part is dedicated to chapters giving empirical evidence about the changes in existing marginality and its possible future implementations.

The conclusions of the book aim to summarize the various, and sometimes conflicting aspects, of marginality and its 'images' both in space and in time.

Pisa, Barcelona and Harare

Heikki Jussila, Roser Majoral and Chris C. Mutambirwa

1 Introduction

HEIKKI JUSSILA AND ROSER MAJORAL

At the beginning of July 1997 a meeting on Past Present and Future Cultural, Social and Economic Parameters of Marginal and Critical Regions was held in Harare, Zimbabwe. This was the first meeting of the IGU Commission on Dynamics of Marginal and Critical Regions, created during the IGU General Assembly held in The Hague, August 1996, on the occasion of the 28th International Geographical Congress.

This Commission was preceded by a Study Group on Development Issues of Marginal Regions that worked during the period of 1992-1996 and held five meetings (Taiwan 1993; Cesky Krumlov, Czech Republic 1994; Delhi 1994, India; Mendoza, Argentina and Santiago de Chile 1995 and Glasgow 1996). During the congress in The Hague, the Study Group had special work sessions that synthesized the work done during the period 1992-1996. A summary of the research done was presented at the special State of the Art session. Papers presented in the different annual meetings of the Study Group were published as proceeding by the local organizers. The papers presented in The Hague constitute the first volume of the 'Spatial Aspects of Marginality' -series.

In the course of the work accomplished by the IGU Study Group, it became evident that marginal regions are a multi-faceted and dynamic phenomenon. Although regional policy efforts have been undertaken in many countries, their effects seem to be offset by the current processes of globalization and deregulation. Behind marginal regions stands the concept of marginality, a term which has to be recognised as relative, depending in its manifestation on the scale used. Being a normative concept, it has a subjective touch, i.e., marginality and marginal regions have to be defined specifically. On the other hand, it is not static but highly dynamic: regions may in turn become more or less marginal, depending on the socio-economic and socio-cultural processes at work.

The Commission wants to enhance and develop its former work by more closely focusing in particularly important theme, i.e., the regional implications of globalization and deregulation on regions that are economically marginal and environmentally critical. In this way, it could focus on marginal regions (defined as socio-economically disadvantaged) and on critical regions (defined as regions suffering from lack of resources or potential of survival). The question of environment and sustainability are naturally included.

The focus of the Commission stems from the following considerations:

- Increasingly, economic power is concentrated in the 'hands' of Trans-National Corporations which use the possibilities and the freedom offered by liberalized world political system to enlarge their power and spheres of influence. Decisions on locations are taken according to telecommunication and the possibilities offered by deregulation.
- The public sector is faced with growing demand for deregulation, i.e., of opening up services to competition (public transport, communications, health services) as well as dismantling state protection of particular sectors of national economies. This entails increasing privatization in the service sector, based on the economic cost-benefit logic: profitable services are of interest to investors and have to be privatised, others are not, hence they can be neglected or left to the public domain. In other economic sectors, increased competition will force certain businesses out of operation, thereby increasing unemployment and 'burden' the taxpayer. Current budget deficits and bureaucratic inefficiency are at the base of this tendency. Disadvantaged regions will find themselves with less public support, and consequently their marginal position will increase.
- The privatization process is profit-oriented; regions with less financial potential will be or less interest, hence they will fall behind (negative feedback), thereby questioning the efforts of regional policies. Consequently, the society is becoming even more segmented; deregulation will lead to an increase in regional disparities.
- Regions, which face critical environmental conditions, need to receive special attention. By critical conditions, we mean that those regions are exposed to specific conditions for food production, or they may live together with particular natural and/or man-made hazards.

Severe problems arise out of these processes. Firstly, globalization puts current economic and political structures to a severe test because of the close interrelations between economic and political actors. Its worldwide and relatively short-term outlook is diametrically opposed to the objectives of long-term development policy and efforts to reduce disparities. Secondly, deregulation menaces the equilibrium relations between state, economy and population; who is competent for which kind of service; who formulates demands; who can afford which kind and which level of service; how can certain sectors of the economy survive if no public support is available.

We also believe that global change and the ongoing processes of globalization and deregulation will lead to regional disparities and thus increase the significance of marginalization. Because of this, it is important to further the understanding of the spatial character of marginality and the spatial dynamics of marginalization and critical region development process. From our experience, we believe that the programme for the 1996-2000 period constitutes a solid extension of what has been achieved so far.

The research focus of the Commission during the current period is for this reason dealing with the dynamics of marginality and the specific problems connected to it. The following themes are explored: a) Past, Present and future: cultural, social and economic parameters of marginal and critical regions; b) The consequences of globalization and deregulation on marginal and critical region economic systems; c) Sustainability issues and ecological consequences of globalization and deregulation policies in marginal and critical regions and d) Policies and strategies in marginal and critical regions: summary evaluations.

The first of the themes was worked out in Harare (Zimbabwe) and the contributions are published in the present volume. The other themes will be elaborated in the following three meetings that are going to be held in Coimbra (Portugal), August 1998, in Albuquerque (New Mexico), July 1999 and in Korea, August 2000. The final evaluation of the four year period will be during the 29th International Geographical Congress to be held in Seoul, Korea, August 2000.

The meeting in Harare is the first that the group of people that has been carrying research first on Highlands and later on Marginal Regions, has held in the African Continent. This gap in the spatial sphere of the Commission's research was filled out: with thanks to the generosity and effort made by the colleagues at the Department of Geography at the University of Zimbabwe lead by Professor Chris Mutambirwa.

Part one

Theoretical and methodological approaches

2 Towards typologies of socio-economic marginality: North/South comparisons

LAWRENCE M. SOMMERS, ASSEFA MEHRETU AND BRUCE WM. PIGOZZI

Introduction

Socio-economic marginality is a condition of socio-spatial structure and process in which components of society and space in a territorial unit are observed to lag behind an expected level of performance in economic, political and social well being compared with the average condition in the territory as a whole. Generally, distressed communities and spaces are revealed where there is a convergence of economic, political, and social marginality. The purpose of this paper is to discuss the fundamental differences between processes and forms of marginality found in the more developed countries (MDCs) of the North and the less developed countries (LDCs) of the South. The first general North/South difference lies in development process (Figures 2.1 and 2.2). This has to do with the relative significance in North and South economies of competitive forces of modernization and hegemonic forces of centre-periphery in the overall allocation of investment that ultimately determines the spatial organization of development. Generally, in North countries, free market forces play larger roles whereas in South economies, especially those with colonial histories, hegemonic (extramarket) forces are more dominant. This North/South contrast has its roots in the sources of decision-making for the modernization of economies. In the North, decisions for mobilization and allocation of scarce resources for development are largely the result of endogenous market systems. Decision-making in the North arises from the population that is ultimately the beneficiary of the development process. Most of the outputs of the economy are also consumed within a given country. In the South, modernizing forces have always been primarily exogenous in which resource mobilization and allocation have been largely determined by rationales external to local needs. These often led to enclave development

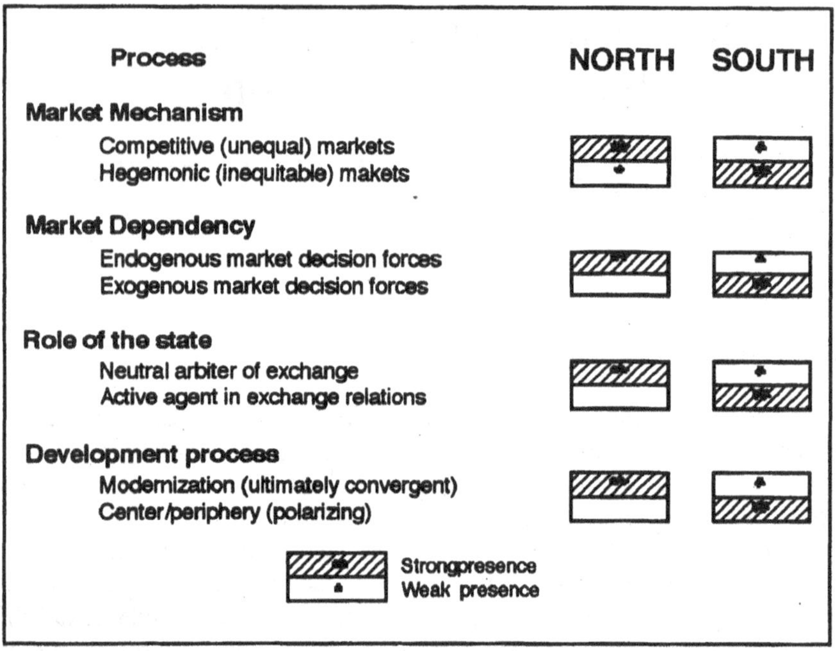

Figure 2.1 Dichotomies of process

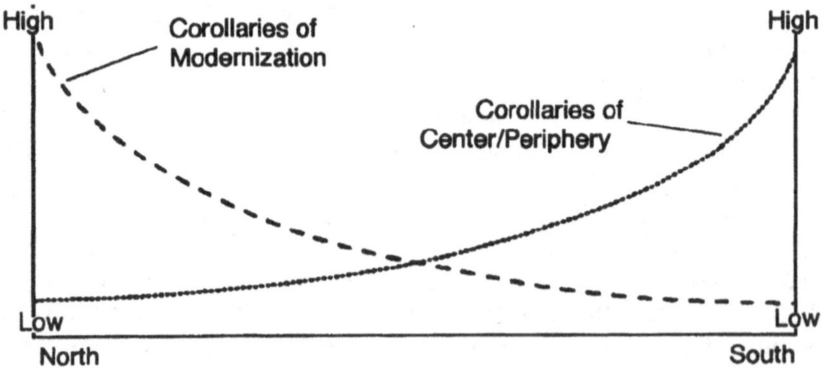

Figure 2.2 North/South variations in magnitudes of presence of corollaries of modernization and centre periphery process

of selected primary resources whose output was almost entirely destined for consumption overseas (Sommers and Mehretu 1992).

Another differentiating factor in North/South process of development is the role of the state government in the triangulation between itself, labour and private enterprise (capital). In the North, the state government, which is generally democratic, is expected to play a more neutral role between capital (private enterprise) and labour by enforcing regulatory provisions for free engagement in the market place. The resulting development process in the North is primarily competitive efficiency within a modernization process which will produce unequal but equitable distribution of development benefits in society and space. In the South, the state government, whose character ranges from pseudo-democratic, to benevolent dictatorship, to totalitarian kleptocracy, generally plays a biased and coercive role with strategic collusion with capital (mostly external) to exploit native labour to 'mine' selected primary resources for export (Ayoade 1988; Callaghy 1988; Mehretu and Sommers 1990). Thus, the development process is primarily dualistic with centre-periphery (urban-rural) polarization of development resulting from hegemonic efficiency with implications for unequal and inequitable distribution of development benefits. The development outcome in the South however may vary from the impressive progress recorded by Southeast Asian Tigers to the poor performance of the Sub-Saharan African nations, the difference lying not so much in the basic nature of the development process or natural resource endowments but in the strategic and catalytic role the state plays throughout Southeast Asia (Kristof 1997).

The second general North/South difference lies in the spatial impress (form or structure) of development and its inertial effect over time (Figure 2.3). In the North, the spatial impress is qualitatively integrated and diffusionist with distance-decay profiles in quantitative magnitudes of development, whereas in the South, the spatial impress is qualitatively dualistic and unintegrated with discontinuities in distance-decay profiles of quantitative magnitudes of development (Figure 2.4). The 'pawl-effect' of the spatial impress in the North is relatively weak, progressive, and allows the propagation of development waves to reach peripheries through spread-effect mechanisms which facilitate the free flow of factors of production between growing and lagging regions (Myrdal 1957; Hirschman 1958). That is, the increments to infrastructure and fixed capital are more flexible in the North where large, open economies are more self-adjusting, incorporating a multiplicity of directions. The pawl-effect in the South is relatively strong and polarizing. Hegemonic forces exacerbate both the qualitative and quantitative dualities between the development centre and the under-developed periphery (Dos Santos 1970; Mabogunge 1981; Riddell 1985).

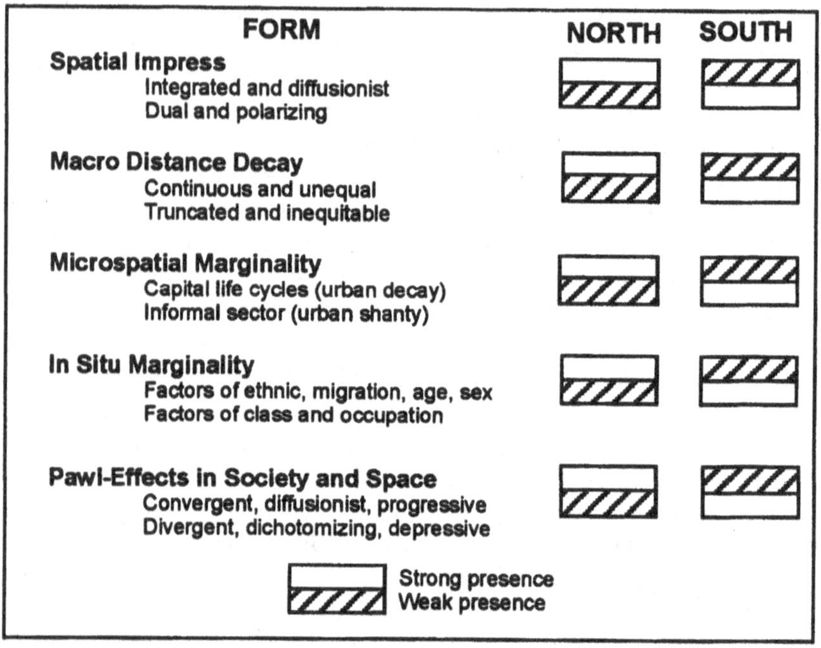

Figure 2.3 Dichotomies of form

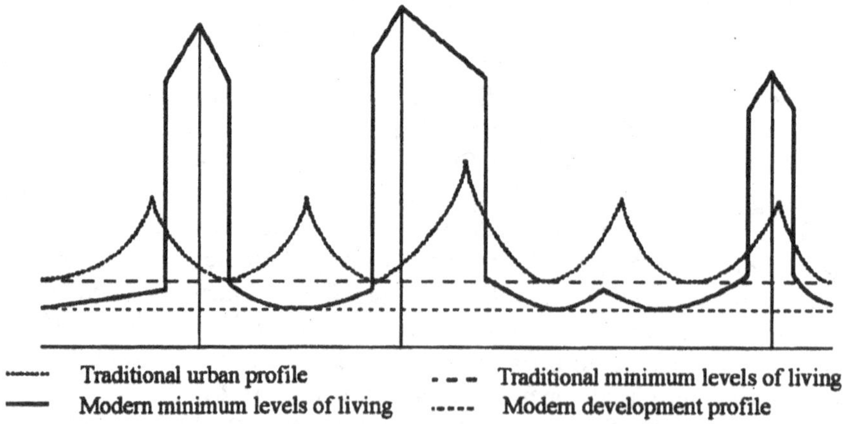

Figure 2.4 Spatial profile of development in the South

The pawl-effect in the South results from the domination of colonial and neo-colonial fixed capital in the trajectory of economies; indeed this domination is so daunting that increments to the fixed capital stock invariably reinforce the colonial and neo-colonial trajectories. This is one of the structural problems of South economies such as those in Sub-Saharan countries that have experienced colonial space organization whose pawl-effect has proved to be enduring and difficult to reorganize (see Mehretu 1989, pp. 33-35, 104-106.).

Uneven development and marginality

Uneven development, which may or may not lead to marginality, is influenced and moulded over time by a variety of physical, historical, cultural, economic, political, and social factors. This evolutionary process of uneven development in any region is the result of the totality of input by ethnic, social, political and cultural groups, as well as by individuals, as influenced by past and present, private and public policy decision-makers, and other important spokespersons. The input maybe in the form of laws, policies and guidelines or the impact of past and present cultural practices, traditions, publications and ideas.

Studies of uneven development by geographers and planners, beginning in the 1930s, were motivated by dramatic economic disequilibria that followed the Great Depression, the Second World War, and the 'Winds of Change' movements for Third World liberation. Each of these momentous changes resulted in significant social and spatial dislocation of communities which were then referred to as 'problem regions' (Friedmann and Weaver 1980, pp. 89-94; Scott and Storper 1992, pp. 3-5). The relative magnitudes of these problems varied by regions. In the North, for many years, they were considered 'temporary and self-correcting aberrations' to the general post-war dynamic of strong growth. It was assumed that communities and territories would fall in or out of favour depending on the impact of lead-lag cycles of economic opportunity and productive factor movements (Scott and Storper 1992, p. 4). For this reason, such regions were often referred to as 'depressed' or 'distressed' and were presumed to be correctable by redistributive interventions (Claval 1983, pp. 118-123). In the case of the South, the regional problems were the result of the core-periphery mechanism of development that continued to prevail after independence and marginalized most of the post-colonial countries to poverty and isolation (Friedmann 1988; Riddell 1985). Relics of grand events like those mentioned above still exist but currently the sources of unequal development and regional disparity in both North and South countries have become more complex and multidimensional.

Structural determinants of marginality: North/South variations

The nature of marginality that pertains to a specific community or territory will depend on the political and economic structure in which it is found. Although it is almost impossible to clearly distinguish between the structural determinants of marginality, it may help to visualize the range of problems of two extremes of structure and agency under which marginality occurs in both North and South economies. As indicated earlier, at one extreme, there is contingent marginality whose occurrence is attributed to the occasional anomalies of the neo-classical economic framework operating in free markets and political democracies in North countries. At the other extreme, there is systemic marginality which naturally flows from controlled political and economic frameworks with radical, pseudo-radical and totalitarian origins which do not allow self-determination and the operation of free markets which is generally the case in South countries (see Figures 2.1 and 2.2.). Marginality within neo-classical variants is contingent as it results from competitive dynamics, which have outcomes that maybe unequal for some communities and regions. Contingent marginality resulting from competitive inequality is considered to be endogenous to the neo-classical framework and is often addressed as 'accidental' or as a 'temporary and self-correcting aberration' of an otherwise equitable framework. It is also assumed that such 'aberrations' are expected to be corrected by the 'self-adjusting' free market dynamics of Northern economies. However, contingent margins in the North due to competitive inequality may in fact persist. The neo-classical framework does not recognize the critical roles that structure and agency play in movement of factors of production and access to opportunities, this framework is incapable of resolving marginality in its social or locational forms. Urban and rural poverty in Northern countries may be attributed to some extent to contingent marginality but it would be quite difficult to isolate the contingent from the systemic as most marginal communities and territories manifest the effects of both competitive inequality and hegemonic inequity in both political and economic benefits (Figures 2.1, 2.2, and 2.3) (Marcuse 1996, pp. 176-216; Wacquant 1996, pp. 234-274; Kuttner 1997).

Systemic marginality occurs within controlled political and economic frameworks with hegemonic dynamics that produce inequities in the distribution of socio-economic benefits and rewards. Systemic marginality resulting from hegemonic inequity is normally exogenously determined. Unlike the neo-classical framework, there is no pretence of a self-correcting mechanism internal to the system to resolve uneven development. In this case marginality is a deliberate construction of an exogenous system which intends to achieve specific desirable outcomes of political control (as in a pseudo-radical regime) or economic exploitation (as in the post-colonial state) (Palmer 1977; Blaut 1993). This is perhaps the most important source of socio-economic marginality in South countries not only because of the pervasive post-colonial mismanagement and corruption associated with pseudo-radical and totalitarian regimes in these countries but also because of the lagged effects of colonial structures that are amplified by acquiescing indigenous elite whose hegemony depends on lucrative compacts with foreign interests, see (Figures 1, 2, 3, and 4) (Rothchild and Chazan 1988; Young 1988).

Vulnerability factors to marginality

Marginality victimizes locations and communities that are characterized by one or more factors of vulnerability (Marcuse 1996, pp. 204-211). Perhaps the best known of such factors is poor relative location and deficient natural resources (Claval 1983; Wiberg 1994). Communities that are characterized by such locations and ecologies have been vulnerable to marginality. Aridity, rugged terrain, a short or non-existent growing season or terrain with swamps and similar ecological liabilities combined with relative remoteness from core areas of development have played critical roles in marginalizing certain regions. Some of the most impoverished areas in the world manifest these vulnerabilities. Post-war concerns on unequal development were concentrated on such North regions as the US Appalachia, Southern Italy, and Northern Scandinavia (Clout 1975; Garofoli 1991). There were similar concerns in South countries especially in post-colonial times. But they had less to do with spontaneous settlements that happened to be in marginal areas as in North countries, but had more to do with deliberate relocation of colonized peoples to remotely situated marginal lands in order to appropriate better resources and locations for colonial enclave settlements (Witthuhn 1976; Palmer 1977; Mandaza 1986).

While locational and ecological factors continue to be important in both North and South countries, an array of social factors are emerging as even more crucial factors to make communities and places even more vulnerable to marginality. With increased freedom of movement and development in transportation, communication and other technologies, physical factors of vulnerability have become less victimizing when compared to social factors of vulnerability. Social factors of vulnerability to marginality include historical background, ethno-cultural characteristics, minority status, immigration status, age, gender, and educational status. Some of the social factors of vulnerability such as ethnicity and immigration status are of particular importance to marginality (Harris 1995, pp. 21-55; Gans 1996).

In the North, as in the case of the American South, the deleterious effects of the history of slavery continue to marginalize a major segment of the rural and urban populations. Historical factors of vulnerability to marginality may victimize minority populations at a much higher rate than they do majority populations. However, especially in places where such histories are strong, majority populations are often captured by the same marginalizing phenomena that continue to have adverse effects on the whole region. Conditions in poorer southern states in the US are good examples. In South countries, historical inertia in discriminatory policies of colonial governments and settler regimes, as experienced by countries such as Kenya, Zimbabwe and South Africa, continue to polarize populations along ethnic lines because of the pawl-effect of lagged structures that create inequities in socio-economic opportunities and life chances (Palmer 1977; Mandaza 1986).

Currently, ethnicity and culture are important vulnerability factors leading to marginality. In the North, such marginalities range from the self-selected benign forms of marginality as that shown by the Amish communities in Pennsylvania to the hegemonic 'outcast ghettoes' of New York City, Chicago, Detroit and Los Angeles (Marcuse 1996, pp. 178-188; Tosi 1996; Wacquant 1996). The 'outcast ghetto' is a peculiar form of marginality that is characteristic of large metropolitan centres in the United States. The term derives from the 'unwanted' and 'excluded' nature of the 'underclass' isolated in the ghetto in which, it is claimed, the 'culture of poverty' dominates (Knox 1994, pp. 302-320). Most recently, this has also been aggravated by homelessness in major cities in Europe as well as North America. Homelessness, whether created within the ghetto or elsewhere, adds to the overall malaise of the urban poor (Tosi 1996, pp. 104). The ethnic factor in vulnerability to marginality varies from region to region. In North America, it primarily involves the African American population, although in some localities Hispanics, Asians and Native Americans also experience the same vulnerability (Darden 1989). In Europe, ethno-cultural vulnerability depends on where you are. It affects the gypsies all over Europe, Turks in Germany, North Africans in France and Italy, the Sami (Lapps) in northern Scandinavia, and Sub-Saharan Africans and Caribbeans in the UK. Europe does not have the pronounced coincidence of social and spatial marginalization as in the outcast ghettoes of North America. In Europe, the phenomenon of 'outcast' or 'underclass' population is most commonly a social construct without the clearly demarcated territorial designation that is found in North America.

In South countries, the ethno-cultural factor operates in two ways. The first is based on polarities that exist between vestiges of colonial foreign settlement domains and those of the indigenous populations. Although most of the tyranny of minority regimes has come to an end with the demise of apartheid in South Africa, traditional hegemonies with co-opted indigenous elite continue to operate in many South countries by virtue of structural pawl-effects that have proved unyielding to post-independence development policies (Kitching 1980; Riddell 1985; Chazan 1988; Callaghy 1988). The second ethno-cultural factor is based on internal cleavages along ethnic lines sometimes exacerbated by religion. In some African and South Asian countries, ethnic differences, that were used as means to divide and rule by colonial regimes and that remained dormant after the independence euphoria, have now resurfaced along with complaints of inequities and are challenging governments for political redress and territorial concessions. Attempts at resolving such issues with moves for independence by Western Sahara and Eritrea may have been thought of as positive developments by many but old ethnic animosities still simmer in the respective regions. Ethnic polarities with deadly conflicts continue in the Sudan between northern Arab Moslems and southern Christians and animists. The same is true between the Hutu and Tutsi in central Africa. The balkanization of Somalia along clan lines is of the same genre of ethnic polarization. Basic to all of these cleavages are inequities in political power and economic opportunities that have ethnic underpinnings.

Somewhat related to the ethno-cultural factor of vulnerability is immigration status. In North countries, with the exception of the outcast ghetto in the North America, which is dominated by African Americans, immigration status more often goes hand-in-hand with the ethno-cultural factor in most other countries. Immigration status is perhaps one of the most insidious factors of vulnerability for marginalization and exploitation worldwide. Immigrants, legally or undocumented, who arrive mostly to seek low-wage employment, face a variety of discriminatory pressures. As they have little political and legal recourse, they become scapegoats and are susceptible to stereotyping, random treatment, exploitation and even violence with impunity. Recent successes in anti-immigrant legislation in

France and California have exposed immigrant communities to political and economic marginalization leaving them helpless and without mitigation (Harris 1995, 186-214). In the South, immigrants are of three types. The first are from rich countries some of who are remnants from the colonial times. They often carry with them finance or human capital and are rarely vulnerable to marginality. On the contrary, they make compacts with local power elite and wield tremendous power over local affairs. The second group consists of historical migrants from poorer nations such as Indians in East Africa. The third are migrants or refugees, usually from neighbouring countries. The second and third type may fall victims to exploitation and political marginalization as experienced by Indians in Uganda decades ago and presently by Hutus in the Republic of Congo (Zaire).

Age and gender are other important factors for vulnerability to marginalization. In northern countries, households with many children and those headed by females have a higher likelihood to be marginalized. According to a recent study by the Population Reference Bureau (PRB 1996), in the United States, 50 % of the people below poverty income are not in the working ages; 40 % are under age 18, and 10 percent are over age 65. It is also observed that poverty rates of families rise with number of children in the family. Over 53 % of families with five or more children under 18 are in poverty. Gender-inequity is another persistent problem that affects employment and income potentials. Female-headed households are especially vulnerable to marginality. In the United States, the highest percent of households below poverty is for single mothers with children (see also Massey 1994, pp. 175-248; McDowell 1995; Christopherson 1995; PRB 1996, p. 18). In the South, the role of age and gender in marginality is somewhat different. The elderly are more respected and protected by the extended family and the community. Nevertheless, in times of economic and political stress, the old and the very young are the first to suffer especially in food distribution. In the South, the most severe form of marginality is that experienced by women and their young children. Women not only receive less food than men but they eat foods that have less nutritional value (Leghorn and Parker 1981; World Bank 1990). Women also bear more than their share of work burdens in farming and home-making. They also spend a significant amount of their time and energy in performing routine activities such as fetching water, gathering firewood and doing the laundry all of which require head or back-loaded weights which have to be carried over long trips by foot (White, *et al.* 1972; Mehretu and Mutambirwa 1992).

More recently, vulnerabilities caused by structural changes in post-fordist economies are becoming increasingly important in unequal development and marginality in both North and South countries. In the North, the development of foot-loose manufacturing with patterns of flexible production and accumulation has made significant changes in the human capital requirements for industrial location. A shift in industrial employment is taking place with adverse consequences to old industrial regions in advanced economies. Contemporaneous with fragmentation of manufacturing is the increasing segmentation of labour within a process sometimes referred to as 'dualization' and 'bipolarization' (Castells 1993, pp. 172-228). A bipolar occupational structure would favour professionals, engineers, and those that can be absorbed by high-technology-based industries. At the same time, those who continue to depend on low-skilled manufacturing jobs become vulnerable to downsizing and reduced rewards from employment. In North America, such bipolarization also has clear ethnic and gender implications in which majority males are favoured by the transformation whereas minorities and women become more vulnerable to marginality (see Benko and Dunford 1991, pp. 3-23; Castells 1993, p. 179-184). In South countries, industrial structural changes follow the dictates of centre-periphery relations in which transnational investments in the South search for the cheapest, most productive and least organized (and less politically conscious) labour pools often dominated by young women (Galtung 1971; Barnet and Muller 1971).

Spatial manifestation

The territorial or regional scale that marginality takes depends on factors of vulnerability to marginality. Three spatial scales of marginality can be abstracted. At the high end of the scale is macrospatial marginality. Macrospatial marginality applies to regional disparities in levels of living between communities in central (core) locations of economic activity and those which manifest vulnerabilities because of their peripheral and remote locations and/or areas with poor natural resources (Friedmann and Weaver 1980, pp. 140-143; Massey 1994, pp. 50-66; Mehretu and Sommers 1994). Macrospatial marginality can be a product of market forces that produce competitive inequality in which the vulnerability factor is locational or physical limitations. Since competitive inequality is a free-market characteristic, the marginality is assumed to be, at least theoretically, contingent and ultimately convergent. However, marginal regions like the Mezzogiorno of Italy and the Upper Peninsula of Michigan, do not lend themselves to convergent resolutions and would require much more than what the market mechanism can offer. An even more serious case of marginality at the macro-scale is that produced by hegemonic inequity in which locational and ecological vulnerabilities are systemically constructed and hegemonically maintained in the national space. Such macrospatial margins are intentional gerrymanders in space to either appropriate land and resource assets and/or contain communities within exclusionary zones as 'tribal' reserves or labour camps. This was the case for 'Tribal Trust Lands' in colonial Zimbabwe and 'Bantustans' in South Africa. Macrospatial margins also apply to all cases in which indigenous populations have been restricted to designated 'native reserves' for the sake of political, social and economic advantages that accrue to exogenous hegemonic agencies.

The second spatial scale of marginality is termed microspatial marginality. Microspatial margins are distressed localities within relatively small territories such as the built-up areas of cities and metropolitan regions. Microspatial margins are mostly the result of social vulnerabilities that are often aggravated by hegemonies associated with the dominant political and cultural order. Although vulnerability factors such as history, age and gender are important in microspatial margins, the most visible forms are those based on ethno-cultural distinctions, migration status and economic bipolarization, the last of which may be associated with cyclical forces within an economy. These cyclical forces may be related to the evolution of individual firms at the micro level (Burns 1934) or evolution of entire industrial sectors at the regional scale (Kondratiev 1935, Mensch 1979). Thus, within North countries, capital is 'fixed' for only a given duration and capital reinvestments often involve locational adjustments (see Figures 2.3 and 2.4).

In Europe and North America, microspatial margins are usually located in the centres of major metropolitan areas and are often blamed on endogenous factors that have created a 'culture of poverty'. It is also recognized that there are exogenous forces that include 'social gatekeeper' agencies that manipulate historical, cultural and ethnic stereotypes to derive windfall financial rewards in real estate and housing markets. Microspatial margins exist in those areas in which there is a convergence of many of the stereotyped vulnerability factors. In some North American cases of microspatial margins, factors of vulnerability, such as ethnicity, play the role of an 'anchor' with which other vulnerability factors join and link to produce some of the worst cases of microspatial margins. This is the case with the 'outcast ghetto' which is a hegemonically contained and highly impoverished area in the central part of major post-fordist cities

(Darden 1989; Knox 1993, pp. 27-29; Cadwallader 1996, pp. 366-368; Marcuse 1996, pp. 176-216; Wacquant 1996).

In South countries, microspatial margins in urban and other more developed spaces have two manifestations (Figure 2.4). The first is the case of less Europeanized metropolitan areas which contain developed spaces with both modern and traditional sectors, the latter relegated to the extremely poor, living in substandard or shanty dwellings, often with rudimentary to non-existent urban amenities. A whole array of informal activities and cheap labour are produced by this sector and the resulting community sometimes looks like the extension of the countryside. The second case of micromarginality in South countries is manifested by colonial cities whose access to African urban residents was strictly controlled. The normal pattern was to have segregated urban domains with Africans relegated to their 'native township' margins, often in detached zones outside the city proper (Mehretu 1989; Sommer 1976). In this case, marginality is not only economic but also social, political and cultural.

The third spatial typology is termed in situ marginality. This refers to unequal development within very small geographic units like census tracts or city blocks in which poor and marginalized households and prosperous households share neighbourhoods. In North countries, in situ margins are a consequence of many factors of vulnerability. However, most important are ethnicity, immigration status and labour segmentation. The intersection of vulnerability factors for in situ marginality can be very complex. But here again, their outside manifestation may be dominated by an 'anchor' factor like ethnicity or immigration status. Disparities in levels of living within in situ marginal areas can be very high. In many cases, well-to-do households may be residual from better days in a neighbourhood in which residents have maintained the quality of their housing stock either by choice or subject to hegemonic containment. In situ margins may also be due to developments of enclaves of better neighbourhoods within blighted inner cities often influenced by area-based urban renewal programs and/or gentrification (see Figure 2.3) (Hayter and Barnes 1992; Knox 1994, pp. 258-261; Cadwallader 1996, pp. 367-366; Sommers, Pigozzi and Mehretu 1996).

In South countries, in situ margins are generally a function of class and occupational segmentation of the urban population. Urban residents who are in the socio-economic margin are those who carry out informal functions such as domestic servants, porters, guards, street peddlers, wage labourers and other members of the lumpen population. These people often reside not too far from the home and work places of their more prosperous counterparts and sometimes within the same compound as in the case of 'servants quarters' (see Figure 2.3).

Conclusion

This paper has focused on the fundamental differences in process and form of sociospatial marginality in North and South countries. The aim is to indicate not only the complex nature and source of marginality in North and South countries but their differential impacts in society and space. An attempt has been made to abstract the principal features of marginality in North and South countries and indicate the factors that dictate social and spatial vulnerabilities that result in marginality. The role of market (competitive) and non-market (hegemonic) forces and their relative significance in North and South has been dealt with. It has been demonstrated that the process of development often produces both inequality and inequity in society and space. Whether the distribution of development benefits is equitable or inequitable is dependent on the framework of the development process and the relative magnitudes of competitive and hegemonic forces found in the economy.

Generally, in North economies, unequal development may or may not lead to marginality. If inequalities are pure functions of competitive markets and free from extra-market pressures on the disadvantaged people in the system, marginality is not expected to occur because the dynamics of convergence and spread-effects are expected to kick in and forestall temporary inequalities from becoming permanent. However, in reality they do occur as in many instances the market fails to prevent contingent marginalities from degenerating into systemic marginalities. When this happens, it is hard to distinguish between marginalities that result from competitive inequalities and those that are produced by hegemonic inequities. It is often the case, though, that when unequal development, due initially to competitive weaknesses that victimizes the same communities and spaces over a long period of time, hegemonies often creep in and take advantage of class divisions and other vulnerabilities that have been engendered.

In South economies, inequitable relations are established from the outset because of the structure of the economy and the role of the state in the allocation of development resources. In such cases, marginality in space and society is dichotomous and polarizing. Under hegemony, the best case scenario is a benevolent dictatorship in which extreme cases of poverty and exploitation may be prevented by paternal leadership styles. East and South-east Asian systems like in Korea, Taiwan, Singapore, Malaysia and

Sri Lanka are examples of such hegemonies. The worst case scenarios are apartheid-like regimes and variations of kleptocracies.

With increasing globalization and international competition for trade and development, both physical and social vulnerabilities will usually increase. In less developed countries, physical vulnerabilities are more likely to dominate the process of marginality because of political instabilities, population growth, increased density on cultivated lands, degradation of land resources, poor technologies for agriculture and slow industrial growth. In most LDCs, the effect of physical factors will be aggravated by hegemonies that arise from non-democratic regimes, corrupt officials, dualistic economies, religious fundamentalism, ethno-linguistic tribalism, and sectarianism. In many African countries such as Algeria, the Sudan, Somalia, Ethiopia, Liberia, Republic of Congo (Zaire), Burundi and others, such factors have led to serious internal civil conflicts. In some countries, the instabilities have led to civil wars culminating in anarchy, large loss of life, and the break-up of the nation state.

In more developed countries, technology may lessen physical vulnerabilities to marginality. Here, the conventional social factors of vulnerability of ethnicity, age, gender and immigration status will continue to operate. Their effect on marginalized communities and places may in fact worsen as increased globalization leads to bipolarization and segmentation of the national work force. The role of transnational corporations and the evolving new international division of labour will adversely affect significant segments of the national majority populations. They will continue to experience increased vulnerability because of international competition and lack of education and skills needed to retain or attract post-fordist (flexible manufacturing) and neo-fordist (high-technology information age) industries. As unemployment and underemployment rates increase among the majority populations, political pressures are likely to increase on the central government. In some cases, as recently in France, it may also enable the far right political parties to become more visible and afford them platforms to blame, unfairly, already marginalized minority and immigrant communities.

In conclusion, there are significant North/South contrasts in process and form of development. Certain countries in both areas illustrate a transitory stage in the continuum between the two extremes of economic development (Figure 2.2). Central America and Eastern Europe in the North, and Northern Africa, Southern Africa and South-Asia in the South contain transitional countries. The significance of high levels of economic production in competitive markets in the North propelled by internal market forces, with the state playing an arbiter and monitoring role, contrasts with the low-level of industrial output dominated by primate cities in the South. Here external market forces are the major motivating force for the modern economic sector and the state to play an active role in ownership of factors of production, economic decisions and allocations of scarce factors.

Spatial process and form in development in the North is characterized by integrated economic space with free-market competitive macrospatial distance decay functions. This is in contrast to the South where regional developments occur within hegemonic markets that result in dualistic, discontinuous and polarized development. The comprehension of the nature of these contrasts in process and form of development is central to research and policy for development in both North and South countries.

References

Ayoade, J. A. (1988), 'States without Citizens: An Emerging African Phenomenon', in D. Rothchild and Chazan, D. (eds.), *The Precarious Balance: State and Society in Africa*, Westview Press: Boulder, CO, pp. 61-82.

Barnet, R. and Muller, R. (1975), *Global Reach*, Simon and Schuster: New York.

Benko, Georges and Mick Dunford (1991), 'Structural Change and the Spatial Organization of the Productive System: An Introduction', in Georges Benko, G. et al. (eds.), *Industrial Change and Regional Development*, Belhaven Press: London.

Blaut, J. M. (1993), *The Colonizer's Model of the World*, The Guilford Press: New York.

Burns, A. F. (1934), *Production Trends in the United States*, National Bureau of Economic Research: New York.

Cadwallader, Martin (1996), *Urban Geography: An Analytical Approach*, Prentice Hall: Upper Saddle River, NJ.

Callaghy, Thomas M. (1988), 'The State and Development of Capitalism in Africa: Theoretical, Historican and Comparative Reflections', in Rothchild, D. and Chazan, D. (eds.), *The Precarious Balance: State and Society in Africa*, Westview Press: Boulder, CO, pp. 67-99.

Castells, Manuel (1993), *The Information City*, Blackwell: Oxford.

Chazan, Naomi (1988), 'Patterns of State-Society Incorporation and Disengagement in Africa', in Rothchild, D. and Chazan, N. (eds.), *The Precarious Balance: State and Society in Africa*, Westview Press: Boulder, CO, pp. 121-148.

Christopherson, Susan (1995), 'Changing Women's Status in Global Economy', in Johnson, R. J. et al., (eds.), *Geographies of Global Change*, Blackwell: Oxford.

Claval, Paul (1983), *Opposition Planning in Wales and Appalachia*, Temple University Press: Philadelphia PA.

Clout, Hugh D. (1975), 'Regional Development in Western Europe', in Clout, H. D. (ed.), *Regional Development in Western Europe*, John Wiley and Sons: New York.

Darden, Joe (1989), 'Blacks and other Racial Minorities: The Significance of Color in Inequality', *Urban Geography*, Vol. 10.

Dos Santos, T. (1970), 'The Structure of Dependence', *American Economic Review*, 40 (2), pp. 231-236.

Friedmann, John (1988), *Life Space and Economic Space*, Transaction Books: New Brunswick, NJ.

Friedmann, John and Clyde Weaver (1980), *Territory and Function*, University of California Press: Berkeley, CA.

Galtung, J. (1971), 'A Structural Theory of Imperialism', *Journal of Peace Research*, 21.

Gans, Herbert J. (1996), 'From 'Underclass' to 'Undercaste': Some Observations about the Future of the Post-Industrial Economy and its Major Victims', in Mingione, Enzo, (ed.), *Urban Poverty and the Underclass: A Reader*, Blackwell Publishers: Oxford, UK.

Garofoli, Gioacchino (1991), 'The Italian Model of Spatial Development in the 1970s and 1980s', in Benko, George et al. (eds.), *Industrial Change and Regional Development*, Belhaven Press: London.

Harris, Nigel (1995), The New Untouchables: Immigration and the New World Worker, Penguin Books: London.

Hayter, R. and Barnes, T. J. (1992), 'Labour Market Segmentation, Flexibility, and Recession: A British Colombia Case Study', *Environment and Planning C: Government and Policy*, Vol. 10.

Hirschman, A. (1958), *The Strategy of Economic Development*, Yale University Press: New Haven, CT.

Kitching, Gavin (1980), Class and Economic Change in Kenya: The Making of an African Petite Bourgeoisie, Yale University Press: New Haven, CT.

Knox, Paul L. (1993), *The Restless Urban Landscape*, Prentice Hall: Englewood Cliffs, NJ.

Knox, Paul L. (1994), *Urbanization*, Prentice Hall: Englewood Cliffs, NJ.

Kondratiev, N. D. (1935). 'The Long Waves in Economic Life', *Review of Economic Statistics* 17:105-115.

Kristof, Nicholas D. (1997), 'Tiger Tales: Why Africa Can Thrive Like Asia', *The New York Times*, May 25.

Kuttner, Robert (1997), 'The Limits of Markets', *The American Prospect*, No. 31.

Leghorn, L. and Parker, K. (1981), *Women's Worth: Sexual Economics and the Third World Women*, Routledge and Kegan Paul: Boston.

Mabogunje, Akin L. (1981), *The Development Process: A Spatial Perspective*, Holmes & Meier Publishers, Inc: New York.

Mandaza, Ibo (1986), Zimbabwe: The Political Economy of Transition 1980-1986, CODESRIA: Dakar, Senegal.

Marcuse, Peter (1996), 'Space and Race in the Post-Fordist City: The Outcast Ghetto and Advanced Homelessness in the United States Today', in Mingione, Enzo, (ed.), *Urban Poverty and the Underclass: A Reader*, Blackwell Publishers: Oxford, UK.

Massey, Doreen (1994), *Space, Place and Gender*, University of Minnesota Press: Minneapolis, MN.

McDowell, Linda (1995), 'Understanding Diversity: The Problem of of/for Theory' in Johnson, R. J. et al. (eds.), *Geographies of Global Change*, Blackwell: Cambridge, MA.

Mehretu, Assefa (1989), *Regional Disparity in Sub-Saharan Africa*, Westview Press: Boulder, CO.

Mehretu, Assefa and Mutambirwa, Chris (1992), 'Gender Differences in Time and Energy Cost of Distance for Regular Domestic Chores in Rural Zimbabwe: A Case Study in the Chiduku Communal Area', *World Development*, 20(11), pp. 1675-1683.

Mehretu, Assefa and Sommers, Lawrence, M. (1990), 'Towards Modeling National Preference Formation for Regional Development Policy: Lessons from Developed and Less Developed Countries', *Growth and Change*, 20 (3), pp. 32-47.

Mehretu, Assefa and Sommers, Lawrence, M. (1994), 'Patterns of Macrogeographic and Microgeographic Marginality in Michigan', *The Great Lakes Geographer*, Vol. 1, No. 2.

Mensch, G. (1979), Stalemate in Technology: Innovations Overcome the Depression, Ballinger: Cambridge, MA.

Mydral, G. (1957), Economic Theory and Underdeveloped Regions, Duckworth: London.

Palmer, R. H. (1977), *Land Racial Discrimination in Rhodesia*, University of California Press: Berkeley, CA.

Population Reference Bureau (PRB) (1996), *Population Bulletin*, Vol. 51, No. 2.

Riddell, B. (1985), 'Urban Bias in Underdevelopment', *Tijdschrift Voor Econ. een Soc. Geographie*, 76 (5), pp. 374-383.

Rothchild, D. and Chazan, N., (eds.) (1988), *The Precarious Balance: State and Society in Africa*, Westview Press: Boulder, CO.

Scott, Allen J. and Storper, Michael (1992), 'Regional Development Reconsidered', in Ernste, Huib et al. (eds.), *Regional Development and Contemporary Industrial Response: Extending Flexible Specialization*, Belhaven Press: London.

Sommer, John W. (1976), 'The Internal Structure of African Cities', in Knight, C. Gregory and Newman, James L., *Contemporary Africa: Geography and Change*, Prentice-Hall: Englewood Cliffs, NJ, pp. 306-320.

Sommers, Lawrence M. and Mehretu, Assefa (1992), 'Trade Patterns and Trends in the African-European Trading Area: Lessons for Sub-Saharan African from the Era of the Lome Accords 1975-1988', *African Development*, 17(2), pp. 5-26.

Sommers, Lawrence M., Pigozzi, Bruce Wm. and Mehretu, Assefa (1996), '*Issues of Urban Marginality in Detroit, Michigan*', Paper read at IGU Study Group on Development Issues in Marginal Regions, Glasgow, Scotland. July.

Tosi, Antonio (1996), 'The Excluded and the Homeless: The Social Construction of the Fight Against Poverty in Europe', in Mingione, Enzo, (ed.), *Urban Poverty and the Underclass: A Reader*, Blackwell Publishers: Oxford, UK.

Wacquant, J. D. (1996), 'Red Belt, Black Belt: Racial Division, Class Inequality and the State in the French Urban Periphery and the American Ghetto', in Mingione, Enzo, (ed.), *Urban Poverty and the Underclass: A Reader*, Blackwell Publishers: Oxford, UK.

White, Gilbert F., Bradley, David J. and White, Anne (1972), *Drawers of Water: Domestic Water Use in East Africa*, University of Chicago Press: Chicago.

Wiberg, Ulf (1994), 'Swedish Marginal Regions and Public Sector Transformation', in Wiberg, Ulf, (ed.), *Marginal Areas in Developed Countries*, CERUM, Umeå University: Umeå.

Witthuhn, Burton O. (1976), 'The Impress of Colonialism', in Knight, C. Gregory and Newman, James L. (eds.), *Contemporary Africa: Geography and Change*, Prentice-Hall: Englewood Cliffs, NJ, pp. 30-38.

World Bank (1990), *World Development Report*, Oxford University Press: New York.

Young, C. (1988), 'The African Colonial State and its Political Legacy', in Rothchild, D. and Chazan, N., (eds.), *The Precarious Balance: State and Society in Africa*, Westview Press: Boulder, CO.

3 The application of spatial theory to intensive agriculture in developing countries: Findings from the Jos study

DAVID GROSSMAN, LEO M. VAN DEN BERG AND HYACINTH I. AJAEGBU

Introduction

This chapter intends to reflect on the application of theory to the findings of a study of market gardening that was conducted in the Jos area (of Nigeria) between 1993 and 1996. It focuses on some of the major findings and attempts to identify the inter-relationships between the fieldwork and geographical theory. The subject is both practical and of academic interest, i.e., the study should be evaluated on the basis of its contribution to academic knowledge, and not solely based on its immediate applicability.

The fact that our study deals with a developing area is academically important in itself, because most of the general theories and models are based on the dynamic patterns of the developed nations. Third world nations mostly have a different socio-economic and spatial structure, which requires different and specific models. The problems of inadequate infrastructure, land use patterns, and insufficient flow mechanism of information, or inadequately applied existing information, are subjects which geography is clearly concerned with. The application of the spatial models to the findings of our Jos-Bukuru study is presented in the second section of this paper.

This article focuses on a strictly geographical model, that of the impact of the spatial factor on the economic rent and other activities. There are, of course, non-spatially-based theories or models, which have direct bearing on the use of land, water, and other resources. They include some of the classical social, economic, and political models, which are of paramount significance to all social scientists, and belong to the framework of the presently fashionable 'political economy' school.

Space limitations do not allow us; however, to consider non-spatial models and the discussion will be devoted here to the spatial impact.

However, it must be recalled that the classical rent distance-decay models, such as that of von Thünen (Hall 1966), are based strictly on the principle of self-interest, i.e., on the profit motive of 'economic man'. They do not deviate, thus, from the spatial economic impacts. Von Thünen assumes no external regulations or interference with rational behaviour. We find it difficult to stick to this principle, because it precludes outside (e.g., government) interference. However, the original Thünen model is much more complex than the form presented in most textbooks. It considers forms of 'transportation costs', such as the monetary value of grains fed to the draft animals on the way to the market. His 'intensity model' takes into account the spatial pattern of input costs, which are probably the most important part of his theory which applies to developing societies (Hall 1966; Morgan 1973).

The intensity model is certainly not less important than the ring model, which applies solely to market economies. Most geographers tend to focus on the latter model, which applies to rural-urban spatial relationships in a commercial economy. One reason for this popularity is that in the intensity model 'costs' and benefits do not necessarily have a monetary value and are not easily quantifiable. They can be measured by time input, i.e., by 'buying leisure', or even by a benefit: treating farming as a recreational (hobby) activity. It is this flexibility, however, which makes the intensity model particularly suitable for the developing countries. Even so, our discussion, just as geographical research, still focuses mainly on the ring model.

The Thünen mathematical formula has never been challenged. Mathematics is universal. The basic logic of his assumptions (e.g., that space is isotropic etc.), are also unchallenged, although they are often misunderstood. However, the most important basis of the model, that transportation costs are the leading force behind land use patterns, cannot be universally applicable. The dynamic nature of technology, especially in the modern world, is mainly responsible for the highly volatile, and highly variable, nature of the existing spatial patterns. The recognition of this and other forces led scholars like Sinclair (1967) to offer a new model, which reverses the Thünen rings at the urban periphery. Its explanatory power for the present day conditions of the sprawling American and European cities has subsequently proved to be highly useful. On the other hand, Horvath's (1969) model, which was based on Addis Ababa's periphery, was meant to apply to Third World conditions. It showed that the land use rings of this city closely resembled those of the original 'isolated town' as presented by von Thünen in the early 19th century for European cities.

Our own spatial analysis, as also the study of other researchers, demonstrates that the spatial patterns of land use are much more complex than those of Addis Ababa. However, we intend to show that our own study, which was conducted in the peri-urban periphery of Jos-Bukuru of Nigeria, tends to confirm the main principles of model although it was conducted about two decades later. It demonstrates, as we intend to reveal that intensity of cultivation is still high in the inner rings. However, the technological impact is not totally absent.

The impact of transportation and communication

The ability of the farmers and gardeners to overcome the friction of distance is often impressive. In a separate study, conducted in the mid-1960s, it was observed that firewood (which in the original Thünen model occupied the second ring), was brought by lorries into the Enugu market of south-eastern Nigeria from as far as 30 km away, i.e., from a 'ring' located beyond that of most food crops, even though this low cost commodity is very sensitive to transportation costs (Grossman 1976). The reason for the extended firewood belt was that it depended on lorry transportation while the local crops were mostly brought to the market by more expensive head portage.

Motorized transport is still quite dear where living standards are as low as they are in Africa. In our Jos study we have recently recorded shipment costs by pick-up vans which climbed 50 percent when the distance increased from 20 kilometres or less, to about 40 kilometres from the market (from 10 Naira to 15 Naira per basket; Ajaegbu *et al.* 1997). However, the very change from head portage by modern means, such as lorries or vans, makes a great difference. The fact is that even the poorest rural Africans use the combustion engine, which is the major contributor to the twentieth century expansion of the built-up areas. The Third World's motorized transportation networks, as also the various means of modern telecommunication, such as telephones, radios, and, increasingly, internet, lag far behind those of industrial nations, but the very availability of the modern systems and the existence of some form of infrastructure, crude as it may be, makes a great difference. It is clear that an early nineteenth century gentleman could not use radios and electronic mail in the way that some of the poorest Africans are able to do so today.

Land values and urban farming

The issue of land cost (the concept of 'rent', which measure the income 'earned by land'), is at the heart of spatial-based models. This is another reason for the existence of a relatively high degree of universal interest in present day spatial models, and why such models, particularly in urban fringe locations, have strong planning implications. Throughout the world, and not only in the developed countries, land values tend to rise and the land market is highly dynamic (see Van den Berg 1984). We have found that even in Jos, there is a wide zone of speculation and uncertainty, and farming is consequently phased out of the urban periphery. The high demographic natural growth rate, the expanding migration rate, the growing densities, and the growing demand for land by the public and industrial sectors, as well as by the growing class of affluent people and the uncertainty which accompanies their speculative operations, result in the spread of the Sinclair model even in Sub-Saharan African countries. To this list, we have to add additional causes of uncertainty, such as tenurial systems of water supply. There are, on the other hand, some significant differences between the developed North and the developing South in terms of economic response to urban sprawl, which are clearly visible in the nature of the landscape. These differences are primarily the result of the differences in living standards, and in their manifestations in the level of commodization and other forms of transitional modes of living. The social transformation associated with the transition from traditional to modern economic systems, accompanied with the two-way transition between the upper (formal) and lower (informal) economic modes of life, are closely reflected in the spatial patterns. This is clear in the Jos-Bukuru area, which shows that agriculture is not confined to specific, well-defined peri-urban rings, but, rather, starts from the very heart of the city, from where it tends to rise toward the periphery before it declines again, as a result of the strong impact of the transport factor. This results from the low impact of the land market close to the urban core, and from the high impact of transportation costs. However, where roads are adequate, the friction of distance is fairly low. Products may be shipped hundreds of kilometres to the major markets, but since the road network in most rural areas is rudimentary; many localities are poorly served. Consequently, a short distance (even ten-km) may preclude any engagement in trade. Spatially, the existence of two (upper and lower; formal and informal) economic circuits is most important. The upper circuit generally resembles the developed models. However, we have dealt in our study almost exclusively with the lower, traditional circuit. Prevailing price levels in this circuit are adjusted to the local low standards, but this means that the services of most official economic institutions and their benefits are beyond the reach of the Jos gardeners. Capital is in short supply and bank loans are mostly inaccessible, probably even unthinkable, to the Jos farmer and gardener. Consequently, investment is low. Essusu clubs, which may be the equivalent of the banks in the lower circuit are only partly effective (e.g., Ben-Yami 1996). Consequently, our findings reveal that most of the small amounts of capital are obtained from self or family sources.

Government spatial impacts

Other important spatial impacts are associated with the government factor. Government interference is not considered by the original Thünen model, but the effects of its actions could be learned from Boal's (1971) model, which illustrates how a purposely modified model can function as a planning device. However, while the latter represents the impact of actual policy, the Nigerian (or Plateau State) model, which we construct, is totally hypothetical. It refers to a scenario that is unlikely to materialize in the near future. Even so, it differs substantially from the British-based Boal model. It can be seen, once more that the optimal scenario which we considered, takes into account the need for widening the urban farming zone in the urban core and fringe, while the British model is concerned with the preservation of open spaces. This trend is even more pronounced in other European countries, and is now particularly prevalent in Dutch models. Even in Israel, which since its establishment held farming to have the highest priority in land use planning, there is now a tendency to replace the goal of farm preservation by open space preservation. In Nigeria, if adequate planning is imposed, priority must still be given to the preservation of space for food production. The potential impact of government interference to regulate farming in the Jos urban fringe is shown in Figure 3.1b (compare with Figure 3.1a). Unfortunately, it is more likely that the deterioration shown in Figure 3.1c will prevail.

The role of uncertainty: land and water tenure

The general nature of both urban and rural landscape reflects the low standard of living conditions, but the impact of capital scarcity is most pronounced in the agricultural landscape, where external investment tends to be low. Spatially, as already noted, there is, nevertheless, some similarity

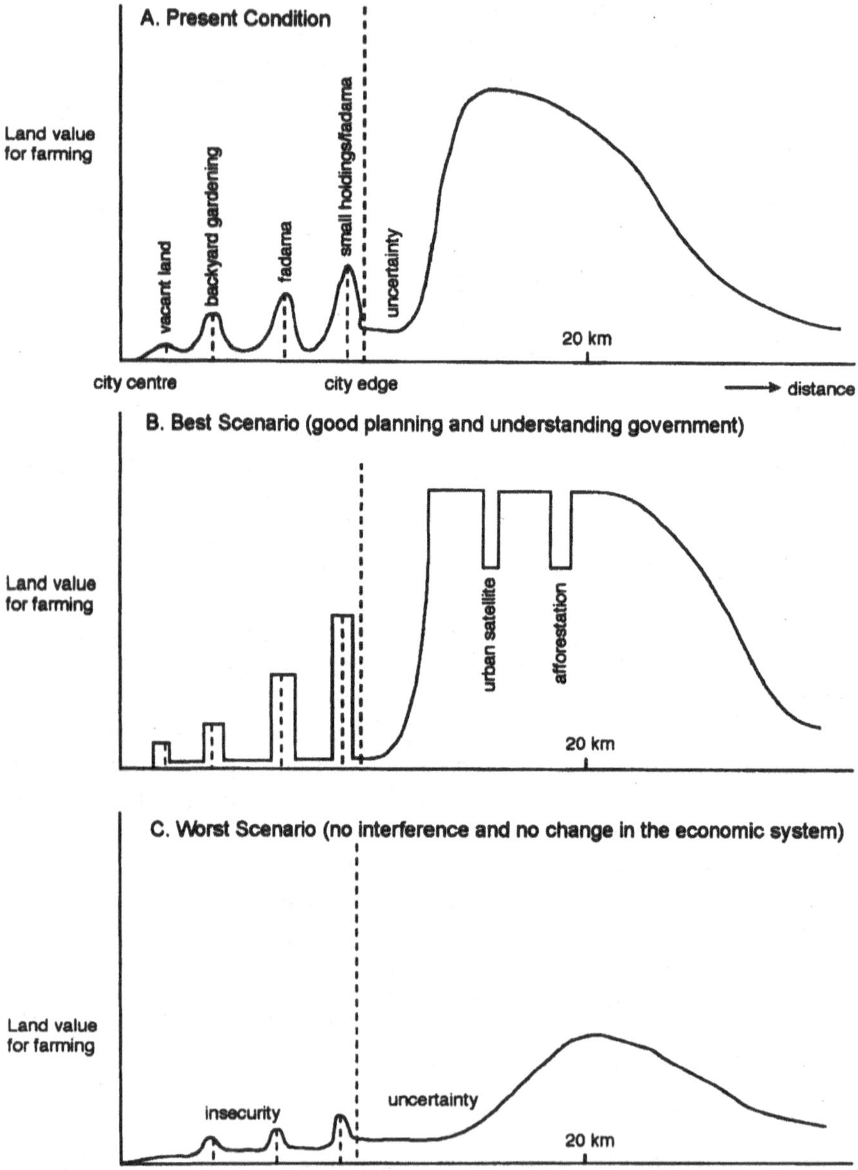

Figure 3.1 Model for urban and peri-urban farming – three scenarios involving hypothetical forms of political conditions

between the modern based model and the Developing Countries model, which is presented in this study. In both, there is a zone of uncertainty in the ring closest to the city. However, unlike the developed countries, in the developing ones there is no large-scale abandonment of farming in the ring subject to urban sprawl. Instead, if there is any large-scale commercial farming, which does withdraw, it is replaced by smaller scale, informal or caretaker farming. The small-scale farmers and gardeners are used to operating within an unstable economy. Their operations are often carried out under conditions of poorly defined tenurial practices. Ownership rights (where they are legally registered) are often ignored, and squatting is common. The fact that most crops are annuals, rather than permanent (trees) also facilitates continuous short-term or seasonal agriculture. The gardeners are not easily scared away, therefore, when the speculators and contractors threaten to remove them, and may insist to continue operation until the actual construction starts. The most visible effect of this attitude is the tendency to farm in all possible open spaces inside the city itself, even where such operations are illegal. The new site of the University of Jos, in the city's northern periphery, is a good example. The new staff houses are approaching one of the main sites of the irrigated gardening operations. The gardeners are aware of the encroachment, but have obtained permission to continue their operations as long as the site is not actively utilized by the University.

Surface and underground water are another example of dynamic resources, which are sensitive to technological change. There is no spatial theory which is equivalent to the classic von Thünen's theory, but it is possible to draw broad models, which represent the varied nature of water use, even though the shape and geometrical dimension (such as circular, linear etc.) account for the difficulty for modelling its availability and distribution. To the rainfed farmer its significance is vital for domestic use, not for farming. Only for the irrigation-based gardener are the quantity, the seasonal fluctuation, and the spatial pattern of prime significance. In the study area the dependence on streams and flooded former tin-mining pits, accounts for the generally linear pattern of the vegetable garden zone. This pattern is clearly different from that of Israel, as also from most other irrigated areas in developed countries. The difference is the spatial expression of the fact that in the developed countries water supply is centrally delivered by public or private companies in an extensive network of pipes and channels. This method has several advantages that are discussed in some detail in our study report. However, one of the important advantages is that it frees the user from direct dependence on local sources. (The same advantage applies to other forms of networks, such as power transmission lines.) In the study area, the water is not centrally distributed in rural areas. As in the case of land, water tenure is poorly defined, or even totally undefined. Access to water may be unrestricted, but more often rights of use are claimed by the local residents, i.e., by the community where the source is located. This can raise the classical problem of the 'tragedy of the commons' (Hardin 1968; see also Ostrom 1990), but the very fact that 'ownership' or 'use rights' depend on location, results in a number of difficulties for realizing the full potential productivity of the land. Consequently, water constrains the development process and reduces alternatives for resource exploitation. Water supply can be improved, obviously, if the government is able to invest in projects which increase its availability by exploiting underground aquifers, providing pipe networks, and helping to even out the seasonal disparities by constructing storage systems. But these infrastructural improvement are not necessarily the highest priority expenditures in a country like Nigeria, which is beset by more pressing critical needs. It must be realized that because of the typically large distances between settlements in rural areas, such a project requires many kilometres of pipes, several pressure pipes, and pumps. It is bound to be very expensive. It may result, furthermore, in drawing the farmers to the few pipelines, and this would accentuate the regional disparities between the waterline belt and the rest of the rural areas.

Technology and development implications

Technology is behind much of the land and water patterns described above. However, even though technology is probably the most important factor of production, it is difficult to measure quantitatively and, therefore, it gets relatively little attention from economists (Galbraith 1966, 46). Its spatial impact is perceptible only through time, and this may account for the difficulty to model its impact by geographers. Its spatial impact is responsible, in fact, for much of the dynamic nature of the land uses already mentioned. Technology, particularly in the form of communication facilities, which supply information about available means of production and market potential, can play a major role in shaping the gardening location, the gardens' size, and the ratio between capital input and labour input in these operations. Under conditions of low access to modern communication, cultivators get practically all their information by the face-to-face method. Written material, where available, is potentially useful for the literate only. Radio can play an important role even for the illiterate, but the use of more costly means of communication is of little help. The problem is magnified by the frequent breakdowns in the rudimentary national infrastructure (electricity, telephone wires, and Facsimile systems). Various parts of the study dealt with the problems of inadequate infrastructure, and the insufficient flow of information. Unfortunately, much of the available information is inadequately applied even if it is available. Personal contacts by the extension staff are of vital significance under these circumstances, but we have found that this service, as many other Government ones, was not effective. This brings us back to the organizational and political problems, which run through most of our report. The poor performance of the 'top-down' system partly accounts for our decision to carry out our pilot project, which was based on personal contacts. It gave the cultivators an opportunity to learn about the potential uses of new products, tools, and techniques that could assist them in meeting the constraints they encounter. We do not believe that we can by-pass the local administration either by this or by other means, but we are sure that working through, and with, the community can generate progress, which will have a positive impact on government as well. We do recognize, however, that this approach is not devoid of pitfalls.

The water use issue is closely related to the abuse issue. Pollution has a clear spatial pattern because urban-industrial users are the greatest 'culprits'. However, sustained land use for farming clearly depends on the quality of the ecological resources. Leaders of developing countries complain, quite often, that they have hitherto spoiled the environment far less than developed nations; and that while the developed nations are those who have deteriorated the global environment by imprudent use of resources, the rich are now preaching to the poor 'to behave themselves' and refrain from destroying nature.

This approach is not necessarily correct. In fact, at least on a local level, many political authorities in the developed world are now devoting many resources to protect their environment. The Dutch, in particular, provide a good model.

The magnitude of the ecological problem in the poor nations is, indeed, quite often, greater than that of industrial ones. A useful illustration is the tin mine land near Jos. It may be argued that the Colonialist regime is to blame, but this does not help to change the landscape. This example, and many others, brings up the essential cause for the problem: lack of funds and, often, lack of awareness or know-how. This applies obviously to the Jos water pollution problems. Elsewhere it would be quite unthinkable that a small stream, which is used for vegetable gardening, would be as polluted as the Delimi and its tributaries. The pollution originates in the sewers of Jos and in a number of factories, including a steel mill. Unfortunately, there is not even a laboratory, which can examine the chemical composition of the water. The absence of trained technical personnel, lawyers, effective municipal officers, and other qualified persons, is probably more severe than the lack of funds.

Conclusions

This point brings us to the real 'bottom line': It is the 'human resource' that accounts for the problems named here. This applies to the spatial discussion (better use of the farmland and water; the ineffective political institutions and their inability to affect the pattern or assist farmers, in both the production phase and the marketing phase.

The spatial models are more of an explanatory than applicable nature, but the discussion reveals that they can be used at least for predicting potential future scenarios or routes of development if local conditions are known. There are a number of ways that distinguish the land use systems of the developing countries from those of developed ones and from the classical models. The clear deviation from the 'normal' Thünen models is that rings are not clearly defined, and agriculture can be encountered, therefore, even in the city centre. They are more sensitive to transportation constraints, but Horvath's (1969) model, which is based on this assumption, is not fully unsatisfactory. Van den Berg (1984) provides more detailed information, which is based on a review of a wide range of studies on this subject.

Despite the information that we were able to assemble, we must confess that there is much more to learn. More studies are needed before our understanding of the developing countries reaches a stage which approaches that of the massive information we have of the developed North.

References

Ajaegbu, H.I., Grossman, D. and van den Berg, L.M. (1997), *Market gardening, urban growth and sustainable income generation on the Jos Plateau, Nigeria*, Final Report, Submitted to NIRP.

Ben-Yami, M. (1996), *Credit and rural small-scale producers*, Paper presented at a workshop on market gardening, farm associations and food provision in urban and peri-urban Africa, Netanya, June 23-28.

Boal, F.W. (1970), 'Urban growth and land value patterns: Government influences', *The Professional Geographer*, 22, 79-82.

Galbraith, J.K. (1966), *The New Industrial State*, Houghton Mifflin: Boston.

Grossman, D. (1976), 'Von Thünen rings and contemporary settlements', Paper presented at the IGU Congress, Moscow, *International Abstracts*, Sec. 8, 18-29.

Hall (1966), *Von Thünen's Isolated State*, (ed. and English Translation), Pergamon Press: Oxford.

Hardin, G. (1968), 'The Tragedy of the commons', *Science*, 162, 1243-48.

Horvath, R.J. (1969), 'Von Thünen's Isolated State and the area round Addis Ababa, Ethiopia', *Annals, Association of American Geographers*, 59, 308-23.

Morgan, W.B. (1973), 'The doctrine of the rings', *Geography*, 58 (4), 301-12.

Ostrom, E. (1990), Governing the Commons: The evolution of institutions for collective action, Cambridge University Press: Cambridge.

Sinclair, R. (1967), 'Von Thünen and urban sprawl', *Annals, Association of American Geographers*, 59, 72-87.

Van den Berg, L.M. (1984), *Anticipating Urban Growth in Africa*, Zambia Geographical Association: Lusaka.

4 The marginality and marginal regions in Slovenia

STANKO PELC

Introduction

The Study Group on Development Issues in Marginal Regions in four years period of its work did not exactly define the contents of marginality from geographical point of view. Leimgruber's article (1994) is the largest and the most holistic step towards the definition of marginal regions. This work formed a loose framework for the research, but in practice a multitude of 'marginalities' was presented, and not always with a definition. The differences between some cases were bigger than the differences between marginal areas of some countries and the central areas of these same countries. However, if we consider that the term 'marginal region' is relative and not an absolute notion, then this is acceptable, and according to the relativity of the term was most commonly accepted.

The problem of Slovenia

Slovenia is a very small country (20,254 km^2) that in 'geo-political' terms is located on the border of the central and south-eastern Europe. Culturally Slovenia belongs to the Central Europe, because Slovenia was a part of Habsburgh Monarchy for much longer than the Republic of Yugoslavia. Slovenia is not only on the border of cultural regions but it is divided between four different macro regions, which are the Pannonian Basin, the Alps, the Dinaric mountains and the Mediterranean. Slovenia is therefore geographically quite diversified country. On a day trip through Slovenia one can enjoy the landscape scenery of small hills with vineyards and orchards at the edge of the Pannonian basin, the high peaks of Julian Alps, the magic beauty of the Karstic underground and finally the warm embrace of the Adriatic.

Currently Slovenia borders with two EU member countries (Italy and Austria) and she is a candidate for a future member. In 1994, Vojvoda wrote about Slovenia as a marginal state, and, in deed, from the point of view of the EU countries, Slovenia is peripheral and has little importance, due to a small market with only 2,000,000 inhabitants. However, it is possible to argue about the 'level' of Slovenia's marginality and, e.g., Vojvoda (1994) gives only few arguments for his statement on the 'marginality' of Slovenia. Vojvoda (1994) derives Slovenia's marginality mainly from the geographical position in between different natural regions, and from the existence of different language groups (Roman, German, Hungarian and Slav) and finally on the 45-year-long period between two political and economic systems after the World War II. Based on this Slovenia's marginality by using the terminology of Leimgruber (1994, 8) is geometrical.[1]

However, it does not matter how Slovenia is defined, marginal or not, since like any country or region Slovenia has own marginal regions. Belec (1996, 175) claims, that half of the Slovene territory consists of peripheral, mainly high-altitude, marginal regions that are usually depopulating, economically less developed and demographically endangered with gradual abandonment of farming, with an uncontrolled process of forestation and increased share of grassland. However, Belec (1996) did not define any criteria for the defining the 'marginal' areas of Slovenia. The case studies of Vojvoda (1996) and Pelc (1996) dealt with the alpine mountainous area of Bohinj and pre-alpine high hill area around the village Vojsko. Pelc (1996) considered in Vojsko as marginal those areas that are situated in hilly regions high above the sea level and near the state border. Besides, areas in high hills have a border 'position' from the point of view of the settled land, and therefore this consideration is more or less within the geometrical approach toward marginality. According to Vojvoda (1996) there are two main marginal regions in Slovenia: high mountainous alpine region and the Dinaric Karst Region. Besides these, Vojvoda (1996) considers that the whole hilly region in Slovenia is marginal due to the depopulation process currently taking place in there. The main argument for the marginality of the mountainous regions is that 'no matter how great the input is, the productivity of such regions reaches at most only 60% of lowland production' (Vojvoda 1996, p. 187).

This very brief overview of Slovene approaches towards marginality in Slovenia shows that, they are very general. Authors are not using objective criteria to define the marginal areas of Slovenia. Consequently, a geometrical approach is prevailing which may be due to its simplicity. According to Leimgruber (1994), geometrically defined marginal regions would be 'the (geometric) periphery of a state or a province (the border region)'. However, it should be noted that as marginal it is possible to interpret only those regions, which are underdeveloped and/or demographically endangered.

What about a slightly different approach?

Leimgruber (1994 p. 6) distinguishes marginality from peripherality and finds marginality as a notion with 'much more negative connotation' than peripherality. Especially 'if defined from the point of view of an industrial (or service) society'. If we take into account that by The Oxford Dictionary of Modern English the word margin also means a blank space round printed or written matter on the page we can claim that the difference between margin and its antonym (the written matter) is essential. Marginal is therefore something that is on the margin, which means something else than the rest of the page. The role of the margin is aesthetic while the role of the rest of the page is to produce information (which can also be aesthetic but in a different way). What we write on the margin is never a part of the text even though it may correct or comment it. Central and peripheral areas are opposite parts of the same 'coin', while marginal areas or regions differ from the central and even from the peripheral areas. In the case of the Republic of Slovenia this means that marginal areas would be, those that are so much different that they have no or very little resemblance with what we generally consider as Slovenia.

In order to get an idea where these 'totally different areas' could be located; several statements about Slovenia were made. Firstly, only those characteristics that can be provided by the census were chosen because they are available on the settlement scale while economic and social data are available only on a larger, macro scale. The statement, which was used to get an idea about marginality in Slovenia, was the following:

> 'Slovenia is a nation with a very small share of illiterate people'.

The hypothesis was:

> 'The groups of settlements with the proportion of illiterate people exceeding very much the national average are situated in the same area and this indicates the marginality of the area'.

This hypothesis was used when making an analysis of the 'measurability' of marginality in Slovenia.

Illiteracy in Slovenia

In 1991, the share of illiterate among 15 years and older inhabitants was under a half per cent (0.46%). The above statement regarding illiteracy rate therefore holds firmly. However, to prove or disprove the above hypothesis it was necessary to analyse the share of illiterate people by the settlements. The problem, that complicated this work, is the rank size of Slovene settlements. In Slovenia there are numerous small settlements with less than 30 inhabitants (921 settlements with altogether 15.235 inhabitants), while the capital of Slovenia, Ljubljana, has around 300,000 inhabitants. The second largest city, Maribor, has approximately 100,000 inhabitants.

The majority of Slovene population lives in villages (population less than 1,000) and in small towns (population between 3,000 and 10,000). The most numerous groups of settlements are villages with 30-299 inhabitants that consist of 68.1% of all Slovene settlements. The number of settlements with less than 100 inhabitants was considerably high (49,1%), but the share of population living in those settlements was only 8.1%. In order to exclude the coincidental factor only settlements with 100 inhabitants or more were analysed (Figures 4.1 and 4.2, Tables 4.1 and 4.2).

The highest share of illiteracy among all 15 years and older inhabitants had the village of Hudeje with 26 illiterate among 125 15 years and older inhabitants (19.4%). This village was followed by the villages' Dobru*sh*ka[3] vas and Stra*zh*a pri Krki but with considerably smaller shares (11.5% and 10.4%) and numbers of illiterate were (15 and 13). The largest absolute numbers of illiterate can be found in Ljubljana (457), in Maribor (201) and in Novo Mesto (123). The first two are the major cities while the third one is a regional centre. Consequently, despite high absolute numbers the share of illiterate in these centres was small. The fourth in the ranking of 'absolute' numbers of illiterate was the village *Ch*ernelavci with 96 illiterate people. This number (96) equals that of Koper, which had almost twenty times more inhabitants than *Ch*ernelavci and that is one of the major towns in Slovenia. *Ch*ernelavci had 1,117 inhabitants older than 15 so the share of illiterate was 8.6%.

The average rate of illiteracy in settlements with 100 or more 15 years and older inhabitants was 0.7% with a standard deviation of 1.1%. There were 38 settlements where the share of illiterate people exceeded the average share by at least three standard deviations. In these settlements, where the share of illiterate people was 3.9% or above, were altogether 516 illiterate people while the number of all 15 years and older inhabitants in these settlements was 8,007. This shows a considerable concentration of illiterate people into some smaller settlements. The spatial distribution of these settlements was analysed. In Slovenia, there are four main areas where it is possible to notice the concentration of the settlements with very high share of illiterate people.

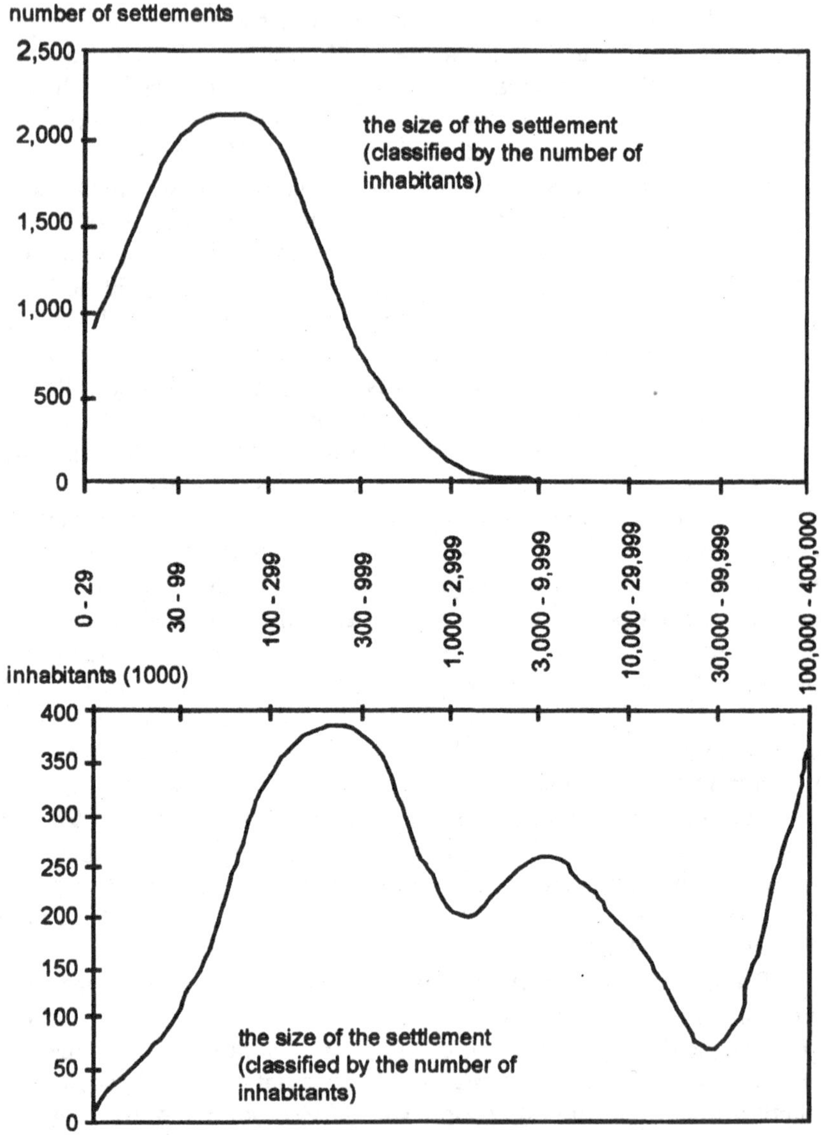

Figure 4.1 **The number of settlements and the number of inhabitants by the size of the settlement in Slovenia**

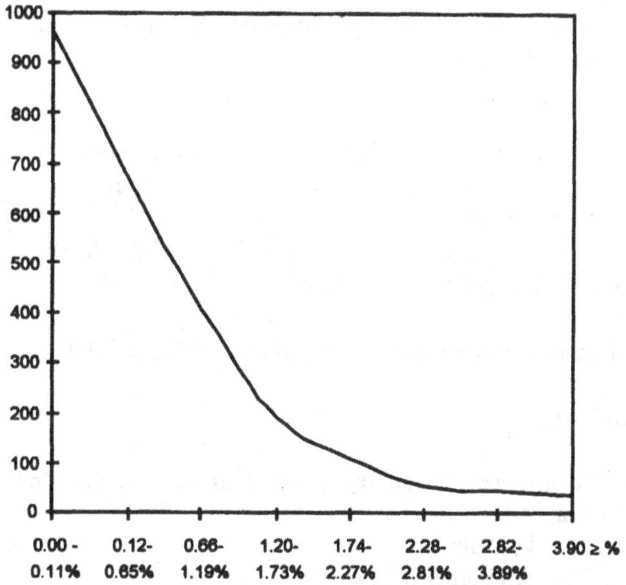

Figure 4.2 **The share of illiterate inhabitants in settlements with 100 and more inhabitants older than 15 years**

Table 4.1 **The number and the share of inhabitants in Slovene settlements by the size of the settlement**

The size of the settlement	Number of settlements	Share of settlements	Number of inhabitants	Share of inhabitants
0 - 29	921	15.6%	15,235	0.8%
30 - 99	2,016	34.1%	122,963	6.3%
100 - 299	2,008	34.0%	348,364	17.7%
300 - 999	772	13.1%	378,728	19.3%
1,000 - 2,999	132	2.2%	208,365	10.6%
3,000 - 9,999	50	0.8%	260,119	13.2%
10,000 - 29,999	11	0.2%	184,077	9.4%
30,000 - 100,000	2	0.0%	77,166	3.9%
>100,000	2	0.0%	370,969	18.9%
Total	5,914	100.0%	1,965,986	100.0%

Source: Statistical office of the Republic of Slovenia, Census 1991

Table 4.2 The number and the share of illiterate and with no schooling

Inhabitants	Number	Average share[2]	Maximum share	Standard deviation
15 years >	1,409,046			
illiterate	5,804	0.7%	19.4%	1.1%
no schooling	210,952	21.4%	62.1%	10.5%

Source: Statistical office of the Republic of Slovenia, Census 1991

These areas are:

- *Sh*avrinsko gri*ch*evje in south-western part of Slovenia along the border with Croatia,
- Upper Savinjska valley,
- Western Dravsko border hills and
- Western Gori*ch*ko in north-eastern part of Slovenia along the border with Austria.

The rest of the above mentioned settlements were more dispersed mainly in eastern parts of Slovenia (Figure 4.3). All these settlements belong to demographically endangered areas.[4] Economic data for smaller units than municipalities are not available, which somewhat complicates and disguises problems. For instance, the settlements with very large share of illiterate people in *Sh*avrinsko gri*ch*evje do not seem to be economically 'problematic'. It is a part of the Koper municipality, where the average monthly gross earnings per capita in paid employment were above the average for Slovenia. The reason for this is that the municipality has of one of the important regional centres and the only Slovene harbour, Koper. However, the depopulated and demographically endangered hinterland of *Sh*avrinsko gri*ch*evje belongs to this municipality.

The municipalities that include the areas of Upper Savinjska valley and Western Dravsko border Hills have income levels under the average for Slovenia mainly around 20%. Western Gori*ch*ko is partly in municipalities which are near the average level of income and partly the area consists municipalities which have income levels that are 11.3% to 25.6%

Figure 4.3 Areas with grouped settlements with extra large share of illiterate people

under the average (Table 4.3). This shows that the available economic data are not suitable for examining marginality. Municipalities are not homogenous enough to allow an analysis of marginality in a small scale. Therefore two sample areas with higher concentration of illiterate people were defined in order to investigate the presence of marginality:

with the analysis of demographical (census) data in first step and
with the analysis of the data collected by questionnaire in second step.[5]

The first sample area chosen was *Sh*avrinsko gri*ch*evje and it includes all the neighbouring settlements with very large share of illiterate people and those located between them. The area consists of 44 settlements and 29 of them had an illiteracy rate that exceeded 4%. The second area is smaller and consists out of eight settlements. Six of them had shares of illiterate people larger than 4%. The first area is considerably larger but it had only 2,522 inhabitants (15 years or older) while the second considerably smaller

Table 4.3 Average monthly gross earnings (=MGE) per person in paid employment (1995)

Area	Municipality	average MGE	index
Upper Savinjska valley	Luche	102,579.00 SIT	91.6%
	Ljubno	85,124.00 SIT	76.0%
	Gornji Grad	93,595.00 SIT	83.6%
Western Dravsko B.H.	Dravograd	89,573.00 SIT	80.0%
	Muta	87,272.00 SIT	77.9%
*Sh*avrinsko G.	Koper	121,670.00 SIT	108.6%
Western Gori*ch*ko	Cankova-Tishina	110,663.00 SIT	98.8%
	Gornji Petrovci	83,302.00 SIT	74.4%
	Kuzma	95,504.00 SIT	85.3%
	Puccnci	99,292.00 SIT	88.7%
	Rogashevci	109,726.00 SIT	98.0%
Slovenia	average	111,996.00 SIT	100.0%
	minimum	63,049.00 SIT	56.3%
	maximum	170,578.00 SIT	152.3%

Source: Statistical office of the Republic of Slovenia, Statistical yearbook 1996

had 1,982 inhabitants. These two areas were chosen because they are situated naturally, economically, and culturally in different parts of Slovenia.

Brief demographical overview of the sample areas

Both sample areas have a rate of illiteracy that is very different from Slovenia on average. As shown in Table 4.4 these areas had a very small share of above 15 years or older inhabitants, 0.2% and 0.1% respectively. However, together, they had 3.3% of all illiterate people in Slovenia and 2.2% of all people without schooling in Slovenia. The share of illiterate in both sample areas was more than 10 times larger than in Slovenia. The share of people with no schooling was also considerably above the Slovene average, especially in the area of *Sh*avrinsko gri*ch*evje.

The ageing index [6] of the *Sh*avrinsko gri*ch*evje was 104.2%, which is twice as much as in Slovenia. The situation was quite different in the Western Gori*ch*ko. In there, the ageing index was only 70.7%, which is not very much above the Slovene average (53.1%). The dependency ratio [7] shows a similar condition in respect to the Slovene average, which was

2.17. This means that theoretically one dependent member of Slovene population (either too young or too old to be employed for full time) was supported by a little more than two people (from age groups of population capable of supporting themselves and the rest of population). The dependency ratio was only slightly more unfavourable in the Western Gori*ch*ko (1.97), while in the *Sh*avrinsko gri*ch*evje it was under two (1.70).

Table 4.4 The number and the share of illiterate people and people with no schooling in sample areas in comparison with Slovenia

Area	*Sh*avrinsko Gri*ch*evje	Western Gori*ch*ko	Slovenia
15 years ≥	2,522	1,982	1,561,628
no schooling	122	88	9,909
	41.2%	25.9%	16.4%
illiterate	139	103	7,234
	5.51%	5.20%	0.46%
15 years ≥ (share in Slovenia)	0.2%	0.1%	
no schooling	1.2%	0.9%	
illiterate (share in Slovenia)	1.9%	1.4%	

Source: Statistical office of the Republic of Slovenia, Census 1991

The population structure by age and sex in Western Gori*ch*ko was not that much different from the Slovene average. The shares of age groups of women 0-4 years and 15-19 years and of the age group of men 10-14 years old were even greater in Western Gori*ch*ko than in Slovenia (Figure 4.4). We can not see something similar for the age structure in the *Sh*avrinsko gri*ch*evje. The shares of all younger age groups were considerably smaller than in Slovenia. The only exception was the age group of women 5-9 years old which slightly exceeded the average share for Slovenia. The shares of older age groups especially those of women considerably exceeded the average shares for Slovenia.

It is obvious that the illiteracy in the area of the *Sh*avrinsko gri*ch*evje in great deal is a consequence of the age structure of the population. However, so many illiterate old people in this area may also be the consequence of the marginality of this area in the past. On the other hand, the same conclusion is not possible for the area of the Western Gori*ch*ko. The demographic structure there is so close to normal for Slovenia that the illiteracy cannot be the consequence of a large proportion of elderly people.

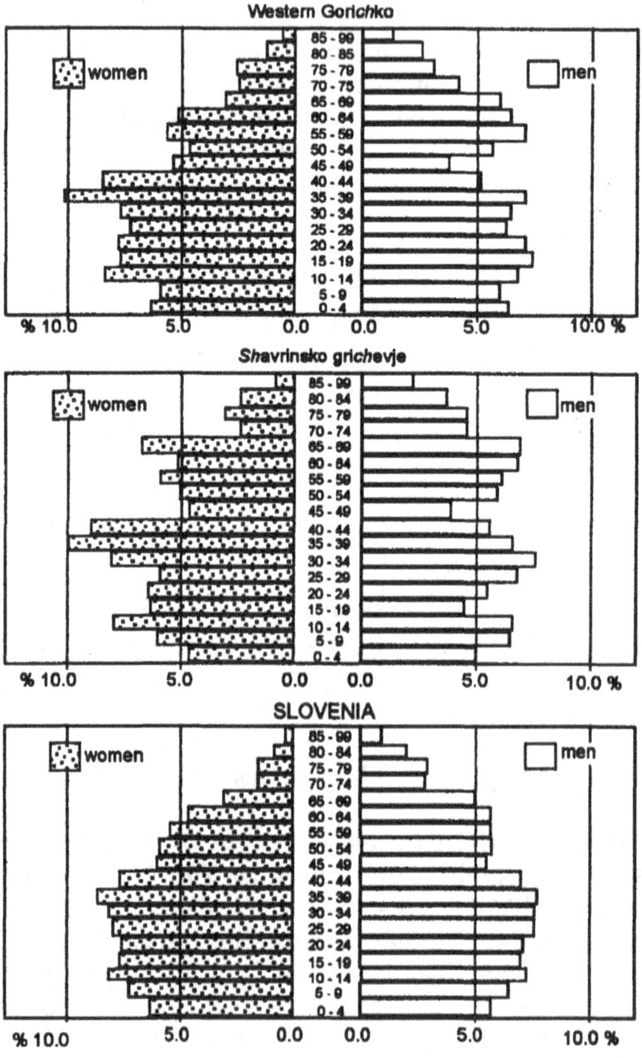

Figure 4.4 Structure of population by sex and age in sample areas and in Slovenia

However, it is possible to assume that the high illiteracy rate may be a consequence of the ethnic structure in Western Gori*ch*ko. Six out of eight settlements around Lake Ledavsko that were included in sample area had smaller or larger parts settled with Roma (gypsy) population. However, statistical data only partly supports the hypothesis proposed. The share of

Roma population in this sample area was 15 times greater than in Slovenia (0.12%), but it was still surprisingly small (1.8%). The most surprising is the fact that all of the 45 members of the Roma ethnic group lived in only two settlements. The data may not be adequate to the situation because four settlements with the Roma parts have no declared Roma population. There are two possible explanations for that:

- the Roma ethnic group in those settlements was not included into the census or
- the Roma ethnic group members declared themselves as Slovenes (or other).

The second case study area, however, supports the hypothesis of the illiteracy because of ethnic structure of these settlements. The two settlements with no Roma parts had the shares of illiterate of 2.8% and 0.6% while the settlements with the Roma parts all had these shares greater than 4.0%.

Conclusions

The presented case study is still going on and therefore only partial conclusions will be presented.

Slovenia is not a marginal new independent nation, in geographical, in political, or in economic sense. There is a lot of evidence for that due to Slovenia's geographical location, rather central than peripheral.

Slovenia as a country may have its own marginal regions or areas. The extent of these areas is directly dependent from the definition of marginality that is used. Areas or regions within a country can be treated as marginal if they are fundamentally different from the national average within at least some field, and they at the same time a have strong effect on landscape and way of life.

Two sample areas analysed were chosen, since they are fundamentally different from the rest of Slovenia, due to the high share of illiterate people. This is only a consequence of a potentially marginal position of these two areas. The reasons for this and the consequences for the landscape and the way of life in the areas are yet to be discovered.

The first sample area consists of eight villages located around Lake Ledavsko near the Austrian border on the edge of Gori*ch*ko hills (relative altitude 100-200 m) on its passage to the Ravensko plane (a part of the Pannonian basin). The geographical location of this area is near the border so the condition for the geometrical approach to marginality is fulfilled.

The presence of the Roma ethnic group in the area makes this area marginal in social sense. However, now there is no available data about economic and ecological situation of the area. The question to be answered in future research is how does the Roma ethnic group affect this area and how do people within this area see themselves (their sense of marginality). The idea is to get these answers directly with the fieldwork.

The second sample area is much larger and consists of 44 villages in hilly hinterland of Slovene coastal region of Koprsko Primorje. The highest peaks of these hills reach over 400 metres above sea level. It is an area, which had a strong depopulation in the past, and currently the demographic structure is not good. This area differs very much from the Slovene average but not as much from many similar regions in Slovenia. Its geographical location is also near the border with Croatia and theoretically, in 'geometrical' sense we can talk about marginality in this case too. The high share of illiterate (old) people makes this area different from other demographically endangered areas in Slovenia, which makes it marginal in social (or demographic) spheres too.

The sample areas are situated in vicinity of two important regional centres Murska Sobota and Koper. The majority of villages in the Western Gori*ch*ko are less than 15 km (a straight line) from its regional centre Murska Sobota and the distance (a straight line) is even shorter in the area of *Sh*avrinsko gri*ch*evje. Accessibility is, however, still not good and particularly time distances, in the past, were considerably longer than one would expect based on aerial distances. Low incomes of households, dispersed population and underdeveloped system of public transportation at the time of industrialization caused depopulation and economic decay in these two sample areas. The extent, to which the population of these two areas can influence on the development of the region where they live in, is certainly weak. Generally speaking, the ability of the people in the case study areas to manage their own area is small or does not exist at all, mainly because of the age and ethnic structure on one hand and the geographical and economic location and situation on the other). This aspect will be studied in the future.

Notes

1. It would be easier to talk about Slovenia as a 'marginal nation', if it would be within the European Union borders.
2. This is not the average share of illiterate from all 15 years and older inhabitants living in the settlements with 100 or above 15 years and older inhabitants. The average of the shares' from individual shares' shows that smaller settlements have higher share of illiterate people.

3. The special Slovene characters, appearing in this text, are transcripted into *ch*, *sh* and *zh*.
4. Areas, which are supported by the state in, order to stop emigration and depopulation.
5. This article includes the presentation of the first step since the research is not yet finished.
6. The number of 65 years and older people compared with the number of people younger than 15 years in percentage.
7. The ratio between those of 15 to 64 years old and the rest of population.

References

Belec, B. (1996), Marginality and the policy of Regional Development in Slovenia. *Development Issues in Marginal Regions II: Policies and Strategies*, Proceedings, Mendoza, Santiago, pp. 175-184.

Leimgruber, W. (1994), Marginality and Marginal Regions: Problems of Definition, *Marginality and Development Issues in Marginal Regions*, Proceedings of the Study Group on Development Issues in Marginal Regions, Taipei, pp. 1-18.

Pelc, S. (1996), The Village Vojsko - an Example for the Implementation of Integral Rural Development in Slovenia, *Development Issues in Marginal Regions II: Policies and Strategies*, Proceedings, Mendoza, Santiago, pp. 195-206.

Vojvoda, M. (1994), Developmental Difficulties in Marginal State of Slovenia, *Marginality and Development Issues in Marginal Regions*, Proceedings of the Study Group on Development Issues in Marginal Regions, Taipei, pp. 227-232.

Vojvoda, M. (1996), Developmental Issues in the Slovene Alps after Independence - Bohinj Case Study, *Development Issues in Marginal Regions II: Policies and Strategies*, Proceedings, Mendoza, Santiago, pp. 185-194.

5 The emergence of capitalism and struggling against marginalization in the Russian North

MARKKU TYKKYLÄINEN

Aims

This article presents two case studies undertaken in a research project, which aims to analyze rural transition in the Russian North[1] and in Hungary. The overall project compares rural survival strategies in several communities in these countries (see Tykkyläinen *et al.* 1998). In this paper, relevant theoretical elements of this research are discussed and the empirical part of the study investigates strategies to develop business and livelihood in two small localities, Värtsilä and Helylä, both which are located in the Karelian Republic, near the Finnish border. The development of sawmills in these communities is depicted and analyzed as the manifestations of the emergence of capitalism and the struggle against socio-economic marginalization.

Transition

Socio-economic transition has proved to be a long-term process in rural places of Eastern Europe and especially of Russia. Individuals and various local groups have encountered difficult adjustment processes. The worst situation is in the countries where production has declined most. The average annual change of GNP per capita between 1985 and 1995 was -17.0% in Georgia, -15.1% in Armenia, -11.7% in Lithuania, -9.2% in the Ukraine and -8.6% in Kazakhstan (*The State in a Changing World* 1997, 214-215). The study areas in this research project, Hungary and Russia have not suffered from the depression as greatly as the above-mentioned countries, although the economic depression has had severe impacts on rural people in both countries. The average change of GNP per capita between 1985 and 1995 was –1.0% p.a. in Hungary and – 5.1% in Russia (*ibid.*, 215). Karelia, the region where field research for this paper was undertaken, has also suffered from industrial decline but nonetheless remains relatively wealthy.

The percentage of the population living in rural areas remains considerable in Hungary (36%, 1994) and Russia (27%) compared with the high-income economies (23%). Of the total labour force, only 5% are engaged in agriculture in the high-income economies, whereas the shares of the labour force involved in agriculture are 15 and 14% in Hungary and Russia, respectively (*From Plan to Market* 1996). Population growth has ceased in both countries, and the meager supply of job opportunities in urban areas does not attract many people from rural outlying areas.

Russia and Hungary represent two unique ways of the dissolution of socialism. The rural economic structures have been reorganized differently in both countries during transition. This uniqueness has been especially discernible in rural resource communities, as land has been privatized in Hungary but not in Russia (Süli-Zakar *et al.* 1998). Moreover, Russian industrial towns are much more isolated from western markets and technologies than the Hungarian ones. The recovery of the Hungarian economy began in 1994, but the economic decline in Russia remained persistent between 1990 and 1996. A slight economic recovery dawned in 1997 (*Russian Economy* 1998).

Survival strategy

Rural transition is associated with the concept of 'survival strategy' in this project (Tykkyläinen 1998). The term has been introduced in different connections in social sciences, but it is usually related to *social reproduction* when discussed in social theory. In the most abstract sense, the content of the term is considered to express the reproduction of capital-labour relations, but it also has more concrete meanings.

The reactions of families and family members to restructuring are investigated in the sociological research tradition related to marginalization. This first approach to marginalization investigates the pressures on families caused by socio-economic restructuring. A restructuring process accompanied with both high unemployment and declining welfare spending (increasingly squeezed by budget pressures) leads to the seeking of alternative sources of livelihood. Individuals must develop new strategies to restore incomes, for instance, an increase of self-enterprising work including reciprocal barter exchanges with friends and neighbours, the adoption of various forms of informal or casual activities, and external contributions which make the maintaining of present lifestyles possible. Geographically, 'marginalization' takes place in various spatial scales and contexts (Jussila *et al.* 1998).

This first approach to marginalization is sometimes based on Mingione's assertions. Mingione (1991) analyzed the reproduction of labour in the terms of formal work, informal work, domestic and self-provisioning work and second jobs. His analysis took place, however, before the crises of the great socio-economic turmoil of the 1990s in Europe. Even for the 1990s, Mingione's conclusion holds true, that economic crises have led to the informalization of work in Western countries. At the very general level, it is true that socio-economic restructuring in the transitional countries has led to similar responses. For instance, the 'second' economy in Hungary is one example of this informalization, which has prevailed and even grown, as early as the initial phases of transition.

There are also other traditions of how to cope with restructuring. One of these approaches is how different rural communities, such as small towns or the working community of a factory, etc., cope with restructuring (Neil *et al.* 1992). The case studies of that book highlighted how entire localities have transformed their economic and social structures during crises, and how different strategies of survival were implemented at the community, usually town, level (Neil *et al.* 1992). The book also showed the power of the welfare state concept: restructuring was possible to manage utilizing the abundant financial means of a welfare state.

The later case studies revealed that the actors reacting to the pressures of restructuring are not great in number but rather a handful of people both in a community and from outside it (Neil and Tykkyläinen 1998). These actors are comprised of both local and external individuals, newly formed groups, and *ad hoc* organizations. Individuals and groups respond to restructuring for selfish motives. Restructuring usually supersedes the borders of a single community and brings together new resources (skill, funds, etc.). It is not realistic to expect that a traditional community – a local authority or local residents – will operate as a collective and coherent organization in the restructuring phase. The consequence of the heavy pressure to restructure is usually disorder rather than increased cohesion. Development takes place selectively.

The third relevant approach is related to the 'economization' of the countryside. This process has pursued in order to increase the efficiency of farming and rural industries. Economization strategies deal explicitly with economic modernization policy supported by authorities. For instance, the EU is engaged in such policy. The countryside constitutes an arena of various efficiency-seeking processes, which are leading to the active search for new business strategies. The first-mentioned, sociological research tradition is focused more on the marginalization processes whereas this economized viewpoint is focused more on entrepreneurship and business strategies – often the successful elements of restructuring. Oksa (1996) and Jussila *et al.* (1992) discuss rural strategies, which cover the entire domain of winners and losers in the rural economic struggle. In Russia, society is not organized in such a way to permit the efficient implementation of development policy by regional and local authorities. Nor are the regional and local authorities authorized with the necessary power or equipped with the necessary financial resources for implementing such policy at present, but the potential of development depends on old societal structures and emerging capitalism. The struggle for survival is largely a matter of individual coping within the old and new structures in society.

After this contextualization of the concept of 'survival strategy', it is easier to define what would be the precise domain of a survival strategy. The definition is, of course, contractual, but it seems that it should contain the following attributes (a1 to a9):

a1. Include measures to improve the socio-economic situation of an actor;
a2. Have individual, household or family participants;
a3. Be the strategy of a local community, such as a co-operative, a working community, a group of entrepreneurs or an informal group of locals, behaving in a co-ordinated fashion and aiming for the common goal of improving the conditions from which to earn their livelihoods;
a4. Be a recognizable and legal set of actions by which an actor attempts to solve the problems of earning a livelihood;
a5. Involve socio-economically meaningful action, i.e. have an observable impact on the life of individuals;
a6. Be a bottom-up activity, i.e. the strategy is an invention or choice of local people, but it can be developed together with authorities and organizations;
a7. Be an observable behaviour, not a vision or an expected behaviour;
a8. Be possible to be learned by others; and,
a9. The overall strategy of a community should further be segmented into strategies.

Because former research reveals the importance of groups and individuals, it makes sense to concentrate on economic development issues from the standpoints of individual actors. Local governance is powerless in creating development in transitional countries. In the outlying areas, such entities do not have many revenues, and local people remain dependent on benefits provided by factories. In general, most do have not much ability to promote development and, hence, they are not prime actors in development.

There are 3,130 local districts (municipalities) in Hungary and 26,000 in Russia (Horváth 1997). The average size of a municipality is 3,300 and 5,700 inhabitants respectively, and in many cases, in outlying rural areas, the boundaries of a local administrative district coincide with the boundaries of a village or a town. Working communities, i.e. the factories and the associated provision of services (infrastructure, housing, central heating, etc.) still predominate in many places in Russia, and local authorities play a minor role especially in the Russian North. The issue of providing public services seems to be problematic especially in Russia, as the case studies in this paper will indicate.

In order to find what really happens at the grassroots level in rural areas and to avoid the complex issues related to the varying jurisdiction of local districts, the research of survival strategies is most fruitful when focusing on individuals, households, groups, entrepreneurs and investors. The reactions of individuals and *ad hoc* -groups are direct, spontaneous and unaffected. As concluded from earlier research, the non-uniform social structures in communities need to be taken carefully into consideration. A community consists of different skills and capabilities, different occupations and generations and, of course, different values and attitudes of individuals.

Compared with the concept of development, one of the benefits of the 'survival' concept is that it concentrates on development at a very local, individual level, where actual decisions are made within the context of a neo-capitalist society. The idea of capital-labour relations is developed further in this paper by the investigation of the conditions of capitalism at a micro level. The concept is utilized in explaining the emergence of economic activities in contemporary Russia.

Theoretical framework - the venue of development

Survival strategies and their institutional contexts

It is defined above that a survival strategy consists of measures to improve the socio-economic situation of an actor, such as an employee or family member. What does this mean in practice? At a more concrete level, the life of an individual consists of living conditions, way of life and participation in production. These elements, in turn, constitute the survival strategy of an individual.

A working paper of this project (cf. Oksa 1998; Tykkyläinen *et al.* 1998) outlined a theoretical framework, which consists of the local and non-local 'environments', which form the venue for interacting factors. First, there are supralocal transition processes (such as privatization, market economy rules, etc.) as the main external factors. Secondly, local development processes are locally specific, implying that they are based on the unique configuration of population, infrastructure, local economy, institutions and local cultures. These supralocal and local processes overlap and local survival strategies emerge in the interface of these processes.

The local and supralocal structures – and their interacting processes – form the central environment with which the individuals and communities interact. It is also an environment, which, together with human agency, creates the conditions in the rural environment for the development of a resource community, that is a community utilizing rural resources for local and supralocal use.

Previous work undertaken with this topic, resulted in the conclusion that, in order to understand local restructuring in any given context, it is necessary to take into account a combination of various factors which profoundly influence local development (Tykkyläinen and Neil 1995; Neil and Tykkyläinen 1998). It was inferred that the four causal factors, which are general, sectoral, political and local factors, along with the role of human agency (as the individual factor), proved to be fundamental in explaining development. This idea is reviewed and developed further to illustrate the role of a survival strategy in development processes in postsocialist conditions (Figure 5.1). Survival strategies represent individual responses in a community (Figure 5.1).

The factors reflect numerous kinds of causal processes, which influence the development of a community (Figure 5.1). The factors also reflect the variety of circumstances in which local economic development takes place. The most important manifestation of the *general factors* was the introduction of capitalistic economic principles in Russia and Hungary in the early 1990s. Consequently, the principles of neo-liberal economic doctrine were widely propagated in many rural communities. An ideological shift from socialism to capitalism took place at a general level and the impacts of the shift did reach to the outlying localities.

The economic landscape of the former Soviet Union was formed by political dealing, and that legacy is still echoing (Tykkyläinen and Jussila 1998). Everyday political decisions, constituting the *political factors*, regulate local development. For example, it has been a result of national policy that privatization has proceeded slower for the northern natural resource-based companies in Russia than elsewhere in the vast country.

The opening up of East-West co-operation in the Barents Region is an example of the decisive influence of (supranational) political factors in the Russian North. On the other hand, economic protectionism, which prevents the proper implementation of modernization, is also a matter of politics, a political factor that can be regulated.

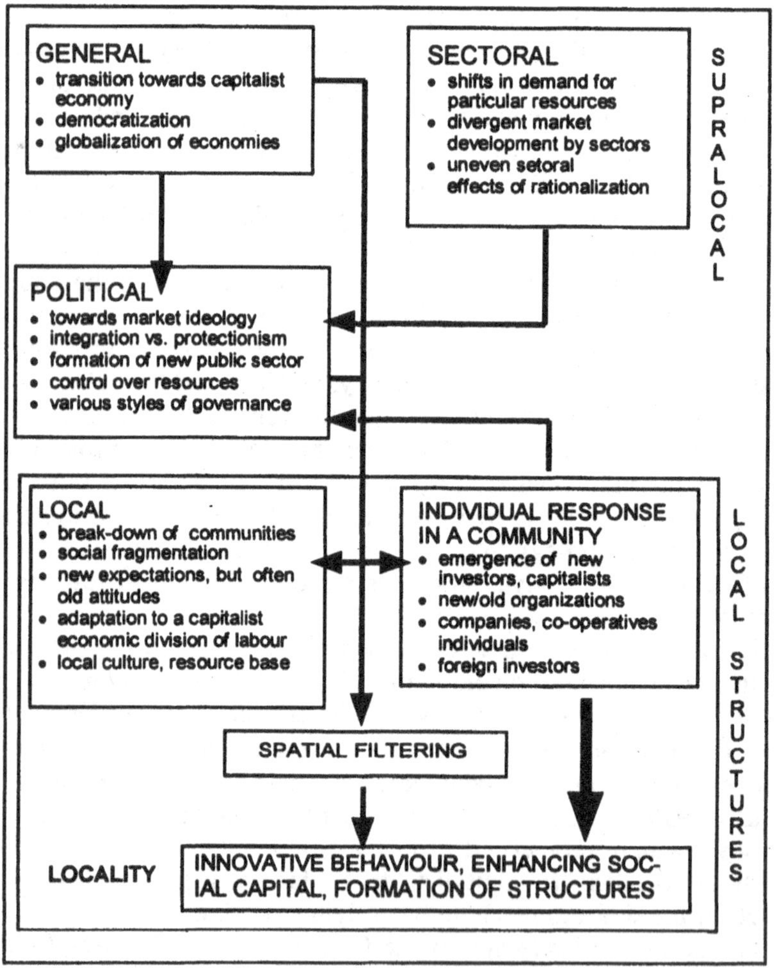

Figure 5.1 Factors affecting communities in transition and human response

When economies develop, some sectors grow faster than others, resulting in spatial implications. *Sectoral factors* often explain why certain types of regions lag behind in development or why others rapidly develop. Economic sectors (agriculture, fishing, forestry, etc.) develop divergently from one another. The communities in the marginal areas are usually small and their economic base is narrow. For example, two villages on the White Sea were both formerly dependent on fishing, decisively influencing people's life in the villages (Varis 1998). Similarly, in the case of Hungarian rural villages, the dramatic decline of demand for agricultural products caused severe shocks for villages, which were dependent on agriculture. In addition, industrial communities are very susceptible to sectoral booms and busts in marginal areas, which need to be taken into account in regional and spatial planning.

The *local factor* is a bundle of locally derived processes and agencies which act at the local level, such as local initiatives, locally-specific projects and policy-making and grassroots actions, etc. A local factor is primarily socially determined (i.e. by human actions), but moreover, a local factor also constitutes the attributes of a place, such as the natural resources and the environment. Earlier research (Neil and Tykkyläinen 1998) revealed the decisive role of the local factor, as a representation of social capital. Each community possesses a socio-economic legacy of its own, but this legacy is not fixed. Social capital can be enhanced though education, training and research. The legacy of institutions and attitudes are, however, difficult to change rapidly.

Individuals are both actors of development and recipients of the benefits of development. They are the fifth, responsive, factor (or rather agency) of restructuring. This *individual factor* must be interpreted in a broad sense, constituting human behaviour and the various coalitions of individuals aiming at fostering development. Neil and Tykkyläinen (1998) do not emphasize traditional collective action as a response to a socio-economic crisis, but rather individuals, groups, enterprises and *ad hoc* organizations as prime actors of development. Certain 'layers' of the population, such as staff and managers of local companies for instance, are active in furthering industrial development, but it is often difficult to anticipate who will be the actors of development. Development is evolutionary – not planned or predetermined.

In conditions of turmoil, development originates from pressure on communities to change. This means that the general, political and sectoral factors exert pressures on villages, towns and rural areas to restructure and, in more general terms, foster the development of a community. These factors attempt to filtrate various possible outcomes to each place. In other words, the impacts of the above-mentioned factors vary by place as each place consists of unique social and physical circumstances and spatial relations. Individuals and groups react to these pressures, and these reactions may be called survival strategies. People react in various ways, for instance, to resist change, to passively adapt to changes or to attempt to be innovative. Innovative behaviour, in turn, lends to the 'development' of a community. Whatever the strategy is, the influence of the various factors (and the interaction of them with actors) produces different spatial outcomes called *spatial filtering*. However, the final outcome is totally dependent on individuals who establish local reactions.

Structure and agency – and selective spatial modernization

Economic turmoil in Russia has been persistent and economic restructuring has been slow compared with the small East-Central European countries. A promising approach for explaining development in North-western[1] Russia has been to analyze how the former structures hinder development, and on the other hand, to appreciate human actors in their attempts to establish and enhance development (Tykkyläinen and Jussila 1998). In social sciences, one of the traditional debates of relevance in explaining Russian socio-economic development is the relationship between structure and agency. That debate deals with many details of the nature of geography (Thrift 1983), but this paper refers only to the basic settings of the formation of structures by human agency. It is essential to situate survival strategies in social geographic theory. The upper part of Figure 5.2 depicts this theoretical setting and the lower part depicts the actual observed processes in Russia.

The role of human agency is fundamental in reactions to structuration processes. The case study of two villages on the White Sea revealed the varying significance of community action, national policies and individuals in spawning development (Varis 1998). Development is bound to place, time, opportunities and human actions. Thus, no ideal, fixed model of local economic development will ever be suitable for all communities.

Human activity shapes everyday livelihood and generates the economic viability of a community. Simultaneously and from the viewpoint of geographical social theory, human activity is an evolutionary process which creates economic, spatial and social practices and, finally, structures. Local development processes are learning processes with feedback. Human agency, comprised of a complex web of actors, is central in creating conditions and acquiring benefits from any economic transformation.

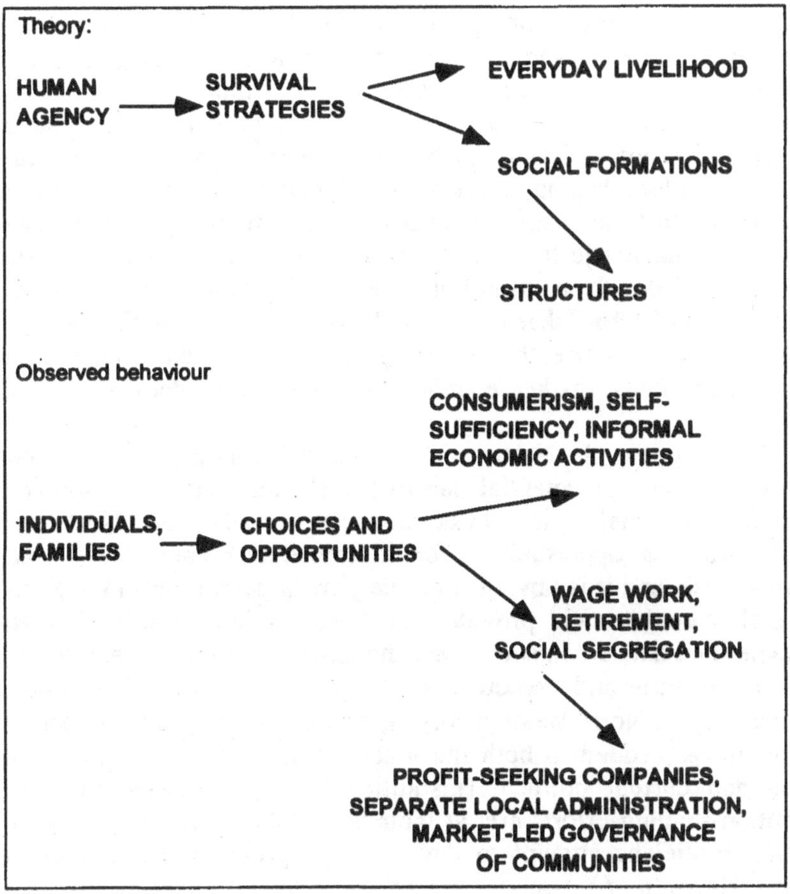

Figure 5.2 The place of survival strategies in social theory, and their practical and theoretical outcomes

The transformation toward a market economy is a more complex process than seems on the surface. There are a bundle of political factors, such as changes in national governance (for instance, property rights, trading quotas, the regulation of business practices by legislation, etc.) which all influence the development of a community. Sluggish development of Northwestern Russia demonstrates how the inherited institutional, service and organizational structures hamper development (Tykkyläinen and Jussila 1998). Initiatives and the opportunities and obstacles of development vary locally.

The lessons to be learned from the North-western Russian transition indicate that modernization is an intentional process (involving various actors) with certain socio-economic regularities (such as profit-seeking) and is affected by the past social system (i.e. institutions, organizations and economic structures). The past poor performance of industrial plants and the former division of labour, based on non-market pricing, have induced a profound and long-lasting restructuring of industry. Furthermore, modernization shows that the post-socialist economic systems have developed in an endogenous manner in the sense of being able to spawn a unique form of capitalism (cf. development in Poland and Hungary as depicted by Loboda *et al.* 1998 and Süli-Zakar *et al.* 1998). Russia is developing its specific form of transition, currently consisting of a combination of laissez-faire, a more conventional market economy as well as modernized socialistic practices.

The analysis of the North-western Russian economy revealed a contradictory development potential due to the abundant natural resources and the inefficient social capital (Tykkyläinen and Jussila 1998). North-western Russia provides opportunities for investments because of its natural resource base, and it is obvious that the growth derived from the European and global markets will provide incentives for industrial modernization. Obstacles and barriers in society are the inherited structures and the legacy of infrastructure and remoteness. The obstacles to rapid innovative restructuring in North-western Russia, as viewed from the western standpoints, are embedded in both the inherited socio-economic fabric of the region and current political (institution-shaping) choices. Endogenous, institution-shaping efforts are, at their best, enhancements of local social capital. Politicians attempt to develop semi-protected economies in the Russian North (*ibid.*). Such efforts are often supported by local companies in order to safeguard their own interests (e.g. Avakjan 1998). The operations of endogenous forces mean that a 'market' economy exists only within a certain political environment and that this political factor may profoundly shape modernization and the formation of economic and spatial structures.

The above development theory 'of innovative restructuring of industry' in Russia results in the conclusion that there are two main forces of restructuring: path-dependency, in the sense of inherited structures and legacy, and path-forming processes, in the form of striving for new economic order. New spatial structures of industry are results of this struggle. The processes of restructuring occur quite differently within each company, location and community. Restructuring is a spatially uneven process, which will lead to the complete reforming of the former 'landscapes of priorities'.

Politicians have no other real options other than to allow the modernization of the industrial bases of North-western Russia. It means that modernization will increasingly take place in locations that are suitable for profit-making. Capitalism selects locations on the grounds of profitability, and hence, innovative restructuring takes place in *favourable pockets*. Upon realizing this, the cleverest local politicians will improve the locality's competitive position by abolishing socio-economic barriers and releasing the factors of production for global use. Furthermore, many endogenous elements, such as the compartmentalization of the Russian economy and insider-led privatization, compound such spatially-selective development. The pattern of uneven spatial development is discernible if one examines development in individual locales, as shown by the case studies in this book.

Spatially uneven modernization of the marginal areas of Russia will most likely proceed as innovative business diffuses from one place to another, even over long distances, creating spin-off effects in the environs of the production sites. However, technological innovations diffuse more quickly to industrial locales located in favourable environments where they can further benefit the business endeavour and produce higher returns. Viewed from a geographical angle, this process of restructuring can be called *selective spatial modernization*.

Methodology - how many swans are enough?

This paper presents two case studies. Research has been carried out in Värtsilä and Helylä, in the western parts of the Karelian Republic. Is a small-scale case study an appropriate method in attempting to explain development? The fundamental divide in methods dealing with the research approach of this study is the difference between statistical inference and analytical generalization. The main difference between these approaches can be depicted by the following analogy: only one coloured swan is enough to prove the existence of a species of coloured swans in analytical generalization, whereas a group of coloured swans is required to prove the spatial distribution of coloured swans when statistical inference is prescribed to. It is clear that these two approaches address two different issues: existence and generality. The interest of this research is primarily focused on the existence of innovative survival strategies and the emergence of new economic institutions and structures.

A second important issue deals with the methodological setting, whether it should be focused on at a highly abstract or concrete level. This methodological discussion also refers to the discussions of the validity of compositional theory and contextual theory as the main framework for a study. The results of many case studies refer to the latter type of theorizing as a valid methodology in attempting to investigate survival strategies in poor, marginal conditions. Nevertheless, there are no arguments to reject the ideas of compositional theory but, rather, an attempt to intertwine the useful parts of both to the methodological setting should be undertaken. It would be better to interpret the relation of the two approaches in such a light that the contextual approach can significantly lend to and enrich the compositional approach, and *vice versa*. Moreover, the contextual approach brings the geographical diversity and uniqueness to the explanation of restructuring.

One way to approach this methodological dilemma is to convert it to the general – specific dimension. The pivotal point is the articulation of the general with the specific to explain the emergence of different outcomes in different places. Both broad-based, general settings and detailed, local and idiografic settings are suitable methodological principles of survival strategy research, as survival strategies can be studied from different perspectives. Epistemological positioning should be open to new methodical ideas (cf. Philip 1998). The applicability of a method, primarily, depends on how the aims of a study have been formulated. As a conclusion, it is useful to use the most economical methodological approach, which can fulfil the research aims of a study. Thus, for this research, two observed cases are enough to prove the existence of a strategy.

Conditions for development: the case studies

Takeoff strategy

Voronkov (1995) blames Soviet attitudes for the turmoil in Russia. Formerly, the optimal mode of societal behaviour consisted of minimizing efforts and still obtaining the same predetermined amount and type of reward. Societal difficulties now emerge because such rewards have been abolished in the new, neocapitalist economy. According to Voronkov (1995, 30), "[p]overty today is not only a result of circumstances; it is no less a result of mental inertia and unpreparedness of the people with regard to other modes of life that they did not know before". If so, how can capitalism emerge in such an environment? And, where to find people who are prepared for change?

There are only few examples of successful business developments in rural North-western Russia. The following two examples represent strategies which attempt to create development in declining communities. The strategy of the two case studies is called 'takeoff' because it represents a dramatic change compared to the strategies generally derived and accepted through traditional means. Namely, people hope for a gradual change based on the former socio-economic structures supplemented with the most beneficial ideas of a market economy. This popular, widely accepted conception does not generally work, at least in the majority of today's industrial communities of the Karelian Republic. In order to be successful, development strategies must be much more radical than previous gradual strategies, as the following case studies indicate.

Värtsilä

Värtsilä is a small industrial community just on the Russian side of the Finnish-Russian border. The main employer in the community is the Värtsilä Iron Works, which employed 1,000 people during the Soviet era. The number of employees in the company has since declined to 600 by 1998. The community struggles for life as it attempts to cope with the economic decline. Authorities and company leaders have attempted to broaden the economic base of the community several times, and many co-operative plans have been constructed with various actors. As an example, a consulting company arranged for an enterprise park to be developed as a Finnish-Russian joint venture in 1994, however, (Kari-Kärki and Kotoaro 1995), the project is still on hold.

Karlis Ltd., a sawmill company located in Värtsilä, is one of only a handful of flourishing examples of successful transition and the emergence of profitable industrial activities in the Russian North. The successful operation of the company also constitutes a survival strategy for those people who have found a new source of livelihood as employees of the company. The sawmill is owned by four Russian and one Finnish partner. The Finnish co-owner previously worked for Finnish customs prior to becoming an entrepreneur and subsequently managing a timber company, Sirius Oy, which exports timber from Russia (Purmonen 1998). The Russian partners own 75% of the sawmill shares. The sawmill investment is a genuine greenfield investment, for equipment and premises are new and they are based on advanced technology. The sawmill was constructed in spring 1994 and commenced production soon after.

The sawmill produces 40,000-70,000 cubic metres of sawn timber per annum and employs 35 people, working over two shifts. Roundwood is acquired from a logging company in Suojärvi, over 100 km east of Värtsilä, and moreover, Finnish logging entrepreneurs cut forest in close proximity and sell timber to the company. Three-fourths of the roundwood acquired by the sawmill is delivered to the mill by a Russian logging company from Suojärvi. The mill saws medium-sized logs, whereas the logging companies export large logs and pulpwood to Finland. The operation of the sawmill fits well with the timber market situation in the border area as the supply of medium-sized timber is abundant and the demand for pulpwood and large timber in Finland is robust. The saw was founded partly because of this market situation.

Karlis Ltd. produces sawn timber mainly for export and less so for the domestic market. Lorries pick up deliveries from the sawmill, and according to the manager; these lorries stay on the Russian side of the border only for one hour (Pazhlakov 1998). Only 10% of sawn timber is destined for Finland, with the majority of production being delivered to other countries. The company can deliver cut-to-size timber just-in-time to customers via its agents. This kind of business concept is not very common in contemporary Russian conditions and JIT-deliveries have been possible because of the vicinity of the border, the conscious adoption of western business practices and the use of modern technology. The Finnish co-owner emphasized the crucial role of communications technology (NMT and GSM connections) in everyday business management in both the border area and up to 100 km from it (Purmonen 1998). He considered that bureaucracy on both sides of the border hinders development and there is not much knowledge on the part of authorities to alleviate it. The technical manager of the sawmill considered that the adoption of new business and working cultures was the most difficult obstacle faced by the sawmill to overcome (Pazhlakov 1998).

About a half of the employees of the sawmill are from the village of Värtsilä. Others live near Värtsilä, especially in Puikkola where a closed state farm is located. One employee commutes from Finland. The Russian owners are not local, and the Finnish co-owner has an office just on the Finnish side of border, where he conducts logging and timber business.

The competitiveness of the sawmill is based on the rich local raw materials, the relatively low costs of production and successful business strategy and management. Wages at the sawmill are about 1/8-1/10 of the respective wages in Finland, but compared with Finland, a larger labour force is needed on-site. On the other hand, the company does not provide social and community services (shops, kindergartens, etc.) as companies used to do during the Soviet era. Nonetheless, the company occasionally assists the local community by financing municipal services (Purmonen 1988). Technology is modern and safety rules are as strict as in Finland. In general, the sawmill's operating procedures contrast with those of many existing Russian companies which attempt to modernize their production, but still adhere to the former institutions and habits of the Soviet era.

For the people of Värtsilä, this sawmill represents a chance to improve their livelihood compared with the bleak situation of unemployment. Work in the Karlis sawmill is a survival strategy for those – apparently only the most proactive – who have succeeded in securing employment in the company. The sawmill is a medium-sized facility, undertaking only primary processing of timber. With continued success, as is expected, the company will be able to expand and develop production. Alternatively, other industrial activities could be fostered, as the sawmill owners possess 8 hectares of land (a former barracks area) which could act as production sites for other companies in the near vicinity. An electronics company operated here in 1998.

In short, the sawmill represents an innovative solution, an economic takeoff, in the Russian context utilizing foreign technology and know-how and local production factors. This case study revealed that successful operations of a joint venture in Russia mean that the foreign partner must find a niche for its business operation and be flexible and adapt itself to Russian conditions. On the other hand, a partner can significantly contribute to production technology and business practices adopted in Russia.

Helylä

Helylä is a suburban community of the town Sortavala. The town district has a population of 36,000. A former ski, furniture and parquet company is located in Helylä, a few kilometres from the town centre. This company has been responsible for supplying the needs of Helylä and its 4,000 people. The main plant was in Helylä, but the company also had a farm in the vicinity as well as a subsidiary plant in Harlu. When the company operated at full capacity, the number of employees was 2,500. The company reduced its labour force in the 1990s, and in 1997, the company employed only 700.

The company went bankrupt in the beginning of 1998. The reasons for the bankruptcy were the costs resulting from the obligations to provide municipal services, the high price of oil, obsolete equipment and machinery and a low turnover (Tsaplin 1998). The turnover for 1997 was an insufficient 4 million USD and the company could not meet its obligations. For example, the plant's electricity was, at times in 1997, cut off.

When the company collapsed, the social obligations of the Helylä community were transferred to governmental authorities. The discarding of social obligations made it possible for company managers to begin new economic activities without the burden of providing social services to the entire community. In February 1998, the machinery and premises were in the possession of a bankruptcy trustee, and recently-established companies were waiting for opportunities to buy and utilize the most attractive real capital assets of the former company.

The strategies of survival and development among the most proactive former employees of the company focused on forming three business ventures in early 1998. First, a new company was established to manufacture furniture. The operation of the furniture company was still in its infancy in February 1998, with the business strategy of the company being to produce furniture and kitchen fixtures. The new company has premises in the town of Sortavala. Second, there will be a continuation of the production of skis and ice-hockey sticks, but under the auspices of a new company. Third, a small-scale sawmill has begun to operate on the premises of the company's farm, commencing production in January 1998.

The sawmill machinery was settled in the farm of the former company. The farm still had 50 cows and grassland fields of 160 hectares in 1998, but some parts of farm were devoted to the sawmill operation. In the winter of 1998, the sawmill operated in an old and unheated cattle house. Non-heated facilities are common for sawmills in any country, but social premises need to be heated and otherwise adequate.

The sawmill company had one main saw and sawn timber was cut to smaller sizes by another machine. Cut-to-size timber was transported outside of the cattle house by manual labour. The company operated in two shifts during the first two months, and in February 1998, they decided to operate in three shifts from the beginning of March. The company had 28 employees in early 1998, but the company planned to recruit more people when the three-shift operation began and production increased.

The sawmill company is not of local origin. The venture capital has been put together from investors from Hungary, Lithuania and Russia with respective shares of 40/33/27. Sawn timber is exported to Budapest, Hungary by lorries. Roundwood is transported to the mill from as far as 40 kilometres away, and the company has an agreement for logging 10,000 cubic metres of roundwood per annum. Cutting is 250 cubic metres per hectare and the company pays five USD per cubic metre as a stumpage price to authorities. The sawmill is very small in size and the price of standing timber is 1/10 of the stumpage price on the Finnish side of the border. Nevertheless, the prices are not directly comparable because of different forest management, taxation and logging costs.

Evaluating the nature of a survival strategy

The two sawmills differ greatly from each other in technology and productivity. The Karlis sawmill is clearly superior in the sense that the company has been able to achieve a modern business and working culture in the company, thus representing a mental 'taking-off' from the complex Russian business atmosphere. Nonetheless, the company has utilized the local network of vital production factors. It is also a takeoff strategy in the sense that the enterprise has clearly been able to create development in the form of incomes, profits and more secure jobs for local residents. The strategy of these kinds of 'takeoffs' must be seen as one of the successful development options in the outlying places of Russia. Without successful companies, local residents would be forced to live on infinitesimal welfare, working in almost insolvent companies and undertaking a self-sufficiency economy, for instance. In this context, the described strategy represents a takeoff from poverty.

Nine attributes for a survival strategy were presented in the first part of this paper. They should be met in order that an action could be deemed a survival strategy. Do these two concrete developments meet the criteria of a survival strategy? Moreover, would it be possible to find any general guidelines for devising fruitful strategies for survival?

In both the Värtsilä and Helylä cases, the strategies of development were not created by the local authorities, but each development plan was solely the result of emerging capitalism, originating from the necessity to earn profits and incomes. Initiating a sawmill is a true survival strategy for the local people, because a firm (as an employer) improves the livelihood of wage-earners and their families (cf. attribute a1 in the list). For each family, a job in a company comprises a strategy (a2). The two first conditions of a survival strategy, listed earlier in this paper, are thus fulfilled, even if the business initiative of supralocal actors has been the outcome in these cases.

When suggesting that a strategy is community-based, it must be taken into account that a community is socially reformed during economic turmoil (a3). It is impossible, in practice, to retain jobs and social security – and even the actual administration of a community – as it experiences transition. Actually, one implicit aim of transition is to change the distribution of incomes and to change the social stratification of society in the name of efficiency. As the case of Helylä indicates, a former community structure may be a lagging factor for development. Old organizational structures cause lags in development (cf. Tykkyläinen and Jussila 1998). Responses to transition come from individuals and organized group responses usually arise due to selfish economic goals. Both case studies show the importance of external linkages, which makes possible the introduction of new technology, market contacts and capital.

When an economy consists of a great variety of modes to conduct business, as is the case in Russia, the question of the legitimacy of new (business) strategies is often raised. Enterprises, which conduct both recognizable and legal business represent an advocated strategy of development (a4). All business is not such in Russia because of the wide informal sector, comprised of barter and illegal trade. Moreover, whether the continued business activities of insolvent companies are legal and recognizable, is often a matter of dispute.

The consequences of some businesses, such as detrimental speculation and the demolition of real capital are alarming. The investigated two business endeavours produce socially and economically meaningful actions; i.e. they have 'observable', expected impacts on the lives of individuals (a5). Employees are dependent on the operation and profitability of the sawmills. Part of the revenues of the companies is distributed as wages and salaries, which give livelihood to individuals and indirectly to their respective families.

As the sixth attribute (a6), it is assumed that a survival strategy consists of bottom-up activities, implying that the strategy is an invention or a choice of local people. Notwithstanding, it can be developed together with supralocal authorities and organizations. On the other hand, the case of the small sawmill in Helylä proves the existence of strong local desires to restart business, but on the other hand, proves the necessity of external linkages in the forms of capital, technology and markets to turn these local aspirations into reality. Perhaps unrealistic expectations exist locally that development would originate solely from a local community. The cases show that development is a combination of production factors at a wider geographical scale. Local aspirations are necessary conditions for development but they alone are not sufficient.

Authorities in Russia continuously bring up for discussion many plans and visions of how development might happen, what kinds of companies are supposed to be established and how people are expected to react to transition and new opportunities. As stated in the first part of the paper, a real survival strategy must be an observed behaviour, not a dream or intended behaviour (a7). The takeoff strategy meets this criterion.

For a strategy to be fruitful, it must be learned by other people (a8). The business experiences of the case study communities can be transferred to other localities. Such takeoff strategy is possible to be learned by others and, thus, similar strategies can be implemented elsewhere and within different industrial sectors.

Finally, it was reasoned at the beginning of this paper that the development of a community consists of various plans and desires intended to produce improved livelihood (a9). The observed strategies generate incomes and tax revenues in Värtsilä and Helylä. Of course, the significance of each strategy varies by locality. There are fewer possible strategies in a one-company community compared with a metropolitan environment. Improving livelihood in a community consists of one or more of these strategies.

The lesson to be learned: how to takeoff from turmoil

Paths to an economic recovery

There is no single panacea for local economic development in the Russian North and economic development emerges from the necessity to earn a living. The outlying areas of Russia are the arenas of slowly emerging capitalism and the lifting of authorities' restrictive actions. Up until 1998, only a very small number of managers and investors have succeeded in creating successful business endeavours, or in a broader sense, a takeoff strategy for themselves and their companies and employees. The continuing economic stagnation in the Russian North attests to the very small number of success stories.

Successful economic cases, such as those observed in Karelia, cannot be repeated as such elsewhere. Nonetheless, they indicate two important points. Firstly, successful business operations point to the path of how to overcome the obstacles and barriers of development in the Russian North. Secondly, with overall development being as slow as it is and with only very profound restructuring yielding sustainable solutions (as the case studies indicate), authorities are provided with clear indications as to which direction they should carry out development policy for the various geographical levels.

The formation of new structures

The study of Tykkyläinen and Jussila (1998) concluded that there are various obstacles and barriers, which hinder development and lead to stagnation in the Russian North. Somewhat analogous to trimming an airline to descend, the experiences with recent development in Russia lend themselves to the idea that the regional economy is *trimmed* (by various policy measures and inherited structures) resulting in economic stagnation. In these conditions, all business ideas must be exceptionally hardy in order to overcome these barriers.

Spatio-economic development is and will be a spatially uneven, selective process in Russia. The findings of this research suggest that economic growth takes place in only a few enterprises, which are located in conducive pockets of development linked to advanced technology, capital, business practices and markets. Russian industrial communities are on the way to social fragmentation rather than moving towards increasing cohesion. Existing communities will be split and re-developed. Nevertheless, the structures of the former local institutions and the ones of a market economy are often so incompatible that new structures (such as enterprises, working cultures, organizations, social responsibilities and obligations, etc.) do not emerge as the logical continuation of the old structures but from recently adopted neo-capitalist principles. It is clear that this development will lead to socio-spatial marginalization. More importantly, this transition will also lead to human counteractions against marginalization as the case studies evidence.

Note

1. The areas referred to as the North (Murmansk Oblast, Karelian Republic, Arkhangelsk Oblast, Vologda Oblast and the Komi Republic) and the Northwest (St. Petersburg, Leningrad Oblast, Novgorod Oblast and Pskov Oblast) are, together, termed Northwestern Russia (Tykkyläinen and Jussila 1998). To avoid confusion in mentally placing the case study localities, the Karelian Republic is considered to be in the 'North' region as it is in statistics. Regardless, local authorities in Karelia usually do not perceive to be living in the 'North' but rather in the north-western parts of Russia.

References

Avakjan, V. (1998), Manager of the private bakery Asid, also the chairman of the Association of Entrepreneurs in Sortavala. Personal communication 20.2.1998.

From Plan to Market (1996), *World Development Report 1996*, World Bank, Oxford University Press, New York, 241 pp.

Horváth, T. (1997), 'Decentralization in public administration and provision of services: an East-Central European view', *Environment and Planning C: Government and Policy* 15(2), pp. 127-252.

Jussila, H., Leimgruber, W. & Majoral, R. (1998) (eds), Perceptions of marginality: theoretical issues and regional perceptions of marginality in geographical space, Ashgate Publishing, Aldershot, 299 pp.

Jussila, H., Lotvonen, E. & Tykkyläinen, M. (1992), 'Business strategies of small retail shops in a peripheral region', *Journal of Rural Studies* 8, pp. 185-192.

Kari-Kärki, M and Kotoaro, M (1995) (eds.), *Teknologiakylä Värni*, University of Joensuu, Continuing Education Centre, 36 pp.

Loboda, J., Rog, Z. & Tykkyläinen, M. (1998), 'Market forces and community development in rural Poland', in Neil, C. & Tykkyläinen, M. (1998) (eds.), *Local Economic Development, A geographical comparison of rural community restructuring*, pp. 97-124, United Nations University Press, Tokyo.

Mingione, E. (1991), Fragmented Societies, A Sociology of Economic Life beyond the Market Paradigm, Basil Blackwell, Oxford. 512 pp.

Neil, C., Tykkyläinen, M. and Bradbury, J. (1992) (eds.), *Coping with Closure: an International Comparison of Mine Town Experiences*, Routledge, London and New York, 427 pp.

Neil, C. & Tykkyläinen, M. (1998) (eds.), *Local Economic Development, A geographical comparison of rural community restructuring*, United Nations University Press, Tokyo, 368 pp.

Oksa, J. (1998), 'Conceptual Framework of a Village', in Tykkyläinen, M. Varis, E. Oksa, J., Piipponen, M., Varis, E., Nágy, I., Kiss, É., and Mátray, G. (1998), Rural Survival Strategies in Transitional Countries, pp. 28-37, *University of Joensuu, Karelian Institute, Working Papers* 2/1998.

Oksa, J. (1996), 'Rasimäen neljä tulevaisuutta', in Kyläläiset, kansalaiset, Tulkintoja Sivakasta ja Rasimäestä, pp. 239-258, *University of Joensuu, Publications of Karelian Institute* 114.

Pazhlakov, G. (1998), *Director, Karlis Ltd, Värtsilä*, Personal communication 18.2.1998.

Philip, L. J. (1998), 'Combining quantitative and qualitative approaches to social research in human geography – an impossible mixture?', *Environment and Planning A* 20(2), pp. 261-276.

Purmonen, P. (1998), *Director, Sirius Oy, Niirala*, Personal communication 20.3.1998.

Russian Economy (1998), *The Month in Review* 2/1998. Bank of Finland. Institute for Economies in Transition, 4 pp.

Süli-Zakar, I., Sántha, A., Tykkyläinen, M. & Neil, C. (1998), 'Coping with socialist restructuring and the transition to a market economy in rural Hungary', in Neil, C. & Tykkyläinen, M. (1998) (eds.), *Local Economic Development, A geographical comparison of rural community restructuring*, pp. 125-153, United Nations University Press, Tokyo.

The State of in a Changing World (1997), World Development Report 1997, World Bank, Oxford University Press, New York, 265 pp.

Thrift, N. (1983), 'On the determination of social action in space and time', *Environment and Planning D* 1(1), pp. 23-57.

Tsaplin, V. (1998), Technical manager, a former ski and furniture factory in Sortavala, Personal communication 20.2.1998.

Tykkyläinen, M. & Neil, C. (1995), 'Socio-Economic Restructuring in Resource Communities: Evolving a Comparative Approach', *Community Development Journal* 30(1), pp. 31-47.

Tykkyläinen, M. (1998), 'Theoretical and methodological underpinnings of the study of rural survival strategies in transitional countries', in Tykkyläinen, M. Varis, E. Oksa, J., Piipponen, M., Varis, E., Nágy, I., Kiss, É., and Mátray, G. (1998), Rural Survival

Strategies in Transitional Countries, pp. 5-14, *University of Joensuu, Karelian Institute, Working Papers* 2/1998, 57 pp.
Tykkyläinen, M. & Jussila, H. (1998), Potentials for innovative restructuring of industry in Northwestern Russia, *Fennia* 176(1), pp. 223-245.
Tykkyläinen, M. Varis, E. Oksa, J., Piipponen, M., Varis, E., Nágy, I., Kiss, É., and Mátray, G. (1998), Rural Survival Strategies in Transitional Countries, *University of Joensuu, Karelian Institute, Working Papers* 2/1998.
Varis, E. (1998), 'Restructuring and articulation of the modes of production in Russian Karelian villages', in Neil, C. & Tykkyläinen, M. (1998) (eds.), *Local Economic Development, A geographical comparison of rural community restructuring,* pp. 154-170, United Nations University Press, Tokyo.
Voronkov, Viktor (1995), Poverty in Modern Russia: Strategies of Survival and Strategies of Research, in Segbers, K. and De Spincgeliere, S. (eds.), Post-Societ Puzzles, Mapping the Political Economy of the former Soviet Union, Vol IV, pp. 23-38, Nomos, Baden Baden.

Acknowledgements

The project pertains to the Academy's Research Programme of Russia and Eastern Europe, project No. 38812. The financial support of the Academy of Finland is highly appreciated. Interviews in 1998 were undertaken during the Sortavala excursion, which was organized as a part of Nordplus co-operation.

6 Another way of perceiving Argentine marginality dynamics: Qualitative indicators

MARIA ESTELA FURLANI DE CIVIT, JOSEFINA GUTIÉRREZ DE MANCHON AND PATRICIA BARRIO DE VILLANUEVA

Introduction

The theoretical contents and case studies discussed by the IGU Study Group on *Development Issues in Marginal Regions* during the last four years brought up a synthesis of various aspects of the subject. On one hand, marginal regions are now viewed as relative, multiphasic, and dynamic phenomena in close dependence on the scale and subjective elements. This is the reason why their definition calls for a deep search of the indicators best suited to the understanding of the various prospectives and interpretation of their specificity, carefully avoiding diagnostics derived from partial views. On the other, attention was placed on the globalization effects that, not only alter marginality situations, either by stressing or weakening them, but also by inducing a tendency to uniformity not inconsistent with local diversity. Thus, an occasion is perceived for the alleviation of marginality without loss of cultural identity, all of which makes a plurality of viewpoints for its understanding not only possible but also necessary.

These were the ideas that framed our previous article in which we gather considerable evidence about two marginality scales concerning agriculture in Argentina: at world level and at national level. In addition, we verified the subsistence of the problem in two different periods: 1880-1930 and 1980- up to the present time, periods characterized by the country's opening to the international economy. The definitions of these marginality situations results from the coincidences found in the perceptions of historians, sociologists, economists, and geographers of the incidence of such processes upon the country's territory and society.

Our first perception, we feel, remained incomplete and slanted towards an interpretation that makes the asymmetric relations between centre and periphery the cause of marginality. In this article the scale and perspective are changed, and now we look into aspects concerning the country itself – its intrinsic conditions, be social or cultural, territorial or structural – and look for them in sources expressing life experiences, feelings, motivations, and intuitions. It is through this new reading that other signs for a more exact understanding of marginality situations are searched.

The authors chosen for this purpose are writers of essays concerned with Latin American and national reality. The choice of this literary genre, very common in Spanish-America, and in special in Argentina during the nineteenth and twentieth century, is not fortuitous. Indeed, it is a current form for the interpretation of the political and social problems that have afflicted the Spanish-American scene. In them, the appeal to history as a tool to find the key to the problem in question is very common. Finally, the essay exerts, either in an intended or in a suggestive way, a strong evaluating and persuasive pressure upon the reader.

The selected essays are: *Historia de una Pasión Argentina*, by Eduardo Mallea, *Radiografía de la Pampa*, by Ezequiel Martínez Estrada, and *Teoría de la Ciudad Argentina* by Bernardo Canal Feijoo. The three authors belong to the same generation, and their works involve, with unequal intensity, a critical appraisal of the historical, political, and cultural result of the first Argentine apperturistic plan (1880-1930). They also show differences. The first two authors were born in the most prosperous region of the country, the Pampa, and wrote their reflections during the thirties, whereas the last author, an intellectual from the interior of Argentina, was putting down his ideas in the forties.

Both Mallea and Martínez Estrada are deeply immersed in the cultural pessimism that followed the First World War, and the Argentine situation in the thirties. In fact, they are under the influence of Spengler's irrationalism, and of the intuitionistic and tellurian sociology of Ortega y Gasset, Waldo Frank, and the Count Keyserling, writers that visited Argentina after 1916 (Borello, 1981, p. 482). It is also in the thirties that the calamitous national situation brought up a feeling of hopelessness among intellectuals and politicians that led some of them to suicide. What had happened in Argentina? The 1930 mark the end of an era in Argentina. The 1929 world economic depression brought up a worsening of the social situation (strikes, unemployment, etc.), and was the beginning of an economic policy that, as in the rest of world, marked the end of classical liberalism. On the political scene, the revolution in 1930 deposed the ineffective Hipólito Yrigoyen, and took General José Felix Uriburu to the presidency. For most intellectual observers this rupture of the constitutional order was the beginning of a deep political project that led to an unmitigated failure.

Between 1932 and 1938 the presidency is occupied by Agustín P. Justo, who reaches the first magistrature through rigged elections. Important changes occurred in the country during his mandate. Yet, power in the hands of a few, corruption of leaders, either official or opposition, and the protection of alien economic interests led to an immense frustration, both in the growing nationalist sectors, as well as in those claiming for a political regeneration.

Canal Feijoo's essay was produced within a different historic and cultural context, and was signed by the presence of encountered national positions. The 1943 revolution put an end to the political regime of the previous decade, and was the starting point for the vertiginous political ascension of the still obscure colonel Juan Domingo Perón. His arrival to the presidency through the 1946 elections meant the crystallization of a new Argentina. In his first years as president, Perón appeared as a nationalist, continuator of the industrialistic and autarchic program of his predecessors. In those years, the statization and planification of the economy acquired a significant importance.

As Borello points out, the author from Santiago del Estero belongs to the group of Argentine intellectuals that 'were in search of rational ways for the understanding of the world they were living in' (Borello 1981, p. 583), position that differentiates him radically from the two other selected authors. Thus, *Teoría de la Ciudad Argentina* has been written with an objective and scientific intention in mind, and has a clearly positive character, for, although it digs into structural disarrays, it also points out the possibilities of overcoming them.

Martínez Estrada and Canal Feijoo look at Argentina from a historical prospective, not so Mallea who writes on the present of his country. In the first author, the determinant category is that of space as a natural element, antagonistic with that of civilization. The geographic determinism leads Martínez Estrada's intuition of Argentina. On his part, Mallea, in the Agustinian thinking manner, deals with the inner man's spiritual categories in a way that allows a correlation with the country's geography. The contribution of Canal Feijoo puts a link between geography and history of political ideas. This way he creates a history of Argentine spatial structuration from the city, process that gave origin to two organization types.

Methodologically and to reach the proposed objective, here we have selected those geographic categories tied to the notion of marginality, categories that appear in a dichotomic way and in close mutual relationship, as the various edges of a unique reality: 'Argentina and the World', 'The two Argentines: Buenos Aires and the interior', 'The city and the country', 'Nature and Society, or Civilization and Barbarie'.

Argentina and the world

The three texts carry reflections on Argentina itself, not on its external connections, because they were written in a period when the country was closed to the world. Nevertheless, although minimal, there are some references to the subject.

While analyzing the second half of the nineteenth century Canal Feijoo makes reference to two closely related processes: modernization of the Argentine nation, and its incorporation to the world trade (Feijoo 1951, p. 108, pp. 136-7, pp. 157-8):

> Another material, the external pressure, along with penetration ways of expansive, imperialistic capitalism. ...that the modern Nation is not introspective but prospective, that it looks not inwards but outwards; that it carries a demand of world recognition, of its entrance to the circle of world powers. ... The nations in the nineteenth century come to existence for the world rather than for themselves - at least in the realm of the imperial and colonialistic grand policies within which they are condemned to come into existence.

This glance to the outer world through the mediation of its capital, Buenos Aires, is the subject of a Martínez Estrada's comment when he says (1957, p. 61) that 'lines between Buenos Aires and Europe were established before their existence with the interior'.

The two Argentines: Buenos Aires and the hinterland

Argentina's internal fracture is perceived under the form of two geographical domains: the City of Buenos Aires and the country's hinterland. However, it must be made clear that the definition of these categories is not identifying but rather takes varying shades according to the authors. Mallea, for instance, concerned with the psychology of the Argentine man rather than with the territory, speaks of two Argentines, the visible and the invisible one, the former being ruled by appearance and representation. With regard to it, he (1981, p. 75) says:

> And these men that I met every day, that were filling University class rooms, science labs, arts supporting institutions, magistral college halls, not a few schools, not a few academies, that spread themselves and ran as a thick wave flooding the parliament benches, the exclusive clubs, the official administration offices, had an adjective function not a substantial one in our world, whose foremost important function was to represent, not to be (...) And these men had managed not to live like men, not to hate like men, not to have passions like men, (...) but to live, love, suffer, hate, have passions, have devotions, as 'men in search of an appearance'.
>
> The visible Argentina was the country of their fiction.

This type of man, usually living in cosmopolitan Buenos Aires, had the characteristics pointed by the author: a disordered intelligence and a weak cultural formation (Mallea 1981, p. 68-9):

> ... On a first examination, the man from Buenos Aires shows a surprising intelligence and an aptitude for culture assimilation no less surprising. But, it is in this organic precocity of his intellect where his true defects push in their black roots. Because, that facility, that as a mean would be magnific, as an end means nothing;, as an end is a trap, because it wraps the subject in a sort of malignant net from which he cannot escape.
>
> And that man, that man that then was coming to meet me in Buenos Aires, was opposing to all free cultural streams a blood devoid of resistance, without selective power, with no refusal -intellectually speaking, a white blood. It is from this that stemmed his confusion of believing (...) that a mere erudite is substantially more cultured than a peasant of a sage race, or, than an Aztec Indian.

In Mallea, the denomination of invisible man is a reference to that traditional and historic Argentina left behind by the progress tide of nineteen-century apperturistic Argentina. That human type, as in Agustinian God's City, may settle in any place, and represents the Hispanic virtues that made home in the country's hinterland. Says our author (Mallea 1981, p. 90-1):

> When this invisible man became visible to me, when, in the capital city or in any other city of the hinterland, I drew close to his countenance, grave without solemnity, silent but resentless, merry without alacrity, active without greed, hospitable without expectation of return, spontaneously prodigal; friend of the stars, of plants, of the sun, of rain and open spaces, ready to friendship, hard to discord, bent to human solidarity up to the most unexpected and sudden sacrifice(...), manly, temperate when vehement, moderate in life, -moderate in his greed- not scared of death's gestures- for nothing is taken away from him that he has not already offered with human dignity; when I came close to that man – and I always saw him lonely, surrounded by a land out of proportion that, in

> Pascal's manner, brought him suffering, not only material but also spiritual - I felt with happiness to have found the live heart of my land. An experience that can only compare with the strange joy of finding, all of a sudden, the object of a vague not yet localized love.

In Martínez Estrada's *Buenos Aires and the rest of the country* are presented as a confrontation between centre and periphery, where the success of the former corresponds to the failure of the latter. As Mallea, the essayist deems that the situation crystallized from 1880 on (Martínez Estrada 1957, pp. 217-8, p. 219, p. 220):

> It is since then, because Buenos Aires has been the centre around which life in Argentina has turned: national organization, culture, and wealth. Alberdi said: 'There are not two parties, there are two countries, nor they are Unitarians and federalists, they are Buenos Aires and the provinces.
>
> And Buenos Aires remained as the centre of a circumference made of populated and cultivated points in the interior. They are all equidistant; they are periphery in the way that that one is the centre.
>
> Buenos Aires' victory meant the death of the interior.

For Canal Feijoo, the structural problems of Argentina have a more remote historical origin: the Spanish conquest and colonization. For this writer the way that that feat took place created two differentiated spaces: the Mediterranean or concentric city, and the harbour or eccentric city. The former concept concerns the foundation process of Argentine cities by the early colonizing streams, that, descending from Peru and Chile advanced blindly into the depths of Argentine territory. These early settlements, that took the form of a rosary, did not seek an exit to the Atlantic, they only intended the annexation and union of territories (Peru with Paraguay), thus explaining the adjective Mediterranean that Canal Feijoo applies to them. They were children of the post-medieval Spanish mentality.

For the author the foundation of Buenos Aires in 1580 represents 'the appearance of the second archetypical Argentine city' (Canal Feijoo 1951, p. 35). It broke the logic of the first foundations: it was born under the impulse of the 'empirical dissatisfaction' (Canal Feijoo 1951, p. 50) of another generation – the so called land's children – with an already modern mentality and a biological need of an oceanic opening.

From the beginning the difference between Buenos Aires and rest of the country appears as modern the former and traditional the latter, because different were their origins, as different was to be their future.

The city and the countryside

Many are the pages of these essays with an account of urban predominance and solitude of Argentine countryside. Mallea (1981, p. 30) say's:

> Desertic lands and large cities -thus was the whole country, desertic lands and large cities, vertiginous noise and solitude.

The same idea is found in a more elaborated form in Martínez Estrada, when he points out one of the gravest structural problems of modern Argentina: few inhabitants concentrated in cities, and a meager and sparse rural population.

> When travelling from one town to the next nothing is found in between (...). The difference between traveller and travel is infinite. Cohesion is hard to keep in a country whose population is much like birds perching after being disbanded. Because two thirds of its population lives in cities while that in the country remains confined and out of touch. Next immediate stop is a far away city (Martínez Estrada 1981, p. 111).

The described situation was partly due to the civilizing policy imposed from the middle of the nineteenth century on that looks with contempt at the open country. This is the way that Canal Feijoo (1951, pp. 86-7) explains the election between city and country:

> By choice, Argentina patriotic conscience was inclined towards the former. Two evidences supported this decision (...), a realistic and an idealistic one: one according to which the process of historic existence in the country - as anywhere else - was marching towards unity in all forms, fact that politically has the local name of Nation, and another according to which the City is the supreme technical instrument to activate and consecrate such purpose (...) This way the country's history becomes a civilization history (...) systematically ruled and oriented from, by, and for the city.

This political project was applied at a time when the Argentine population was mostly rural. The word of order was, according to the same author (Canal Feijoo 1951, pp. 78-9):

> An aggressive and a still more temerarious negation since at that moment the population in the country was globally larger than that in the cities (up to 70% or more in the country, and 30% or less in the cities). The open country had the whole of all possible basic resources, while the cities lived from the

> country; the open spaces follow one another without interruption, and the cities are at enormous distances from each other; so to say, there is a natural alliance between open spaces and a fortuitous divorce among cities... .

The historic process started at that moment, joined later to the immigration flood that predominantly settled in the country's most important cities, reverted the spatial distribution of the population, according to the picture described by Martínez Estrada.

It is in that part of Argentina, that of the hinterland, forgotten and hidden, where Mallea finds the true Argentine being:

> There finally is a man that lives on that land, which tests, opens, labours, and fertilizes it; a man rarely perceived in Argentina, a man submerged in his labour's secret. The generous plain has given him a form, that of a prodigious fertility. This time soul and heart fertility (...)
>
> There is manhood in this inhabitant of the land that is, substantial humanity, free of human substance. Even his hands are roots, not so his deep quiet eyes about to give birth at any instant to a new love mood' (Mallea 1981, p. 88).

But, in addition, and as to urban Argentina, Martínez Estrada points out a feature common to all cities in the hinterland: the imitation of Buenos Aires, and therefore, the loss of their territorial and historical identity. In addition, upon them, and on the capital city, is weighing the flatness of the Pampa as a victory of nature over man.

> They all have the same soul (...). From Buenos Aires to Rosario, from Rosario to Córdoba, from there to Santiago, to La Rioja, to Jujuy, to Salta, and one remains under the impression that Buenos Aires becomes retrospective, each time smaller and older. Any provincial city stagnant in the past, fifty, hundred, two hundred years behind, is the same as any other of the same age. They lack soul and an authentic expression, rather than search into themselves they try to look like Buenos Aires, the Buenos Aires in the album. The similarity existing between these cities, even between Tucumán and Santa Rosa de Toay, is the Pampa's soul that weighs heavily over the squashed buildings, it is the indolent step of the passer-by... (Martínez Estrada 1981, p. 117).

Society or nature, and civilization or barbarism

The three authors' vision when doing America and Argentina was one against an abysmal nature. This assertion, however, admits gradations. In

Martínez Estrada, it is an all embracing concept. Indeed (Martínez Estrada 1981, p. 10-1, p. 116):

> Over an immense land, an unchangeable reality, man's precarious works would have to rise. ...To work, to yield to the demands of Nature, however little, meant defeat, to become a barbarian.
>
> Nature is inside and over everybody, that monotonous, flat, eternal land. On its surface, the human being lives a flat geometrical existence.... .

In a description of the Argentine Pampa he says:

> The width of the horizon, ever the same as we proceed, or the whole plain moving along with us as we advance, appears as something illusory in this rude reality of the land. Here the field is mere extension, extension that looks like no other than the unfolding of an unbounded interior, the dialogue with traveller's God. Only the conscience of moving, fatigue and anxiety to arrive yield the measure of this latitude that seems not to have any. It is the Pampa, the land where the man is alone as an abstract being about to begin, once more, the history of the species, or to put an end to it (Martínez Estrada 1981, p. 12).

As in Martínez Estrada the man-nature dialectic is a struggle in which the former is the weaker, the society he assigns to the city also participates of la Pampa characteristics: monotonous, flat, undifferentiated. He says:

> Those villages are like aerolites, inhabited star pieces fallen on the land. On arriving you would say that, once more, you are arriving to the town just left, and that the trip was but an illusion (...) There is no difference between town and country, the town depends on it, and that's all... It is there just to provide sustentation to the peasants (Martínez Estrada 1981, p. 113).

In Eduardo Mallea, the idea of the space as something without measure, hard to control, also appears, although not as the central concept of his message:

> American history is the history of man face to the rebelliousness of space. As this space is nature, that is, form, the struggle is that of man with an unchained form, with the primitive and pushing form, with the not yet created. Spiritual, material, political, it all has to be created by that man, has to be reduced and left as a construction raised by an act of predominance, and -as all predominance over matter- of creation. His manner of conquest is the hardest of all (Mallea 1981, p. 94).

For this author the other term of the relation is a mirror of the characteristics of the Argentine man. Thus, there are two types of societies as there are two types of men, the visible and the invisible one. Yet, as the latter is who has led the nation destinies, Argentine society is weak, labile. This subject comes up when analyzing the results of the immigration process at the end of 19th century. The masses that arrived in the country brought abundant energy, energy that had to be organized and inserted into the local cultural matrix:

> It is obvious that this matrix could be no other than the spiritual form of our people. But, something more serious has happened. And that is, that in the measure that the foreign human masses were enriching more and more our soil through harbours, railways and roads, our spiritual form, our conscience and soul capital were becoming explicitly weaker along the whole extension of the country. I have emphasised the term explicitly. I have done it because, to my understanding, such a degeneration, such a weakening of our spiritual physiognomy, may only be attributed to a present and persistently changing spiritual, intellectual, moral mood of the men expressing our country, that have been doing it, or better, that have taken possession of its expression all along our century (Mallea 1981, pp. 70-1).

Canal Feijoo is the most geographic of our authors, and, paradoxically, the least concerned with the forces of nature. In a text about territorial distances between the earliest foundations, he comments:

> But, what distances are those? On which units were they originally reckoned? We now that the distance between two stations, as well as the distance between two old mail posts, not always were reason enough to promote or justify a city. Because, in truth, it is a distance measured in deep human, superhuman endurance, may be, what measures the space of authentic possibilities from one city to another' (Canal Feijoo 1951, p. 21).

Rather, in this author predominates the consideration of how the new American environment was not incorporated into the mentality of the first Spanish settlers. Because:

> ...beyond its native boundaries, the 16th century European mind was still lacking the capacity for the perception of the landscape -the discerning aesthetic feeling of nature-... (Canal Feijoo 1951, p:14).

This limitation moved to America. In the earlier settlers one could perceive:

> ...that alienation, the thorough lack of concern with the *paysage* with which the first cities were conceived. One could say that rather than being founded they were stamped on the ground as a square mesh; they arose as a superposition of a linear and plane geometry with the essentially spatial geometry of nature-*paysage* (Canal Feijoo 1951, p. 16).

Closely related to this subject is the ideological category 'civilisation or barbarism', coined by Sarmiento in the middle of the nineteenth century, and incorporated to the political language up to the present one. Canal Feijoo explains the meaning of this category:

> All of a sudden, the notion of barbarie is thus transferred to the countryside, and through it to Nature; but it will not stop there, since in a last representation, already afflictive, to the idea of desert, in which the hypostasis Nature-Barbarie becomes an extraordinary paradox. And pay attention, that all enlightenment, the chair, be it sacred or profane, science, poetry, the country is proud of, are and have all been the work of individuals from the city... In brief, since the open spaces generate monsters, the cities conceive archangels (Canal Feijoo 1951, pp.76-7).

This is the reason why, as the author explains, the political task of civilizing consisted in denaturalizing by producing citizens, new ethical, rational, democratic men.

The dichotomy civilization and barbarie are also present in Martinez Estrada's writings (e.g., Ciriza 1990), but not as a politico-ideological project, but rather as a pessimistic verification that such a project turned to a failure. These considerations put in evidence the geographic determinism of the author, that is, of the dominance of nature over man, all of which means nothing other than the argentine society failure.

These categories are also implicitly present in Mallea, though with a value sign opposite to that of Sarmiento and Martínez Estrada. For although for the author the visible and invisible man does not have a rigorous position in space, it is also clear that the city, specially Buenos Aires, produces an undesirable human type, the man that pretends but is not. On the contrary, the man in the hinterland, the invisible one -invisible because he is far removed from power and hence is hidden- the traditional one, he who still retains the Spanish habits (Sarmiento's barbarian?), he who simply is, that one is the authentic Argentine man for Mallea.

Conclusions

The conclusions derived from the comparative readings of the three essayists express a dismay at evaluating the Argentine weakness face to other realities, in special, the European. We perceive a negative perception as a marginality feeling in their interpretation of some visible and invisible elements, natural, territorial and social that defines the country. That way, when making reference to the internal structure they verify the existence of two Argentines, of two realities: one that was born and grows towards the outer world, and opposite to it, the rest of the country, whose various components, while having greater territorial identity, live in function of the other. The domination of the Pampean region is one with that of the city of Buenos Aires, and this representativity coincides with the relevance that the three authors assign to the Argentine urban phenomenon. Their discrepancies notwithstanding they agree in blaming the excess of urbanization for the territorial and social unbalance.

In their reports the countryside is always viewed as Nature's special condition -large extensions, distance, uniformity- remarking its solitude, lack of population, and slighting its relevant productive function.

Their penetrating description of territorial problems becomes hard criticism when dealing with Argentine society. In fact, among other shortcomings, they point out the lack of depth, dominance of the fictitious, materialism, possessions avidity, individualism. In a last instance, these negative characteristics are attributed to two dominant territorial features: the implacable natural environment, and the excessive urban concentration.

It is alarming to recognize more than half a century later that the territorial structure remains the same, and that the problems have become more acute still. Although it is risky to make predictions about society, we dare to anticipate a further deepening of the negative features.

The foregoing considerations place us face to the obligation of assuming our vulnerable flanks, that have become more exposed in an apperturistic moment inclined to the uncritical acceptance of external models.

Our brief search has confirmed the questions stated in the introduction, that is, that to evaluate marginality it is necessary to have at hand qualitative and quantitative indicators, as well as a graduation of the internal and external factors effects.

To plan the future one must have an evaluation of the past and the present, and therefore, in our attempt to obtain an appreciation of argentine marginality we will continue our search with the study of contemporary writers.

References

Borello, R. (1981), El ensayo 1930-1970, in *Historia de la literatura argentina*. 4. Los proyectos de la vanguardia. Buenos Aires, Centro Editos de América Latina, pp. 481-504.

Canal Feijoo, B. (1951), *Teoría de la ciudad argentina*. Buenos Aires, Sudamericana.

Ciriza, A. (1990), Martínez Estrada, las categorías de 'Civilización' y 'Barbarie' en el discurso de un intelectual del Siglo XX. *Revista de Historia de la Ideas*, nº 10, pp. 139-152.

Furlani de Civit, M. E. and Gutiérrez de Manchón, M. J. (1996), A perception of Argentine Agrarian Marginality Dynamics, in H. Jussila, W. Leimgruber and R. Majoral, (eds): *Perpections of Marginality*, Ashgate, Aldershot, pp. 195-216.

Majoral, R., Leimgruber, W., Jussila, H. (1996), Research Forum and Specific Objetives for the Period 1996-2000. Mimeo.

Mallea, E. (1981), *Historia de una pasión argentina*. Buenos Aires, Sudamericana.

Martinez Estrada, E. (1957), *Radiografía de la pampa*. Buenos Aires, Losada.

Schmidt, M. (1998), An Integrated Systemic Approach to Marginal Regions. From their difinition to the development policies, in H. Jussila, W. Leimgruber and R. Majoral (eds) *Perpections of Marginality*, Ashgate, Aldershot, pp. 45-66.

Part two

Cultural and socioeconomic views

7 The importance of cultural links in a marginal area: Terra Alta (Catalonia, Spain)[1]

HUGO CAPELLA-MITERNIQUE AND
JAUME FONT-GAROLERA

Introduction

Aim of the article

The aim of this paper is to reflect on various aspects of the concept of the marginal area. To date, this concept has largely been defined by socio-economic parameters. Here, however, we centre our focus on a study of the role played by cultural links. We begin from the hypothesis that these links ought to be considered fundamental in the definition of the marginality of a given area and that their mere existence provides a certain guarantee for the future of the area. This study has been conducted in the *comarca* (regional subdivision) of Terra Alta, which is considered marginal within Catalonia. Based on this case study, we conclude by proposing a general classification of the various situations in which cultural links can be found in marginal areas.

General reflections on the concepts of 'marginality' and 'cultural links'

What is meant by 'marginality'? When we speak of marginality, we consider a certain area to be in a position of disadvantage vis-à-vis other areas, based on a number of given comparative parameters and spatial units. Thus if, for example, we consider an economic parameter such as income per head, a given area will not occupy the same rank in the hierarchy on the regional or national scale as at a global scale. Marginality is, therefore, a relative concept, which depends on the spatial scale of analysis and the parameter chosen (gross domestic product per inhabitant, income per inhabitant, quality of life).

These economic parameters, together with those of a territorial (geographical situation and location, peripheral nature) and social nature (population density, ageing index), are used in determining the thresholds which establish the areas to benefit from the policies of regional development and territorial adjustment within the European Union.

It remains undeniable that the parameters outlined above are of considerable weight – the role played by economic activities, infrastructure, service provision and the demographic structure continue to be fundamental – but in order to understand the conditions and the possibilities for the endogenous development of an area, the state of its cultural links should similarly be considered fundamental.

What are 'cultural links'? Cultural links can be defined as the set of relations and activities arising from the uninterrupted interaction of a certain group of people with 'their' territory or geographical medium. It is this interaction which creates an identity that is reflected in local political and social power and in the mechanisms by which autochthonous interests are defended. Seen in this light, cultural links might be considered as the motor of a territory or rather as constituting, in the words of Leimgruber (1996), the native potential, which is to be found in the community and in the territory.

Taking wine as a metaphor, we might liken the cultural links established in a territory with the history and vintage of a wine. That is, the quality of the wine is determined by the layer which forms on the surface of the must and which gives the wine its particular and distinctive taste according to the year. Man's uninterrupted labour in a given geographical area, creates certain cultural links which constitute its maternal identity, which confers on each territory an unmistakable and genuine personality. This personality can be likened to the concept of *genre de vie*, developed in classical Regional Geography (Vidal de la Blache) and to ideas in Humanistic Geography.

If we return to our wine metaphor, today it is possible to obtain a given taste with certain chemical additives. Similarly, public initiatives in a territory might be conducted via an external interventionism. Notwithstanding, there is an important difference between the two systems. The former is concerned with the fostering of its own internal processes (the wine and the territory have their own identity), while the latter is concerned with mere external intervention, where success is not guaranteed and the application of measures is never easy.

An understanding of a territory's cultural links should not be seen in terms of a strictly qualitative evaluation (Cosgrove, D., 1996). The objective is not to establish a relationship between marginality and the extent of development of the cultural links, but rather one of considering the mere existence of such links as a basic requisite so that policies of regional development might be successful.

Seen in this light, cultural links should constitute a new set of complementary variables, which will serve to evaluate, from an endogenous point of view, the actual efficiency of these policies and their adaptation to each territory. The main problem, however, is the difficulty involved in determining which parameters need to be selected in establishing these links.

Here, two variables are chosen for the analysis of cultural links: the so-called native potential of a given local economy and the state of the cultural landscape. The native potential can be defined as the result of a dual behaviour: on the one hand, the initiatives carried out by the inhabitants who are normally resident in the territory itself (the autochthonous population), and on the other, the behaviour of the non-resident population who, nevertheless, feel attached in some way to the area, be it through having been born there or any other type of link. Frequently the vitality of a marginal area depends on this second group, which consumes regional products, rents or buys second homes and participates in the social life and the organization of cultural activities and events of public interest or even protest.

The study area

Terra Alta was chosen as a case study as it is one of the most characteristic of the marginal areas in Catalonia and because it presents, at the level of the municipality (territorial subdivision), a certain variety in the condition of its cultural links.

Terra Alta (see map) has one of the least developed demographic, social and economic structures of the Catalan *comarcas*. It is a peripheral territory and is relatively isolated from the main nodes of dynamism in Catalonia. Similarly, and in spite of being close to the Mediterranean coast, it remains far-removed from this coastline because of a deficient communication network. However, it is surrounded by territories which are considered to be more marginal, constituting in turn the peripheral *comarcas* of Aragon (the eastern section of the province of Teruel) and the Comunidad Valenciana (the northern section of the province of Castellon). This large area, which coincides with the southern foothills of the Iberian Mountains, is one of the most heavily depopulated in Spain and should be considered as one when establishing a regional policy. Today, four regional governments intervene in this frontier territory Catalonia, Aragon, the Comunidad Valenciana and Castilla-La Mancha.

Demographically, the *comarca* is clearly suffering a recession. In 1920, it was at the height of its population with 23,000 inhabitants, but since then demographic decline has been constant. Recent data show that the population fell 7.42% between 1975 and 1991, leaving it with just 12,945 inhabitants at the last census (1991). The population density is 17.5 inhabitants/km^2 compared with a density of 190 inhabitants/km2 for the whole of Catalonia. The *comarca* also suffers a high population-ageing index, which, together with a low birth rate, places the territory in real danger of desertification.

The economic resources of the *comarca* are based on traditional agriculture (50% of the working population is engaged in the primary sector), dedicated primarily to the small-scale cultivation of vineyards and olive trees. Together they account for 29,516 hectares (approximately 40% of the area of the *comarca*). Industry provides work for 20% of the working population, building for 10% and the service sector for another 20%, from which the relative insignificance in the economy of the *comarca* of the secondary and tertiary sectors can be seen. This weak economic base means a low income per head (around 7,000 US$), which is 22.1% lower than the Catalan average.

It is its poor economic state which has meant that Terra Alta has benefited from the European Union's development policies, having been selected as a region under Objective 5b (development of rural areas). The *comarca* has applied for and been granted two LEADER plans (Community Initiative 6), which have gone largely to promoting initiatives of endogenous development based preferentially on the fostering of tourism.

Endogenous development and cultural links: the case of Terra Alta

Here, we analyze three aspects of the cultural links: the capacity to manage regional development initiatives from within the *comarca*, both at the general as well as at the local scale (LEADER plans I and II); the importance in the *comarca* of the non-resident population, which feels attached to the territory and acts as a dynamic factor within it; the analysis of the so-called native potential.

The management of Regional Development Initiatives (LEADER plans)

The mere concession of two LEADER plans to the *comarca* of Terra Alta is in itself an indicator of the existence of a certain degree of dynamism. The plans need first to be drafted and an application made at the petition of the interested party. This is then evaluated by the relevant bodies of the European Union, before definitive approval can be granted.

The management of the two LEADER plans has been and is the responsibility of the *Consell Comarcal* (local council), a government body established in the laws of Territorial Organization of Catalonia, enacted in 1987. Both plans have a duration of four years and cover both public and private initiatives.

These initiatives have focused, in both cases (LEADER I, now terminated, and LEADER II, currently being applied) on two priorities: 1) promoting those economic activities already in existence in an attempt to ensure their continuation (fostering endogenous potential). 2) promoting the diversification of the economic structure of the *comarca*, so as to avoid an exclusive dependence on the primary sector, both at the level of the *comarca* and the municipality.

The money from LEADER plan I (a larger financial subsidy), was used in improving basic infrastructure and services, both at the level of the *comarca* and the municipality. Among the main tasks undertaken were the joint financing of an Ecomuseum in Horta de Sant Joan (the municipality with the greatest potential for tourism), a jetty in the municipality of La Pobla de Massaluca (to facilitate tourism on the River Ebro) and a farm-school in La Fatarella (an agricultural municipality). As regards private initiatives, a part of the investment went to improving and modernizing the agricultural co-operatives while the rest went to building and modernizing tourist infrastructure. In the case of the latter, the general principle was applied of giving incentives to one installation per municipality (restaurant, hotel, etc.), so as not to give rise to competition between the municipalities and inside a same one. In order to obtain the subsidies the installations had to be managed by residents in the same municipality.

The LEADER plan II – currently being applied – is not such a large financial subsidy and is oriented towards the promotion of tourism, in general, and towards the promotion and commercialization of regional products, through the establishment of *appelations d'origine* for the main products (wine and olive oil). The part dedicated to private initiative is aimed at providing incentives for specific projects, which have first been submitted to a viability study. In this case, priority is also given to those projects which are not in direct competition with already existing activities. In awarding the grants, two factors were taken into consideration: the links the applicants had with the *comarca* (thus promoting the autochthonous potential) and discrimination in favour of young entrepreneurs (so as to encourage young people to stay in the *comarca*).

The application of these policies has revealed two findings. Firstly, the lack of initiatives forthcoming, which has been seen by the *Consell Comarcal* as an indicator of a certain lack of vitality in the area; and secondly, that the granting of incentives to certain projects has been interpreted by a section of the population as favouritism towards certain individuals.

The non-resident population linked to the area: second homes

Second homes in Terra Alta make up between 40 and 60% of the total number of residences and they are occupied in the main (around 90%) by people born in the *comarca* (Sabaté, J., 1993). This population, although it does not live permanently in the municipality, exercises considerable weight in the cultural dynamism of the *comarca*. Therefore, when we refer to the autochthonous potential we need to include not only those normally resident but also (and perhaps increasingly more so, given their greater entrepreneurial spirit) those natives who have second homes in the *comarca* and whose family and cultural ties continue to bind them to the area.

Recognition of this fact allows us to see the depopulation of the area in a more relative perspective. That is, if in given periods of the year (summer and Christmas holidays and weekends) we were to consider the second homes as being fully occupied (let's suppose each is occupied by four persons), the total population of the *comarca* would be 21,613 inhabitants; that is, virtually double the 12,945 permanent inhabitants, according to the 1991 census. Thus, the total (permanent residents + temporary residents) is similar to the maximum population of 23,365 recorded in 1920. The Table 7.1 reflects these calculations at the scale of the municipality and for the whole *comarca*.

However, an analysis of these data reveals considerable differences between municipalities. Prat de Comte, for example, has an estimated population of 462, just half its maximum recorded in 1920 (814 inhabitants); whereas, at the other extreme there is Gandesa – the capital of the area- which with an estimated 4,195 inhabitants is now clearly larger than the figure of 3,648 inhabitants recorded in 1920. In this case, many families from the *comarca* have preferred to establish their second home in the capital, which has better services than the village of their birth.

Generally speaking, we might conclude that a certain native potential has been maintained due to the maintenance of the cultural links. This potential might prove to be the key in maintaining the dynamism of these territories. In any case, what can be seen is that while the permanent population has declined, the villages themselves have developed urbanistically, constantly improving their appearance (many old houses have been renovated and many new homes built outside the village centres).

Similarly, with the improvement in transportation and communication networks and the increase in the standard of living and leisure time, the native population which has migrated from the territory now finds it easier to maintain its links with the homeland. All this is reflected in the construction and renovation of housing, in the widespread consumption of autochthonous products (wine, oil, horticultural products, fruit and confectionery) and even in the promotion and recuperation of traditions and participation in cultural activities.

Table 7.1 Terra Alta, 1991: population, and first and second homes

Municipality	First home	Population 1991	Second home	Estimated Population[2] 1991	Population 1920
Arnes	173	534	223	1,426	1,520
Batea	619	2,002	304	3,218	3,331
Bot	265	906	136	1,450	1,474
Caseres	116	343	66	607	752
Corbera d'Ebre	321	1,122	114	1,578	2,143
La Fatarella	411	1,383	170	2,063	2,497
Gandesa	806	2,651	386	4,195	3,648
Horta de Sant Joan	454	1,328	338	2,680	2,447
el Pinell de Brai	328	1,170	149	1,766	1,931
la Pobla de Massaluca	140	471	93	843	1,048
Prat de Comte	79	222	60	462	814
Vilalba dels Arcs	239	793	128	1,305	1,724
TERRA ALTA	3,951	12,945	2,167	21,613	23,365

Sources: INE: Nomenclator, 1991 and INE: Censo de población, 1920

Parallel to this, and as a result of the present-day crisis suffered by the urban areas, many young people are choosing to remain in the *comarca*, as it is here where they now have some chances of employment (in areas with these characteristics the underground economy is of considerable importance). Furthermore, today there are many examples of people returning to live in the *comarcas*. They include both those who in their day emigrated but have now reached retirement age as well as their young descendants. The role which this fluctuating population plays over the next few years will need to be analysed. Given this newly arising situation, can we still talk of desertification or rather should we be analysing the territory from other perspectives?

'Native Potential'

One of the most notable features in the case of Terra Alta is the awakening, to a certain extent, of the so-called strength of social reaction (Leimgruber: 1996), which can be defined as the capacity to react to external impositions. In this case, the awareness of an individual identity has recently been manifest, with the appearance, in some municipalities, of independent representatives of Terra Alta, thus breaking with the traditional moribundity at the ballot box. Another example is the massive turnout in protest at reforms in the provision of education, which has closed down various schools in the *comarca*.

Further evidence of this native potential can be seen for example in the growing interest for the study of the local history and ethnography of the *comarca* (the establishment of study centres), the publication of journals (Fatumer) and the organization of cultural activities. In all cases, the participation of the temporary residents is extremely high.

The state of cultural links at a municipal level

The municipalities of the area can be grouped on the basis of classic socioeconomic parameters as well as those of a sociocultural nature, defined according to cultural links.

A) *Dynamic municipalities*: Included in this group are Gandesa and Batea, which together account for 40% of the population in the *comarca* (4,673). Their socioeconomic variables are quite favourable compared to the rest of the *comarca* and active cultural links are to be found. Both areas have preserved a weak yet varied socioeconomic structure.

B) *Agrarian municipalities which survive thanks to their cultural links*:This group includes Bot, Corbera d'Ebre, La Fatarella, Pinell de Brai and Vilalba dels Arcs. They are all predominantly agricultural and are characterised by a certain economic and demographic stagnation. Here, the main factors of dynamism arise from the influence of the non-resident population which remains attached to its place of origin and contributes to the activation of the local economy (buying regional products, the return of emigrants on retirement, who usually take up residence for long periods in the municipality and the restoration and construction of housing).

C) *Municipalities with a tendency towards marginality*: Included in this group are Caseres, La Pobla de Massaluca and Prat de Comte. These are areas which are suffering a severe state of abandon, evident in the deterioration of housing and the fields. There are few economic activities and the cultural links have not been maintained because of the breakdown of the economic and demographic structure. In these case all policies are non-viable: they constitute territories which no longer exist as such and which have become dependent on others.

D) *Centres which have developed their tourist sector*: This group includes Arnes, Horta de Sant Joan and a part of the municipality of La Pobla de Massaluca (the area around the River Ebro). These are municipalities which, having seen their economic and demographic structures and cultural links deteriorate, have identified tourism as an incentive to restore their economy, in accordance with the general tendency of many rural and marginal areas in Europe. Tourism, however, in exploiting the environment and the heritage, might eventually fossilize the territory, turning the cultural links into mere folklore, if it were to become the only viable economic activity. In Horta de Sant Joan the natural and cultural potential (Picasso Museum, architectonic patrimony) have transformed what was a varied traditional rural structure into one which is increasingly dependent on tourism. In La Pobla de Massaluca a German tourist centre has been established based on the tourist resources of the River Ebro (fishing, water sports). It might be argued that it is an area which operates in complete isolation from the area (even in direct opposition to its interests).

Conclusion

Many of the marginal areas of the European Union, defined as such by socioeconomic parameters, are increasingly becoming mere recreational areas dependent on the central areas. This phenomenon of assimilation may well, in the long run, lead to the loss of their potential, as autochthonous activities are replaced by those imported from outside.

In some peripheral areas of the European Union (the Greek Islands, southern Italy, southern Spain, Portugal and parts of Ireland) which still boast a degree of native potential, cultural links need to be considered as a fundamental variable when it comes to establishing regional development policies. The maintenance of the dynamism of these small territories represents, in the final resort, the best guarantee for ensuring the stability of the population in these territories and helping to correct regional imbalances.

Terra Alta is a varied territory in which cultural links are still to be found, in spite of the process of depopulation and a weakened economic structure reliant upon traditional agriculture. Here, thanks to the survival of a certain cultural element, policies will have a greater effect in the long term, as the territory has its own capacity to channel aid and initiatives.

The cycle of cultural marginalization a classification

The diagram below (Figure 7.1) shows the distinct states cultural links might adopt in a hypothetical region. The diagram focuses on the evolution of one region, though each state can exist independent of the others and the cycle need not always follow the same sequence.

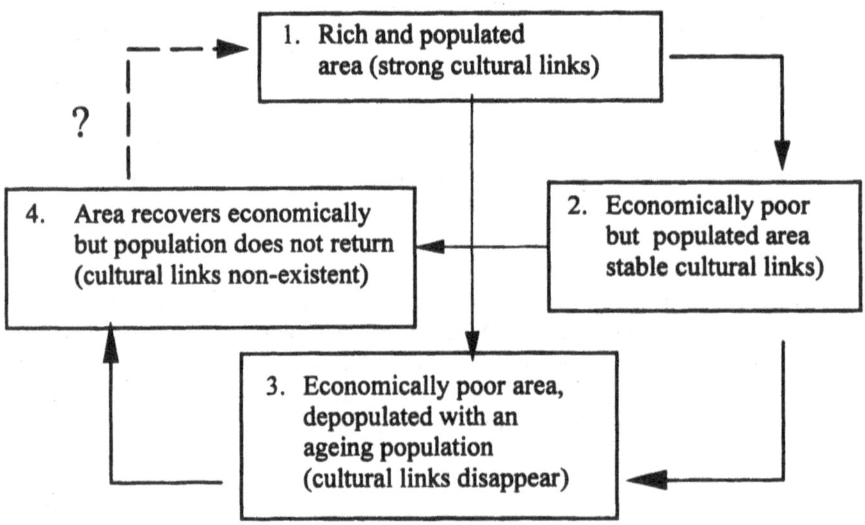

Figure 7.1 The cycle of cultural marginalization [3]

We begin with an area (preferably European) whose economic and demographic parameters are excellent and where cultural links have led to the formation of a separate identity with which its inhabitants fully identify (1).

This same area, due to structural changes (industrialization, changes in trade routes for example) undergoes a shift and as a result its wealth is affected. However, the population can still live there, thanks to the stability of the previous cultural links (accumulated wealth), and the roots which tie the population to the territory (2).

Following the decline of the remaining productive structure (no longer competitive from an economic viewpoint and lacking in potential for renewal), the population is forced to migrate towards new points of production. It is at this point when the cultural links begin to branch off to other territories and spaces. In this way, external colonies can be formed, while the original regions become forgotten and largely abandoned (3).

Finally, the economy of these marginal areas can enjoy a certain recovery, when their very state of abandonment transforms them into a tourist resource for the central areas. In this way, certain rural areas of the United Kingdom, the Alps, Germany and the centre of France have become destinations for family holidays, areas of settlement for the retired or places for rediscovering an idealized paradise lost (4). In Europe this phenomenon has extended itself from the marginal areas of the most highly developed and urbanised countries to the peripheral areas of the continent.

The native potential provides hope for the peripheral areas of Europe that life might be reintroduced in defending and ensuring the future of a territory. The partial return of emigrants and their descendants, and the establishment of new communities (which has already occurred in some cases) and their resulting influence (buying of products, initiatives, capital investment) might ensure the future survival of these regions (4 to 1).

Notes

1 This paper has been prepared as part of the research project entittled Delimitación y Análisis de las áreas marginales en Cataluña, funded by the Dirección General de Investigación Científica y Técnica (DGICYT) of the Ministerio de Educación y Cultura (Research Project: PB95-0905).

2 Estimated Population, 1991: the estimated population of the municipality is the addition of the 1991 population census plus the estimated population in the second homes – four people per home.

3 Within the cycle of varying cultural links, two further possibilities are included. First, certain areas which are transformed directly from traditional rural areas to picturesque spaces, thanks to the strong pressures of tourism. This situation often occurs in areas close to large urban centres which become anthropological museums (2 to 4). Second, a region can go directly from being in a strong socioeconomic situation to a being a poor, depopulated region as a result of a natural or human disaster (1 to 3).

References

Cosgrove, D., Duncan, J. & N., Jakson, P. and Mitchell, D. (1996), 'Exchange: There's no such thing as culture? (debate)'. *Transactions of the Institute of British Geographers*, núm. 21/3, pp. 572-582.

Fundació Enciclopecia Catalana: (1984), Terra Alta, in *Gran Geografia Comarcal de Catalunya,* F. E. C. Barcelona.

García, B. (1997), *La sociedad rural ante el siglo XXI,* Ministerio de Agricultura. Madrid.

Instituto Nacional de Estadística (1994), *Censo de la población y viviendas. Nomenclator, Provincia de Tarragona, 1991,* INE, Madrid,.

Leimgruber, W. (1996), 'Marginal Regions: a Challenge for Politics: Local Development Efforts: Native Potential and People Participation', *Development issues in Marginal Regions II: Policies and Strategies,* Universidad Nacional de Cuyo, Mendoza, pp. 143-160.

Majoral, R., Font Garolera, J. and Sánchez-Aguilera, D. (1996), 'Regional Development Policies and Incentives in Marginal Areas of Catalonia', *Development issues in Marginal Regions II: Policies and Strategies,* Universidad Nacional de Cuyo, Mendoza, pp. 27-48.

Majoral, R., Andreoli, M. and Cravidao, F. (1997), 'Perceptions of Marginality. A view from Southern Europe', in Jussila, H., Leimgruber, W. and Majoral, R. (eds.), *Perceptions of Marginality,* Ashgate, Aldershot, pp. 147-164.

Sabaté, J. (1993), *La Terra Alta estructures productives i evolució social,* Caixa d'Estalvis de Catalunya. Barcelona.

Sánchez Aguilera, D. (1995), Evaluating Marginality trough Demographic Indicators in R.B. Singh & R. Majoral: *Development issues in Marginal Regions. Processes technological developments and societal reorganizations,* Oxford & IBH Publishing, Delhi, pp. 133-148.

8 Local government among marginalized ex-nomads: The Israeli Bedouin and the state

AVINOAM MEIR

Introduction

The semi-nomadic Bedouin of the Negev semi-arid region of Israel have sedentarized and settled in various types of settlements in the recent decades. Most of this process may be attributed to lack of other options left for them by the Israeli government. Consequently, there have been many conflicts between this community and the government over issues of land tenure, allocation of economic and social resources (economic opportunities and provision of public goods such as essential services), and distribution of local political power (Meir 1997). The latter issue has become among the Bedouin one of the most critical arenas of protest and conflict with the state. Being the most marginalized ethnic group in Israel (both functionally and spatially), it symbolizes for them their willingness to be able to maintain in different versions significant elements of their traditional pastoral nomadic ideology, even within a sedentarized context. In particular, they desire to maintain spatial marginality, which in the past (Kressel 1993) provided considerably for their well-being. Such ideology stands at the focus of their conflict with the state over recognition of many Bedouin hamlets, villages, and towns as municipal entities, and the transfer of local political power from the state to local people, so that space is produced and managed locally by the Bedouin rather than nationally by the state. This paper will discuss this issue, particularly the evolution of the problem, the growth of public protest over it, and the struggle of the Bedouin over gaining local political power.

The ideological perspective

Pastoral nomadic societies are often at a tension with governments. This tension carries spatial-territorial as well as functional dimensions. The tension originates in the conflict between traditional pastoral nomadic centrifugal ideology and modern state centripetal concepts and tendency (Meir 1988). The centrifugal ideology of pastoral nomads stems from various sources: their nomadic ideology, which ensures maximum spatial and ecological flexibility for pursuing an opportunistic range management strategy (Behnke and Scoones 1993); tribalism, which provides for socio-political well-being in terms of a deterrent power to guarantee the protection and availability of pastoral and human resources; and ethnicism, to ensure the sustenance of cultural identity against external forces.

This ideology, which carries disintegrative forces and impacts, stands in sharp conflict with the centripetal ideology of the state, its *raison d'être*. The latter ideology implies maximal control of peoples and resources. With regard to pastoral nomads in particular, it means that governments usually perceive of them as irrational economic actors in their pursuit of traditional pastoral nomadism (Harbeson 1991).

These conflicting tendencies result in opposing forces of space production. While the spatial and functional manifestations of the centrifugal ideology of pastoral nomads result in a tendency for maximum locational flexibility, divergence, and dispersion, the centripetal tendency of the state implies maximum spatial-territorial and functional centralism, convergence, and concentration.

The tension between these conflicting ideologies may be considerable at the nomadic setting of pastoralists. However, it may intensify further under sedentarization, particularly when this takes place within a government-initiated context. The main reason is that these ex-nomads may still maintain their traditional centrifugal tendency in an encapsulated form for a relatively long period even though they appear to be succumbing to the state. Previous elements of this ideology, which may be thought of by state agents as obsolete and *passé*, may be reactivated by the settling nomads in order to preserve their culture and protect it against the far reaching implications of the social, economic, and political consequences of sedentarization.

One of these ideological elements is their self-reliance, particularly spatio-political freedom from any obligation to an external political authority (such as the state). These elements are of great worth to them, yet often the capability of these elements to also affect nomads' rationalization of their sedentary behavior is ignored or overlooked by governments. This freedom previously ensured ripping the fruits of spatial and functional marginality which was beneficial when the state did not, or could not, interfere with their affairs. Under the context of the modern powerful state one may assume that these 'power of freedom' and 'power of marginality' of the ex-nomads disappear. It is precisely this assumption which is challenged here in discussing the case of distribution of local political power among the Israeli Negev Bedouin.

The dynamics of Bedouin 'power of marginality'

The historical dynamics of Bedouin 'power of marginality' in this century may be briefly summarized within the centripetal-centrifugal tension model of their relationships with governments that ruled Palestine (Meir 1997). Under the Ottoman Empire (until 1917) and the British Mandate (1921-1948), centrifugality was manifested by the Bedouin in their Negev territories within a pastoral nomadic context with little interruption. In general, these governments took relatively few initiatives to enforce their power upon the Bedouin. Centrifugality was thus constrained only by internal forces and affairs, that is inter-tribal or inter-group relationships, encoded within the traditional Bedouin law and socio-political order.

Since 1948, however, under the State of Israel and for the first time in their modern history, Bedouin centrifugality and 'power of marginality' became constrained by an external force. Bedouin freedom to sustain this cultural system was thus greatly reduced by strong centripetality applied by the state. This centripetality took several forms. The Bedouin were relocated in 1948 into a militarily-administered zone, the *seig*, which was in effect until 1966 (Figure 8.1). In the early 1950s the government, by interpreting and adopting versions of the old Ottoman Land Law, declared many Bedouin territories as state land. The Bedouin were left with little alternatives, and were compelled to intensify processes of sedentarization that begun earlier on a voluntary basis. They thus gradually abandoned their traditional livestock and dry-farming economic ventures, and settled in spontaneously erected small hamlets within the *seig* (Ben-David 1982).

Beginning by the early 1960s, the government initiated a project of further relocating the Bedouin into seven semi-urban towns, into which only about fifty percent of the Bedouin have by far moved. The towns were initially planned with little regard to Bedouin needs in terms of number and size of towns and their internal layout. These towns, let alone the other unplanned Bedouin spontaneous settlements in the periphery of the *seig*, have always suffered from deficient allocation of public resources such as

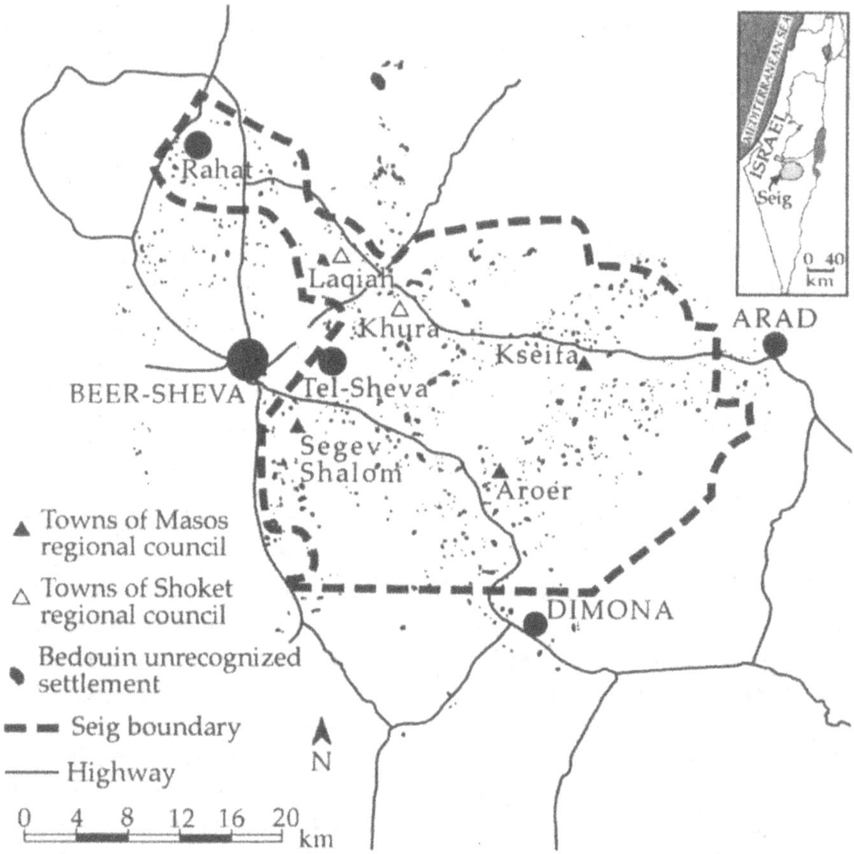

Figure 8.1 Bedouin towns, regional councils, and unrecognized settlements

establishment of an economic base and provision of health, education, welfare and other services (Ben-David 1992, 1993). This was manifested in deficient spatial and functional availability and accessibility, but most important in lack of cultural relevance to Bedouin's particular needs (Meir 1990). Finally, and most important from the perspective of the present article, until the mid-1980s, and for many practical purposes even at present, the distribution and decentralization of political power from the state down to the local people has been an extremely slow process.

Thus, at least until the early 1980s, Bedouin centrifugality and 'power of marginality' were reduced considerably. However, these ideological elements of their pastoral nomadic culture have not disappeared. They have been institutionalized into their culture to such an extent that they were kept by them in their cultural reserve. Beginning by the late 1970s they began to reactivate them gradually, now within a rural settled and a semi-urban context, in an attempt to regain some of the previous advantages of marginality. This reactivation took form in both public protest and self-empowerment action that were aimed at revitalizing their centripetal tendency.

Bedouin protest and action over local political power

The issues discussed above reflect the attempts by the state to impose a centripetal force on the Bedouin. This force affected both the ability of Bedouin groups to reside in a particular location, the nature of the settlement, and the manner in which they could comfortably conduct their autonomous life there. These issues, which originate primarily in the centrifugal-centripetal tension, considerably exacerbated the tension between the Bedouin and the Israeli government. During the military administration, until the mid-1960s, the state was capable of suppressing manifestations of this tension. Therefore, Bedouin civil protest in those years was quite minor.

The growth of Bedouin civil protest began in the late 1970s, and is accounted for by several events and processes. First, the implementation of the state's urbanization policy began to gain momentum. This resulted in a second wave of spatial and functional turbulence in Bedouin society within a period of three decades, the first wave having occurred during relocation into the *seig* in the late 1940s. Second, more than a decade of freedom from military administrative restrictions has contributed to increasing interaction of the Negev Bedouin with both the Jewish and Israeli-Arab populations. Associated with this process is the growth of civil identity among the Bedouin at the expense of ethnic identity, resulting in growing assertiveness among them.

In order to understand the evolution and dimensions of Bedouin protest and action, a survey of protest events as reported by the media since 1976 on all issues of their relationships with the government was conducted (Meir 1997). The Bedouin have been conducting various kinds of public protest, including press conferences, lobbying Arab and Jewish Israeli politicians and public functionaries, appeals to the Supreme Court of Justice, demonstrations, and schooling and sit-down strikes. They received external assistance of various kinds in their protest, and learned with time to recruit the media to promote their cause.

The issues on which the Bedouin were protesting were broken down into four categories as follows (in descending order of frequency of events): land ownership; allocation and internal distribution of public social resources (namely provision of public services); sedentarization and urbanization (that is the nature, structure, size and number of settlements – towns and villages – allowed by the government); allocation and internal distribution of agro-pastoral resources; and finally distribution of local political power.

Bedouin protest in all issues combined has grown considerably and steadily in the last two decades. However, the protest over distribution of political power, particularly in relation to self-management of Bedouin local and regional municipalities and state recognition of new ones, has begun to emerge only since the early 1980s, and was relatively minor and slow. Yet, in recent years it has gained momentum and, together with the policy of the government regarding the general nature of Bedouin settlements, has become a leading issue.

The consequences of this protest have been leading to action by the Bedouin and eventually to governmental gradual retreat from its centripetal tendency in many of the issues mentioned above, including the issue of local political power resources. This took place in several forms. The first one concerns local leadership. The government has constantly attempted to control the Bedouin population via co-optation of sheikhs and tribes, but this has had a boomerang effect. Until 1972 there were only eleven officially recognized tribes and sheikhs. For various internal and external reasons, Bedouin groups in towns and in the periphery have been demanding state recognition as independent and official tribes, despite the decline in the strength and importance of tribal organization and in the status of sheikhs. In some cases these groups took advantage of special circumstances while in others they exploited their good connections with government officials, and the general political-electoral game in Israel. This resulted in a centrifugal effect of a more than fourfold increase of the number of official tribes and sheikhs to forty eight in 1995 (with several more under consideration (Meir 1997). Although the nomination of sheikhs and the institution of tribes means relatively little in terms of external benefits, particularly given processes of detribalization that have taken place, its significance lies in diffusion of some internal political power and honor to groups that previously had little or no access to it.

The second, and more important form of action is the process of municipalization. It involves two sub-processes: the transfer of municipal power from the state to the Bedouin in terms of self-management, and recognition of spontaneous settlements that were not initiated by the government. These are discussed in length below.

Municipal self-management

In their initial stages, Bedouin towns that were established during the late 1960s and early 1970s had no municipal status. They were managed directly by the Ministry of the Interior with no local officers and offices. Public services were not available within them until only a later stage. These towns (Tel-Sheva and Rahat, see Figure 8.1) were simply assemblages of dwellings laid out according to a certain plan prepared by external planners. The plan of the first town, Tel-Sheva (estab. 1966) in particular did not fit Bedouin dwellers' socio-cultural needs, and therefore was slow in its growth process (Frenkel-Horner 1982). This attests to the lack of local political power that, if given by the state to the Bedouin, could have resulted in more appropriate approach to planning the early Bedouin towns. Lessons learned by planners from the initial failure of Tel-Sheva were more successfully applied in the second town, Rahat (estab. 1972).

Indeed, the growth and development of Rahat was smoother and rapider than that of Tel Sheva, and it became the first Bedouin town that received, in 1983, the municipal status of a 'local council'. This status is the second and lower ladder (below a 'city') of municipal status given to individual non-rural settlements in Israel. However, a Jewish mayor and officials were appointed for this town by the Ministry of the Interior, with only few local Bedouin representatives allowed on the town council. True, this method of municipal management has been common in newly established Jewish towns as well, serving to position them on the proper development track until municipal autonomy and local elections are approved by the Ministry. Yet, in the case of the Bedouin the government has been reluctant to renounce state control of this population and its affairs.

This municipal management policy was thus found particularly convenient, presumably since it constituted a civilian control substitute for the military administration that was abolished in the mid-1960s. It took several more years, until 1989, before local elections in Rahat were approved, since when the town of Rahat became municipally managed by its own people. Its growth process was accelerated, due to natural increase and further voluntary relocation of Bedouin families from the peripheral spontaneous settlements. Becoming the largest Bedouin town (Pop. ~28,000 in 1996, (Negev Center for Regional Development, 1996)) and the third largest urban settlement in the Negev at large, the municipal status of Rahat was even upgraded in 1995 from a local council to a city, making it eligible for expanded allocation of resources according to state regulations. Whether these resources have been allocated in sufficient and justified quantity and quality has been another issue, but this is beyond the concern of the present discussion.

The case of the other town, that of Tel Sheva (which, it is recalled, was established earlier), was more complicated. Due to initial ill-planning, its growth process was slower. The success of Rahat yielded newer and more appropriate planning ideas for Bedouin towns which were then implemented in Tel Sheva. Consequently, this town begun to grow faster beginning by the early 1980s, and was declared local council by 1986. Yet, the same municipal management approach by the Ministry of the Interior was adopted there as well. However, local people in Tel Sheva learned from the experience of Rahat, and used a tactic which became quite common among Bedouin elsewhere at later stages. They appealed to the Supreme Court, and by 1991 were able to reach a ruling against the Ministry which was compelled to call for local municipal elections. Since then the town has been ran independently by its own people. The significance of this case is that despite the smoother growth of this town during the 1980s compared to the 1960s and 1970s, and the development of a cadre of local, educated and able candidates for municipal posts (mayor and council members), the Ministry did not voluntarily yield its power of controlling the local population but only following legal action.

Thus, two decades were to lapse from the introduction of the urbanization program, and only following Bedouin public protest and struggle, before they were able to extract the political power resources from the state for towns that were already holding a municipal status.

Further implementation of the program of settling the Bedouin in towns continued afterwards in two waves. The first wave took place in the early 1980s, and included the towns of Aroer (1981), Kseifa (1982), and Shgieb (1984); the second wave of the late 1980s included Khura (1989) and Laqiah (1990) (Figure 8.1). The case of municipal management of these five planned Bedouin towns has, however, been even more complicated than the first two towns. Due to small population size (several hundreds on average), rural settlements in Israel at large cannot provide services efficiently and at equal cost to their population, and therefore hold no independent municipal status. For reasons of economies of scale, the law requires that a number of such neighboring settlements become incorporated into 'regional councils' which act as regional municipal management bodies for the efficient provision of public and municipal services and collection of municipal taxes. The Chairman ('mayor') of the council is elected by residents of these settlements, and council members are in fact elected representatives from the elected local committee of each settlement. These local committees have to coordinate their activities, and function side by side, with the regional council. The number of settlements included in a regional council may range between less than ten to more than forty, with the average ranging between fifteen and thirty. By 1990 there were fifty four such regional councils in Israel (Newman and Orgad 1991).

However, from a local management perspective, the case of the Bedouin has been different. While internal planning of these five new Bedouin towns was made with considerable participation of the various Bedouin groups that were to settle there (Fenster 1995), no local participation was sought by the Ministry of the Interior with regard to local management. The Ministry decided to enforce the above rural municipal management model upon these Bedouin towns. Therefore they were not awarded with an independent municipal status, but rather were incorporated into two regional councils (Masos, estab. 1988 and Shoket, estab. 1990).

This enforced policy raised several issues that constituted an exception with regard to municipal management norms elsewhere in Israel. The first issue relates to control of territory. The regional council of Masos incorporated the towns of Aroer, Kseifa, and Shgieb (Figure 8.1). These towns are quite separated spatially from each other, whereby the inter-towns periphery is interspersed with many small municipally unincorporated and unrecognized spontaneously erected Bedouin settlements. No Jewish settlements exist within this periphery. However, only the designated planned territories of these towns were included within the regional council. The inter-town areas remained thus outside the jurisdiction of the regional council. This spotty municipal territorial control and lack of spatial continuity is an exceptionally unique situation among regional councils in Israel, where the entire farming and non-farming areas within the council's boundaries are under their full municipal control. Such control ensures coordination of land-uses to minimize conflict, optimizes utilization of environmental resources, and ensures efficient provision of services to the settlements. In Masos, the special spatial situation has carried a potential for conflict between town dwellers and extra-town village dwellers which belong to no municipal body.

The second issue of an exceptional nature in terms of municipal management refers to the socio-political aspect of the location of council offices. Inter-tribal competition has always been quite sharp among the Bedouin, particularly at present given the constraint imposed upon the various traditional livelihood resources. Therefore towns were established based upon the principle of maximum internal tribal homogeneity, such that each was composed of groups of similar tribal origins with minimal inter-tribal mixture (Ben-David 1993). Thus, the towns that became incorporated into the regional council were each of a separate tribal origin. But then an issue was raised regarding the location of the offices of the municipality. This issue caused considerable debate, as the people of each town demanded their town to be chosen as a host for this facility. Therefore, due primarily to lack of internal agreement among the local people, the facility was eventually sited in a neutral location in Beer Sheva, the Jewish regional capital city of the Negev.

Although there have been some precedents among Jewish municipalities, this extra-territorial location of municipal government is exceptional in Israel. The problem as regards the Bedouin is twofold. First, Beer Sheva has historically been a regional central place for the Bedouin in terms of government, services, retailing, and other business (Gal-Pe'er 1979). Yet, before the state of Israel it was an Arab town. The present Jewish nature of Beer Sheva to some extent constitutes an alien cultural environment. Yet, the Bedouin are compelled to commute to this city for conducting their routine municipal affairs in the council's offices, such as tax payment, receiving various permits (building, business, etc.), and application for various kinds of support and welfare, in addition to non-municipal engagements such as agricultural and grazing permits and other government engagements. Given the fast growth rate of Bedouin town's population and their housing and other social and economic needs, the intense and complicated nature of Israeli governmental bureaucracy, and the fact that dealing with government is a relatively new cultural reality for the previously 'independent' nomadic Bedouin, this situation imposes considerable stress upon them. Spatial difficulties add further to this distressful situation, especially in light of the low motorization level among the Bedouin and the fact that the frequency of public transportation lines to Bedouin settlements is relatively low. Residents of Kseifa, for example, are in a particular hardship as their town is located about forty km. away from Beer Sheva (see Figure 8.1).

Second, town-dwelling has been an entirely new spatio-psychological experience for the Bedouin. The problem arises particularly from the increased population density in the town environment which requires new cultural and behavioral codes for maintaining social and spatial order (Rapoport 1978). The development of these codes has been naturally slow, part of the slow adjustment to modern urban life. Together with the economic adjustment required for integration into the capitalistic labor market, this has been causing considerable stress among the resettlers. Many local conflicts, some quite violent, have erupted among Bedouin groups over various issues such as the struggle for siting desired public facilities (schools, clinics, sport clubs, mosques, etc.) in a certain neighbourhood, the desire to avoid unwanted facilities in a certain neighbourhood, or over various social issues such as privacy, honour, dignity of women and so forth (Keidar and Meir 1995). The ex-territorial and remote location of the council's offices reduced considerably the ability of officials to intervene in real time for calming the conflicts or even preventing them. This, in fact, reflects lack of municipal control over local issues which is particularly required in the highly sensitive cultural situation within which the Bedouin are situated.

The third and most important issue regarding municipal management has been that of the regional council's chairmen and council members. The process in Masos was similar to that of the initial stages of Rahat and Tel Sheva, namely the appointment of a Jewish chairman and some Jewish council members by the Ministry of the Interior. True, the vice chairman was a Bedouin, but he received little co-operation from tribesmen of tribal origins other than his, a situation which reflects the internal competition for political power resources among the Bedouin. In contrast, throughout his entire tenure in post, the Jewish appointed chairman enjoyed considerable appreciation and support of residents of the towns under his jurisdiction to such an extent that interviews with residents revealed that all other things being equal, many would have preferred his tenure extended. They thus expressed their acceptance of his tenure in post as a solution to many inter-tribal rivalries and conflicts.

However, other things have not been quite equal. Despite the basic similarity between Masos and Rahat or Tel Sheva, the situation in Masos was considerably more complicated. In addition to the problems described above, which caused considerable hardship to residents of the three towns, it should be noted that soon after the establishment of Masos these towns begun to grow, and already in the early 1990s each numbered several thousands of residents. Such a population size of a single rural settlement that is incorporated within a regional council is an exceptional situation in Israel, being far greater than the average population size of Jewish rural settlements. The growth in size of these towns generated growing inter-town conflicts over allocation of resources by the regional council to each town. These conflicts were severe especially given the already constrained resources allocated by the state to the Bedouin community at large, a situation which generated a considerable development gap with the non-Bedouin population in Israel (Arab and Jewish alike). The conflicts were deep to such an extent that the council was often unable to reach decisions or to implement decisions that were reached following fierce and bitter council deliberations. In addition to these problems, unrest has grown from the local people over the very issue of Jewish remote-control from Beer Sheva of local Bedouin affairs, a situation which they have increasingly began to regard as a form of dependency and cultural-political patronizing. Consequently, pressure has emerged with time from various local groups who begun to demand that the above described system of rural municipal management is reformed.

This pressure has accumulated particularly as the Bedouin have increasingly become convinced, through observing reality among Jewish rural settlements elsewhere, that the total population size of the regional council has reached a threshold that justifies transfer of municipal management to their own control. This conviction came about also through their realization that their society has developed and progressed sufficiently to produce internal resources of political leadership and municipal expertise, particularly as a number of the professional officers in the regional council as well as members of the council itself were Bedouin by origin. However, their attempts to persuade the Ministry to reform the municipal management system failed.

As was the case with the towns of Rahat and Tel Sheva, the Ministry was once again reluctant to pursue this reform. There were various reasons for this reluctance, not the least important of which was the fear of yielding control over Bedouin affairs. Another reason was economies of scale (saving on facilities, salaries, and various resources) that were accrued, in the Ministry's eyes, from retaining this particular municipal management system. A further reason, which will later on become one of the most criticized procedures by the Ministry, was the Minister's desire for appointment of Jewish chairmen, council members, and officials as part of the internal political-electoral game in Israel.

Thus, by late 1993, five years after the regional council of Masos was established, the Bedouin decided to take action in their attempt to reform the municipal management system. It is recalled that by then the Bedouin have accumulated about two decades of experience in public protest against the government over various issues of their life in the new urbanized environment. A group of Bedouin from the various towns have joined in an appeal to the Israeli Supreme Court of Justice against the Minister of the Interior requiring him to announce within six months municipal elections to the regional council of Masos. This group consisted mainly of members of the younger generation. They took this action despite objection of the older generation of elders, who preferred a merger of each individual town with one of the neighbouring Jewish towns in order to prevent internal inter-tribal struggle over chairmanship of the regional council (Sagi 1997). Few weeks later an agreement was reached between this group and the Minister about elections to be taken during 1994. Following some deliberation regarding the validity of this agreement, the Supreme Court ruled to approve it.

However, by early 1994 another group of Bedouin appealed to the Supreme Court requiring that the agreement and the ruling are canceled. Once again, internal Bedouin politics, and presumably fear of involvement of the radical Islamic Movement, were responsible for this appeal (Sagi 1997). Instead, a new ruling was requested, namely that the Ministry announces local elections in each of the three towns. In their explanation they raised many of the issues that were described above. Yet they also argued that the pace of relocation of additional population from the periphery to these towns is expected to accelerate in the forthcoming years, which could better reflect the true balance of power between the towns rather than the temporary one which could have been reached under the proposed elections to the regional council at that time. They also suggested that it would be acceptable to them if the local elections take place within two years, a solution they assumed would be acceptable also by the Ministry.

In its response to the appeal, the Ministry proposed a public committee to investigate the case and to suggest a solution. This response followed considerable public pressure and media exposure, which persuaded the Ministry about the irrationality of its objection to the dissolution of the regional council. By late 1994 the public committee indeed recommended that the regional council of Masos is dissolved, and each town becomes a local municipality, with elections to be taken within two years. Yet, it took the Ministry a whole year, until early 1996, to dissolve Masos and award the status of local council to Kseifa, Aroer, and Shgieb. The opportunity was then taken to adopt the same solution as well for the other regional council of Shoket, which incorporated the towns of Khoura and Lakhia and which suffered from the same problems as described above for Masos. It should be noted, however, that this decision by the Minister of the Interior was reached a few months before the general parliamentary elections in Israel and, according to some Bedouin observers, was taken presumably as part of the electoral campaign.

Yet, while the Bedouin were highly successful in this part of their campaign to reform the rural municipal management system, the Ministry still insisted on maintaining the old model of appointed council chairman and members. Being thus loyal to its centripetal desire to continue its control of the Bedouin population, it refrained from calling for local elections.

True, by early May 1996, few days before the general parliamentary elections and presumably again as part of the electoral campaign, the Minister of the Interior publicly announced local elections in each of the five towns within a year.

However, the political upheaval in Israel in 1996 as an outcome of the general elections caused a change in government, and a new Minister of the Interior was appointed. The new Minister decided to ignore the decision of his predecessor. He ordered the municipal offices of the five towns to remain in Beer Sheva, housed within the office buildings of the two previous regional councils. More seriously, however, he appointed a Jewish mayor and vice mayor for each of these local councils. All the appointees are outsiders, living outside the Negev region altogether, and some are even carrying additional municipal posts in their place of residence. Experience so far has revealed that they manage these towns on a remote-control basis from their Beer Sheva offices or elsewhere, visiting their communities once or twice a week. This has been considered by the Bedouin a regression even from their previous achievement whereby the vice-chairmen of the regional councils were Bedouin persons. Finally, the new Minister decided that from among nine council members in each local council, only four were to be appointed from within the Bedouin population, ensuring thus a Jewish majority on the council which will facilitate sustained control of the Bedouin population.

These decisions were reached by the new Minister in order to provide lucrative jobs with generous side benefits for his political affiliates, some of whom lack municipal management qualifications altogether. These appointments were to remain effective for four years, with the possibility of extension for another term. The Bedouin have regarded this as a total despise of their society and its ability to manage their affairs independently. By late 1996 they appealed once again to the Supreme Court in order to reach a ruling that calls for free local elections, but as of mid-1997 the situation has not changed. On the contrary, the remote-control system of management, and lack of qualifications of the appointee persons, have generated further stress among the Bedouin and caused several crises with quarrels among Bedouin groups in some of the towns. In a television broadcast on Israeli General Television (May 25, 1997), the spokeswoman of the Ministry of the Interior explained this policy on the grounds that 'many of the appointee persons (which are members of a particular political party, A.M.) are closest to the Arab mentality by virtue of having been born in Arab countries, speak their language, and are thus preferable over members of other political parties who are alien to this mentality'.

The Bedouin's campaign is still going on. Their case was widely publicized, and generated much public interest. Following this campaign, the present norm by which an appointed local council's mandate should not be extended beyond a two years period was recently passed as a new law in a first reading in the Knesset. Also, most recently a proposal was made by the Ministry that local elections in the Bedouin towns will take place in 1998, together with the next scheduled municipal elections in Israel. The Bedouin, from their perspective, are unwilling to wait, and are continuing their campaign for immediate local elections in their towns. They have been demanding also that, in the meantime, the offices of their local councils be relocated from the previous Beer-Sheva office buildings (which still carry the sign-posts of the previous regional councils) into their appropriate towns. The reason was not only that the officials become more closely acquainted with their local community and its problems, and that the local population enjoys a higher degree of municipal well-being, but also that the municipality can function better *in situ* rather than in the Beer Sheva location where all the officials and functionaries of all towns are now crowded into the same municipal building of the previous regional council. In this area the Bedouin have been also successful, as recently the Ministry approved some budget for gradual relocation of municipal offices into towns.

The issue of unrecognized settlements

A related issue to the Bedouin community's campaign for a reformed municipal management has been their campaign regarding the unrecognized settlements. These settlements, which were established spontaneously, are located within the inter-town rural periphery. There are thirty six such settlements, as defined by members of Bedouin community, which contain about fifty percent of the ~100,000 Bedouin population. This population is reluctant to relocate into any of the seven planned towns. Various reasons are raised by them, such as their land ownership claims and therefore land dispute with the state, quality of life within the towns, and their fear (based on their kin's experience) that urban life is detrimental to traditional Bedouin culture. These settlements are devoid of any municipal status and are therefore mostly non-eligible for independent allocation of public resources. Hence, many of their services are provided by the other Bedouin municipalities or directly by the government ministries but, as revealed elsewhere, are at considerably lower quality and quantity compared even to the those provided in Bedouin towns.

Yet, unlike the towns these unrecognized rural settlements are quite homogeneous in their internal ethnic (tribal) structure, and are considered by their residents as a more appropriate solution for a culturally relevant settlement policy by the state. Thus, despite their relatively small size, their residents have been demanding state municipal recognition. These demands have begun to be voiced already in the late-1980s, upon Bedouin realization of the negative socio-cultural consequences of relocating to towns and that progress in the solution of their land claims was rather slow. Many of their residents have attempted to build permanent homes on what they consider as their land. The government, refusing to recognize these settlements, let alone as municipal entities, has been declaring this act as illegal home construction on state land, and many homes have been demolished in the course of time. The government has also been investing much effort to relocate residents of these settlements to the towns, but with relatively little success.

In recent years, following intensive protest by the Bedouin and publicity of this issue in the media, the state has begun to somewhat relax its obstinate centripetal policy, and to consider other, non-urban alternatives for Bedouin permanent settlement. This represents a further successful step in Bedouin's centrifugal campaign. One of the most vivid examples concerns a Bedouin village which was cut-off from its direct access to the main road to Beer Sheva due to construction of a four-lane highway in 1996. Following considerable protest, and contrary to the original plan, the state was compelled to construct a special junction at the entrance to this village that allows an easy access. While this represents an informal state recognition of this village, the state is still insisting that these settlements receive no independent municipal status.

As a further step in their campaign, members of Bedouin community's elite in the Negev have established in late 1996 an independent Bedouin Strategic Planning Committee (BSPC), based in Rahat. Its purpose, endorsed by the wider Arab community in Israel, is to act as an internal independent Bedouin body in front of governmental planning agencies, and represent Bedouin's view of their cultural and civil needs and future. This self-empowerment act is meant to prepare a strategic long term development plan for the Bedouin community that will counterbalance from below those governmental plans from above.

One of the issues that was given top priority is that of the unrecognized settlements, in regard of which the BSPC begun to take action in early 1997. During the recent annual Arab Day of the Land ceremony in the Negev, it announced its own self-recognition of one of the unrecognized settlements, located east of Beer Sheva. It also decided to post sign-posts with the names of these settlements in the entrance to each settlement. Soon after, the BSPC announced independent local elections to be taken shortly in these settlements, whereby each will elect a local committee. These committees will then convene to establish a regional council which will be regarded by the BSPC as a formal municipal body, with an elected chairman and council members. A special fund has also been established for funding the initial budget of this regional council. Elections for this informal regional council indeed took place in June 1997, and it now incorporates twelve unrecognized settlements. The Ministry of course refuses to recognize this Bedouin regional council.

By thus taking these acts, the Bedouin intend to create unchangeable facts of self local municipal management. The Ministry of the Interior has of course responded by declaring the proposed elections illegal and by removing the sign-posts. In response, the BSPC published a press release saying that it regards these acts by the Ministry as 'a serious offense against the Bedouin right for a social, geographical, and historical identity. The sign-posts are the identity card of the settlements, and the police should take action against the intruders who removed them...' (*Kol HaNegev* 1997). The BSPC has also decided to repost new post-signs and to appeal to the Ministry to register residents of these settlements according to their real place of residence, arguing that this is their undeniable civil right.

Conclusions

The recent events described above demonstrate the Bedouin's determination that the reality of municipal management that prevailed so far is not repeated when the unrecognized settlements, or at least some of them, become recognized. They signify a further stage in Bedouin conflict with the state, because they involve also the most basic issue of this conflict, one from which many of the other issues stem: their claim for the right to build their permanent homes on lands for which they claim ownership. While this issue has been resolved for the those Bedouin relocated to towns, it is still a very pressing one for those still living in the periphery.

It is for this reason that the Bedouin have become so active, demanding, and assertive in their campaign for a reformed municipal system within their communities. They are motivated by their desire to control their own territorial, social, economic, and cultural resources. They desire this control in a manner that can enable them to regain some of the 'power of marginality' which they lost during the recent decades of sedentarization and modernization. This power, that previously was built into their culture through the values of nomadism, tribalism, and ethnicity, has become a normative behavior for this, as well as for many other pastoral nomadic societies elsewhere. Being thus built into their culture it has become the major force in their centrifugal ideology and tendency.

Yet, as many students of cultural change have argued, culture is a mechanism of social reproduction (Castells 1983). It contains a reservoir of institutionalized alternatives from which the members of the transformed society choose those that are best suitable for their changing environment (Salzman 1980). That is, even when the circumstances that created these cultural values disappear, they tend to persist within the changing society. In the case of the Bedouin's campaign for a reformed municipal management system, spatial and functional centrifugality, through the desired 'power of marginality', enables this social reproduction. The persistence of this deeply rooted psychology is the major reason for conflict with the state. But it is also the dialectics between this ethnic persistence and the emergence of civil awareness and identity under the modern state that is paving the road for the ex-nomadic Bedouin in compelling the Israeli government to gradually relax its centripetal ideology and tendency.

References

Behnke, R.H., and I. Scoones (1993), 'Rethinking Range Ecology: Implications for Range Management in Africa', in Behnke, R.H., I., Scoones, and C. and Kerven (eds.), *Range Ecology at Disequilibrium: New Models of Natural Variability and Pastoral Adaptation in African Savannas,* Overseas Development Institute: London.

Ben-David, Y. (1982), *Stages in the Development of the Bedouin Spontaneous Settlement in the Negev*, Ph.D. Dissertation, Department of Geography, The Hebrew University: Jerusalem (Hebrew).

Ben-David, Y. (1992), *Turnaround in Negev Bedouin Urbanization in the 1980's – The Case of Kuseifa,* The Jerusalem Institute of Israel Research: Jerusalem (Hebrew).

Ben-David, Y. (1993), *Bedouin Settlement in the Negev – Policy and Practice, 1967–1992,* Ministry of Housing and Jerusalem Institute for Israel Research: Jerusalem (Hebrew).

Castells, M. (1983), *The City and the Grassroots: A Cross-Cultural Theory of Urban Social Movement,* Arnold: London.

Fenster, T. (1995), Participation as a Political Process in Enforced Resettlement Projects: The Bedouin in Israel, *Geography Research Forum,* 15, pp. 33–48.

Frenkel-Horner, D. (1982), Planning for Bedouins: The Case of Tel Sheva, *Third World Planning Review*, Vol. 4, pp. 159–176.

Gal-Pe'er, I. (1979), 'Beer-Sheva and the Bedouin', in Gradus, Y., and E. Stern (eds.), *The Book of Beer-Sheva*, Keter: Jerusalem (Hebrew).

Harbeson, J. W. (1991), 'Post-Drought Adjustments Among Horn of Africa Pastoralists: Policy and Institution-Building Dimensions', in F.A.O. (ed.), *Report of a Sub-Regional Seminar on the Dynamics of Pastoral Lands and Resource Tenure in the Horn of Africa, Mogadishu, 1990*, Food and Agriculture Organization of the United Nations: Rome.

Keidar, R., and A. Meir (1995), Locational Conflicts Over Public Facilities Among the Bedouin, Unpublished paper, Department of Geography and Environmental Development, Ben-Gurion University of the Negev: Beer-Sheva (Hebrew).

Kol HaNegev (1997), 'Bedouin Steering Committee Convened Following the Green Patrol Action', April 11, 1997 (Hebrew).

Kressel, G.M. (1993), Nomadic Pastoralists, Agriculturalists and the State: Self-Sufficiency and Dependence in the Middle-East, *Journal of Rural Cooperation*, Vol. 21, pp. 33–49.

Meir, A. (1988), Nomads and the State: The Spatial Dynamics of Centrifugal and Centripetal Forces among the Israeli Negev Bedouin, *Political Geography Quarterly*, Vol. 7, pp. 251–270.

Meir, A. (1990), Provision of Public Services to the Post-Nomadic Bedouin Society in Israel, *The Service Industries Journal*, Vol. 10, pp. 768–785.

Meir, A. (1997), *As Nomadism Ends: The Israeli Bedouin of the Negev*, Westview Press: Boulder, Co.

Negev Center for Regional Development (1996), *Statistical Yearbook of the Negev, 3*. Ben-Gurion University of the Negev: Beer-Sheva (Hebrew).

Newman, D., and A. Orgad (1991), *The Regional Councils in Israel*, The Regional Councils Association: Tel Aviv (Hebrew).

Rapoport, A. (1978), Nomadism as a Man-Environment System, *Environment and Behavior*, Vol. 10, pp. 214–247.

Sagi, I. (1997), The Bedouin Regional Councils, Paper presented at the Annual Symposium on the Bedouin, Sede Boker (Hebrew).

Salzman, P.C. (1980), *When Nomads Settle: Processes of Sedentarization as Adaptation and Response*, Praeger: New York.

9 Land tenure in rural marginal Western Pampa in Argentina

ANA MARIA PETAGNA DE DEL RIO

Introduction

This chapter derives from the research on theory and explanation about marginal western Pampa. The Pampa region is one of the most profitable temperate plain of the world. It runs from the Atlantic Ocean to the central hills and central shrub. It occupies about the 20% of the territory. Its marginal western area was incorporated during this century. The behaviour of this area seems to be similar to the Pampa core but there is some kind of complexity that allows to consider it a marginal one.

In an earlier study on marginality we compared this area with a chaotic behaviour system because the results are always undefined (Petagna, 1996). As we could see in that opportunity there are many factors that take place to define rural marginal western Pampa. We are asking now if land tenure is one of them.

In this region the yield of cereal and animal production depends on the size of farms. There is a certain kind of relation between land tenure and the size of rural enterprises. It is well known, that it was during the second half of the nineteenth century, when the great grasslands of the world were being opened up, the economy of Pampa began to emerge.

Pampa is a plain covered by temperate grassland. The dominant plants are the grasses, the most widespread and successful group of land plants. It occupies Buenos Aires Province and the eastern La Pampa Province, southern areas of Santa Fe Province, Entre Ríos Province and Córdoba Province.

In Argentina there are few areas of concentration of population and more empty and nearly empties spaces which remain largely because of their historic and natural conditions. The most crowded region of Argentina is Pampa. It is located in midlatitude zone with a humid subtropical marine climate with four different seasons. Some of the most important cities are on the Atlantic coast.

Rural marginal western Pampa

The boundary between the Pampa region and the Thorny Wood, called Espinal, is considered as a part of Pampa Region since rural patterns of the Pampa emerged in this area with the occupancy by migrants. There was a migration chain since many migrants followed in the footsteps of those who have previously migrated. They came from Eastern Europe and they founded small villages. It took place during the beginning of this century (Figure 9.1).

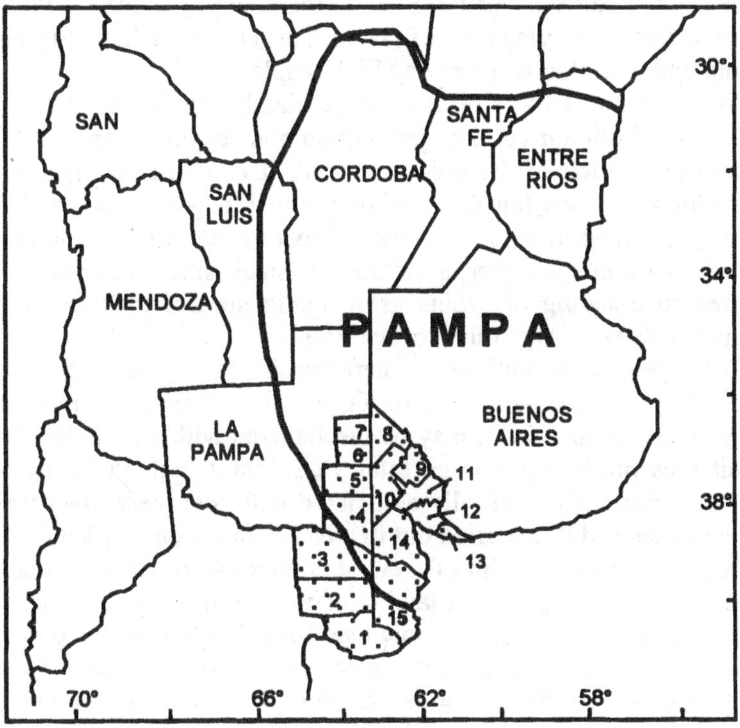

1= Adolfo Alsina	6= Guatrache	11= Tornquist
2= Conesa	7= Atrelico	12= Bahia Blanca
3= Pichi Mahuida	8= Adolfo Alsina	13= Cnel Rosales
4= Caleucaleu	9= Saavedra	14= Villarino
5= Hucal	10= Puan	15= Patagones

Figure 9.1 Argentine South-western marginal borderland [1]

These immigrants could buy the public land. The government sold small and large farms which were taken from the destroyed thorny wood. There was a conversion of unsuitable areas to arable agricultural and this created significant migration and subsequent colonization in the area.

It is this space which is considered a marginal region in regional scale. First of all we ponder on ecological and geometrical marginalities (Leimgruber, 1994). In this sense we consider that these areas are ecotones (Petagna, 1996). Ecotone is a transition between two different biomasses. The transition happens from east to west and physically prairie contacted with wood of leguminosae before human activities took place. Seconly, an economic marginality is occuring due to the natural conditions, while at he same time there are symptoms of social marginality such as out-migration of young and educated workers and high employment.

Nowadays the area is used as a grassland with scattered tress. From 1965 to 1985 both agricultural production and retention for some farm or non farm population of the area increased. It is a part of Argentine rural sector which assumes the function of producing goods and raw material preferably oriented to external market. Most of the farms are large (estancias), while a minor number is medium or small sized. The use of land is dedicated to breeding or grains growing. In general the field system is extensive such as in Argentine core prairie.

This type of rural activity is characterized by relatively low levels of input and output per unit area of farmland. Farming in large holdings employs little labour, and it may be mechanized with a relatively low cost per unit area producing a large total yield and a high yield per worker. Extensive agricultury is usually associated with relatively low rural population densities and it is carried out in areas distant from markets.

From an economic point of view, it is possible to consider, that the net income of crops on a parcel of land may be very low, while there may be a large net income for using the same land for cattle rearing. In this case the land is marginal for crop cultivation (especially wheat) and the farmer is likely to transfer his capital and labour to cattle rearing. In both cases total revenue only covers farmer's total costs in some years.

There is no doubt that the transformation of the ecotone into agricultural and cattle rearing space has generated this marginal area called Arid Pampa, in Argentina. Much of the literature tends to generalize as a whole and from this point of view it is considered a subregion from the Pampa Region. However it is culturally and physically heterogeneous. The use of land by agriculture and rural activities in general is not always productive and successful. The land value and rent vary quickly in response to yield variations.

The changes happen between the increasing time of agricultural and declining time of it. The relation between the basic elements of the production process, labour land and capital, varies according to the type of productions. However, physical conditions, especially the weather, are fundamental in the variety of yields during sowing and harvesting seasons. The yield of animal breeding varies clearly (Figure 9.2) in this space. High yield of cattle and sheep breeding goes away from the ecotone. It is necessary to have one and a half hectare per cattle. That's a low receptivity. This land needs to produce about 40 kg per hectare just to be profitable, but this production is not common. It is not easy to have a higher yield with lower costs in these physically marginal areas (Figure 9.3).

Population is wide spread (Figure 9.4). High density occurs in the central subcounty, Bahía Blanca city and its hinterland while the lower density occurs in the south and in the west. The rest of the space looks empty except for the main subcounty cities. In the latter areas population did not rise since last census 1980. Bahía Blanca city is the nodal point in a converging transport network by acting as a centre of employment, by being a seat of local government, by functioning as a central place. The size and status of the settlement make it to act as the focal point of the area. The city provides goods and services for the benefit of this area despite some subcounties belong to an other county. The influence comprises both rural district and smaller and dependent settlements (Figure 9.5).

The origin and progress of land transference in Pampa Region

The government was the owner of most of the land since the independence of the country in 1810 to the end of the last century, and when the Pampa was brought into production the problems of property appeared very soon.

The laws, called Indian Laws, were the first rules that came from Spanish authorities in Spain. According to these laws the sovereign was the owner of the land but it was allowed to make some transference or to sell them to private people.

There were three types of owner in the end of eighteenth century:

a) 'Militaries and public officials' received large areas, about 40,000 Hectares. This type of transference was free of duties. Perhaps these properties were the beginning of the large estancias which were the pattern of the way of living of upper social classes;

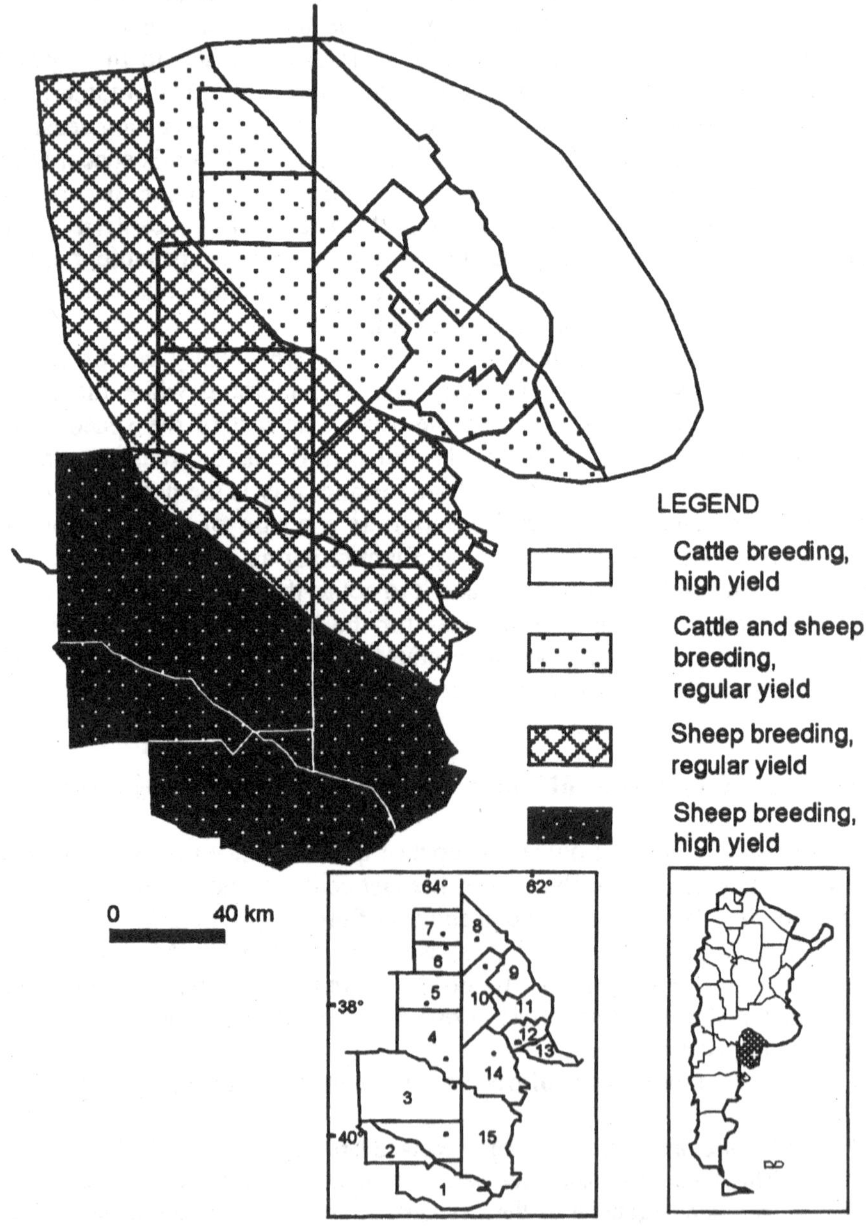

Figure 9.2 Animal breeding areas of the marginal borderland

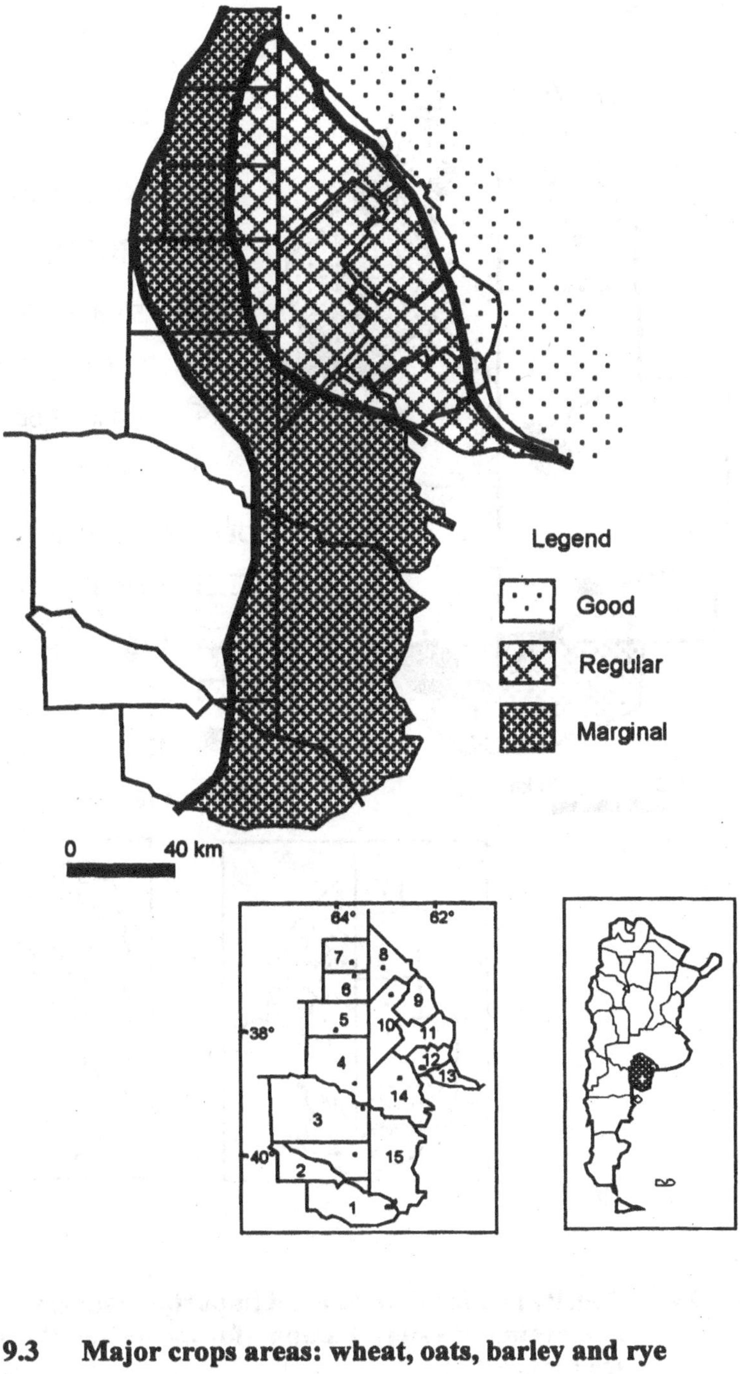

Figure 9.3 Major crops areas: wheat, oats, barley and rye

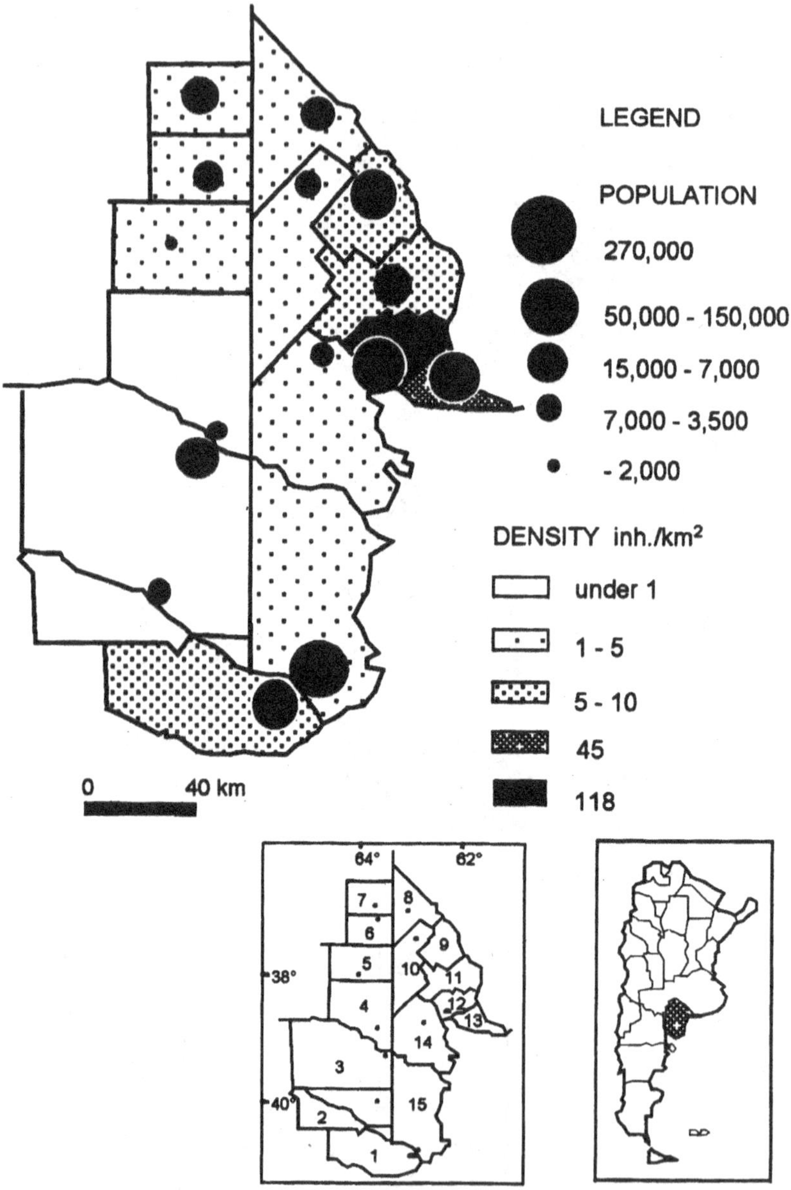

Figure 9.4 Density and location of most important villages and cities in marginal Western Pampa (for the names of regions see Figure 9.1)

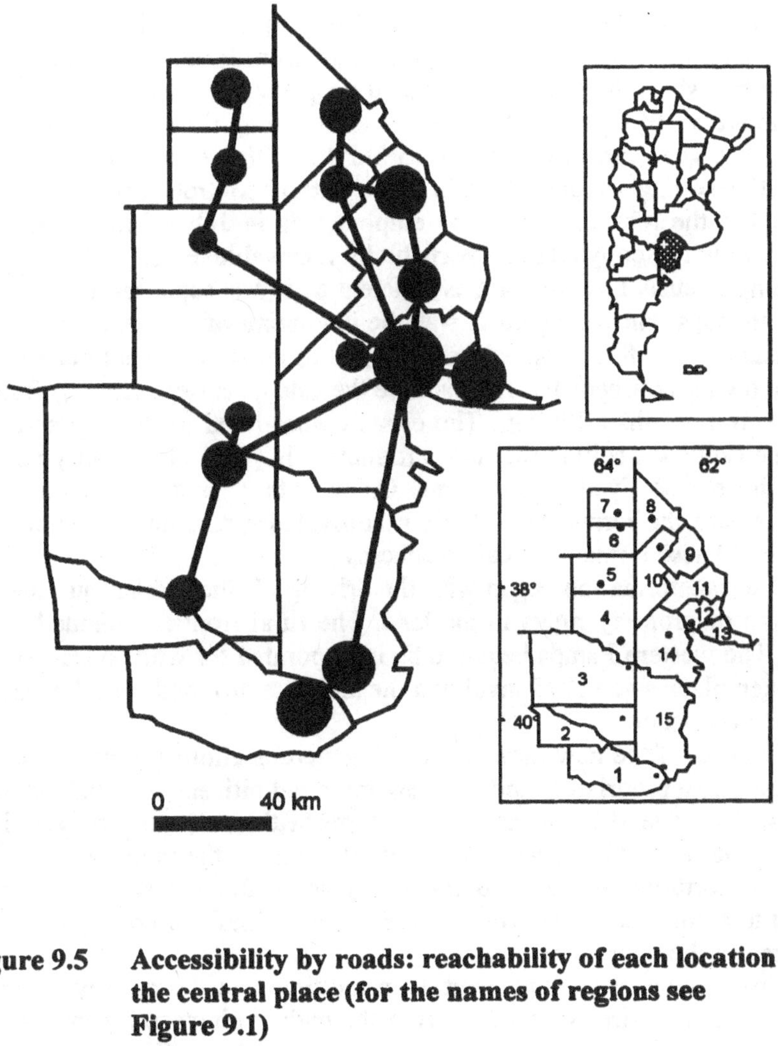

Figure 9.5 Accessibility by roads: reachability of each location from the central place (for the names of regions see Figure 9.1)

b) 'The small owners' were the founders of villages and settlements and received about 1,875 Hectares. These properties were small units because it was not possible to breed an enough quantity of animals to make the property profitable. These were called suerte de estancia;

c) 'Poor people' who occupied the land that belonged to the government without permission. These lands were called realengas (or the land of the king). The lands, owned in this way, were not productive ones. The Indians occupied many places of the plain. It was not easy to run the risk of trying to set up any kind of settlements. Few people wanted to run it.

After 1810, when Argentina got its freedom from Spain, it was necessary to try to take the land from the Indians in order to extend the public land. Meanwhile the theme of the land property continued being a problem, above all trying to find a way for establishing urban and rural settlements. The government decided to forbid the selling of land in April 1822 when the selling of public lands went out of control. The government authorized the renting of land by emphyteusis in July of the same year. This is a kind of copyhold or a perpetually renewable lease.
The Emphyteusis Law was not as efficient as it was supposed to be. Some literature says that emphyteusis was the beginning of the very large farms in hands of very few people who belonged to an upper social class called 'estate owner bourgeoisie.' At this time the estancias were close to Buenos Aires, no more than 300 km. The estate owner lived in the city and they become rich soon selling the rural products. They had farm managers who were those who lived in the farms. On the other hand there were small farms where the farmers lived. They cultivated grains and other primary products. These farms were called chacras.

The transformation began with the driving off the Indians and the distribution of property rights in the land. The rural frontier extended to the West. The western Pampa began to be incorporated for white occupancy. It has taken place since 1875 involving the area in a new and complex pattern of land occupancy.

The size of the new farms reflected generous allotment by a nation of abundant unappropriated land and few favoured citizens for establishing a rural seat with land for livestock. The form of the properties reflected the carrying out a random system of survey. It begun in the vicinity of Buenos Aires in north-western and south-eastern areas and the survey extended inland to form successive properties of various sizes and convenient regular form on the unbroken plain.

This occupancy took place at the same time that the railway extended beyond Buenos Aires province during the end of nineteenth century. The road pattern followed the orientation of property lines. The only through roads were those along side railways. Uniformity of the land and lack of rural concentrations were suggested by the spacing of railways and placement of stations regularly 12 miles (20 km), with occasional exceptions. The railway pattern of the Pampa region clearly suggests how it gets inside the thorny wood. This native closed thorny wood of shrubs and trees which belong to the family of Leguminosae (Prosopis sp.) was cut by white occupancy in order to make vegetal coal, sticks and timbers. The railways were necessary to carry out the goods. The wood was half destroyed and the denuded land was incorporated for cropping and breeding.

Agricultural law and land tenure in Argentina

There were many laws that guaranteed private property since 1900 but the Colonization Law 12636 of 1940, was the one that introduced rules of regulation of land use, land tenure and size of farms in order to organize the land charge register. This rule introduced the theme of 'economic land unit', as a way to protect small farmers from the risk of agricultural production above all in marginal and less productive areas.

An economic land unit is defined as the smallest unit of land necessary to obtain enough profits. It is a spatial measure that depends on many conditions such as physical, above all climatic conditions and economic ones as the market prices and investments of farmers. Cereal production per hectare is taken to decide if a farm may be considered as an economic land unit. It varies year after year. For example last year it was 600 Hectares and ten years before it was 700 Hectares. It means that the yield during last year increased considerably and that a farm of 600 Hectares was enough rentable.

The implication of this Law allowed to clarify the rights of those who were the owners and to consolidate the fields that emerged after Desert Expedition.

Many Laws fixed rules about smallholdings (minifundio) and large landed estate (latifundio). Smallholders are people who belong to lower classes depending largely on subsistence agricultural. This social class is common in the marginal western Pampa

Nowadays land tenure is the system of land ownership and of title to its use. It takes a number of different forms. National Agricultural Censuses have been undertaken since 1940 but they are not taken at regular intervals. Last Census took place 1990. In spite of this it took the same types of data for the same system of spatial units. The agricultural enterprise is the unit for which census data are recorded and published. The Census units are called the EAP. It means Agricultural and Livestock Enterprise, that is the economic concept of farms (Table 9.1).

The main types are:

1 'Owner occupation': The user or occupier is the owner. That is self management.
2 'Tenancy': Where the user or occupier is not the owner and where the user either pays the owner rent or he makes payment as labour or share cropping.

2.1 'Farm lease': The producer is called lease holder (to let on lease).

2.2 'Share farming or Sharecropping': The producer is called share farmer or sharecropper. In this case if the production is lost the risk is both for the owner and for the sharefarmer. Agricultural Law 13246, article 21, states the difference between share cropping and share breeding. The first is when the land is shared and the latter when the animals are shared.

3 'Mixed contract': It is stated by Agricultural Law 13246, article 44. It represents the join between farm lease and share farming. In this case the owner receives a percentage of production and some money.

Table 9.1 Types of land tenure in Argentina 2

	EAP	Hectares
Owner	274,000	134,000,000
Farm Lease	15,100	6,200,000
Share Cropping	3,800	710,000
Others	72,000	31,890,000
Public Land	14,100	5,200,000
Total	379,000	178,000,000

Source: Argentina Agricultural National Census

There are other types of land tenure which are sometimes guaranteed by a contract. For an example we can mention that type where the tenant contributes only with work and tools.

Argentine agricultural country has 178,000,000 Hectares and 379,000 agricultural fields. Approximately 72% of them are used or occupier by the owner and 23.75 are in hands of tenant farmer (Table 9.2). This condition is the result of a legal process. It allowed the immigrants to buy the farms where they were working.

The data of the table above are showing a similar situation between the Pampa Region and the whole country. About 66% of agricultural enterprises are used or occupied by the owners. The Pampa Region has the 34% of the agricultural enterprises of the country and with the Patagonia Region joins together about the 60% of these enterprises. The lesser data about farm lease and share cropping show that the tendency is the use and occupancy of farms by the owners, both in the country and in the Regional Pampa. Public lands are insignificant and those which belong to military institutions and scientific institutions are considered in this type.

Table 9.2 The Pampa region, number of enterprises and surface occupied by different types of land tenure

	EAP	Hectares
Owner	83,300	21,000,000
Farm Lease	18,000	1,900,000
Share Cropping	1,200	220,000
Others	22,180	19,718,000
Public Land	520	162,000
Total	125,200	43,000,000

Source: Agricultural National Census 1995

Conclusion

The land tenure in rural western Pampa Region (Table 9.3) is not very different of the whole country and of the Pampa Region. Large farms commonly held by the owner are more common (70%) such as in the whole country. These farms occupied the 82% of the surface. This means that the most of the rural land is in hands of the owners. We can make a small difference inside the marginal region between the subcounties. There is a gradient from the East to the West (Figure 9.6). The amount of slope is about 30%. The south-western subcounties Pichi Mahuida and Adolfo Alsina show the most percentage, about 90%. These amounts have a historic cause. After the Desert Expedition those lands that were taken from Indians were given to the people, above all militaries, who participated in the expedition.

There were large uninhabited spaces in barren lands. They seemed to be not productive. Nowadays these lands have a high value because of their good possibilities for livestock, especially sheep breeding. The economic process agrees with conditions for capitalist agriculture. The political impact upon the wild landscape in the end of ninteenth century is still expressed through the actual rural landscape.

The landscape resulting from the transformation of both grassy Pampa and thorny wood is characterized by a simple rural pattern. There are not important differences between the core and periphery talking about land tenure. Historical and political economical factors draw the actual territory.

Table 9.3 Number of agricultural enterprises (EAP) in marginal Western Pampa in 1995

Subcounties	Total	Owners	Farm Lease	Share Cropping	Others
A. Alsina	581	468	20	29	64
Gral. Conesa	403	308	21	31	43
Pichi Mahuida	540	468	25		47
Atreucó	524	347	41		136
Guatraché	685	468	35	3	179
Hucal	544	385	14		145
Caleu Caleu	233	183	17		33
Bahía Blanca	348	218	15	13	102
Cnel. Rosales	169	102	20	3	44
Patagones	1,073	800	38	11	224
Villarino	1,347	970	48	14	315
A. Alsina (B.A.)	1,021	602	38	65	316
Puán	1,156	691	60	5	400
Total EAP	8,624	6,010	392	74	2,148
Total Hectares	9,600,000	7,890,000	460,000	385,000	865,000

Source: Argentine National Agricultural Census 1995

There is on other kind of marginality. It depends on the qualities of land for cropping and breeding. There are micromarginalities reflecting this economic marginality. They are social marginalities which depend on spatial conditions above all the small size of the farms and economic marginalities such as margin of cultivation. We think that these micromarginalities may be studied as we proposed in our previous study (Petagna, 1994), trying to understand processes as in a chaotic system.

Argentina is a country where the free market is sometimes disrupted in different degrees. However, the production and land tenure are determined by private decisions rather than by the state control. Nowadays the main problem is the size of the agricultural enterprises. Perhaps it is necessary to restructure them legally and economically to survive. The large scale farm operations and large field size are well suited to industrial capitalism.

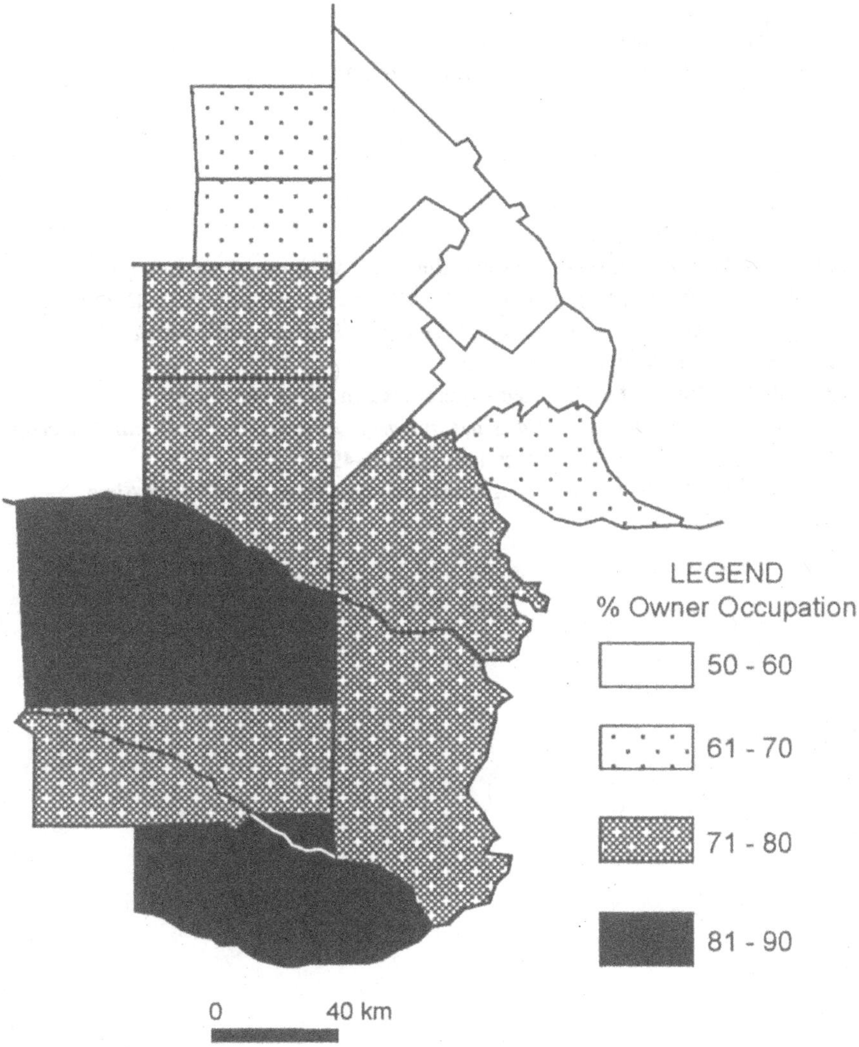

Figure 9.6 Land tenure and owner occupation (for the names of regions see Figure 9.1)

Notes

1. 23% of The Pampa Region.
2. 72,3% of Enterprises (EAP) are in private hands and 23,75 % are in tenancy.

References

Gould, P. (1985), *The Geographer at work*, Routledge and Kegan Paul: London.

Leimgruber, W. (1994), 'Marginal regions: a challenge for politics', in M. E. Furlani *et al.* (eds.), *Development issues in marginal regions II Policies and Strategies*, Universidad Nacional de Cuyo: Mendoza, pp 143-161.

Petagna, A. M. (1994), 'Marginal agricultural area in pampeano thorny wood', in M. E. Furlani *et al.* (eds.), *Development issues in marginal regions II Policies and Strategies*, Universidad Nacional de Cuyo: Mendoza, pp 485-497.

Taborda Caro, M. S. (1978), *Derecho Agrario*, Editorial Plus Ultra: Buenos Aires.

10 Demographic factors in characterizing and delimiting marginal lands

RICHARD E. LONSDALE AND J. CLARK ARCHER

Introduction

Analysts concerned with marginal lands have often acknowledged the problems faced in characterizing and delimiting such lands. One obstacle has been the lack of broad consensus on a definition of marginal lands. In an effort to make some modest progress in this regard, this paper examines a number of basic demographic measures to see if they might provide one basis for characterizing and delimiting these lands. There are of course other bases for doing this, e.g. physical environmental and economic, but a demographic approach would seem to be more promising. After all, it has been said many times that 'population is the essential geographic expression'. As Trewartha put it in his 1953 Association of American Geographers presidential address, 'Population is the point of reference from which all the other elements are observed and from which they all, singly and collectively, derive significance and meaning. It is population which furnishes the focus' (Trewartha, 1953, p. 83).

The importance of demographic factors in marginal lands research has been generally recognized, yet rather few analysts have made extensive use of demographic data. In a review of the many published works by members of the I.G.U. Commission on Marginal and Critical Regions in its current and earlier forms, and of the books issued by the PIMA group (Planning Issues in Marginal Areas), there are only a small number of papers dealing extensively with demographic factors.

The focus in marginal lands research has been more on the origins of marginality, ways to alleviate it, and the many developmental issues involved. This is thoroughly understandable. Demographic problems have been seen mostly as symptomatic of marginality, not as a cause or a solution. But if demographic problems are a symptom or a reflection of marginality, then demographic factors should also provide a basis for characterizing and delimiting marginal areas, much as Sanchez-Aguilera (1996, pp. 133-48) did in Spain and Andreoli (1992, pp. 24-44) and Tellarini (1992, pp. 193-210) did in Italy.

At the International Geographical Congress in The Hague, Cullen and Pretes presented the results of a highly useful survey of perceptions of marginality. Respondents were asked to examine each of 30 statements, indicating their level of agreement on a five point scale (1=agree and 5=disagree). Two statements dealt with demography. One read, 'Marginality is usually associated with areas of low population density'; the result was a mean score of 3.25 and a standard deviation of 1.30, indicating quite divided responses. The other statement read, 'Marginality is associated with net population outmigration'; the result was a mean score of 2.83 and a standard deviation of 1.05, suggesting neutrality or uncertainty about the statement. These rather ambiguous responses may be the result of some persons seeing marginality as primarily rural while others see it as both urban and rural (Cullen and Pretes, 1996). Whatever, the results are somewhat distressing, and it is hoped this paper will help to clarify the situation.

Characterizing marginal lands

There are many kinds of demographic indicators, but the following five proved to be most appropriate for the purposes of this study.

Population growth

Negative growth or population loss is generally seen as a sign of regional dysfunction, an indication that the region's future is in question. It unleashes a negative multiplier effect, i.e. central place functions gradually diminish, jobs are lost, and property values decline. It erodes public services (Bylund, 1989, pp. 24-36) and reduces the overall quality of life.

Net migration rate

Net outmigration is often the major reason for population loss, and it characterizes most marginal lands (Majoral *et al*., 1996). Generated primarily by employment factors, it deprives a region of its best educated people (Gade, 1991, p. 22; Walsh, 1992, pp. 23-36). It can involve much personal hardship as people feel forced to leave families and friends (Tellarini, 1992, pp. 193-210). Because young adults are much more likely to migrate than older people, an 'aging in place' process can occur in conjunction with net outmigration (Plane and Rogerson, 1994, p. 370). It can create what Andreoli (1992, p. 37) calls a 'deteriorated demographic structure', i.e. a concentration of elderly people and therefore low birth rates and few children. Retarding or reversing net outmigration is a major objective in many nations' regional policies (Leimgruber, 1994, pp. 1-18; Jussila and Toiviainen, 1995, pp. 13-31; Belec, 1996, pp. 175-84; Cozzani and Parra, 1996, pp. 537-45).

Natural growth rate

This is the crude birth rate minus the crude death rate (per 1,000 of population, divided by 10). A low or even negative natural rate of growth is rather common in marginal areas, though it is not a consistent characteristic. Though many such areas do indeed have higher death rates than birth rates (Sanchez-Aguilera, 1996, p. 136), there are also many instances of high birth rates and therefore rather strong natural growth rates in marginal lands. This tends to occur when educational standards are low, women often remain outside the labor force and fertility rates are correspondingly high.

Race or ethnicity

Marginality may be found in areas where a particular racial or ethnic group is concentrated. Such areas may be ones with low per capita incomes, low educational levels, high birth rates, a history of discriminatory practices and/or environmental neglect. This has been examined by Sommers, Mehretu and Pigozzi (1996, pp. 249-59) in their micro marginality studies in the Detroit region where there is a strong African American component in the population.

Share of population living in poverty

In the U.S. the poverty rate is the proportion of the population whose income falls below the government's official poverty level, which is adjusted each year for inflation. Areas where poverty is common and persistent generally suffer from a host of social problems and are therefore perceived as places where the quality of life is low and future prospects for the area questionable.

There are other demographic indicators that were considered (e.g. population density, age structure, percentage of population urban and employment category), but they were deemed to be too inconsistent as an indicator and less appropriate for purposes of this study.

Delimiting marginal lands

It requires a bit of courage to draw a line on a map outlining a marginal area. After all, marginality is a relative concept, and there are degrees of marginality. But with the aid of some detailed maps it can be done. Using the United States as an example, maps were prepared using data from U.S. Bureau of the Census publications (1993, 1996), matching the data with locational references using Atlas*GIS procedures. With these kinds of maps as a guide, it was possible to construct a map delimiting a plausible set of marginal lands for the 48 contiguous states.

Some 635 counties or equivalent units (one fifth of the U.S. total) lost population. Certain clusters of losing counties are evident. Most obvious is the agricultural heartland embracing all of the Great Plains and the western part of the Corn Belt. Also fairly easy to delimit is the lower Mississippi Valley. Less obvious is a central Appalachian region (a bituminous coal mining area) centered on West Virginia and eastern Kentucky. As it turns out, a good case can be made for designating all three of these regions as marginal lands. Not so evident until one studies Figure 10.1 carefully is the large number (47) of metropolitan counties or equivalent units in the northeastern U.S. that are losing population (some do not show up well because of their small areas, e.g. units embracing Boston, Bronx and Brooklyn Boroughs of New York City, Jersey City, Newark, Philadelphia, Baltimore, Washington DC and St. Louis). Most of these counties have one or more older industrial cities, usually with some deteriorating inner city areas. It is in such an environment that Sommers, Mehretu and Pigozzi (1996, pp. 249-59) have done their work on micro marginality. These 47 units are collectively labeled the northeastern dispersed metro centers.

The geographic pattern of net outmigration is very similar to that for population loss shown in Figure 10.2, and outmigration is clearly the most important component of population loss. There are some differences in the two patterns. This map indicates a somewhat larger lower Mississippi Valley region, more clearly extending to the Gulf of Mexico. Two additional marginal regions are suggested, namely the Southern Coastal Plain, long an area of poverty, and the New York/New England area which embraces many of the northeastern dispersed metro centers.

Counties with a negative change, i.e. deaths in excess of births, show up most prominently in the agricultural heartland and to a lesser degree in central Appalachia. But the natural population change is quite positive in the Southern Coastal Plain and through much of the lower Mississippi

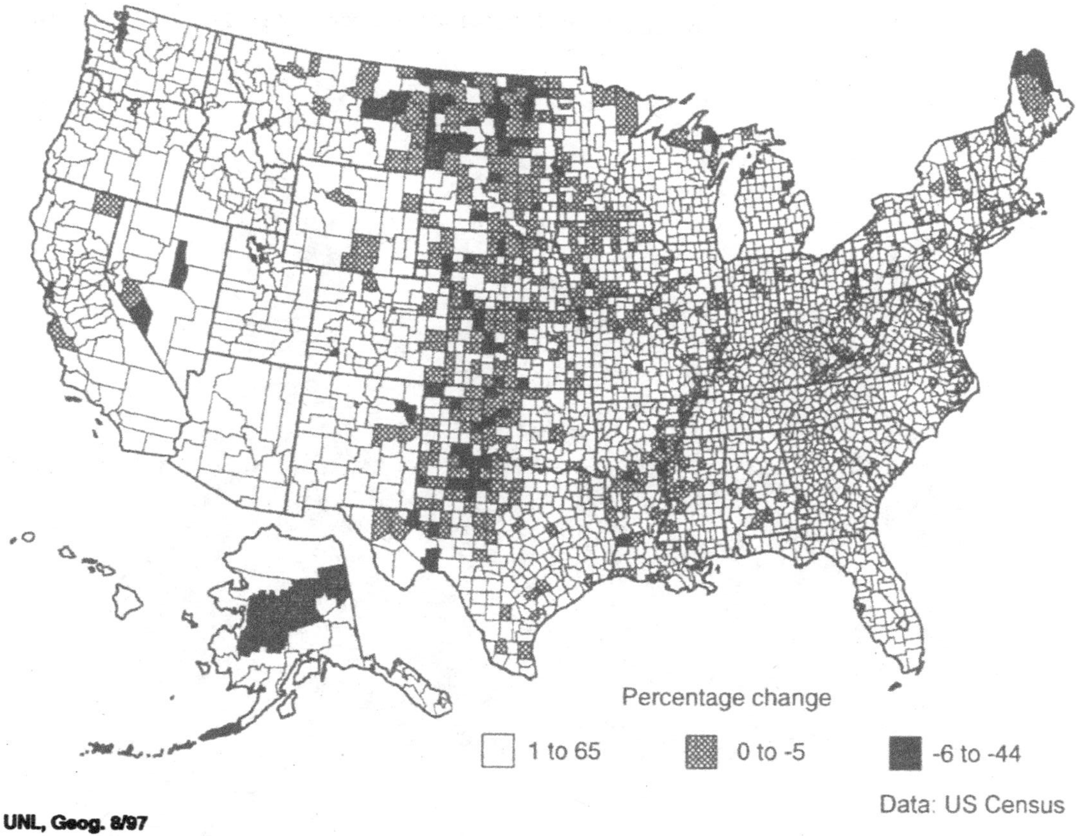

Figure 10.1 Map of population loss, 1990-95

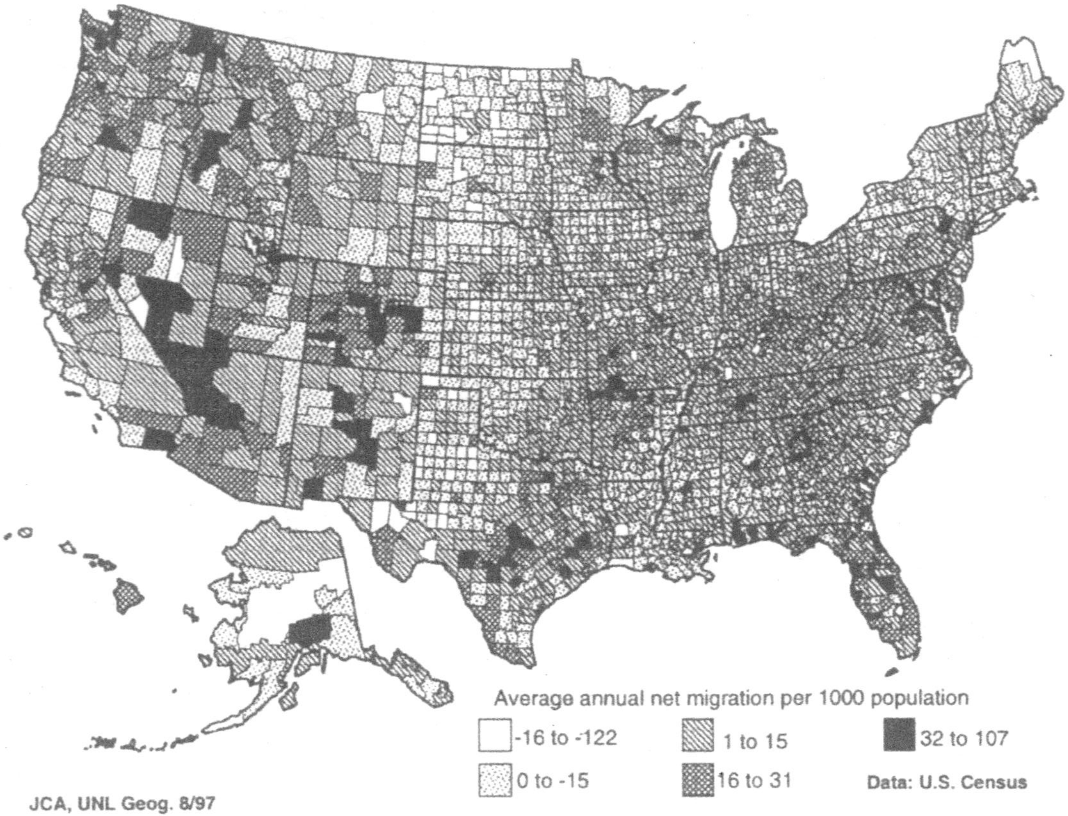

Figure 10.2 Map of average annual net migration, 1990-95

Valley and the New York/New England area. In the latter three cases, natural population growth results from average to above average birth rates (the U.S. mean is about 15/1,000 per year) and somewhat below average death rates (the U.S. mean is about 9/1,000). Thus some areas are losing population because of both net outmigration and natural population decline (agricultural heartland and central Appalachia), while others are experiencing net outmigration but more than make up for it in natural population growth (Southern Coastal Plain and the New York/New England area). The lower Mississippi Valley would appear unique with most counties having natural population growth while experiencing both net outmigration and population loss. The key to all this is found in differences in birth rates, and this has a clear racial/ethnic dimension.

Included here are African Americans, Hispanic Americans, and Native Americans, the three groups usually classified as disadvantaged minorities in the United States. African Americans, here largely the result of the 19th century slave trade, still have a major presence in the old cotton producing areas of the Southern Coastal Plain and the lower Mississippi Valley. Migration to the northern industrial cities began after World War I, assuming major proportions after World War II, and their share of the population in many of these cities is substantial. The Hispanic Americans were present in the four border states (CA,AZ,NM,TX) before the arrival of the Anglo Americans, but their numbers have increased dramatically in more recent times as net inmigration, in particular from Mexico, has come to exceed 500,000 a year (based on data in De Vita, 1996, pp. 24-25). Concentrations of Native Americans are most evident in the 'four corners' area (AZ,NM,CO,UT), Oklahoma and in or near Indian reservations in the northern Great Plains. High birth rates are associated with all three groups, in particular Hispanic Americans (De Vita, 1996, pp. 14-15), which helps to explain the geographic pattern of natural population growth shown in Figure 10.3. This pattern alerts us to the possible location of conditions leading to marginality.

The geographic association between poverty and minority population is abundantly evident in comparing Figures 10.4 and 10.5. Several areas experience poverty levels well above the U.S. mean (about 13 % in 1989-90). Notable in this regard are the Southern Coastal Plain, the lower Mississippi Valley, the lower Rio Grande Valley and the south central Rocky Mountains. Equally notable is central Appalachia with almost no minority population. Not exhibiting much poverty are large sections of the

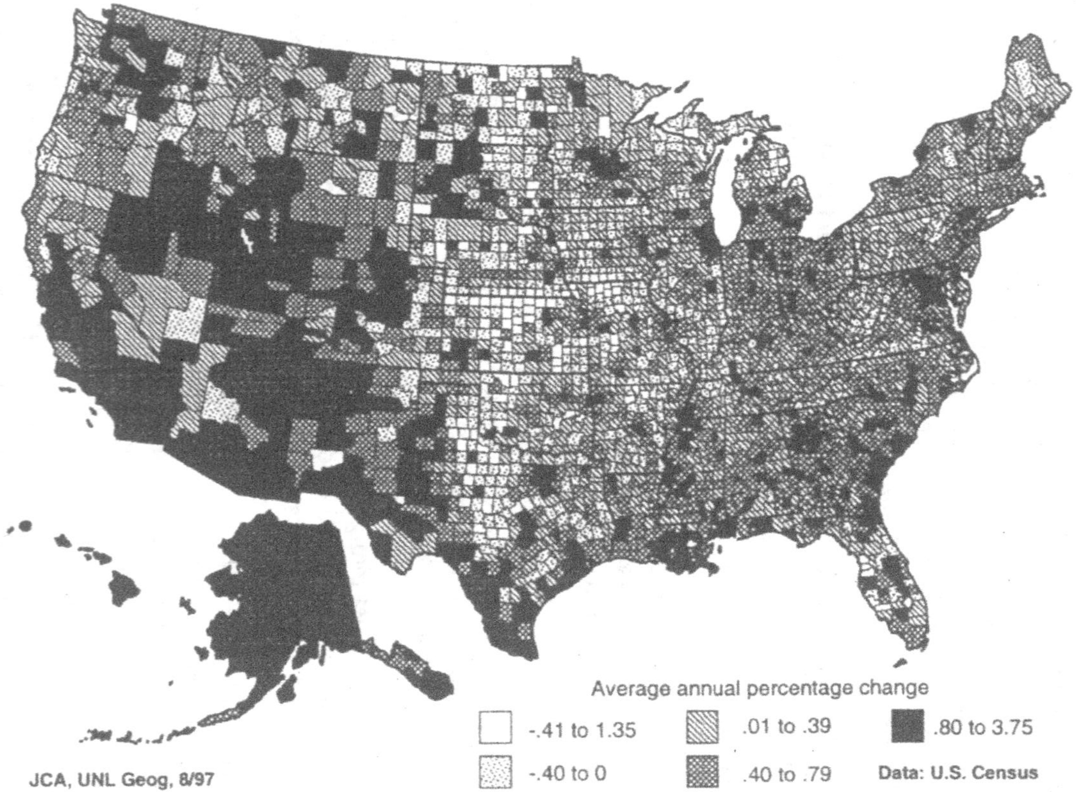

Figure 10.3 **Map of natural population change rate, 1990**

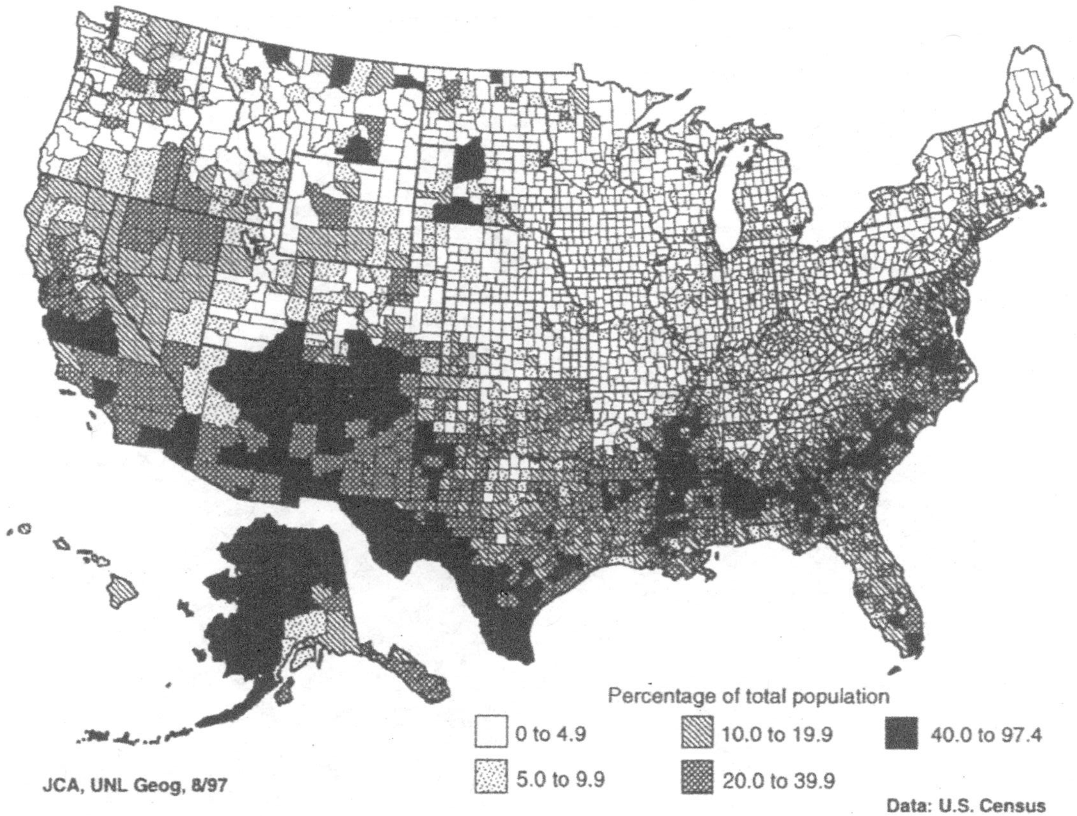

Figure 10.4 **Map of minority population as a share of total population, 1990**

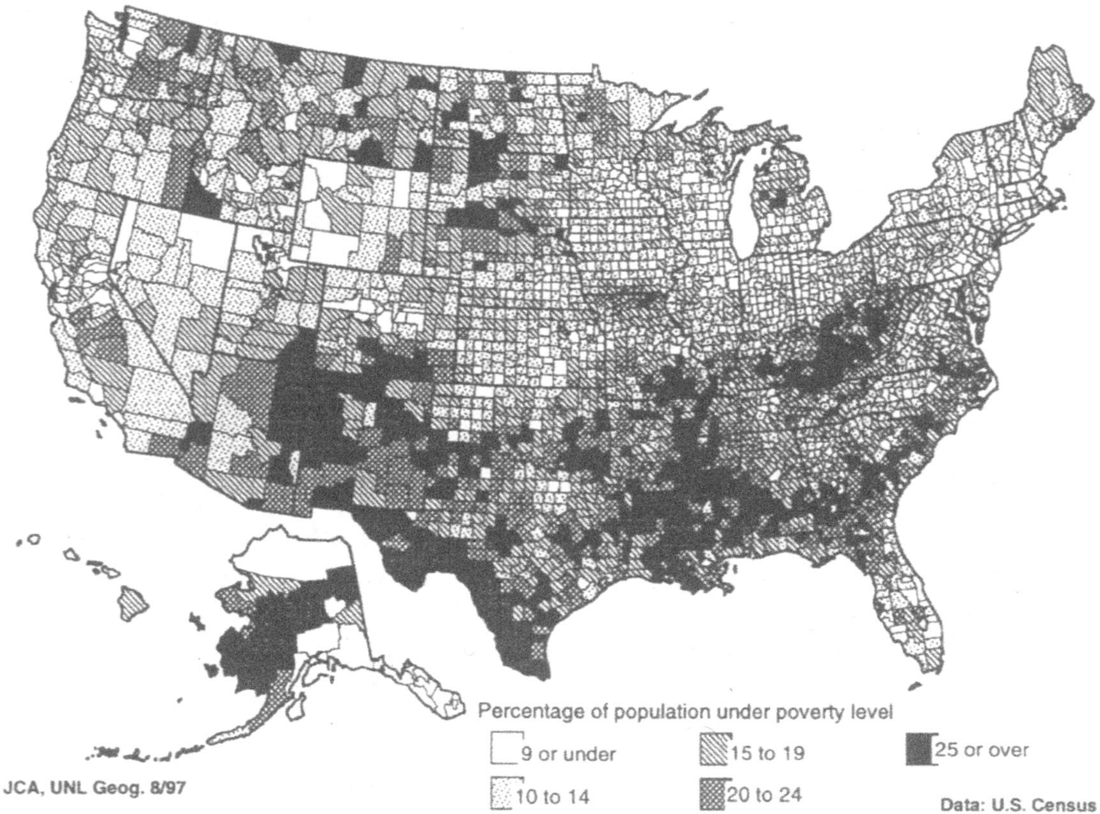

Figure 10.5 **Map of percentage of population under poverty level, 1989**

agricultural heartland and the northeastern dispersed metro centers. People in poverty are certainly present in these metro centers, but most counties also contain higher income districts which neutralize county averages.

The final map of marginal lands

The five population maps provided the basis for identifying regions thought to be candidates for designation as marginal lands. Should all the regions be so designated? Precisely where are the boundaries to be drawn? Inevitably there is a good amount of subjectivity in these decisions, but such is often the case in cartographic regionalization, e.g. constructing maps of climatic regions, economic regions, etc.

Seven regions were designated 'marginal lands', though the case for inclusion is stronger for some than for others (Figures 10.6 and 10.7). The 'most marginal' land would seem to be the lower Mississippi Valley with a combination of net outmigration, population loss, many people in poverty and poor prospects for improvement. The agricultural heartland sets the standard for net outmigration and population loss, with no change in this trend evident, but it is not an area of extensive poverty except in portions of the far north and far south. The lower Rio Grande Valley and the south central Rocky Mountains both enjoy population growth but suffer from high levels of poverty which show no sign of abatement. The Southern Coastal Plain and central Appalachia share net outmigration, some areas of population loss and high poverty levels, but in both areas there has been a noticeable weakening of these problems in recent years. The northeastern dispersed metro centers, where marginality is more localized, are included because of the large numbers of people involved and the enormity of the problem. Of the eight candidate regions, only the New York/New England area is excluded because its declining metro counties are already included and otherwise the only extensive problem is with net outmigration.

Conclusion

As far as characterizing marginal lands is concerned, there should be little doubt about the utility of demographic data. Measures such as population loss, migration rates, people in poverty, etc. tell us a great deal about these places and provide valuable insights to the problems that exist there. When it comes to delimiting marginal areas, demographic measures can be very

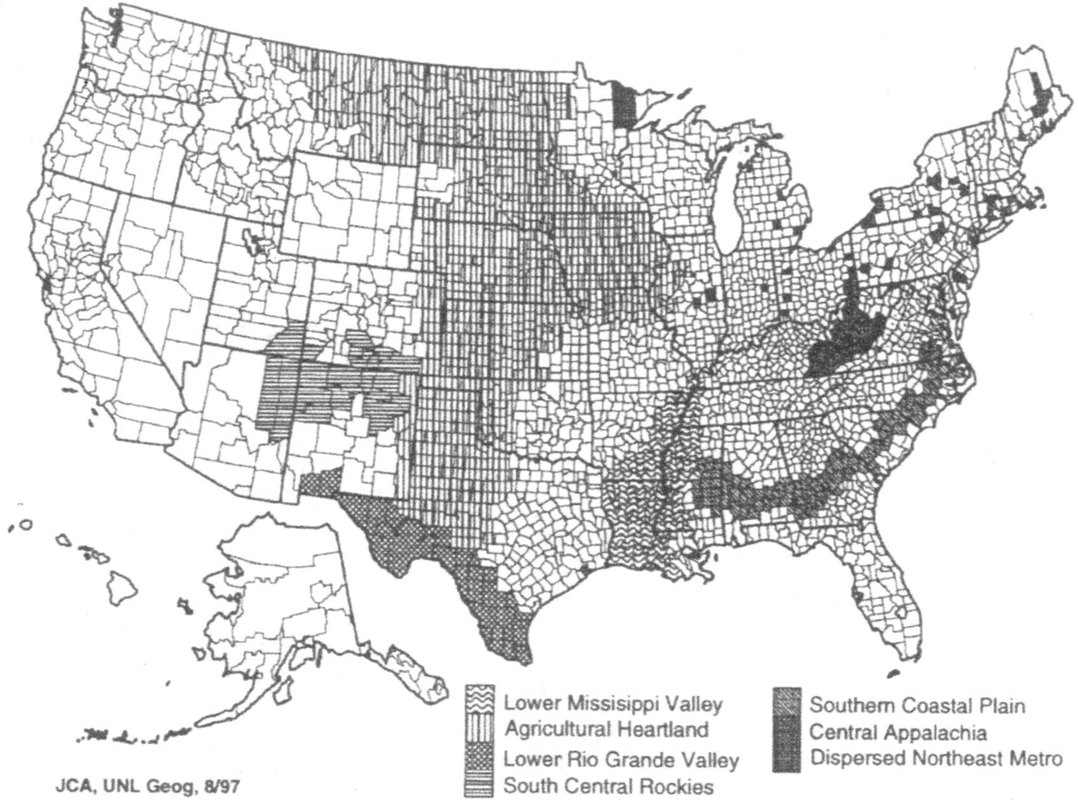

Figure 10.6 **Marginal lands**

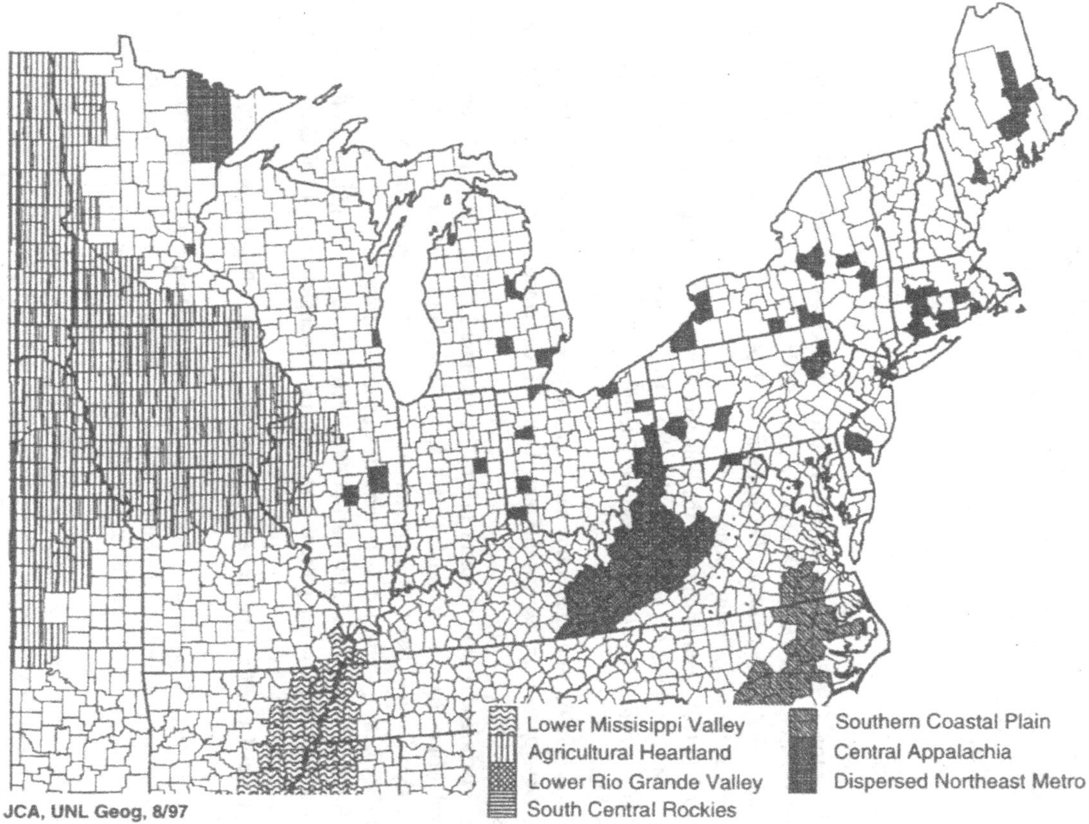

Figure 10.7 Marginal lands of north-eastern USA

helpful, but one must proceed with considerable caution. The analyst must 'know the territory', as the expression goes, and be able to recognize where demographic conditions do indicate marginality and where they do not. Geographers, good at integrating diverse data to understand the character of places, should be able to manage it quite effectively.

References

Andreoli, Maria (1992), 'An Analysis of Different Kinds of Marginal Systems in a Developed Country: The Case of Italy', in Gade, Ole (ed.), *Spatial Dynamics of Highland and High LatitudeEnvironments*, Dept. of Geography and Planning, Appalachian State University: Boone.

Belec, Borut (1996), 'Marginality and the Policy of Regional Development in Slovenia', in Furlani, M.E., Pedone, C., and Dario, N. (eds.), *Development Issues in Marginal Regions II: Policies and Strategies*, Facultad de Filosofia y Letras, Universidad Nacional de Cuyo: Mendoza.

Bylund, Erik (1989), 'Regional Policy and Regional Research in Sweden', in Gustafsson, G. (ed.), *Development in Marginal Areas*, Dept. of Geography, University of Karlstad: Karlstad.

Cozzani, Maria and Parra, Graciela (1996), 'Concentration and Depopulation through Internal Migrations in Marginal Areas', in Furlani, M.E., Pedone, C., and Dario, N. (eds.), *Development Issues in Marginal Regions II: Policies and Strategies*, Facultad de Filosofia y Letras, Universidad Nacional de Cuyo: Mendoza.

Cullen, Bradley T. and Pretes, Michael (1996), 'Perceptions of Marginality in the United States and Canada', paper presented at 28th International Geographical Congress, The Hague, Aug. 4-10.

De Vita, Carol J. (1996), 'The United States at Mid-Decade', *Population Bulletin*, Vol. 50, No. 4.

Gade, Ole. (1991), 'Dealing with Disparities in Regional Development, The Intermediate Socioeconomic Region', in Ole, Miller, V.P. Jr., and Sommers, Larry M. (eds.), *Planning Issues in Marginal Areas*, Dept. of Geography and Planning, Appalachian State University: Boone.

Jussila, Heikki and Toiviainen, Esko (1995), 'The Future of Marginal Regions: Networking, Knowhow and Integration as Motors for Regional Development', in Singh, R.B. and Majoral, Roser (eds.), *Development Issues in Marginal Regions*, Oxford & IBH: New Delhi.

Leimgruber, Walter (1994), 'Marginality and Marginal Regions: Problems of Definition', in Chang, C.D. (ed.), *Marginality and Development Issues in Marginal Regions*, National Taiwan University: Taipei.

Majoral, Roser, Andreoli, Maria, Tellarini, Vittorio, and Cravidao, Fernanda (1996), 'Regional Perception of Marginality: A View from Southern Europe', paper presented at conference of I.G.U. Study Group on Development Issues in Marginal Regions, Glasgow, July 30-Aug. 4.

Plane, David A. and Rogerson, Peter A. (1994), *The Geographical Analysis of Population*, John Wiley: New York.

Sanchez-Aguilera, Dolores (1996), 'Evaluating Marginality through Demographic Indicators', in Singh, R.B. and Majoral, Roser (eds.) *Development Issues in Marginal Regions*, Oxford & IBH: New Delhi.

Sommers, Lawrence M., Mehretu, Assefa, and Pigozzi, Bruce W. (1996), 'Factors in Microspatial Marginality in Southeastern Michigan', in Furlani, M.E., Pedone, C., and Dario, N. (eds.), *Development Issues in Marginal Regions II: Policies and Strategies*, Facultad de Filosofia y Letras, Universidad Nacional de Cuyo: Mendoza.

Tellarini, Vittorio (1992), 'Some Questions about Socio-Economic Marginality in Rural Areas of Developed Countries', in Gade, Ole (ed.), *Spatial Dynamics of Highland and High Latitude Environments*, Dept. of Geography and Planning, Appalachian State University: Boone.

Trewartha, Glenn T. (1953), 'A Case for Population Geography,' *Annals Association of American Geographers*, Vol. 43, No. 2.

United States Bureau of the Census (1993), *1990 Census of Population and Housing; Summary Tape File 3C; United States Summary*, U.S. Government Printing Office: Washington DC.

United States Bureau of the Census (1996), *USA Counties 1996 on CD-ROM*, U.S. Government Printing Office; Washington DC.

Walsh, James A. (1992), 'Economic Restructuring and Labour Migration in the European Periphery: The Case of the Republic of Ireland',in O Cinneide, M. and Grimes, S. (eds.), *Planning and Development of Marginal Areas*, Centre for Development Studies, University College Galway: Galway.

11 Length of unemployment as an indicator of social exclusion in Finland: A GIS viewpoint

TOIVO MUILU, JARMO RUSANEN, ARVO NAUKKARINEN AND ALFRED COLPAERT

Introduction

Unemployment is usually examined in relative terms on the basis of the rate of unemployment and in absolute terms by setting out from the number of unemployed persons. These parameters are the points of departure in the unemployment statistics used to draw comparisons between populations, socioeconomic groups or regions.

Decision-making and public discussions often rely on these established ways of measuring unemployment, so that the public administration and politicians in Finland, for example, seem to be interested almost exclusively in monitoring trends in the prevailing record high unemployment rate and in particular observing the extent to which the present government is able to keep to its goal to halve the unemployment rate during its term of office. This is quite understandable, for despite the variety of methods employed to measure it, the rate of unemployment does serve well as a basis for temporal, regional and international comparisons. Extensive research results are consequently available on the changes in unemployment that took place during the economic recession of the early 1990s and its impact on various socioeconomic groups, though it seems that this is not very well communicated to the grass-roots level in the form of actual decisions and measures, in spite of the fact that unemployment is known to be a major cause of social exclusion.

Unemployment is a highly complex phenomenon, within which the rate of unemployment and the number of unemployed persons account for only one, albeit significant, dimension. Mass unemployment nowadays affects concerns such an extensive segment of the population, however, that unidimensional parameters provide an excessively generalised picture of its regional distribution, for example, as not even a small local government district is in any way a homogeneous regional unit in terms of population density and distances, which may distort the interpretation of the results due to ecological bias (Martin 1991). In addition to the rate of unemployment and the number of unemployed persons, attention should also be paid to other factors describing the structural features of unemployment, such as the duration of unemployment (see Walsh 1987, pp. 3-4). According to Pyy (1994, pp. 1-2), the duration of unemployment is also important from the point of view of welfare and the risk of social exclusion, more so, indeed than the fact of becoming unemployed in the first place.

This paper discusses regional changes in the duration of unemployment on the basis of Statistics Finland grid square data for Finland in the recession years of 1993 and 1994, after which unemployment finally began to abate somewhat. It has been observed earlier that the regional structure of unemployment altered in the recession years, in that the highest unemployment figures were recorded not only in the peripheral areas, which had typically been the most difficult areas in this respect, but also in the surroundings and suburbs of the major cities (Muilu *et al.* 1996). It is now clear that the slow improvement in the rate of unemployment has affected the central areas most. We shall endeavour to examine here whether corresponding regional changes have also taken place in the duration of unemployment, e.g. leading to long-term unemployment becoming a permanent phenomenon in some areas.

Changes in the duration of unemployment in 1993-1994

The employment statistics of the Statistics Finland take persons aged 15-74 years who have no work on the last working day of the year to be unemployed. Unemployment data in this statistic is based to register of job seekers maintained by the Ministry of Labour (SVT Population 1997:3, p. 220), in which the duration of unemployment is calculated on the basis of a seven day week, i.e. not according to working days, converting the result to calendar months. This means that if a person has been unemployed continuously for e.g. 5.20 months from the beginning of the year, his unemployment had actually lasted from 1st January to 6th May.

The employment statistics for Finland show the number of unemployed persons to have reached its peak at the end of 1993, when it was more than half a million, five times higher than at the end of 1989. The number began to fall in 1994, for the first time since the onset of the economic recession, and was approximately 43 000 less at the end of the year than it had been at the beginning, the rate of unemployment correspondingly falling from 22.2% to 20.4% (Table 11.1).

Table 11.1 Number of unemployed persons and duration of unemployment in Finland on 31.12.93 and 31.12.94

Year	Number of unemployed persons [1]	Rate of unemployment (%)	Duration of unemployment, total (months)	Duration of unemployment/ person (months)
1993	528,418	22.2	4,055,903	7.68
1994	485,342	20.4	3,952,209	8.14

Source: Statistics Finland

Although the conventional measures thus pointed to an improvement in employment, no corresponding change took place in the duration of unemployment. Although the total number of months of unemployment experienced fell slightly in 1993-1994, the duration per person actually increased by an average of two weeks, to approximately 8 months and 4 days in 1994. The social effects of unemployment were thus not alleviated despite a fall in the rate of unemployment. If the average duration of unemployment had remained at the 1993 level and not increased, there would still have been approximately 515,000 unemployed persons at the end of 1994.

It was not possible to monitor changes in long-term unemployment, i.e. periods exceeding 12 months, as the employment statistics only measure its duration at the annual level. The increase in the duration of unemployment periods nevertheless directly suggests an increase in long-term unemployment, which has already been indicated in a number of investigations. The number of long-term unemployed persons increased in Finland from 3,000 to 140,000 during the five years of the economic recession, i.e. between 1990 and autumn 1995 (Santamäki-Vuori 1996, p. 11). Long-term unemployment can be regarded as a major problem in a number of western countries, both in terms of the national economy and as a factor increasing the risk of social exclusion, and the long-term unemployed constitute almost a half of all unemployed persons in many European Union countries (see Walsh 1987, p. 5, Haughton *et al.* 1993, pp. 1-3, Symes 1995, pp. 3-4, Santamäki-Vuori 1996, p. 15).

Duration of unemployment and regional structure

Although the duration of unemployment increased in 1993-1994, this does not imply that the increase took place in the same proportion in all segments of the population and geographical areas. The employment statistics enable the duration of unemployment to be examined with respect to a number of background parameters, of which the established demographic variables age and sex are selected for use here. In the case of the regions, differences in the duration of unemployment are first compared on the basis of the distribution and size of the local government districts (municipalities), although the main emphasis will be on comparison in terms of population density, which accounts better for the regional structure of settlement. This can be done by applying the GIS technique to employment statistics coded with an accuracy of one sq. kilometre.

Local government districts and population density

Unemployment and its prolongation have traditionally been regarded in Finland as a problem typical of poorly developed areas. According to Sääski (1981, pp. 104-105), for example, the small number of employment vacancies in Northern Finland in the 1970s hampered the finding of jobs and increased the duration of unemployment. The mass unemployment of the 1990's has balanced out the situation, however, in that it has aggravated unemployment in the central areas (Muilu *et al.* 1996, p. 170), a trend which has been typical of a number of European countries for a long time (see Hasluck 1987, Haughton 1993, Symes 1995).

The regional distribution of the duration of unemployment in 1993-1994 likewise does not conform to the observations of Sääski (1981), as the longest average unemployment periods were mainly recorded in Southern and Central Finland and in the commuter districts of the major cities. The longest average unemployment period in one municipality was almost 11 months in 1993, so that the vast majority of the unemployed persons in that municipality could almost be regarded as long-term unemployed (Figure 11.1). The map for 1994 was drawn up using the 1993 quintile classification in order to account better for the increase in the duration of unemployment and the regional distribution of unemployment.

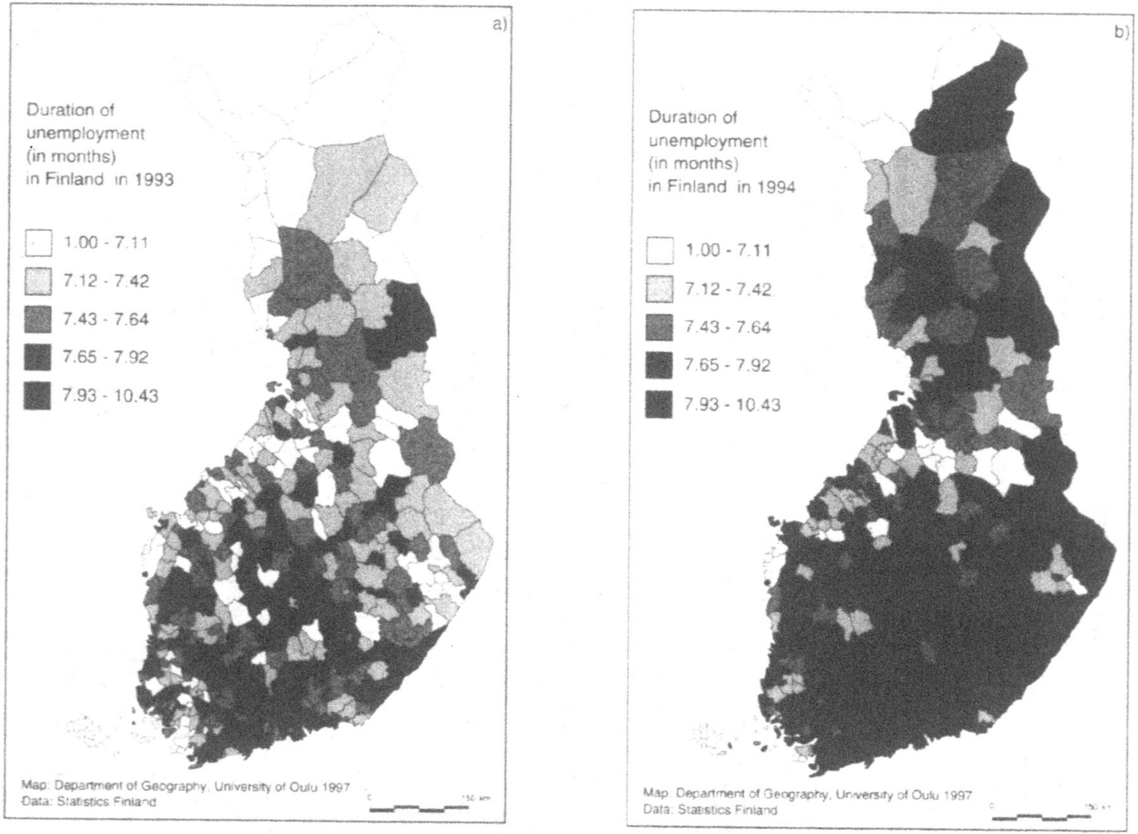

Figure 11.1 Duration of unemployment (in months) in Finland in 1993 and in 1994

One interesting feature of the pair of maps is that some areas and local government districts with the highest unemployment rates (e.g. Kainuu in Northern Finland) in fact represent the lowermost categories in terms of the average duration of unemployment. This would seem to suggest that the current labour policy, and particularly its employment measures, has enabled long periods of unemployment to be interrupted in many cases, a trend also verified by research findings (Aho *et al.* 1996, p. 137, Myrskylä 1997, p. 33). Correspondingly, the large absolute number of unemployed persons in the major urban areas may slow down the measures taken by the labour authorities and lead to a failure by local councils to create a sufficient number of short-term jobs.

The patterns in unemployment relative to the structure of local government can be examined in more depth by comparing districts which differ in population. The proportion of unemployed persons and the duration of unemployment (months) with respect to the situation in Finland as a whole are compared in five population categories in Table 11.2. The result is quite distinct: the districts with a population of at least 10 000 inhabitants had a higher proportion of the total unemployment and also the duration of it than of the total population, whereas the smaller districts were 'under-represented'. In addition, the difference increased over the years 1993-1994 to the extent way that the local authorities with over 70 000 inhabitants, i.e. the ten largest cities, increased their proportion of total unemployment, i.e. the problem can be regarded as having moved over to the cities in both relative terms and with respect to duration. The differences and changes are not as such so very marked, but it should be borne in mind that they took place within only one year.

The average duration of unemployment is compared by population density deciles in Figure 11.2 (for the decile technique, see Naukkarinen *et al.* 1993), setting out from the average duration of unemployment in 1993, i.e. 7.68 months (approximately 7 months 20 days), which constitutes the zero level in the diagram. Each population density decile covers one tenth of the population, with the line indicating deviation in days from the 1993 average. The lines proceed from left to right, beginning with the 1st density decile, about 4,000 inhabitants per sq.kilometre or more, i.e. the city centres and suburbs, and moving towards the 10th decile, i.e. extreme sparsely populated areas with less than 18 inhabitants per sq. kilometre.

In both the years examined here the duration of unemployment was longest in the most densely populated areas. Deciles 5-9, which mainly cover the rural centres and basic rural areas remained below the duration average in 1993, and the pattern was almost identical in 1994 except that

Table 11.2 Proportions of population, labour force, unemployed persons and unemployment duration (%) relative to population in the local government districts of Finland on 31.12.93 and 31.12.94

Population	Proportion of population (%)		Proportion of unemployed persons(%)		Proportion of unemployment duration (%)	
	1993	1994	1993	1994	1993	1994
- 4,999	11.53	11.63	10.34	10.29	10.15	10.04
5,000 - 9,999	16.94	16.60	16.38	15.80	15.92	15.40
10,000 - 29,999	28.42	27.74	29.29	28.00	28.92	27.56
30,000 - 69,999	11.38	12.00	12.22	13.12	12.20	13.07
70,000 -	31.72	32.04	31.77	32.81	32.81	33.93
Total	100.00	100.00	100.00	100.00	100.00	100.00

Source: Statistics Finland

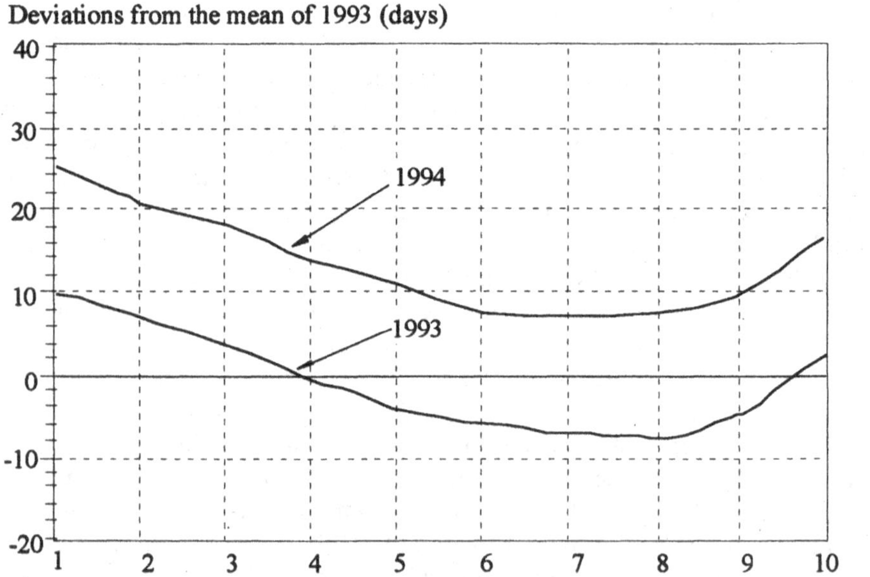

Figure 11.2 Average duration of unemployment compared by population density

the average duration had increased everywhere by approximately two weeks, so that none of the figures recorded fell below the 1993 average. The results thus confirm and in part fill out the earlier interpretations. An entirely new observation was that unemployment lasts longer on average in sparsely populated areas, i.e. in deciles 9-10. It can be assumed that a large number of unemployed persons in these areas do not even actively try to look for work or to become enter one of the job creation schemes administered by the labour authorities. These people could be classified on statistical grounds as excluded from society, though it should be noted that a number of inhabitants of remote rural areas classified as unemployed gain a sufficient living from small-scale farming, fishing and other forms of exploitation of natural resources.

Age structure and population density

Unemployment varies in the extent to which it affects the sexes and different age categories. Unemployment among young people has typically been regarded as a special problem, the rate in the EU countries having risen in the 1970s and 1980s to reach almost double the general rate of unemployment in the early 1990s (Symes 1995, pp. 13-14, cf. Alheit 1994, pp. 2-7, Gould and Fieldhouse 1997, pp. 623-624). This type of unemployment also reached a record high level in Finland during the economic recession of the early 1990s (Santamäki-Vuori and Sauramo 1995, pp. 15-17, Muilu *et al.* 1996, pp. 166-169). The gradual alleviation of this recession has improved the situation, however, though mainly as a result of job creation measures and an increase in the number of persons admitted to further education, whereas the position of older employees in the labour market has weakened.

The employment statistics do not allow any distinction to be made between the factors that contribute to the duration of unemployment and those that hamper employment as such, but a number of investigations have pointed to the role of factors related to age and sex as the most important background variables. It should be noted, however, that this is a cluster of highly complex cause and effect relations, as employment and the duration of unemployment are also dependent on factors such as education, the intensity of seeking work, the number of vacancies, labour force policy, unemployment benefits and labour policy measures (see Sääski 1981, pp. 124-128, Kettunen 1993, pp. 255-259, Symes 1995, pp. 188-194, Korpi 1995, pp. 366-367).

Deviations in the average duration of unemployment from the 1993 average (7 months 20 days) are compared by age category and population density decile in 1993-1994 in Figures 11.3a-c. The results point to major differences between the age categories, the average duration being 20-50 days below the average among unemployed persons aged 15-24 years (Figure 11.3a), for whom the situation even improved in 1993-1994. The poorest trends among young people were observed in population density deciles 2-3, which cover the suburbs of the major cities in particular. The trend among middle-aged persons more or less conforms to the average (Figure 11.3b, cf. Figure 11.2), but that in the oldest age categories is poor, the deviation from the average increasing in all population density deciles (Figure 11.3c).

The results indicate that job creation measures have increased employment among young people, at the same time underlining the fact that general labour policy should pay more attention to the position of ageing employees. Myrskylä (1997, p. 32) notes that it is extremely rare for an unemployed person aged over 55 years to find work in Finland. The concern regarding the fate of the more elderly employees is further emphasised by the threat of a lack of labour as the boom generation reaches retiring age in the 2010s at the latest.

Sex distribution and population density

Unemployment differences between the sexes are mainly attributable to variations in the extent to which they take on paid work and in the structure of the fields in which they are typically employed. Part-time and short-term jobs, for example, are characteristic of female-dominated service sectors, whereas men have been typically employed in full-time industrial and senior salaried positions. These labour market differences are of course also reflected in people's working history, i.e. the relation between employment and unemployment. The unemployment rate was approximately 5% lower among women than among men at the end of 1993 (Myrskylä and Ruotsalainen 1994, pp. 10-11). According to Santamäki-Vuori (1996, p. 57), the relative risk of women who were unemployed in 1993-1994 becoming alienated from the labour market was higher than that for men. Similarly, Mannila (1993, pp. 141-143) found that sex is a discriminating factor which increases the risk of social exclusion among men and women who have problems in finding work and who are consequently unemployed for long periods of time (cf. Gould and Fieldhouse 1997).

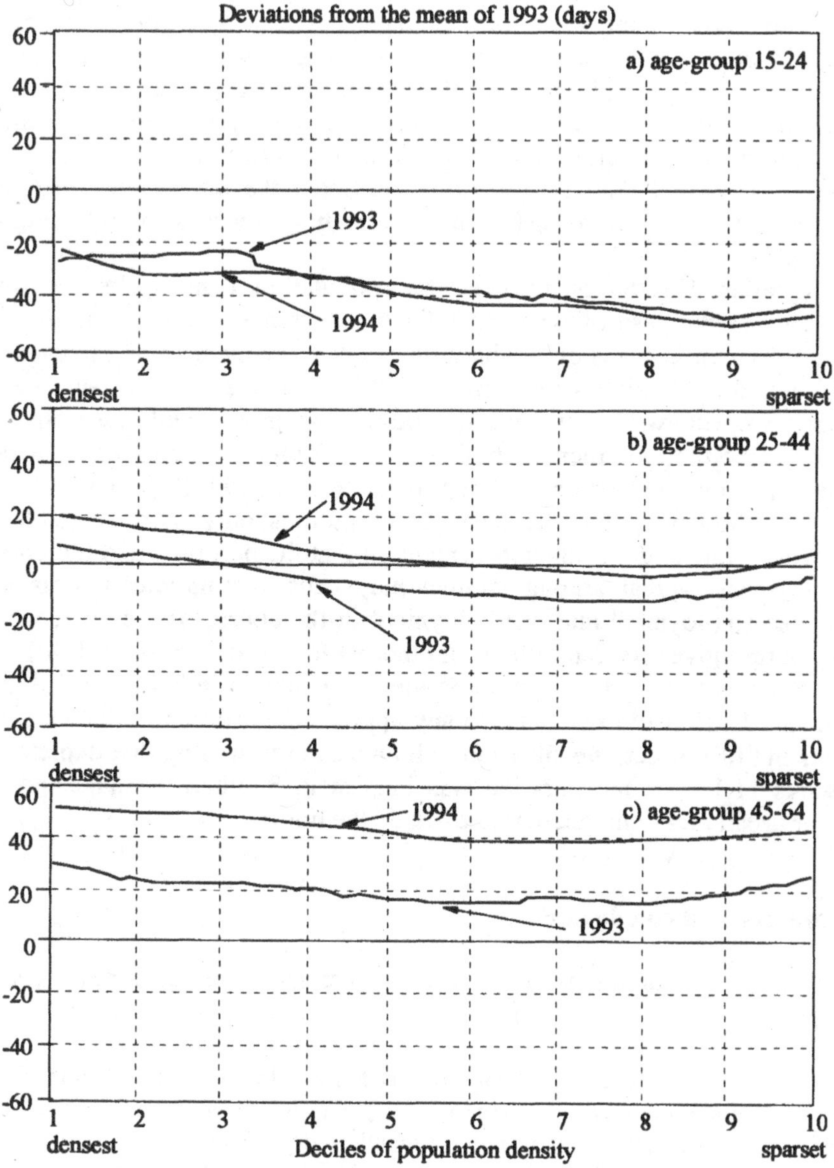

Figure 11.3 Deviations in the average duration of unemployment from the 1993 compared by age-groups and population density deciles in 1993 and 1994 in Finland

Examination of this issue on the basis of population density deciles indicates that prolonged periods of unemployment are typical of unemployed men living in the most densely populated areas in particular. Where the duration of unemployment in the most densely populated 1st decile in 1993 was approximately 20 days greater than the average for the year, it was well over one month greater in 1994. By contrast, even the basic rural areas (deciles 6-9) had figures only just about the average in 1993, the duration likewise increasing by approximately two weeks in 1994 (Figure 11.4a).

Smaller differences between the population density deciles were recorded in the case of women, indicating that the various areas did not differ so much in terms of the duration of unemployment among women. In addition, the situation with respect to the 1993 average was also better among women, whose average duration of unemployment was some 25 days below that for men in both years, although it increased at a rate almost identical to that among men from 1993 to 1994. It should be borne in mind, however, that the average duration is only partly capable of describing the nature of unemployment, in that the part-time and temporary employment typical among women may cause continuous fluctuations between employment and unemployment in the course of the year, which may in turn give rise to problems in other sectors of life (Figure 11.4b).

Examination of the duration of unemployment in individual local government districts did not point to any appreciable differences between the sexes in this respect, the situation in both cases resembling that depicted in Figures 11.1 , i.e. the duration was longest in Southern Finland and the major urban areas and decreased towards the north.

Summary and conclusions

The main findings to emerge from this investigation can be summarised as follows:

1. Although the rate of unemployment fell by almost 2% in 1993-1994, the average duration of unemployment per unemployed person increased by two weeks, so that it averaged 8 months 4 days in 1994.
2. The duration of unemployment is markedly below the average in some of the areas with the highest rates of unemployment, e.g. Kainuu in Northern Finland.
3. The focus in the number and proportion of unemployed persons and the duration of unemployment moved over to the major cities during the years of economic recession.

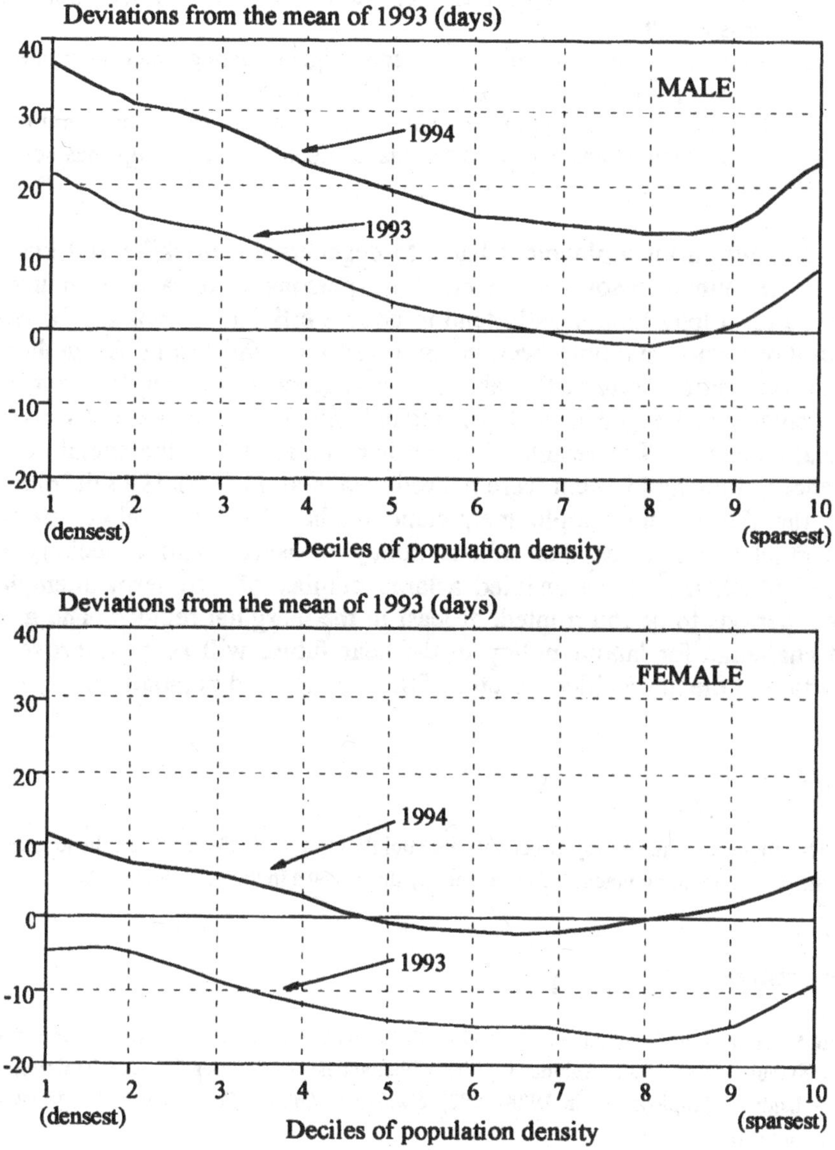

Figure 11.4 Population density deciles and prolonged unemployment among men and women in Finland, 1993

4. The duration of unemployment was greatest in the most densely populated areas in both years.
5. Average unemployment is markedly higher among men than among women, particularly in the most densely populated areas.
6. The position of unemployed young people with respect to the duration of unemployment has improved and that of the oldest age groups has deteriorated.

Long-term unemployment leads to degeneration in skills and knowledge, i.e. human resources. In addition, persons who have been unemployed for a long time usually tend to be less efficient at looking for work than those who have only been unemployed for a short time. A number of the investigations referred to above also suggest that unemployment, and particularly prolonged periods of unemployment can increase the risk of social exclusion. The results obtained here indicate that the social consequences of unemployment were not relieved at all in 1993-1994 despite the fact that the rise in unemployment came to a halt. The regional comparison nevertheless indicates that labour policy measures, and especially job creation schemes, have enabled a large number of long-term unemployment periods to be interrupted, at least in the marginal regions. The greatest challenge for labour policy in the near future will be to improve the position of the more elderly sector of the unemployed population.

Note

1. The numbers of unemployed persons are slightly more than 1% less than those given in the published employment statistics, mainly due to gaps in the coordinate data

References

Aho, S., Nätti, J. and Suikkanen, A. (1996), Työvoimakoulutuksen ja tukityöllistämisen vaikuttavuus 1988-1992 (Summary: The Effectiveness of Labour Market Training and Subsidized Employment in 1988-1992), *Studies in Labour Policy* No 144, Ministry of Labour: Helsinki.

Alheit, P. (1994), *Taking the Knocks, Youth Unemployment and Biography - a qualitative analysis*, Cassel.

Gould, M.I. and Fieldhouse, E. (1997), Using the 1991 Census SAR in a multilevel analysis of male unemployment, *Environment and Planning A* 29, pp. 611-628.

Hasluck, C. (1987), Urban Unemployment, Local labour markets and employment initiatives, Longman.

Haughton, G., Johnson, S., Murphy, L. and Thomas, K. (1993), *Local Geographies of Unemployment*, Avebury: Aldershot.

Kettunen, J. (1993), Re-employment of Finnish Unemployed Workers, *ETLA, The Research Institute of the Finnish Economy, Series A* 17, Helsinki.

Korpi, T. (1995), Effects on Manpower Policies on Duration Dependence in Re-employment Rates, The example of Sweden, *Economica* 62: 247, pp. 353-371, The London School of Economics and Political Science.

Mannila, S. (1993), Työhistoria ja syrjäytyminen, vaikeasti työllistyvien terveysongelmaisten elämänkulusta (Abstract: Work Career and Social Marginalization, On the Life course of Marginal Jobseekers with Health Problems), *Studies in Labour Policy* No 58, Ministry of Labour: Helsinki.

Martin, D. (1991), *Geographical Information Systems and their Socioeconomic Applications*, Routledge.

Muilu, T., Rusanen, J., Naukkarinen, A. and Colpaert, A. (1996), Työttömyyden alueellinen rakenne ja sen muutokset Suomessa 1989-1994 (Abstract: Trends in the regional structure of unemployment in Finland in 1989-1994), *Terra* 108:3, pp. 160-171, Geographical Society of Finland: Helsinki.

Myrskylä, P. and Ruotsalainen, K. (1994), Työttömät 1993, selvitys työttömien taustoista (Abstract: The Unemployed in 1993, A study on the backgrounds of the unemployed), *Studies in Labour Policy* No 78, Ministry of Labour: Helsinki.

Myrskylä, P. (1997), Nuori ikä ja korkea koulutus nostavat työttömän työllistymistodennäköisyyttä, *Kuntapuntari* 2/1997, pp. 28-33, Helsinki.

Naukkarinen, A., J. Rusanen and A. Colpaert (1993), The Future of Rural Settlement Structure in Finland, *Geography Research Forum* vol. 13, pp. 61-70.

Pyy, M. (1994), Nuorten työllistymisen kuvaaminen elinaika-analyysin menetelmin, *Government Institute for Economic Research, Research Reports* 22, Helsinki.

Santamäki-Vuori, T. and Sauramo, P. (1995), Nuorten työttömyys Suomessa vuosina 1993-94 (Summary: Youth Unemployment in Finland in 1993-1994), *Studies in Labour Policy* No 107, Ministry of Labour: Helsinki.

Santamäki-Vuori, T. (1996), Pitkäaikaistyöttömien työmarkkina-kokemukset lamavuosina 1993-1994 (Summary: Labour Market Experiences of the Long-Term Unemployed in Finland in 1993-1994), *Studies in Labour Policy* No 131, Ministry of Labour: Helsinki.

Statistics Finland, Employment Statistics 1993-1994, Unpublished grid square data, Statistics Finland: Helsinki.

SVT Population 1997:3, Työssäkäyntitilasto 1994-1995 (Employment statistics 1994-1995), Statistics Finland: Helsinki.

Symes, V. (1995), *Unemployment in Europe: Problems and Policies*, Routledge.

Sääski, N. (1981), Työttömyyden kestoon vaikuttavat tekijät (Factors affecting to the duration of unemployment), *Työpoliittisia tutkimuksia* N:o 28, Työvoimaministeriö, Suunnitteluosasto: Helsinki.

Walsh, K. (1987), *Long-Term Unemployment: An International Perspective*, MacMillan Press.

Acknowledgements

This study has been financed by Kunnallisalan kehittämissäätiö and Jenny ja Antti Wihurin rahasto.

12 Living on the margins: The case for the elderly in Zimbabwe

LAZARUS ZANAMWE

Introduction

The population of the elderly is increasing worldwide in both absolute and relative terms. This is especially true of countries in the developed world. Here populations aged 65 and over form 15-20% of the total population. Populations of the elderly are set to reach in the 21st century to as much as 25 to 30% of the total population in developed countries (Weeks 1986).

For developing nations, the problem does not currently seem acute. National figures show only 3-4% of the population as being aged 65 years and over. However, as is well known, national figures can mask vast differences or variations in the vertical and spatial distributions of a phenomenon (Zanamwe 1989). Closer examination of figures at more disaggregated levels is therefore needed before the problem is dismissed as not being acute or serious.

Further, there is a need to question the wisdom of using the accepted definition of the elderly as being 65 plus in countries where life expectancies are generally below the age of 60 years (UN 1994). At the same time, because of generally economic hardships brought about by economic recession and structural adjustment programmes, a number of developing countries, especially those in Africa south of the Sahara, have introduced programmes of early retirement. Most such early retirement packages are aimed at persons aged between 50 to 59 years. Since the elderly are considered to be the retired, what are the implications of these early retirement policies on the definition of the elderly?

The analysis sets out to examine the composition of the elderly in Zimbabwe based on the 1992 census. It will justify the use of the term elderly as referring to those in the age 60 years and above in view of some of the observations made above as well as the need to study the population of the elderly. It will then highlight the broad vertical and spatial distribution of the elderly in Zimbabwe both at the provincial and district levels.

Justification for analysing the elderly population

Research on age structure in developing nations has mainly concentrated on investigating children, youths, women of reproductive age and those in the working age population. This was justified on the basis of the rapid nature of population growth which required a full knowledge of the structure of the youthful population in order to plan adequately for future needs in the health, education, housing and employment fields. Even now, attention still needs to be focussed on these age groups though calls for attention to be focussed on the elderly age groups are beginning to be heard (Madzingira personal communiction).

The demographic transition model shows that the elderly explosion is inevitable as the population of the world ages (Weeks 1986). What is more, the developing countries, such as Zimbabwe, will face the burdens of still having a youthful population along with a growing number of the elderly. This springs from the fact that outside forces brought in medical science which was able to control both infant, child and adult mortality at the same time. This resulted in increased and improved life expectancy with fairly high annual population growth rates. Annual growth rates exceeded 2.5% per annum for Africa since the end of World War II while life expectancies rose from around the mid-forties to nearly sixty in the 1990s. The spectra of a twin burden of a youthful population with a fairly large proportion of elderly persons therefore found its roots in these rapid medical advances which lowered infant and adult mortality and increased life expectancy.

Following the acceptance of the likelihood of facing the twin burden of the young and the elderly, it is necessary that the distribution of both groups be studied. Enough studies have been done on the children and the youths. Less have been directed on the elderly. Indeed, in the Inter-Censal Survey of 1987, the elderly were not even disaggregated by gender, yet, the Ministry of Health has pointed out the need for statistics on the elderly, if only to provide for their health needs (CSO 1989). These statistics should highlight gender as well as spatial distribution by area of residence even in broad categories such as urban and rural.

A further reason for interest in the elderly is the increased realization that with the HIV/AIDS pandemic on us, the elderly are likely to bear the brunt of bringing up the orphans. Already, FACT has reported that in Manicaland the burden for elderly parents of looking after the orphans of AIDS victims is fairly heavy. In Bulawayo, it was reported that a 92 year old grandmother who was unemployed was looking after five orphans with very little resources in terms of food and financial support to keep these orphans in school (The Herald, 21 Feb. 1996). Thus, if for nothing else but this, the spatial and temporal distribution of the elderly need to be known.

Definition of the elderly

As pointed out above, the elderly are supposed to be composed of the retired population. This population is generally considered to be aged 65 years and over. The definition is borrowed from developed countries were ages of retirement are clearly defined. This author has queried the wisdom of using this definition even if it is an internationally accepted one in a situation were the life expectancy is only beginning to reach 60 years. The bulk of the population, it would seem, ages and dies before this age. At the same time, the AIDS scourge is going to make significant inroads into the chances for a long life for most people, such that maybe the concept of the elderly needs revisiting.

To this end, this analysis will use the age 60 and above as the elderly population. The choice is based on the noted life expectancy at birth (CSO 1994) as well as the consideration that with early retirement policies in place, some people are now leaving work at the age of 55 years. Sixty will therefore seem to be a reasonable compromise for defining the elderly in the Zimbabwean, if not the Sub-Saharan African context.

Anywhere, the Cairo Conference on Population and Development held in 1994, analysed the rate of growth of the elderly based on those 60 years and above. It noted that in developed countries, one in every six persons was above the age of 60 and that the proportion will be close to one in four by the year 2025. The same conference noted the need to pay attention to this age group, particularly in situations of rapid fertility decline and especially for women who outlive men in developing countries. Thus, the concept of the elderly as being aged 60 years and over has international acceptability and recognition (UN 1994).

Inter-censal patterns of growth among the elderly

The argument has been made that the proportion of the elderly has been increasing in Zimbabwe due to increased or improved life expectancy. Table 12.1 gives evidence of these increases. The analysis here is based at the provincial level. This is so because only the broad trends in the patterns of the increase of the elderly needed to be shown (CSO 1994) .

Across all provinces there seems to have been an increase in the population of the elderly in the inter-censal period. The exception is for males in Midlands and females in Harare and Bulawayo. Here there are slight drops in the proportions of the elderly. At the national level, there are positive increases in the elderly in the inter-censal period (6.25% for males and 11.11% for females). The increase in females is almost always larger than that for males in all cases except for the urban areas of Harare and Bulawayo. The largest increases are recorded in Mashonaland East and Matabeleland North Provinces. The main reasons for both the drops noted in the provinces of Midlands, Harare and Bulawayo as well as the increases for Mashonaland East and Matabeleland North might have to do with boundary changes effected during the inter-censal period. The figures shown for the two provinces included the cities of Harare and Bulawayo in 1982. In 1992, these cities now stood as independent provinces in their own right. This had the effect of increasing the proportion of the elderly in Mash. East and Mat. North, because their populations became more rural compared to their position in 1982 (CSO 1985, 1994).

Table 12.1 Percent elderly population 60+ by gender, sex ratios and by province: Zimbabwe, 1982 and 1992

Province	Elderly Population					
	Male		Female		Sex ratio	
	1982	1992	1982	1992	1982	1992
Manicaland	5.1	5.2	4.7	5.3	94.3	87.9
Mash.Cent	5.4	5.8	4.1	5.3	123.5	105.5
Mash. East	4.2	6.3	4.1	6.3	105.3	93.9
Mash. West	5.3	5.5	3.6	4.5	153.0	124.3
Mat. North	4.5	5.7	3.4	6.3	108.7	85.7
Mat. South	6.3	6.4	6.1	7.4	93.7	77.0
Midlands	4.9	4.8	4.6	4.9	101.6	93.8
Masvingo	4.7	5.3	4.8	5.9	88.2	79.4
Harare	3.0	3.1	2.9	2.4	117.6	138.8
Bulawayo	3.7	4.0	3.3	3.2	126.6	126.4
Zimbabwe	4.8	5.1	4.5	5.0	105.1	96.6

Sources: (CSO 1985, 1994; Zanamwe 1989)

The loss registered for males in Midlands Province might also have to do with boundary changes. The province lost Chikomba District to Mashonaland East. As the district analysis shows, Chikomba District has some of the oldest populations in the country.

The larger increases for females as compared to males are expected. These are a result of the well established factor that women tend to outlive their male counterparts (Weeks 1986; Jones 1992). Indeed as there are recorded improvements in life expectancy at birth, the gap between male and female life expectancy also tends to increase. In other words, the more the population tends to live longer, the greater the gap for the expectations of life between the male and female. Zimbabwe is no exception to this rule. It has recorded increased life expectancies between 1982 and 1992 and these would translate into greater numbers of female survivors compared to the males ones in both absolute and relative terms.

The declines noted for females in urban areas are a bit difficult to explain. However, a brief explanation is put forward here. It could bear with further empirical research since it is mostly speculative or based on a few observed and known historical trends in urban and rural development. The first might be linked to the urban history of Zimbabwe. Urban areas used to be predominantly male, since colonial legislation forbade Africans from having permanent residence in these areas which were classified as being European (Zanamwe 1989). Females tended to come into urban areas for very short visits and definitely with no intention to stay. This attitude might imply that at retirement, more females above the age of 60 leave for their rural homes compared to their male counterparts. It might also imply that, because of the retention of the rural home, females might be sent home earlier by husbands on the verge of retirement. Such a situation might be re-enforced or even speeded up under conditions of economic hardships leading to forced retrenchments of labour as has occurred since 1990. Therefore, the economic structural adjustment programme might have led to a loss of the elderly female population from urban areas at rates which are higher than normal and which would then be registered as negative growth in the inter-censal period.

The sex ratio for the urban areas of Harare might support this contention. Due to the loss of females, the sex ratio for the elderly actually increases from 117.6 males per 100 females to 138.8 in the inter-censal period. The increase in the dominance of males would seem to suggest a loss of the female population due to out-migration from the urban area rather than in-migration of males.

In terms of spatial distribution, both for males and females, Matabeleland South had the oldest populations, both in 1982 and 1992. The least proportion of the elderly population were found in urban areas. Even between the two largest urban areas, some ranking is evident with Bulawayo having proportionately more older populations compared to Harare. Thus, it would seem that urbanization does play a role in the spatial distribution of the elderly. The more rural a province is, the more likely that it will contain a significant number of elderly persons.

Spatial patterns of elderly distribution at the district level

Tables A to H at the APPENDIX of this chapter, present the pattern of distribution of the elderly population at the district level as well as the sex ratios. The analysis shall proceed by examining the spatial distribution by gender first, then the sex ratios and concludes by looking at the implications.

As stated under the provincial analysis, Matabeleland South has the oldest populations. If an arbitrary scale is created where any district with 6% or more of its elderly population is supposed to be oldest, then Matabeleland South tops the list with five out of its seven districts meeting the criteria (APPENDIX Table F). Indeed, three of these districts have proportions higher than 7% for either gender (Bulilimamangwe 7.12% male and 8.77% female; Gwanda Rural 7.77% female and Matobo 7.05% male and 8.38% female). These figures can be contrasted to Gwanda Urban with only 3.03% males and 1.73% females being in the elderly category. Other provinces containing districts with fairly large proportions of the elderly are Matabeleland North (4 out of 9 districts; APPENDIX Table E) and Mashonaland East (6 out of 10 districts; APPENDIX Table C).

The provinces containing the districts with the least proportion of the elderly population would seem to be Manicaland and Mashonaland West, according to the above criteria. Makoni in Manicaland is the only district to have an elderly proportion above 6% for both males and females (7.15 and 6.44% respectively, APPENDIX Table A). In Mashonaland West (APPENDIX Table D), only males in Chegutu Rural and Hurungwe actually exceed the 6% criteria (6.79 and 6.37% respectively).

Districts in the remainder of the provinces present a mixed picture. In most, females tend to out number males in terms of districts were the proportion is above 6%. A case to illustrate this point is the province of Masvingo (APPENDIX Table H). Out of eight districts, only 2 (Chivi and Gutu) have males above the 6% mark while four (Bikita, Chivi, Gutu and Zaka) do meet the criteria for the females. Midlands (APPENDIX Table G) also exhibits a similar distribution to that found in Masvingo.

In terms of sex ratios, it would seem that the spatial patterns of the distribution of the elderly follows the urbanization-development opportunity argument presented above. Districts which are highly urbanized, such as Mutare, Rusape, Shamva, Bindura and so on, tend to boast of sex ratios in favour of males. Districts which are purely rural such as Chivi, Gokwe, Mutasa, Nkayi and so on show a female dominance in the sex ratios of the elderly (Zanamwe 1989).

In between are rural districts which are dominated by commercial farming activities. These are found chiefly in Mashonaland Central and West (APPENDIX Tables B and D respectively). They sex ratios also tend to favour males because these are areas of economic opportunities and do provide employment. They are also areas into which a lot of migrant workers are found, mainly from Mozambique and Malawi (Zanamwe 1989, 1995). Because of this, it is postulated that their ability to return to a communal land on retirement is limited. The tendency is to hold onto employment for as long as possible or upon dismissal to squat on the land. Several such cases have been reported in the media, from the two provinces mentioned above.

What other explanations can be offered for these observed spatial and gender distribution of the elderly population and what conclusions can be drawn? It can be argued that the historical patterns of development generated by the settler state have determined the distribution of the elderly population just as it has determined the location of economic activities and the resultant migration patterns. The rural areas, especially the communal lands, still seem to be the reservoirs of labour as well as the dumping grounds for retired and/or retrenched workers from the urban and commercial farming sectors. The result is such areas tend to boast of more elderly proportions of the population compared to their urban/commercial sector counterparts. They also tend to be dominated by the elderly female rather than the elderly male (Zanamwe 1989).

Implications of the growth of the elderly population

As stated in the introductory sections, the population of the world is ageing. This has serious implications, especially in the field of health. In the developed world, health costs have risen as nations battle to look after their elderly. Costs include provision of old people's homes and expensive treatments for these such as hip replacements or treatment of heart problems. For nations in the developing world the problem of the elderly has not received enough attention to date (Madzingira per. comm). This is because these nations were still battling the youthfulness rather than the ageing of their populations. However, it is now time attention was paid to the ageing process, if only to enhance their ability to cope when the time comes.

The analysis above has also tried to show that the complacency with regards to the old age populations in developing countries is also based on the use of aggregate statistics based at the national level. When more spatially disaggregated data are used, as was done in this analysis for Zimbabwe, then the proportions of the elderly in given areas do rise above the national average. Indeed, it is the dichotomy between the rural and the urban areas that tend to keep overall national averages of the elderly low.

What are the implications of the growth of the elderly for Zimbabwe? First, the growth of the elderly provides a challenge in terms of the provision of health as well as social facilities for this group. A clear cut policy should be put in place in terms of who shall provide for the elderly. Currently, the extended family system has acted as a social security system providing for the elderly in old age. Indeed, this is one reason for the late decline in the fertility of Zimbabwe, despite greater access to family planning services compared to other African countries. As long as parents are not assured of security in old age, especially in view of a lengthening life span, more children will be born to look after the elderly parents. The end result will be that the social and economic systems will eventually have to cope with the twin burden of youthfulness and the elderly (Zanamwe 1989, Madzingira per. comm).

Secondly, the growth of the elderly poses challenges for the health and social welfare sector. Do these sectors have the ability to provide the old peoples homes? Do they have the capacity to provide for the expensive medical treatments being provided for the aged, say as in developed countries? and so on. These are some of the issues these sectors will have to address.

The AIDS pandemic has also been mentioned above. With the burden of looking after the orphans of the AIDS victims falling on the elderly, a re-evaluation of their role as retired is needed. Indeed, instead of being secure in old age and being looked after by their children, the old are become a social security system for those who fall victims of AIDS. In providing care both for the sick and the orphans, using what ever meagre incomes they have, the elderly are taking care of one of the major burdens of the state and local governments. Ways and means have to be found to make the provision of resources to the elderly households looking after the orphans possible.

The construction industry and other provider of services will also have to address the issue of the elderly. The construction of public access areas will have to take into consideration their use by the old and frailly. Currently, most buildings were the elderly shop or go for services are built without access ramps and steep steps. Modifications to such buildings will have to take place so that ease of access can be gained by the elderly and the disabled. Thus, the elderly will cause a change, not only in the ways we perceive economic, health and social issues but in other areas as well.

The distribution of the elderly by gender and geographic area is also of major concern. APPENDIX Tables A to H clearly demonstrate that elderly females are to be found in communal lands in large numbers. These are the areas that can least afford to look after them and take care of their health and nutritional needs. Most old peoples homes or social welfare programmes display a distinct urban bias. Due to this, the elderly female is placed at a great disadvantage because she is located faraway from centres that could offer help in her times of need. The disadvantage increases even further if that elderly women has to take care of AIDS orphans. Thus, the distribution of the elderly would seem to indicate the need to locate more facilities within rural areas so that social welfare programmes directed at the elderly can reach them.

Concluding remarks

The analysis has tried to provide a vertical, temporal and spatial picture of the situation of the elderly in Zimbabwe based on the 1992 census. It has shown that, though the elderly form a small proportion of the overall population of Zimbabwe, their numbers have increased in both absolute and relative terms in the inter-censal period. This increase has been smaller for males than females (Table 12.1) and is a result of increased life expectancy due to improvements in medicine, life conditions and nutritional knowledge.

The analysis has further shown that the national level masks great variations in the proportions of the elderly across the country. At a subnational level, the elderly vary from 0.79% females in Ruwa to 8.77% females in Bulilimamangwe District. Further, the rural areas with less in terms of social and health infrastructure to care for the elderly tend to contain more of their numbers than the urban areas. Thus, those who spend their productive years working in urban and commercial farming areas are retired into the communal lands where infrastructure is inadequate to take care of their needs.

The analysis calls for clear policies to be put into place to take care of the elderly. It recognizes that the proportion of the elderly will continue to increase and this will place a different kind of demand on the utilization and provision of services, especially in the health and social welfare sectors. Changes are also envisaged for those in the construction industries while state and local governments need to brainstorm on the best ways of dealing with the elderly.

The analysis is by no means exhaustive. At most, it is a kind of base-line study providing pointers for future areas of research. More detail is required about the distribution and living conditions of the elderly at the household level. More is required about the sources and sizes of their incomes. More is required about their responsibilities especially in the light of the AIDS pandemic and the orphans that it is generating. Indeed, more is required about the mechanisms by which they cope with the loss of those whom their expected to look after them in old age.

References

United Nations (1994), International Conference on Population and Development, Cairo, Egypt.

CSO (1985), Main demographic features of the population of Zimbabwe: an advance report based on a ten percent sample, CSO, Harare, June 1985.

CSO (1989) , Zimbabwe Inter-censal Demographic Survey, CSO, Harare.

CSO(1994) , Census 1992: Zimbabwe National Report, CSO, Harare, November 1994.

Jones H.R. (1990), Population geography. Chapman, London.

Weeks J.R. (1986), Population: An introduction to concepts and issues. Wadsworth, Belmont.

Zanamwe L. (1989), Population change and socio-economic development in Zimbabwe, PhD Thesis, School of Geography, University of Leeds.

Zanamwe L. (1995), From tax registers to census enumerators: nine decaces of census collection in Zimbabwe, Geographical Journal of Zimbabwe, Vol. 25.

Other sources

Madzingira N. (personal communications).

Appendix

Tables A to H (Source for tables is given at the end of table H)

Table A **Elderly population aged 60 years and above by gender and districts: Manicaland 1992**

District	% Male	% Female	Sex Ratio
Buhera	5.60	5.87	80.86
Chimanimani	4.90	5.27	85.88
Chipinge	3.97	4.73	71.13
Makoni	7.15	6.44	99.51
Mutare Rural	5.93	5.50	98.39
Mutasa	5.78	5.87	87.84
Nyanga	5.25	5.52	82.90
Mutare Urban	2.74	2.17	137.36
Rusape	3.40	2.28	143.21
MANICALAND	5.19	5.29	87.92

Table B **Elderly population aged 60 years and above by gender and districts: Mashonaland Central, 1992**

District	% Male	% Female	Sex Ratio
Bindura Rural	4.95	4.17	119.59
Centenary	6.28	5.04	120.94
Guruve	6.91	6.23	101.52
Mazowe	5.11	4.42	114.81
Mount Darwin	6.66	6.54	92.03
Rushinga	5.80	5.54	91.16
Shamva	5.55	4.75	115.12
Bindura Urban	2.72	2.07	137.38
MASH. CENTRAL	5.80	5.25	105.47

Table C **Elderly population aged 60 years and above by gender and districts: Mashonaland East, 1992**

District	% Male	% Female	Sex Ratio
Chikomba	7.63	8.18	83.28
Goromonzi	5.10	4.65	106.30
Hwedza	6.57	6.62	92.47
Marondera Rural	5.83	5.37	108.98
Mudzi	6.52	6.72	83.58
Murewa	6.61	6.70	90.46
Mutoko	7.46	7.49	88.87
Seke	5.79	4.82	120.81
UMP	6.77	6.66	91.13
Marondera Urban	3.48	2.60	129.17
Ruwa	1.83	0.79	300.00
MASH. EAST	6.34	6.27	93.92

Table D **Elderly population aged 60 years and above by gender and districts: Mashonaland West, 1992**

District	% Male	% Female	Sex Ratio
Chegutu Rural	6.79	5.69	117.76
Hurungwe	6.37	5.41	114.71
Kadoma Rural	5.81	5.01	116.84
Kariba Rural	4.52	4.82	90.53
Makonde	4.83	3.58	140.07
Zvimba	5.74	4.24	140.62
Chegutu Urban	3.05	2.66	116.83
Chinhoyi	3.38	2.36	146.32
Chirundu	3.01	0.84	575.00
Kadoma Urban	3.18	2.25	141.42
Kariba Urban	2.37	1.25	223.53
Karoi	2.47	1.84	138.06
MASH. WEST	5.48	4.45	124.33

Table E Elderly population aged 60 years and above by gender and districts: Matabeleland North, 1992

District	% Male	% Female	Sex Ratio
Binga	4.75	5.20	74.35
Bubi	5.94	5.97	99.45
Hwange Rural	6.58	6.72	95.24
Lupane	6.01	6.85	80.30
Nkayi	6.16	6.84	81.42
Tsholotsho	7.26	8.56	70.69
Umguza	5.90	5.24	129.34
Hwange Urban	1.62	0.98	188.21
Victoria Falls	2.70	2.06	177.55
MATABELELAND NORTH	5.71	6.25	85.68

Table F Elderly population aged 60 years and above by gender and districts: Matabeleland South, 1992

District	% Male	% Female	Sex Ratio
Beitbridge	4.66	5.11	79.66
Bulilimamangwe	7.12	8.77	66.76
Gwanda Rural	6.75	7.77	82.06
Insiza	5.99	6.54	86.65
Matobo	7.05	8.38	75.22
Umzingwane	6.03	6.56	87.38
Gwanda Urban	3.03	1.73	188.64
MATABELELAND SOUTH	6.35	7.39	77.03

Table G Elderly population aged 60 years and above by gender and districts: Midlands, 1992

District	% Male	% Female	Sex Ratio
Chirumanzu	6.07	6.62	83.17
Gokwe	8.74	4.71	92.68
Gweru Rural	5.93	6.23	93.39
Kwekwe Rural	5.67	5.31	101.54
Mberengwa	5.69	6.30	80.06
Shurugwi Rural	6.34	6.19	98.07
Zvishavane Rural	5.49	5.85	90.49
Gweru Urban	2.39	1.96	123.61
Kwekwe Urban	2.66	2.00	130.49
Redcliff	2.24	1.44	168.12
Shurugwi Urban	4.63	4.17	100.00
Zvishavane Urban	3.21	2.04	141.18
MIDLANDS	4.82	4.85	93.84

Table H Elderly population aged 60 years and above by gender and districts: Masvingo, Harare and Bulawayo Provinces, 1992

District	% Male	% Female	Sex Ratio
Bikita	5.96	6.77	74.41
Chiredzi	3.24	3.43	86.85
Chivi	6.33	6.79	81.10
Gutu	6.55	7.21	78.07
Masvingo Rural	5.43	6.23	80.17
Mwenezi	4.54	5.07	79.44
Zaka	5.99	6.71	76.57
Masvingo Urban	2.14	1.85	116.77
MASVINGO	5.32	5.93	79.37
Harare Rural	3.82	1.74	250.00
Chitungwiza	1.96	1.56	126.35
Harare Urban	3.31	2.62	138.77
HARARE	3.07	2.41	138.36
BULAWAYO	4.03	3.17	126.43

Source: (CSO 1994).

13 'Basics are now a luxury': Perceptions of ESAP's impact on rural and urban areas in Zimbabwe

DEBORAH POTTS AND CHRIS C. MUTAMBIRWA

Introduction

Throughout Africa people's lifestyles and livelihoods have been fundamentally altered by the impact of structural adjustment policies (SAPs). Ostensibly designed to rectify a host of economic distortions which international financial institutions argue had been caused by government mismanagement, there is so far little evidence that these policies are strengthening African economies in the ways which their promoters have promised. Instead there is an ever-accumulating literature on the devastatingly negative, and sometimes tragic, impact of such policies on people in terms of employment, incomes, health and education (see for example, Corma, Jolly and Stewart (eds), 1987).

The overall interest in this paper is the disparate impacts of SAPs on the economically maginalised communities in the rural and urban areas of Zimbabwe as perceived by new rural-urban migrants who have taken up residence in Harare's high density residential areas, and the consequent nature of the linkages between rural and urban communities.

This paper is the result of research in 1994 amongst a sample of migrant households who had recently come to Harare. The research focussed on how these people perceived ESAP (Economic Structural Adjustment Program) and its effects: the expectation being that in line with other surveys in Harare and Zimbabwe, these perceptions would be generally negative. Beyond this, however, we wanted to find out to what extent people felt that ESAP's impacts varied between urban and rural areas, and whether there was a clear trend in these perceptions. We also endeavoured to find out which aspects of ESAP were regarded as most problematic for different areas, and for the respondent personally.

The researchers specifically adopted a qualitative approach to this topic. The questions about ESAP and its effects were usually open-ended, i.e. there was no attempt to pre-judge the answers or to categorise them during the interview. There was a questionnaire which included many pre-coded questions on general socio-economic status, but the responses to the questions about ESAP were written down more or less verbatim, and prompting for information was kept to a minimum.

This study aims to contribute to the literature on Zimbabwe and SAPs in sub-Saharan Africa in the following ways:

1. It shows which particular aspects of SAPs are considered to be most important by the people affected rather than focussing on macro-level economic indicators or issues judged to be of significance by the researchers/
2. It indicates how people rank the various impacts of SAPs on communities in different geographical settings.
3. It provides meaningful insights into the differential impacts of SAPs on rural compared to urban areas.by focussing mainly on rural-urban migrants who have recently left the rural areas, and who can therefore reasonably be assumed to have a sensible view of rural priorities and livelihoods, as well as urban life,
4. It adds to the researchers's on-going longterm research on migration to Harare which provides information on the nature of how rural-urban linkages are changing under ESAP.

Background to the study

Zimbabwe introduced its Economic Structural Adjustment Policy (ESAP) in January 1991. It is important, in terms of the population's subsequent perceptions of the impact of ESAP which is a key aspect of this paper, to note that it is questionable whether Zimbabwe needed to adjust in this particular way (i.e. adopting the usual SAP package). It was certainly not in the desperate economic straits typical of many other sub-Saharan African countries during the 1980s. Over the decade economic growth rates had, on average (and despite some severe drought episodes), kept just ahead of population growth (c.3.5% per year) at around 4% per year (Economist Intelligence Unit, Zimbabwe Country Reports, 1991-1996) The government had also adopted its own economic austerity measures in March 1984 after an economic crisis. These succeeded in, for example, reducing the debt-service ratio from almost 40% to 20% between 1985 and 1989 (Collin Stoneman, 1996). In non-drought years the performance of the agricultural sector, including the peasant farming areas, had been good. The Productivity of the communal areas was very geographically variable, with some areas relying on drought relief and food programmes in most years and contributing little or nothing to marketed production. However these macro-patterns are to be expected given the pattern of rainfall in the country and other environmental factors (Zinyama, 1988). The population had experienced some really significant improvements in health and education as a result of the government's development programmes in health and education for all citizens by the year 2000 (Government of Zimbabwe, 1981, 1982, 1983). Furthermore, whilst the performance of the manufacturing sector was variable, with the important iron and steel parastatal ZISCO sorely mismanaged, the sector also displayed many strengths and the end of the 1980s saw significant increases in the export of non-traditional manufactured exports (Stoneman, 1996; Riddell (ed.) 1990). This latter growth owed much to an export revolving fund. Neither was the currency hugely over-valued as was so typical in many other African countries: the World Bank estimated the overvaluation to be in the range of 10 to 20% (Stoneman 1996).

Yet the portrayal of the Zimbabwean economy and government policies in World bank documents tends to typify the country as one in specific need of structural adjustment (see Gulhati, 1988). Whilst there were undoubtedly economic problems, such as the size of the budget deficit and the lack of flexibility in import control programmes to the extent that key productive sectors were sometimes held up by lack of necessary inputs, it is arguable that these could have been managed without recourse to a full-blown SAP. Nevertheless, in a continent of structurally-adjusting countries, following a decade of propaganda on the need to 'liberalise' economies and the collapse of 'socialist' economies worldwide, and the lure of easier borrowing (for a while), with a Finance Minister with strong neo-classical economic tendencies, it is perhaps not surprising that Zimbabwe eventually decided to join the crowd. Another more sinister factor may have been a degree of 'sabotage' by the World Bank to divert Zimbabwe from its autonomous policy path (see Riddel, 1990; Stoneman, 1996; Campbell and Loxely (eds), 1989). According to Stoneman (1996), the Bank needs to adjust its tactics to enable Zimbabwe to successfully adjust economically from a position of relative economic strength already.

There have now been several surveys of the impact of ESAP, including specific work on trade unions, the informal sector, health, and women (see for example, Gibbon (ed.), 1995). Most of these have focussed on urban-based impacts, and all of them record the severely negative effects of ESAP for the ordinary people (the povo) of Zimbabwe. These will not be further discussed here, although relevant details will be picked up in some sections below. Suffice it to say, at this point, that the Zimbabwean people have experienced massive income and welfare shocks which mirror what has happened elsewhere throughout 'adjusting' sub-Saharan Africa.

The first phase of ESAP has now ended and the second phase referred to in Zimbabwe as ZIMPREST (Zimbabwe Program for Economic and Social Transformation) was meant to start in 1996. However, there have been difficulties with the IMF, mainly over the budget deficit, with two suspensions of funding in 1995, and in July 1996 the second phase of funding was dependent on the nature of the government budget. One final point about ESAP is that almost immediately after its introduction Zimbabwe suffered two very serious years of drought, which had devastating economic effects. This has obviously made evaluation of the macro-economic effects of ESAP rather difficult, although it is much easier to establish the micro-level effects on specific types of jobs, health, education, food prices etc.

The impact of SAPs is not geographically uniform within a country. The usual policy package includes significant devaluation, cutbacks in public expenditure, liberalisation of trade and abolition of public subsidies, and reform of parastatals. These measures may have a different impact on urban areas compared to the countryside. For example, the widespread loss of jobs in the formal private and public sectors, and the ending of food subsidies are two common outcomes of structural adjustment, and both are felt most acutely in urban areas. On the other hand, the adjustment policies of crop price increases and liberalised agricultural marketing should, theoretically, improve the incomes of farmers.

The surveys

Our research was conducted mainly during April and May 1994 by means of a questionnaire mainly amongst migrants who were resident in Kuwadzana, one of Harare's high density areas (HDAs). Kuwadzana is one of the largest housing areas to be developed since independence in Zimbabwe: it has been funded by USAID and most of the houses have been developed on a site-and-service basis.

The research reported here is part of a long term collaborative project on migrants and migration to Harare begun in 1985. The 1994 survey covered 157 respondents resident in three different unit of Kuwadzana in April 1994, and a sub-sample of 46 respondents from three older townships dating from the colonial era for comparative purpose. We maintained similar criteria for respondents as in our previous migrant surveys (Potts and Mutambirwa, 1990, 1991). A respondent had to be a recent migrant: in the survey this was designated as anyone who had moved to live in Harare since the beginning of 1990. He or she had to live on the plot where they were interviewed, and had to be over 18 years of age. Respondents were identified by our three interviewers going from one plot to another from a common starting point in each unit, and asking if anyone there had moved to live in Harare (but not necessarily to that specific residence) since 1990. Once sufficient respondents had been interviewed in one area the interviewers moved to the next unit. Apart from the minimum age criterion, there were no further restriction on the nature of migrant respondents. In particular we did not wish to restrict ourselves only to household heads, as this makes it impossible to get a rounded view of migrant households and of the views of different types of migrants. For example, since new migrants often live with relatives (whose household head may or may not be a migrant) the common practice of only interviewing household heads would completely exclude such people from this kind of survey. By interviewing throughout the day, and particularly at week-ends we were able to get a varied sample of migrant household heads, migrant spouses of household heads, and various other migrant household members. Apart from the questions specific to the respondents, the interview schedule included some questions about household heads (e.g. sex, age, employment, income, migrant status) which the respondent, if not head, was also asked. Whilst not all such respondents could fill in all details about their respective household heads, this methodology allows much data to be gathered on both the migrants and the households of which they are part.

Profiles of migrant respondents

Social profile

The 203 migrants interviewed were roughly evenly divided between men and women (55% and 45%), household heads (HHHs) and other household members (56% and 44%), and married and non-married people (56% and 44%) (see Tables 13.1 and 13.2). One third of the migrants had never been married, and the age profile of respondents was generally young (see Tables 13.2 and 13.3). Just over a quarter of the respondents who were also HHHs (thirty individuals) had never been married – that is they were generally young people who were living in town on their own. Sixty per cent of this group were aged 18 to 24 years, and 75% were male. However, as would be expected, the age profile of respondents tended to be older than that of the sample as a whole.

Table 13.1 Household status and gender of migrant respondents (%)[1]

Reln. to HHH	All respondents (%)	number	Male (%)	Female (%)
HHH	56	(114)	79	21
Spouse	21	(43)	5	95
Son/daughter	12	(25)	48	52
Brother/Sister	7	(14)	64	36
Other relative	2	(4)	0	100
Others [2]	1	(3)	0	100
All respondents (%)	100	(203)	55	45

Table 13.2 Marital status of migrant respondents

Marital status	All respondents (%)	number	Respondent HHH (%)
Never Married	33	(66)	27
Married	56	(111)	56
Divorced	5	(10)	7
Separated	2	(4)	3
Widowed	4	(8)	6
All respondents (%)	100	(199)	56

Employment status of migrant households

In common with our earlier surveys of migrant households, we found that nearly all (96%) of the migrant HHHs we interviewed were working. This was also true for all HHHs. As explained above the survey also gathered information from 'dependent' migrant respondents on their respective HHHs. Thus the HHH data set includes information on some HHHs who were not respondents in the survey. Since the eligibility for the survey rested on the year of the respondent's migration, non-respondent HHHs need not be recent migrants as classified by our survey, or even migrants at all. Ninety four per cent of the non-respondent HHHs were working. It was notable that all of these were reported to be working in formal sector jobs, as were 92% if the working migrant HHHs.

Table 13.3 Age profile of migrant respondents

Age band	All respondents (%)	Respondent HHHs (%)
18 - 24	34	18
25 - 29	24	25
30 - 34	17	21
35 - 39	9	13
40 - 49	9	16
50 - 59	9	4
60+	0	0
DK	3	4
All respondents %	100	56

Our sample then was almost entirely of people who had formal jobs, or who lived in households headed by someone with a formal job. Significant increases in participation in the informal sector, as structural adjustment policies have reduced incomes and formal employment have been noted in many African cities (Potts, 1997). However, the results of this survey suggest that, in 1994 at least, this strategy has been relatively less important in Harare for HHHs. Only 4% of all the household heads in our survey were working in the informal sector. Interviewers classified jobs as formal or informal according to the basic criterion of whether the person was licensed or not. As it is very often the case in urban Africa, it was particularly female HHHs who were working informally: 56% of this group were women (five out of nine cases), whilst women as a whole accounted for only 21% of sampled household heads. Even for women, however, there is some evidence that ESAP in Zimbabwe (in contrast to SAPs elsewhere on the continent) is reducing their involvement in this sector. A survey of informal sector traders in Harare by Brand (1995) found that between 1992 and 1993 22% had stopped a trading activity, whilst only 5% had started up new ones. According to her ESAP had resulted in more competition and lower returns, leading to a decision that further effort was cost-ineffective. Kanji and Jazdowska (1993) also found that women in their sample (also in Kambuzuma, Harare) had experienced reductions in their informal sector activities and income between July 1992 and January 1993. This was largely ascribed to falling demand due to their customers' increasing poverty under ESAP. It appears, therefore, that the characteristics of the economic problems caused by SAPs in Harare are somewhat different, and on a rather lesser scale, than those which have been typical of many sub-Saharan African cities like Lusaka, Accra, Dar es Salaam or Lilongwe where informal sector activities have become a virtual *sine qua non* for economic survival.

Nevertheless the informal sector did play a part in the economics of our sampled households, Another strategy commonly pursued by urban residents in other African countries when their incomes have been 'squeezed' by SAPs, is to take up second jobs in addition to their primary employment. Eighteen percent of all household heads in this survey were reported as having a secondary income and, in nearly all cases, from another job which was in the informal sector. There were only two cases where the HHH's secondary source of income was not recorded as being from a 'job'.

In complete contrast to the household heads, 'dependent' migrants in the survey experienced a high level of unemployment. Although most of this group of respondents classified themselves as housewives or attending school, 78% (28 out of 36 eligible for work) said they were unemployed and actively seeking work. These unemployed 'dependents' were more or less evenly divided between men and women (54% to 46%). Of the eight who were working, six were women, and two were in the informal sector. Nine 'dependent' respondents also reported that they had some income from secondary activities.

Household incomes

The survey gathered data on the level of the respondent's income, and of the HHHs', if not the same person. In both cases efforts were made to include both primary and secondary sources of income. The average primary income of all heads (i.e. both respondent heads and those reported by 'dependents') was Z$907. The modal earning level was Z$400 and 15% of all household heads were earning exactly this amount. Only 4% had no primary earnings, which corresponds well with the proportion reported as unemployed. The average value of reported secondary income for all household heads was Z$80, although the vast majority (87%) had none. For the 13% who did report secondary earnings, the average contribution to household income was quite substantial at Z$622.

As already established most 'dependent' migrant respondents were unemployed or not earning by virtue of being housewives or in education. Only 6% actually reported a specific primary income, for which the average was Z$38; and 10% reported a secondary income (average Z$32). Thus the income profile of our sample was of generally poor urban households, as would be expected among recent migrant households in high density areas.

Migrants' perceptions of ESAP

We now turn to the issue of how the surveyed migrants felt about ESAP. Our primary interest was not so much on what impacts ESAP had on the migrant households in a quantitative sense, but more so on how they 'perceived' the policies as a whole, and whether they had strong opinions about the differential impact of ESAP on rural versus urban areas. Much of the information gathered is qualitative and in the form of comments from each respondent. The interviewers began this section of the interview with the introduction that the government had introduced economic policies since 1990 known as ESAP, and that they wanted to find out what the respondent felt about how these policies had affected people in different parts of Zimbabwe. Respondents were then asked to rank how they thought ESAP had affected the communal areas (i.e. whether it had made things better, worse, both better and worse, or had not had much effect). They were then encouraged to explain their ranking, with no further prompting about the types of issues they brought up at this point. This process was then repeated for three further areas: on the impact of ESAP on Harare (as a whole); on whether there was any difference in the nature of the impact of ESAP in the communal areas compared to Harare; and finally on how the respondents felt they had been personally affected. The rankings are shown in Table 13.4. They have been desegregated according to the respondents' birthplace in order to test whether the degree of familiarity with life in town or the communal areas affected their perceptions.

As described above, respondents were asked to explain and elaborate on their perceptions of ESAP's impact on the communal areas (CAs). It is these comments, recorded by the interviewers on the interview schedules, which give the true flavour of their attitudes, and which indicate the factors and events which made them form their opinions. As will be seen below, many comments fell into very specific categories and are easily summarised. There were also other, perhaps less frequently mentioned, issues which are of great significance for constructing and understanding of how Zimbabwean migrants perceive ESAP to have affected rural and urban livelihoods.

Impact of ESAP on communal areas

A large majority (87%) of the migrants felt that ESAP had made things worse for the communal areas (= CAs). Only 6% felt that it had improved the situation. The remaining few were divided between those who felt that it had made little difference, or had made some things better and others worse, or could not tell (see Table 13.4). There was some evidence that where a migrant had been brought up made some difference to their perceptions, but this was more because town-born people were, understandably, uncertain about how ESAP had affected the CAs rather than that they were less negative about its impact there. In fact 33% of this group felt unable to rank the impact of ESAP on the CAs.

Table 13.4 Rankings of impact of ESAP by birthplace of respondents (%) [3]

	On Communal areas				On Harare			
Birth Place	Better	Worse	Better & Worse	Same	Better	Worse	Better & Worse	Same
All	6	87	1	1.0	4	95	1.5	0
CAs	6	91	1	0.5	4	96	1.5	0
Towns	5	62	0	0.0	5	90	0.0	0

	On CAs versus Harare				
Birth Place	Better CAs	Better Harare	Worse CAs	Worse Harare	Same CAs & Harare
All	0.5	1	4	84	6
CAs	0.5	1	4	84	6
Towns	0.0	0	5	76	5

On respondent			
Better	Worse	Better& Worse	Same
2	90	1.5	1.5

The explanations for their rankings made it very clear that the most important issue influencing the migrants' perceptions was the very significant increases in prices andwhich they attributed (correctly) to ESAP (see Table 13.5).

Table 13.5 Explanations of perceptions: the impact of ESAP on the communal areas (CA) [4]

Type of Comment	Number
General Increases in prices (excluding farming inputs)	94
of which:	
ending price controls	10
rural shops have monopoly/no competition, so charge exorbitant prices	14
food now very expensive	31
Fertilisers become too expensive	30
Education problems:	
cannot send all children to school	15
cost of uniforms	2
Hospital fees too high	8
Rural-urban linkages:	
return migration 'overburdening' CAs	7
retrenchment in towns leading to loss of remittances	8
Little effect on CAs as people do not have to buy anything or live on farming	7
Helped CA farmers who can sell maize in town for high prices	6

Thus 94 of the migrants focussed on the issue of prices for items other than farm inputs, and this corresponds to 57% of those who made a detailed response to this question. They were particularly worried about increasing food prices, but the ending of price controls generally was also mentioned. A number also made very specific complaints about rural dealers exploiting their monopoly position and charging 'exorbitant' prices now that price controls had gone – clearly this problem is one that would affect rural areas rather than urban areas where competition would tend to discourage such over-pricing. The migrants' new familiarity with urban prices may have focussed their minds on the differentials between urban and rural prices, and higher rural prices would to some extent be due to 'fair' factors such as transport costs and small turnover, but, on the other hand, the ending of price controls definitely gives rural traders the potential to be exploitative, and the respondents may well have noticed that rural prices had increased proportionately more than those in urban areas. The fact that prices for non-farm inputs were perceived as being the main problem for the communal areas is regarded as highly significant: we return to this point in the conclusion.

The second most important category of responses related again to price rises, but this time to the perception that fertilisers had become very expensive. In some cases the respondents made this comment in association with a complaint about the generally increasing expense of farm inputs including, for example, seeds and farm equipment. Again such concerns indicate that any advantages accruing from higher selling prices for agricultural produce are easily offset by the impact of liberalisation on necessary inputs. In relation to many other sub-Saharan African countries, African farmers in Zimbabwe use relatively high levels of fertiliser and hybrid seeds, become important items in rural budgets. On the other hand, a few respondents (6) also pointed out that one advantage rural people had was getting free fertiliser and seed packages: however this policy has nothing to do with ESAP as it was originally a response by the government to help people overcome the appalling impact of the droughts of the early 1990s. The impact of this policy would vary between rural localities, depending on the severity of the drought, and the nature of local politics, which some local newspapers reported to have the tendency of influencing the extent of some of this assistance.

One of the major policy changes introduced under ESAP has been the introduction of user fees for previously free welfare facilities in health and education for example, or huge rises in the prices charged for such facilities. Even primary schools now charge fees in urban areas (but not in the CAs yet), and high increases in the cost of secondary school fees, uniforms, books, paper, exam fees, etc, have placed a heavy burden on parents and guardians. It was evident that this was a serious concern for some of our respondents when thinking about the CAs; presumably many of them have younger relatives at school and some would be asked to help with their education. The thrust of their responses was that it was no longer possible to always send all the children in a family to school: a situation which suggests that some very hard choices had to be made. Some specific comments are reproduced below:

- Some parents prefer to buy food that send their children to school.
- Children cannot afford to continue education beyond 'O' level.
- School fees are so high parents can only send half their children to school.
- Parents cannot afford to send their children to secondary school

Similar concerns were expressed about the expense of hospital and clinic fees since ESAP had been implemented. One migrant felt that, in the communal areas, education and health were now only for the 'privileged'.

Of particular interest to this survey were the responses which related to rural-urban linkages, since these have been a major focus of our long-term research on migration in Zimbabwe. Two very specific types of impacts were identified spontaneously by about 10% of the migrant respondents. One of these was that worsening economic conditions in town were increasing urban-rural 'return' migration, and that these migrants were causing significant problems for CA households who were finding it difficult to support them. The other issue was how ESAP was causing rural families to lose remittances from their urban kin. With one exception in every case where this was mentioned the respondents referred specifically to the problems of retrenchment which were occurring in urban areas, and the type of unemployment as most specifically ESAP-induced. Here are some illustrative comments.

- Retrenched workers are causing over-population in the communal areas.
- People are flooding in the communal areas from town after retrenchment which is leading to land struggles.
- People made redundant in town go to the communal areas, but are not absorbed into communal area activities.
- Economic hardship in town means less money is sent to people in the communal areas.
- Rural people depend on wages from urban workers, but they are being retrenched.
- Retrenched workers are overburdening rural folk so that there is not enough land or food to go round.

The final two categories of comments as shown in Table 13.4 came from respondents who either felt that ESAP had made little impact on the CAs, or that the impact had been positive. In the first case there was a small group who felt that CA farmers were able to avoid the burden of higher prices because they grew all their food and did or did not need to buy things; and in the second the respondents felt that farmers could get such high prices for their maize in town which would more than compensate for general increases in the cost-of-living. The feeling that farmers were making a lot of money from high urban maize prices is easy to understand given the enormous jumps in the price of roller meal which have occurred since ESAP was introduced. For example mealie-meal prices rose 30-35% in April 1991, by 20% at the beginning of 1992 (when super-refined maize rose 83%), by 50% in June 1993, and by about a further 30%

in July 1995 when the price stood at Z$28.80 for a 20kg bag. However this was caused partly by removal of price subsidies and partly by crop price increases. Super-refined maize lost its subsidy in 1992; and in June 1993 normal roller meal lost its subsidy of Z$562.42 per ton. (Economist Intelligence Unit, 1991-1996). Thus peasant farmers have not always seen their own (even nominal) incomes rise in line with the retail price of maize. For example the guaranteed Grain Marketing Board price rose by only 20% in April 1991. On the other hand there have been some major jumps in maize producer prices such as from Z$550 to Z$900 in July 1992, as a response to the drought crisis, where they remained until March 1995 when they rose again to Z$950; a further increase to Z$1200 per ton was announced the following year in May (Economist Intelligence Unit). Maize producer prices rose faster than the cost of living index for most of the 1990s. The perception (though a minority one) that maize sellers were compensated for ESAP price rises by higher maize prices is thus generally correct. However, the majority of our respondents evidently did not feel that this had translated into greater peasant purchasing power on the whole (perhaps because of the numbers of peasants who are net purchasers or sell only very small amounts) and which worsened with falling support from urban kin.

Impact of ESAP on Harare

Perception of the impact of ESAP on Harare were even more clear cut. Nearly all the migrants felt that the situation in Harare had become worse since policies had been introduced. Only 2% felt that there had been a general improvement. Evidently the migrants felt that life for urban residents in general had been made much more difficult and, as can be seen from Table 13.4, this was true no matter where the migrants had been born. It is interesting that the proportion of positive responses from urban-born respondents (whilst still low) was much higher that from migrants born in the communal areas (10% compared to 1%).

The comments made by respondents to qualify their rankings generally fell into distinctive categories as with those on the impact of ESAP on the CAs. These are shown in Table 13.6. Again by far the most pressing concern was the problems caused by price rises in general. Sixty four percent of respondents (116 cases) mentioned some sort of price rise in their comments, and usually recited a list of things which had become too expensive by saying, for example: 'bread, sugar and mealie-meal are now very expensive'; 'hospital fees, electricity and rents are too high'; 'hospital, school fees, transport, water and food are all very expensive'. These general answers have also been disaggregated to indicate the frequency with which specific categories of price increase were mentioned (e.g. rent, transport, education). Some respondents however made only very general answers saying for example, 'the price of every commodity has gone up too high'.

Table 13.6 Explanations of perceptions: the impact of ESAP on Harare [5]

Type of Comment	Number
General Increases in prices	116
of which:	
ending price controls	10
devaluation has caused prices to increase	8
food	37
rent/housing become very expensive	36
transport	24
hospital fees too high	16
education: school fees too high	9
Employment-related:	
retrenchments	66
unemployment	18
overworked/underpaid	16
Other:	
rural-urban linkages	6
crime	5
Positive impact	3

As can be seen from Table 13.6 food costs were particularly worrying, with 32% of 'price' comments specifying food as one of the problems. For low income families, food may already have been the major component of monthly expenditure before ESAP, and even larger in response to the dual pressures of falling real incomes and rising food prices. Such increase can only be managed at the expense of other budget items and are likely to cause real stress for poor families as already detailed in Harare by other studies (see Kanji, 1993; Brand et al, 1995 and Biljmakers et al, 1995). Three specific comments about food prices indicate how severe the problem appeared to some of our respondents:

- People are no longer able to eat lunch in order to cut expenses.
- The higher prices of food means starvation.
- Food prices are alarming.

As will be seen below, the food issue also loomed large in people's minds when comparing the impact of ESAP on Harare and the CAs.

The next most frequently mentioned type of price related problem related to housing costs, specified in 31% of 'price' comments. The majority of the migrant households in the survey were lodgers (53%) and a significant proportion (38%) were owner-occupiers. Housing issues thus fell into two main groups. First were rising rents mentioned by 30 respondents. In the context of ESAP rents are a double-edged sword for the landlords/ladies (most of whom may also live on the premises with their lodgers) who can increase them in line with ESAP-induced inflation (unlike wages) and therefore use them as a hedge against falling living standards. For the lodgers, however, rent rises are just part of the litany of extra costs which have to be met. For most owners, especially those in Kuwadzana who would still be in the process of completing the construction of their houses, the problems were related either to increases in building materials' prices thwarting house development or to the inability to maintain loan payments. These problems are exemplified by comments such as:

- People are being forced to sell property.
- [People are] living in semi-squatter houses.
- People's houses are being auctioned because they fail to develop them due to financial strain.
- So many people lose jobs, they can't finish their houses.

Transport costs were the next most frequently mentioned 'price' problem for Harare, but something not mentioned in the context of the CAs. However, in the context of CAs, health and education fees were viewed as part of the problems caused by ESAP in town. Three respondents stated that rising health fees were making people seek alternative and cheaper forms of healthcare: in one case a resort to n'angas (traditional healers) and in the other two, 'people [forced] to join churches for spiritual healing'. Comments about education costs however were confined to complaints about rising fees: no-one actually said that urban residents were removing their children from school. This accords with results from other surveys in Harare which have all found a low drop-out rate amongst poor urban households (Gibbon, 1995). By contrast comments about education problems in the CAs specifically mentioned that children were being withdrawn from school.

A separate and major group of urban-based problems mentioned in response to this question related to unemployment, poor job conditions and, very specifically, retrenchments. Forty-two per cent of the comments about the impacts of ESAP on Harare mentioned job losses, and the majority of these specified retrenchment (rather than unemployment) and large numbers of workers being laid off by certain employers, often suddenly and, as bitterly recounted by some of our respondents, without any redundancy payments. Fifteen per cent of those who mentioned retrenchments went on to make this point. It is evident that increased vulnerability in the urban job market is one of the most significant perceptions our respondents had of the impact and nature of ESAP.

A small sub-set of comments related to the way in which rural-urban linkages had been affected in Harare. To some extent these reflect the opposite side of the coin to the perceptions, already discussed above, of how the rural end of these links have been influenced. Thus there were comments to the effect that urban people could no longer afford to support dependents or the elderly in the CAs and that retrenchments meant that people had no money for rent and were therefore 'forced to migrate [back to the CAs]'. Two responses specified that parents were having to send their children away to the CAs to cut urban expenditure: one of these identified the cause as high rents.

ESAP was also perceived to have caused an increase in crime. Three respondents commented that retrenchments and/or unemployment caused by ESAP meant that people had no money to live on, and this pushed them into becoming thieves. Another considered that this was also the fate of youths who had to drop out of secondary school ('O' level drop-outs').

Only three people gave some reasons why ESAP had made things better for Harare. In two cases the respondents were traders in the informal sector and praised 'free market' conditions which let them sell their items 'wherever we want as long as we have a license'. The profiles of these two were remarkably similar. Both were unmarried women aged 30-34 (one was divorced) who were born in towns, one in Gweru and the other in Bulawayo, and who had come to Harare in 1992 and 1993 respectively. They both had two jobs: a formal sector job (licensed street vendor and shop assistant) and an informal job which involved selling used clothes. Their respective incomes were Z$350 plus Z$800, and Z$500 plus Z$500. They both stated, unlike many other respondents, that they planned to remain in Harare all their lives. Clearly both of these women, one of whom lived in Kuwadzana and the other in Mbare, were exploiting one of the key niches which had opened up with trade liberalisation – the trade in second-hand clothes. Not only was it easier to bring the clothes in from other countries but the demand for such clothes had increased also as people could no longer afford new clothes. However since the surveys controls on such imports had been tightened up again, but these restrictions apparently had little effect on the trade (see Economist Intelligence Unit, January 1995 , April 1995 and September 1995). Furthermore they could set their prices to reflect their costs: as one remarked when explaining why ESAP had improved life for her personally, 'I can now go to neighboring countries and sell at own prices'.

It was much less clear why the third respondent felt positive about the impact of ESAP on Harare. He was a married man aged 30-34 who stated that it had given 'young people a chance to work, as older workers were retrenched.' He worked as a security guard for a low income of Z$400 per month, and had no secondary job. His wife and children had been left in Mutoko communal land, his birthplace, where he planned eventually to return to farm. He was also positive about the impact of ESAP on the CAs, saying that people there 'could sell crops at high prices, and get free fertilisers from the government.' On the other hand he felt that ESAP had a negative impact on him personally because his 'wages were very low and he had to borrow his bus fare at the end of the month'.

Impact of ESAP on communal areas in comparison to Harare

The results of migrants' rankings of the differential impact of ESAP on the communal areas compared to Harare were also clear: there was a very definite feeling that Harare had suffered the most. This was the opinion of 84% of the migrants (see Table 13.4). There was of course a wide range of types of answers to this question, but most could be categorised by the interviewers quite easily into five rankings shown in Table 13.4. The interviewers had to be careful not to 'push' respondents into certain directions in their answers, and so the responses were recorded as given. To some extent this did leave some opportunity for confusion since the response that the impact of ESAP had been better for the CAs could also be construed to mean that it had been worse for Harare (and most likely did) although, in very few cases, respondents might have meant that things had improved in both places, but the CAs had seen the most improvement. However, not only is it very evident that the major perception was that ESAP had been worse for people in Harare, but also that the explanations given for the rankings generally made it very obvious what factors were influencing the respondents' judgement.

Table 13.7 indicates the nature of some of the specific comments made in response to this particular question. Some responses reiterated the general problems related to ESAP (e.g. price rises) but made no comparison between the two areas, and these have been excluded from the analysis.

Table 13.7 Explanations of perceptions: the impact of ESAP on communal areas (CA) compared to Harare [6]

Type of Comment	Number
Impact worse in Harare	122 [7]
of which:	
urban people must but/pay for everything	79
urban people must survive on their salaries only	10
town people losing jobs	8
urban people cannot supplement incomes (e.g., by growing food)	40
Impact the same for Harare and the CAs	12
of which:	
urban and rural people must buy basics which have increased in price	7
rural people depend on those in town	4
Impact worse in CAs	10
of which:	
exorbitant prices	3
agricultural inputs now too expensive	2
no jobs available in CAs	3

As can be seen, the reasons why most people thought Harare residents were suffering more than those in the communal areas were related to their dependence on cash income from employment to purchase everything necessary for day-to-day survival. Since prices had risen for most essentials, incomes had not kept pace, and job losses were increasing and hence putting financial pressure on urban residents. Whilst urban people had to buy everything, communal area residents could grow their own food, thereby avoiding at least one major urban expense. The ability to grow food was by far the most commonly identified advantage that rural people had in terms of needing less money, although free accommodation and firewood were also mentioned on occasion. The comparisons made were not as simple as 'urban people need money, and rural people do not'; for, although some respondents did say things like 'the communal areas live on farming', in many cases rural cash needs were recognised but not surprisingly judged to be less pressing than urban residents. Illustrative comments included: 'the communal areas can supplement with farming'; 'communal areas survive by farming, especially in good years' (the point that rural people's cash needs varied from year to year depending on the weather was made by several respondents); 'in the communal areas they grow some food'; 'in communal areas people can avoid grocery bills'; 'communal area people, especially those with land can live on farming alone'.

Essentially, therefore, the migrants perceived very strongly that the communal areas were less vulnerable to the exigencies of ESAP because food costs there were significantly reduced, that rural people were not directly affected by the urban-based job losses associated with ESAP, and that some of their other needs (like housing) did not require regular cash payments.

A second group of responses, also shown in Table 13.7, explained why some respondents felt that there was little difference in the impact of ESAP on Harare compared to CAs. This was a minority viewpoint as only 7% of those who gave explanations for their rankings on this issue were of this opinion. Their usual reasoning was that rural people also had to buy many things and price rises affected everyone. These respondents clearly had a rather different perception of the key economic aspects of people's lives in the CAs. A possible reason could be that they came from areas where agriculture was particularly problematic due to a combination of causes such as low rainfall, acute pressure on land and their families having very little in the way of rural productive resources. In these circumstances peasant households could purchase most of their food, or rely on drought relief. People from such areas would understandably not feel that growing food was a particular advantage of rural living.

A secondary set of reasons why people felt ESAP's impact was not geographically differentiated related to the perception that the rural areas were so economically dependent on urban areas to the extent that anything which affected urban incomes adversely was bound to damage rural households as well. The four comments reproduced below are clearly related to perceptions about rural-urban linkages with respect to the impact of ESAP on the CAs alone.

- Retrenched people went to CAs and increased burden there.
- Rural people depend on those working in town.
- Retrenchments in town equal retrenchments in CAs.
- Urban workers support the rural poor.

A final small subset of respondents thought the CAs had suffered the most from ESAP. In their explanations for this viewpoint, the problem of rural retailers exploiting their monopoly position emerged again. One respondent stated that: 'In town prices are low, whereas in rural areas they are double or thrice'. Rising agricultural input prices were deemed by two respondents to outweigh the disadvantages of urban price rises, as did the lack of jobs to earn any income at all in the CAs. Another respondent pointed out that 'during droughts farmers are not able to raise an income.' On the face of it this appears to be a generic problem, rather than one specific to the impact of ESAP. However the coincidence of the commencement of ESAP and the drought would have exacerbated the problems of cash-poor rural households faced with rising food prices. On the other hand another respondent who felt that the communal areas had not suffered as much as Harare said, 'people in the CAs are helped by social welfare, this does not take place in Harare'. It seems reasonable to assume that this refers to drought relief programmes which are separate from ESAP of course, but which would nevertheless have helped rural people avoid the impact of the food prices in the areas where they were implemented. The marked difference in the perceptions of how the CAs have fared, evident in these two comments, is again probably very contingent on the respondents' specific rural experiences.

Impact of ESAP on migrant respondents

The final issue our surveys attempted to explore was how the sampled migrants perceived ESAP had affected them personally. Yet again the answers were overwhelmingly negative, with 90% feeling that they had been disadvantaged compared to a mere 2% who felt better off (see Table 13.4). The majority of explanations given for negative perceptions mirrored those advanced in relation to the generally negative impact of ESAP on Harare as a whole (e.g. prices rises, fewer jobs available, devaluation of the dollar) and will not be considered again here. Instead this section focusses on those responses which refer to particular problems or advantages experienced by the respondent and his or her family. These are summarised in Table 13.8.

Table 13.8 Explanations of perceptions: the impact of ESAP on migrant respondents [8]

Type of Comment	Number
Negative Impact	159
of which:	
job-related	23
education problems (eg children had to leave school)	19
accommodation problems	19
food (e.g. not enough; consumption reduced)	9
clothing (e.g. cannot afford to clothe children)	9
Adverse effect on rural linkages	14
of which:	
'Forced to live separate from family to make ends meet'	7
'Had to join family in Harare to cut expenses'	2
'Cannot go 'home' regularly because of high transport costs'	3
'Cannot afford to support rural relatives properly'	2
Positive Impact	4

The largest single category of personal problems which respondents blamed on ESAP were related to difficulties in either finding or keeping a job. The generally parlous state of the job market was mentioned by many, but 23 respondents had either lost a job due to ESAP or felt that the new economic climate meant that they simply could not find one. As one remarked: 'I cannot find a job regardless of qualification.'

Education and accommodation problems ranked equal second for personal problems. Nineteen respondents said that the increased costs of education had meant that either they or their children had to leave school, or they could not stay at the school of their first choice, or they had not been able to do their exams. Another 19 who specified accommodation difficulties as a major problem fell into two main sub-categories: those who felt that they could now not afford 'decent' accommodation, and those who had the chance to buy and/or develop a stand, but whose incomes had fallen because of ESAP and hence had been unable to complete the building, or had been unable to meet the criteria for eligibility to be included on the housing scheme.

A further 11% of responses related to the failure to meet even more basic needs. Nine respondents very specifically said that they had to reduce their food intakes; and such comments seem to confirm deteriorations in urban households' diets as reported in Kanji (1993), Brand *et al.* (1995), Bijlmakers *et al.* (1995) Sachikonye (1995) and Rakodi (1994). Some specific comments from the respondents are reproduced below:

- We are failing to buy groceries as we used to do in the eighties.
- We are failing to buy enough food for the family.
- We are not able to eat a balanced diet.
- Not getting sufficient food as there are no jobs.
- We have cut down on basics – sugar, mealie meal and meat.
- I can no longer afford enough food for the children.

There were also nine responses which specified that new clothing and/or shoes had become too expensive, so that people had to repair their old ones all the time or 'failed to dress properly'.

Finally there was a small sub-category of migrants (8%) whose main explanations about the adverse effect of ESAP for them revolved around the issue of rural-urban linkages. The curtailment of visit and remittances were specifically mentioned and which can be easily understood in the context of failing incomes. Seven respondents indicated that their main problem was living apart from their family and against their wishes, because it was cheaper to keep some family members in the rural areas. On the other hand, there were two cases where individuals reported that the main adverse impact of ESAP had been that they had to join their families in Harare in order to cut down on the expense of keeping two homes. One of these however was made in the specific context of a woman who had joined her owner-occupier husband in Harare because the 'modern' house which they had been building in the CA could not now be completed. The other was a teacher who for economic reasons requested to be transferred from the town of Mutare to join his wife in Harare.

Discussion

The overwhelming response from our migrant respondents was clearly that ESAP had a very negative effect on virtually every area and aspect of life in Zimbabwe. Both rural and urban areas had suffered economically, people's personal ambitions and plans had been wrecked, and access to employment, health and education was perceived as deteriorating drastically. Again and again the migrants returned to the intolerable burden which was being caused by price increases.

Very clear geographical differences in the nature and severity of the impact of ESAP were identified. people in the urban areas were worst affected, according to the migrants, because all their needs had to be paid for, and prices for everything from food to building materials were rising. The key difference for rural people in the CAs was that they could usually grow some of their own food and this cushioned them from the food price rises.

The lower cost-of-living (in cash terms) in rural areas has, of course, always been the case for Zimbabwe, just like for most African and Third World countries. It is primarily this aspect which draws or forces some people back to the rural areas when urban incomes are curtailed. The importance of not having to pay for one's food has always been recognised, as evidenced by the following comment made by a Harare resident in answer to the question, 'What was the biggest problem about living in town [in the period 1930-70]?

> Eating bought food. At home we eat what is grown.... you know a cucumber? [Here} I buy a cucumber for a shilling. A cucumber which is eaten by a baboon at home! Ah no.... [But here] you put a bought thing in your mouth! A chicken's egg is bought for twenty cents! Two bob! An egg! So that's a hard life. You buy firewood. Are trees bought? No. You go and break it in the bush. No...they are selling my tree to me. That is what was hard about living in town. (Quotation taken from interviews recorded in Barnes and Win, 1992, p.202).

However the evidence of the surveys suggest that this now has a new and urgent significance in people's minds, because food prices have been so drastically affected by ESAP. Food bills have probably never been so prominent in the budget of low-income urban families, and the advantages of 'free food' never been more attractive. Between 1991 and 1992 alone one study in Harare showed that, for the poorest households sampled, real expenditure fell by 12.4% because incomes did not keep up with prices (which rose 45% over the period), and the share of food in household budgets rose significantly (Kanji, 1993). For people whose experience of rural living is very recent, the cost of food in contemporary urban Zimbabwe is quite unbelievable.

It is interesting to note that, despite the fact that urban agriculture has become increasingly important in Harare in the 1990s (see for example Mbiba, 1994) none of our respondents referred to this as a factor which would reduce the harshness of ESAP's effect in Harare relative to the CAs. In fact there were only three responses which made any reference to urban agriculture at all: two were related to the lack of land in town for growing food, although the other noted that 'people have become resourceful, farming everywhere'. It would be interesting therefore to know whether urban agriculture is more commonly practised by longer-term urban residents, perhaps because they 'know the ropes' for obtaining land (albeit usually 'illegally'), or they have less access to rural produce. Whatever the reason for this virtual 'silence' on this important urban economic strategy in our surveys, it seems that this is not seen as a panacea by urban residents themselves for ameliorating the food price shocks.

The emphasis placed on rural-urban linkages by some of those surveyed is also highly significant in terms of assessing the real impact of ESAP. Adaptations in such linkages are already known to be some of the important strategies adopted throughout urban Africa to survive the exigencies of structural adjustment (see Potts, 1995). Variations in Zimbabwe under ESAP have also been noted by other researchers (see Kanji and Kazdowska, 1994). Fewer visits to the rural 'home', sending children to the rural areas, increase in consumption of maize brought in from the communal areas, and return rural migration to avoid destitution in the urban areas are amongst the strategies noted. As this study has shown, the latter strategy is not just perceived as a problem for the individual migrant, but also for the communal areas to which they return. This is because those returning are seen as 'burdening' the rural areas. Obviously people feel that, on the whole, they are unable to contribute enough in terms of added agricultural production to cover their consumption needs of both food and non-food items. This is scarcely surprising given that this is the underlying rationale for migration to town in the first place for many migrants. Indirectly ESAP is also seen as contributing to the land shortage problem in the rural areas as some migrate from towns and cities to occupy land in the CAs.

Whilst rural-urban linkages involve very important flows and transactions in both directions, the responses from this survey indicate quite clearly that the expectations of Zimbabwean people, which might be seen as an element of the Zimbabwean 'moral economy', are essentially that net contributions should be from the urban areas to the rural areas. This is evidenced from the concern displayed about reductions in remittances for rural kinfolk necessitated by the impact of ESAP on urban incomes: many respondents obviously felt guilty about this. There was no suggestion that the shift in the nature of rural-urban linkages was acceptable in some way as a quid pro quo for previous urban to rural flows. Thus the comment that 'Urban workers support the rural poor' was not in competition with any perceptions that nowadays perhaps the rural areas should help the urban poor. Even under the stringent conditions of ESAP, and in the context of a generally-held perception that the urban areas had been hardest hit, the indications are that the structural conditions of life in the CAs are still seen as distinctly disadvantageous compared to those in town.

This point leads on to the general issue of how ESAP is perceived to have affected the CAs. The fact that prices for non-farm inputs were perceived as being the main problem for the communal areas is regarded as highly significant. There is often an assumption by proponents of structural adjustment that improvements in the terms of trade and narrowing the income gap between rural and urban communities will be made if crop and livestock prices are enhanced in real terms. Yet structural adjustment also tends to lead to price increases for food and consumer items. If the latter are important in rural budgets, then any increases in income from agricultural sales may be dissipated by the greater expense for consumption, or even exceeded, leaving rural households worse off. There is an extensive literature for Zimbabwe which has established that many rural households are partly, or even highly, dependent on bought food for a variety of reasons mainly connected with the country's history of land alienation and migrant labour. It is therefore not surprising that this factor was pinpointed by so many of our respondents as being he most important problem that ESAP had created for rural people in the communal areas.

The importance of buying food in many rural budgets is probably not something which policy-makers have taken sufficiently into account, either in Zimbabwe or in Africa as a whole. The migrants who spoke to us in Harare were only too well aware of the problem, and there are a number of other countries where such perceptions would probably be replicated. For example in Malawi most peasant households are not food self-sufficient, and this is probably even more true for South African households in the former 'homelands'. Thus any move in South Africa towards structural adjustment-type policies is likely to have very negative effects on the rural areas, and food prices have already been spiralling upwards there in the 1990s as subsidies are removed.

The issue about bought food is also relevant to assessing methodologies which measure the rural-urban income gap in Africa. For example, Jamal and Weeks (1994) seminal work which considers this topic in the context of a critique of SAPs tends to assume that rural households' food needs in Africa are met from subsistence production and not therefore affected by national food price rises. Such an assumption may be sufficiently realistic to yield useful comparative indices for rural and urban incomes in some sub-Saharan African countries, where land shortages are not a major issue and the history and nature of migrant labour is rather different from that typical of many Southern African countries. However, it may well lead to misleading results in Zimbabwe, South Africa, Lesotho, malawi, Swaziland, Botswana and Namibia.

Another issue to consider, in terms of the advantage gained in rural areas by SAP recommendations to increase prices for crops and to liberalise marketing arrangements, is whether the advantages are sustained. Analysis of specific country experiences shows that seemingly significant price rises in agricultural produce are rapidly eroded by inflation, so that the farmers' gains in real terms are short-lived. This, for example, was true of Malawian maize prices in the 1980s. Furthermore the ending of farmers' subsidies (particularly on fertiliser) may negate crop price rises, and the liberalisation of agricultural trade has often not helped farmers because the capacity of private traders to fill the technical, transport and capital investment gaps left by marketing boards has often been grossly overestimated. Thus arrangements for marketing the 1993-94 maize crop in Zambia were chaotic, and disastrous for the farmers. Our survey indicates that fertiliser price rises have been a particular problem in Zimbabwe, as they were frequently mentioned by respondents. Further very significant rises in fertiliser prices have occurred since the survey as well: they rose 49% in March 1995 and a further 10% in August of the same year, and further increases cannot be ruled out as the Zimbabwe dollar devaluates against the major world currencies.

Returning to urban livelihoods, comparison of our survey with other surveys of the impact of SAPs in urban Africa suggests that the role of the informal sector in Zimbabwe has, so far, been quite different. For household heads in particular the sector was playing a relatively minor part, and even when other contributions to the household income were taken into account, the share of formally-earned incomes was clearly generally predominant. Furthermore, as noted above, other surveys in Harare have suggested that people are being discouraged from entry into the informal sector, or are leaving, because conditions there are deteriorating under ESAP. Falling incomes leading to reduced demand are one problem cited. However the other problem, that there was now too much competition in certain trades (Brand et al, 1995 p.153) suggests that the rate of new entrants had increased, but perhaps this was a temporary 'surge'. Increased competition and falling incomes are however typical of the informal sector in other African cities in the context of SAPs but the sector has 'boomed' nevertheless. The explanation may well lie mainly in the differing severity of economic conditions. Whilst undoubtedly Harare's low-income residents are really struggling with the impact of ESAP and most likely also with its successor ZIMPREST, they have not had the rug pulled from under their feet in quite the way typical of, for example, the poor in Dar es

Salaam or Freetown, where monthly incomes from formal jobs frequently cover only one week's food needs (see Potts, 1997). In such circumstances there may be little choice about participation in the informal sector, no matter how small the returns. Moreover, since the limiting factors which retarded the growth of this sector in the past, and as reported by Rakodi (1995), have been falling away since 1966, participation in the sector by many can be expected.

Any factor worthy of note is the frequency with which housing problems were singled out as being an ESAP-related problem. For those who were trying to build houses, their perceptions are supported by the Central Statistical Office statistics which show that the building prices index has nearly always risen faster than the general retail prices during ESAP. In addition to this there have been very serious problems for the housing sector caused by 'two inordinate increases in the interest rate mandated by the [World] Bank's macroeconomic department during 1991' which led to Zimbabwe's building societies failing to make any home loans to new borrowers for two years thereafter (Bond, 1996). As low-income housing strategies in Zimbabwe (unusual for Sub-Saharan Africa) rely heavily on building society loans, this is clearly a huge disadvantage for the urban poor, and directly attributable to ESAP. ESAP has therefore actively discouraged one of the most productive activities (in both economic and welfare terms) of Zimbabwe's urban low-income population – their investment in housing with or without the participation of the government's national housing scheme.

The disastrous impacts of SAPs on health and education in Africa is now a commonplace observation. The World Bank has now revised its valuation of the importance of such welfare expenditure, but unfortunately the damage has already been done. Zimbabwe's people have not escaped this tragedy, and both health and education issues signified strongly in their perceptions of the negative effects of ESAP in both rural and urban areas. It is interesting to note that the comments of our respondents suggest that rural children may be more affected than their urban counterparts by being removed from school, despite the fact that rural primary schools still do not charge fees. The sense that health was deteriorating under ESAP in Zimbabwe is clearly supported by the facts: a 1996 Harare City Council survey found that infant mortality rates in the city doubled since 1990 (national rates halved during the preadjustment 1980s), and Harare's maternal mortality rates also rose significantly, whilst rural rates doubled.

Conclusion

Both urban and rural people in Zimbabwe appear to have suffered many disadvantages from ESAP. The views of rural-urban migrants, who could be expected to have informed opinions about ESAP's impact on both urban and rural areas, are clearly that both areas have experienced serious economic and social difficulties because of ESAP policies, although the urban areas have been hardest hit because of their strong dependency on a cash economy. Where rural-urban linkages have been affected, the impact has however tended to shift the flows to some extent so that rural areas are no longer receiving as much money from the urban areas as they used to, and are having to cope with extra family members who might otherwise have lived in town. Indeed one of the impacts of ESAP in urban Zimbabwe has been starkly characterised as 'unemployment, followed by return to the rural areas of destitution' (Rakodi, 1994, p.661, emphasis added). Urban destitution is becoming more evident in Harare in the 1990s particularly for those who have no rural alternative such as the landless, widows and orphans. All this indicates the extent to which the rural areas and their communities continue to be marginalised in many ways, even under ESAP. For the urban areas the marginalisation becomes more evident among the urban poor some of whom go to the extent of living in squatter settlements and shacks (see Mutambirwa, 1997). The safety net of the CAs has been vital for urban households (Potts and Mutambirwa, 1990). The ESAP era is providing yet again the significance of that safety net inspite of the hardships the rural communities face.

Notes

1 In all tables: number of cases in brackets. Total number of cases may vary due to some missing values for certain categories of data. Percentages may not add to 100% due to rounding.
2 'Others' were two employees (domestics) and one unspecified.
3 Percentages do not add to 100% mainly because of the small number of respondents who could not rank the impact of ESAP. Urban respondents in particular were uncertain about the impact on the Cas.
4 166 respondents made specific comments about the effect of ESAP on the communal areas.
5 181 respondents made specific comments about the effect of ESAP on Harare.
6 170 respondents made specific comments about the effect of ESAP on the communal areas in comparison to Harare.

7 The answers detailed for this category add up to more than 122 because respondents' answers often included more than one type of comment.

8 171 respondents made specific comments about the effect of ESAP on themselves personally.

References

Adepoju, A. (ed.) (1993), *The Impact of Structural Adjustment on the Population of Africa: Implications for Education, Health and Employment*, James Curry in Association with United Nations Population Fund: London.

Barnes, T. and Win, E. (1992), *To Live a Better Life: An Oral History of Women in the City of Harare, 1930-1970*, Baobab Books: Harare.

Bijilmakers, L., Bassett, M. and Sanders, D. (1995), 'Health and Structural Adjustment in Rural and Urban Settings in Zimbabwe: Some Interim Findings', in Gibbon, P. (ed.) *Structural Adjustment and the Working Poor in Zimbabwe*, Nordiska Afrikainstitutet: Uppsala.

Bond, P. (1996), 'Review Article: Who Foots the Bill? Contrasting Views on the Success of Structural Adjustment in Zimbabwe', *Journal of Southern African Studies*, 22:1.

Brand, V., Mupedziswa, R. and Gumbo, P. (1995), Structural Adjustment, Women and Informal Sector Trade in Harare', in Gibbon, P. (ed.) *Structural Adjustment and the Working Poor in Zimbabwe*, Nordiska Afrikainstitutet: Uppsala.

Corma, G. Jolly, R., and Stewart, F. (eds.) (1987), *Adjustment With a Human face*, Clarendon Press: Oxford.

Drakakis-Smith, D., Bowyer-Bower, T. and Tevera, D. (1994), 'Urban Agriculture in Harare', *Habitat International*, 2:17.

Economist Intelligence Unit (1991-1996), *Zimbabwe Country Reports, Various reports*, EIU: London.

Gibbon, P. (ed.) (1995), *Structural Adjustment and the Working Poor in Zimbabwe*, Nordiska Afrikainstitutet: Uppsala.

Government of Zimbabwe (1981), *Growth with Equity*, Government Printers: Harare.

Government of Zimbabwe, Ministry of Finance, Economic Planning and Development (1982), *Transitional National Development Plan*, 1982/83-1984/85, Vol. 11, Amalgamated Press Pvt. Ltd: Harare.

Government of Zimbabwe, Ministry of Finance, Economic Planning and Development (1983), *Transitional National Development Plan*, 1982/83-1984/85, Vol. 2, The Government Printer: Harare.

Jamal, V. and Weeks, J. (1994), *Africa Misunderstood: or Whatever Happened to the Rural-Urban Gap*? Macmillan: Basingstoke.

Kanji, N (1993), 'Gender and Structural Adjustment Policies: a Case Study of Harare, Zimbabwe', unpublished Ph.D thesis, University of London.

Kanji, N. and Jazdowska, N. (1993), 'Structural Adjustment and Implications for Low-income Urban Women in Zimbabwe', *Review of African Political Economy*, 56, pp. 11-26.

Loxley, J (1990), 'Structural Adjustment in Africa: Reflections on Ghana and Zambia,' *Review of African Political Economy*, 47, pp. 8-27.

MacGarry, B. (1993), *Growth? Without Equity? The Zimbabwe Economy and the Economic Structural Adjustment Programme*, Mambo Press: Gweru.

Mbiba, B. (1994), 'Institutional Responses to Uncontrolled Urban Cultivation in Harare: Prohibitive ot Accommodative?', *Environment and Urbanization*, 6:1, pp. 188-202.

Mutambirwa, C.C. (1997), 'Squatters of the Growing City of Greater Harare City, Zimbabwe,' ch.22, in Fairhurst, J., Booysen, I. and Hattingh, P. (eds.), *Migration and Gender: Place, Time and People Specific*, IGU Commission on Gender and Geography, UP Geography Press.

Onimode, B (ed.) (1989), *The IMF, the World Bank and African Debt*, London, Zed Press.

Potts, D. (1995), 'Shall We Go Home? Increasing Urban Poverty in African Cities and Migration Processes,' *Geographical Journal*, 161:3, pp. 245-264.

Potts, D (1997), 'Urban Lives,' in Carole Rakodi (ed.), *The Urban Challenge in Africa*, United Nations University: Tokyo.

Potts, D and Mutambirwa, C.C. (1990), 'Rural-Urban Linkages in Contemporary Harare: Why Migrants Need Their Land', *Journal of Southern African Studies*, 16(4), pp. 676-98.

Potts, D. and Mutambirwa, C. (1991), 'Low-Income Housing in Harare: Overcrowding and Commodification', *Third World Planning Review*, 13:1, pp. 1-26.

Rakodi, C. (1994), 'Recession, Drought and Urban Poverty in Zimbabwe: Household Coping Strategies in Gweru', paper given at Institute of British Geographers Conference, Panel on Coping with Poverty: Urbanisation During an Economic Crisis, January, 15 pp.

Rakodi, C. (1994), 'Urban Poverty in Zimbabwe: Post Independence Efforts, Household Strategies and the Short-Term Impact of Structural Adjustment', *Journal of International Development*, 6:5, pp. 660-663.

Riddell, R (1990), 'Zimbabwe', in Riddell, R. (ed.), *Manufacturing Africa*, James Curry: London, pp. 337-411.

Sachikonye, L. (1995), 'Industrial Relations and Labour Relations under ESAP in Zimbabwe', in Gibbon, P. (ed) *Structural Adjustment and the Working Poor in Zimbabwe*, Nordiska Afrikainstitutet: Uppsala.

Simon, D., van Spengen, W., Dixon, C. and Narman, A., (eds.) (1995), *Structurally Adjusted Africa: Poverty, Debt and Basic Needs*, Pluto: London.

Sparr, P. (1993), *Mortgaging Women's Lives*, Zed Press.

Stoneman, C. (1989), 'The World Bank and IMF in Zimbabwe' in Campbell, B. and Loxely, J. (eds.), *Structural Adjustment in Africa*, James Curry: London, pp. 37-66.

Stoneman, C. (1996), 'Prospects for the Development of Regional Economic and Political Relations in Post-apartheid Southern Africa: Can the New South Africa Dynamise the New SADC?,' *Ritsumeikan Studies in Language and Culture*, 7:5-6, pp. 297-319.

Watkins, K. (1996), 'Zimbabwe 'Miracle cure' Fails to Save the Poor,' *The Guardian* 26.7.96.

Zinyama, L. (1988), 'Commercialisation of Small-scale Agriculture in Zimbabwe: Some Emerging Patterns of Spatial Differentiation', *Singapore Journal of Tropical Geography*, 9:2. pp. 151-62.

Acknowledgements

The research for this paper was made possible by a grant from the Nuffield Foundation. Computer analysis was aided by funds from the School of Oriental and African Studies' Research Committee. The quotation in the title is taken from a comment made by our respondents. We are grateful to Collin Stoneman for his helpful comments.

Part three

Policies for regional development

14 Marginal regions and new methods for development in the EU:
Comparing Garfagnana in Italy and Kuusamo - Koillismaa in Finland[1]

MARIA ANDREOLI AND HEIKKI JUSSILA

Introduction

The question of periphery and the role of different tools for overcoming the notion of peripherality have become an important issue for regional development in Europe. Information and communication technology has been gaining attention and in many of the European Union development programs there is an element aiming to introduce communication or information technology as one alternative for the regional development. These solutions are connected with the peripherality concept. This concept is usually linked to remoteness from major economic centres of the nation and the 'Europe'[2] and to the density of population as in the case of European Planning Strategy (1992) which used the amount of 100 inhabitants per square kilometre as a limit for rural regions.

The peripherality that arises from these definitions, given above, is different from the one that can be witnessed in the case study areas: Garfagnana[3], in Lucca Province, that is one of the two regions in Tuscany that have had as an Objective-5b area status since the first Community Support Framework (CSF) and has received financial aid under LEADER I, and the municipality of Kuusamo, in Koillismaa, Finland. The area of Kuusamo in Koillsmaa has been included into the regional policy support schemes of Finland and the European Union as an Objective-6 area.[4]

The chapter analyses regional economic development from comparative micro-perspective. The new methods based on communication are used as the base for comparison. In Tuscany all LEADER II program Local Action Groups (LAGs) have included networking and information technology in their Local Action Plan (Di Iacovo and Gouèrec, 1996, 83), but only Garfagnana had a draft plan for the project (Agritec srl, 1996). This makes the comparison with Kuusamo area possible, although Kuusamo case is 'older', since in there this process began over ten years ago (see Development of Local…1997). In Finland the use of telematics is ahead compared to the situation in Italy and consequently, it is possible to see some differences in the process. At the same time it is possible to compare the current results of the Finnish experiment to the 'expectations' and 'hopes' expressed in the Italian project.

Theories for regional development and networking in information age

Current ideas and theories of regional development stress the importance of local activities and local skills (e.g., Andreoli et. al., 1995; Tykkyläinen and Bond, 1996). The people within the region are viewed as the 'actor'. The networking and networks are seen as important. According to this 'model' peripheral areas in Europe are looking for partners of alliance. Theoretically these alliances are co-operation units that are able to compete within 'Pan-European field' of regions. According to the model of Nordgreen (1995) regions become proactive agents (Figure 14.1). The danger in this is that it favours powerful areas and regions that have the skills and knowledge to diversify and enhance their economic base.

Regional development theories usually presuppose that a region is capable of changing its position in the development 'cycle'. Currently economic development theories relying on innovation diffusion (e.g., Brown, 1981) or comparative advantages have been losing ground and, e.g., Bond and Tykkyläinen (1996) talk about 'pocket development' when describing economic development in a peripheral area. When regions start developing and modernising their economic base with the help of fast communication technologies traditional macroeconomics approach is not useful, as the possibilities for obtaining information for development increase.

It is important to develop new ways and modes of regional development that take into account the new changed economic environment. It is in this context that the idea of a 'pocket development' can be taken up (Bond and Tykkyläinen, 1996; Tykkyläinen and Jussila, 1998). Information orientated economic development follows closely the ideas within the theory of 'economic development pockets'. It is important to understand that this approach towards regional development does incorporate a higher degree of regional disparities. The problem with the current theoretical tools is that they do not provide ways for alleviating disparities in the 'knowledge society' where disparities grow from the qualities, qualifications and knowledge levels of individuals and firms in a particular region.

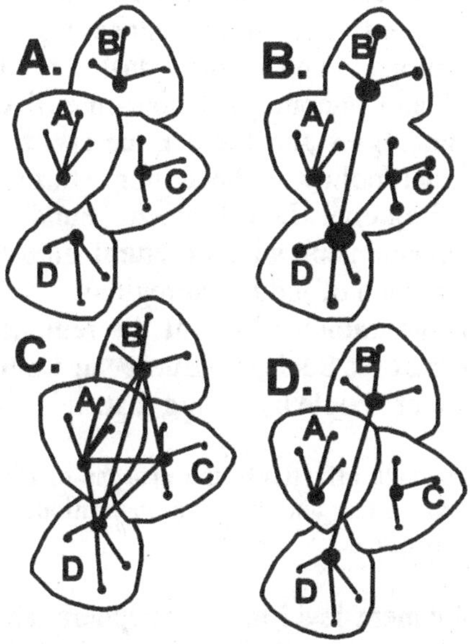

Figure 14.1 Various region systems available for regional co-operation and economic development; (A) mutually equal functional regions, (B) new region formation, (C) region system, (D) region alliance

Source: Nordgreen (1995)

Regional policy and regional development and the and tools

In the European context there is tradition 'to look after' the less favoured regions. However, the ways for 'looking after' have changed markedly in recent years. The most profound change is the introduction of policy that aims at empowering regions, instead of the states. A policy that has been put into practice in varying degrees in different European countries. This has led to an increasing activity within and among the regions. The regions have more than before become the 'responsible actors' of economic development. This has lead to a new type of co-operation in Europe, since there now exists a need to develop more contacts between European regions and areas. It is in this context, that the community regional policy comes into the picture. The European Regional Planning Strategy (1992) of the European Parliament indicates the aims of regional policy and regional development when speaking about 'balanced socio-economic development of the regions' and 'about enhancing competitiveness and productivity within Europe'. The priority task of regional policy is to reduce unemployment and encourage labour-intensive economic sectors based on modern technologies and the service sector. Implementation of the Community regional policy is been done through the ERDF programmes (European Regional Development Fund), whose two main objectives are: (1) development and structural adjustment of backward regions, and (2) reconversion of industrial regions.

While the ERDF programmes look at the regions, the Community's Green Paper on 'Information Society' (European Commission 1996a and 1996b) stresses the role of people by saying that:

> It is important to manage effectively the process of change at all levels and this requires that education and training institutions and business support services have to be involved.

The high unemployment level in the peripheral and marginal areas of the Union has been the reason and the cause to look for new and alternative ways for regional development. The most commonly used tool is promote activities that create new jobs. In this, the service sector is seen very important. In many peripheral areas this has been 'interpreted' as 'tourism' that has been deemed as the 'number one' method to alleviate the 'chronicle' unemployment situation. The use of personal services has also been one that many regions have been looking. The role of them, however, varies greatly from country to country, since the laws dealing with employer taxation or social costs differ markedly. In UK, where most of the social costs have been cut into a minimum, there is 'a blossoming' service sector, but with low paid jobs. The other end of this path are, e.g., Finland and Italy, where employers speak about 'work tax' with what they mean social security payments an employer pays in addition to the salary, and these institutional aspects influence the choices of development tools.

The use of 'new communication technologies' in regional development is something typical for the Finnish approach towards peripheral region development, which might also reflect the social 'climate' of work in that particular society. There is a very strong belief in the society, that 'technology' will assist and help in changing the otherwise 'gloomy' faces of regional development in peripheral northern areas (e.g., Jussila and Segerståhl, 1997).

In Finland the 'information society' is the most used community path. The other paths towards local development, like the 'LEADER', have not been tested very much in Finland. In other the European Union countries, for instance in Italy, the LEADER, however, has proved to be a relatively good way to 'mobilise' people for local development. There are, however, differences in the use of LEADER initiatives between European countries. The use of different development tools is reliant on the cultures in Europe. It is this that makes the role of regional policy difficult. A 'single Pan-European' approach is not possible, since people in different regions react differently to development actions. In certain regions, technology orientated approach, is the best, but in others it is more appropriate to advance with a more 'humanistic' approach (see Jussila, 1998).

The case regions and their description

Garfagnana area in Tuscany, Italy

The Garfagnana region in Lucca province in Tuscany, Italy (Figure 14.2) is mountainous, and consequently, the possibilities for maintaining contacts with the underlying lowland are not that good. This has lead to a relatively 'slow' economic development pattern in the region. The area of Garfagnana region is 533.77 square kilometres and the population density of the area varies (as of 1995) between the high of 218.14 to a low of 12.47, which, at the same time, is the lowest in the whole of the Province of Lucca, whose highest density level is about 1800, in one of the municipalities on the coast. This kind of variation in the population density is important in Italy. The lower the population density, the more probable it is that the region is 'retarded' or being 'marginalized'.

Garfagnana's 'marginalization' is evident when studying the changes in population development within the Lucca Province. Garfagnana has been suffering of out-migration since the 1950s and this continued until the early 1980s. The change that occurred in 1980s is hard to explain, but at least partly, it is due to the 'universal' turn-around effect in migration. Nevertheless, during the last fifteen years the population development in Garfagnana has been less negative (Figure 14.3).

In fact, during the 1950s and the 1960s Garfagnana's loss of population was about 20%. Most of the migrants were young and better educated which created an unbalanced population structure. This accounts for the present problems of ageing, and although the migration balance has improved in recent years population in the area is still, although more

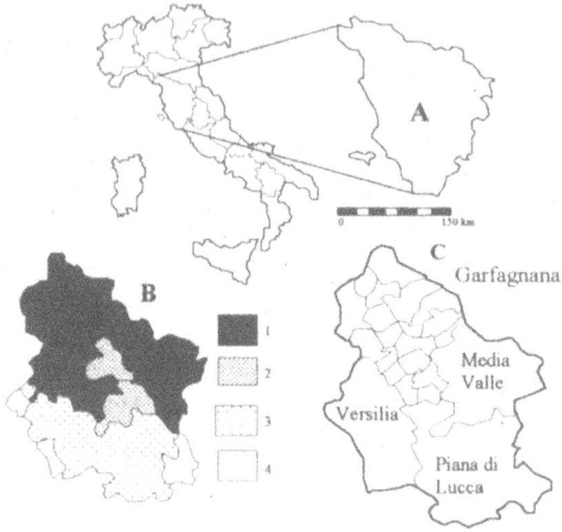

Figure 14.2 The location of the case study area, (A) the Tuscany region, (B) Lucca province, with physical regions: 1= mountains, 2= high hills, 3= low hills, 4= the plain, (C) regions of Lucca Province

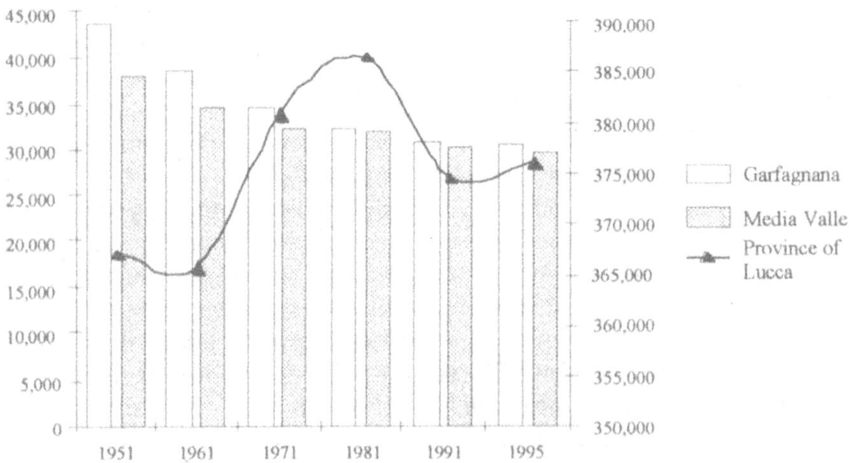

Figure 14.3 The population development in Lucca Province between 1951 and 1995

slowly, decreasing. Between 1981 and 1991 the 'natural rate'[5] has been around -5% and the situation is not very much changed since then, but during this latter period the 'social rate'[6] has improved, passing from 0.81 in the ten years between 1981 and 1991 (about 1/3 of the average provincial level, 2.34), to 0.77 (on a four years basis) which is a half of the average provincial level (1.44). According to Gouèrec (1995) the improving social rate is more due to a decrease of out-migration than an increase of immigration. Besides, while people leave the area for traditional reasons (mainly for occupational problems), it seems that the reasons for entering are quite different from the past, being often related to a new approach to 'space consumption'.

From the economic development point of view the continuing depopulation is not a good sign. The fact that young active population is migrating means that the 'best developers' of the region are also leaving and from this point Garfagnana proves the point. Elia *et al.* (1976) have high-lighted, that in the past there was a sort of 'latent conflict' in Garfagnana, since there were people more willing to break with the 'dominant' way of thinking and they were more open to let innovations arrive to the area.

During the 1950s and in the early 1960s Garfagnana, like most mountainous areas in Italy, had a high proportion of the active labour force engaged in agriculture. The figures for the 1951 and 1961 for Garfagnana were 44.1% and 27.9% respectively. This share has dropped since and today it is under seven per cent (6.9% in 1991). The drop in agricultural jobs was faster than the pace of creating new jobs in other industries and sectors by compelling people to leave the area with the vision of better position elsewhere provided by the Italian 'economic boom'.

The small acreage of farms in Garfagnana (about 3 ha. of agricultural utilised area) makes it almost impossible to live only on the farm income. Nevertheless, it may represent an important component of income coming from different activities and thus encouraging and giving a reason for people to stay on their family holding. The possibility of having a house in the countryside with an orchard and vegetable garden, giving food for family consumption combined with a clean and suitable environment for children could 'urge' people to stay, and Gouèrec (1996, 98) points out that maintaining farms in the area has not only strictly productive reasons. They represent a 'backbone' for the area with regard to their position in the territory itself.

The economic development based on the 'basic rural sector' has not been equal within the area. This applies also to the other sectors, as can be seen in the level of disposable per capita income in 1991 which in Garfagnana varied between 21.2 and 11.9 million of Liras, while the average provincial level was 20.97 million of Liras (IRPET, 1994). At provincial level the lowest incomes can be found in the municipalities of Garfagnana while the highest are on the lowlands near the provincial capital, the city of Lucca, and along the coast. A large share of disposable income in Garfagnana comes from pensions, that in 'backward' areas have often been provided not only for elderly, retired people, but as a sort of 'assistential intervention' to younger people as well. Another form of 'assistential intervention' in these areas is the high rate of employment in public administration in the 'poorer' municipalities of the area.

The industrial structure of Garfagnana area has changed quite radically during the last 30 years (Figure 14.4). The area has gone through the same pattern of economic transition than most Western-European rural regions. In 1961 Garfagnana region was very heavily leaning towards small-scale industrial activities and agriculture, which counted some 73% of the total labour force of the region. This figure had dropped to close 46% (45.8%) by the year 1991, the most dramatic decline because of the decline in agriculture. The decline was approximately 80% from the year 1961.

Initially from Figure 14.4 it seems that Garfagnana went through a lower increase in service sector and a higher decrease in industrial sector jobs. However, when comparing Lucca Province and Garfagnana, it is necessary to realise that in Lucca Province active population increased with almost 14,000 people between 1961 and 1991, while in Garfagnana, during the same period, number of active population decreased with about 2,700 people.

Despite industrial restructuring in Garfagnana and indeed also in the whole Province of Lucca industrial production has not declined as much as in some more heavily industrialised areas of the Western-Europe, the Ruhr in Germany and the area around Liege in Belgium and the industrial centres of the United Kingdom being the most common examples of this change. This has meant that at least in some respect the area has been able to keep its 'potentials' for development, although the last census data of 1991 does not take into account the fact, that industrial employment in the whole province has suffered from the Italian economic crises of the early 1990s.

Nevertheless, statistical data about unemployment in 1991 are able to highlight the situation of Garfagnana in comparison with the Lucca Province. In fact from this point of view the nine municipalities of Garfagnana (accounting for more than 40% of the total population) have an unemployment rate higher than 15% (up to 23.3%) while the provincial average is 13.7%. The worst unemployment situation is among the young people, whose unemployment in many cases surpasses 30%.

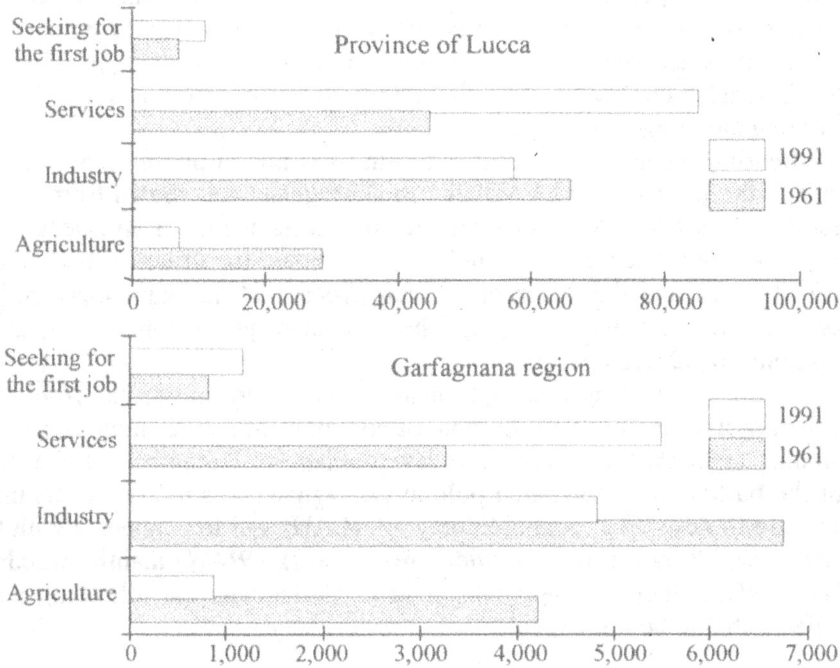

Figure 14.4 The industrial structure of the active labour force in Garfagnana region and the Province of Lucca in Tuscany in 1961 and 1991

As we have previously stated, Garfagnana has been an Objective-5b areas since the first CSF. This means that structural funds intervention implemented during the 1990s could have been able to modify the situation described by means of statistical data of 1991. Besides the 'tangible' changes in the socio-economic situation for which there are already available some first attempts of evaluation, it is important to stress how, for instance, the new development approach of LEADER, based on the participation of local people and on networking, may have contributed to change the local population attitudes, that are so important in achieving good results. From this point of view one of the problems, that need to be faced in Italy and especially in Tuscany is the strongly individualistic behaviour.

This is according to many, the reason why people have not been able to build more networks with inhabitants of other regions and within the region itself. Besides the individualistic attitude which is a common feature of all Tuscany population, people from Garfagnana show also a negative attitude towards risk and, consequently, toward a more entrepreneurial behaviour, since according to Andreoli and Gouèrec (1995, p. 194) the [true] 'Garfagnino' waits for all validity tests to result positive before adopting anything new.

Bearing the above quotation in mind it is not surprising that the first draft of the program for LEADER I in Garfagnana was drawn from a subject outside the area, namely a private consulting agency from Lucca. This draft was then discussed with public institutions, for instance, the Comunità Montana and the different municipalities, and the main local bodies (associations, co-operatives, etc.). The LAG manager of Garfagnana comes from this consulting agency.

At present the Garfagnana, as many other regions in Europe, is looking at the possibilities of utilising modern communications technologies when building and enhancing economic development. In December 1996 a draft for the building of a telematic pole in Garfagnana was presented. Its main aims are to develop a local area network (LAN) and to connect it with the outside world by means of a wide area network (WAN) mainly based on INTERNET. Under the telematic pole in Garfagnana the following main projects should be implemented:

- Building a system able to provide cartographic information for planning (GIS)
- Electronic commerce
- Civic network
- Activities for promoting local entrepreneurship, innovation, etc.

The draft provides information about cost, scheduling and financial resources requirement for the implementation. It gives also information about the professional skills needed in the implementation and management of the telematic pole. However, very little is said about the training of final users, since it is supposed to be discussed later. The draft is not taking into account the need of spreading the new culture and know-how needed for accepting these new tools nor mentioning 'in field surveys' aiming to understand the needs of local population both in terms of personal services and in terms of economic animation and services.

This could be very important since, although during the previous years and using the resources coming under CSF and LEADER they were able to develop the use of information technologies, for example using INTER-

NET for advertising agri-tourism and local products, our interviewees were quite pessimistic on the chance of spreading new technologies among local population. Besides, although they feel the need of networking with other areas, having already had the chance of partnerships with LAGs of other Regions (i.e. Umbria) about promoting tourism and so on, they think that at present there is lacking a common effort at Regional and area level to promote co-ordination. This negative attitude could be also due to the failure of some previous Regional programs aiming at setting up a system of telebooking and at providing training in the use of new technologies in the schools of the area. Besides, the other experiences of building civic networks in Lucca Province have not been successful, at least up to now.

Koillismaa area in Finland

The Finnish case study area is located in the north-eastern corner of the province of Oulu, Finland (Figure 14.5). This area is economically relatively poor and it has one of the highest unemployment rates in Finland, the average in June 1996 was 28,5% and this high level has persisted in 1997 and in 1998. In 1994 the average income per person in state taxation was approximately 65,000 FIM (1 USD = 5.15 FIM). This figure was almost 20,000 FIM lower than in the most affluent areas of Northern Finland with income above 83,500 FIM or that of Finland as a whole with an average of 81,717 FIM.

The case area is very sparsely populated with only about 3 persons in a square kilometre as an average, but two of the three municipalities of the Koillismaa have relatively large centres. They are like small 'cities' and provide services that are, especially in Kuusamo, much higher than in some small towns in southern or western Finland. Table 14.1 shows that the Koillismaa region has been suffering from a decline in population, which in 1995 accounted a population that was almost 18,5% below the 1966 peak year population.

The industrial structure of Koillismaa shows that 'traditional' rural occupations continue to have an important position in the region, although services (public and private) have been climbing in importance. In Koillismaa the smallest municipality of Taivalkoski has suffered, perhaps the most. At first due to the closing down of the iron ore mine in mid 1980s (see Talman and Tykkyläinen 1992) and today (1996-7) due to the closing of the plants of the company that builds railroad carts. These closings have had a very big effect on the economic life and activity level of this particular municipality. The subsequent development of information technology and information based industries has not been so fast as it has been in the other two municipalities of the area, Kuusamo and Pudasjärvi, that have local 'technology villages' to promote economic activities which use information as the 'raw material'.

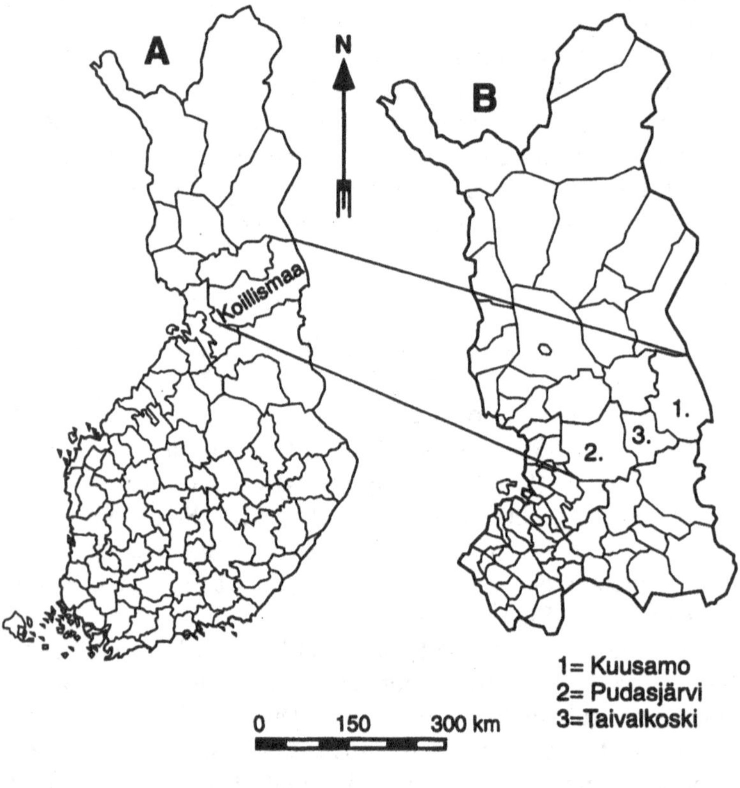

Figure 14.5 The location of Koillismaa region in Finland

Figure 14.6 shows that service have become an important economic sector. This is mostly due to the increase in employment in public services and in tourism, and today tourism is the single most important private employer in the area, especially in Kuusamo. This is evident as one analyses the trends in tourism of Kuusamo by numbers of overnight stays in hotels that have increased rapidly. In 1987 the overnight stays in Kuusamo amounted to 45,000 but by the middle of 1990s this number almost doubled to 80,000, and the total number of stays in Kuusamo rose during the same period by 92% (http://www.ascentia.fi/).

Despite the growth in services as a source of livelihood in Koillismaa in Kuusamo this was not to be enough for the future, and consequently one started looking for other alternatives. During this time – the later half of 1980s – the 'information highway' approach was deemed to be the best solution for Kuusamo to develop something new which eventually would lead to creation of employment opportunities in the municipality and later in the whole Koillismaa area. The report *'Development of Local Telematics Know-how and Information Society in the municipality of Kuusamo - first ten years'* (1997) reveals clearly the reasoning behind choices and the process, which subsequently has led to the creation of the local technology village 'Naturpolis'. According to the information from Kuusamo projects first phase (1987-1990), it is not easy to improve 'know-how' and 'see' results. At the same time the interviewed responsiples stressed that 'there needs to be a real commitment, since all improvements require more resources and time than one would expect. This in turn leads to a slower pace in business creation, and puts a pressure on the 'project' as a whole. It is thus important to have patience when developing something completely new.

Table 14.1 The population in the Koillismaa, its municipalities, Oulu region, the province of Oulu and northern Finland from 1966 to 1995

Population	year 1966	year 1988	year 1995	change 1966-1995
Kuusamo	20,982	17,802	18,687	- 10.9%
Pudasjärvi	15,826	11,202	10,958	- 30.8%
Taivalkoski	6,516	5,673	5,595	- 14.1%
KOILLISMAA	43,234	34,677	35,240	- 18.5%
%-Kuusamo of Koillismaa	48.3%	51.3%	53.0%	+ 4.7%
%-Oulu province	10.2%	7.8%	7.8%	- 2.4%
%-Northern Finland	6.7%	5.5%	5.4%	-1.3%
OULU REGION	107,419	144,499	160,050	+49.0%
%-Oulu province	25.4%	33.2%	35.4%	+10.0%
%-Northern Finland	16.8%	22.8%	24.4%	+7.6%
OULU PROVINCE	422,044	434,847	451,148	+6.9%
NORTHERN FINLAND	641,259	634,688	656,034	+2.3%

Source: Statistics Finland 1967, 1992, 1996.

However, the decisions that where subsequently taken after the first 'KUUSAMOon' project have lead to a positive economic development in information based economic activity. It was during this period that the first enterprises directly involved with the information technology started in Kuusamo. These firms are:

- Koillis-Infot, founded in 1987, sells computer and office equipment.
- Pehmo-Kuusamo, founded in 1990, develops software applications for tourism and organizes training in co-operation with the local Adult Education Centre.
- Ruka-Data began to offer Computer Roadhouse service at the Ruka area, and it is specialized in offering telematics services and premises for meetings, seminars and distance work.

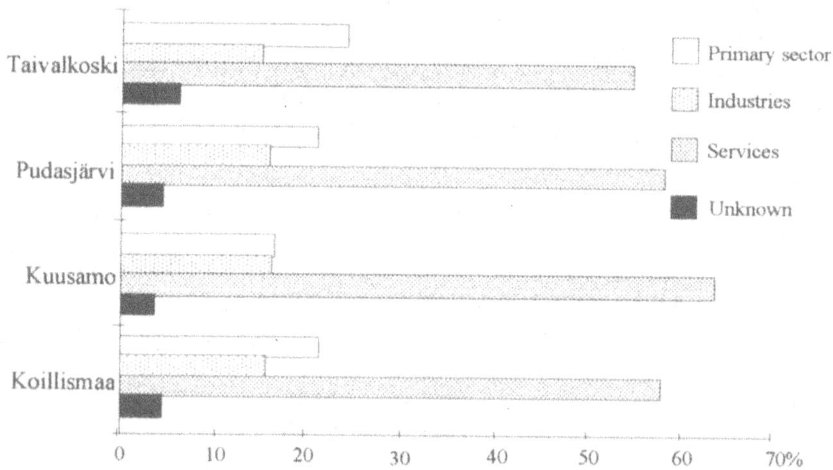

Figure 14.6 Industrial structure in Koillismaa region, 1995

Sources: Tilastokeskus 1996, and URL http://www.fennica.ascentia.fi/

It is this development of small-scale telecommunications 'industries' in Kuusamo that are a sign of the new development. However, it is almost certain that without the backing of the municipality the projects and small firms, that are now developing would not have started. The economic importance of tourism and 'information jobs' has been growing steadily and currently the Koillismaa region has between 89 to 112 jobs per every 100,000 inhabitants in the information or knowledge society sector (Tilastokeskus, Seutukuntakatsaus 1996). This share, although, still small is growing and the local 'technology village', Naturpolis is a vibrant centre for small hi-tech and information production firms. The centre has currently room for some 20-25 small information production firms. The current number of the firms is 16, but according to the interviews done in February 1997 the centre is getting too small and in winter 1997 an enlargement of facilities was in future plans.

The development process has just started, but there is a strong belief that the path chosen has been the 'right choice', although at the beginning there were many that raised doubts and sceptical thoughts about the success of information business in Kuusamo. However, the success of Naturpolis proves that the chosen path has been successful, although the total amount of firms working there is not large. One of the most important signs of the coming of the information era is that the local daily newspaper has been very interested in developing new ways to distribute the local paper. This means that the information production and local interest towards the media as such can be kept relatively high among the local population.

Comparison of experiences

Regional development trends

Regional development is nowadays truly dependent on the local issues. The development projects in Garfagnana and in Kuusamo (Koillismaa) reveal that local people, not those from outside, are the key for development. Local initiatives are the ones' that stand out in the current discussion on regional development in peripheral areas. The problem is, however, that there is always a shortage of people who can work as animateurs of local development.

This places the local efforts into perspective. They are important, but there are many obstacles that need to be overcome. The difficulties regarding local actions for development were constantly present in the discussions with the animateurs in Kuusamo and in Garfagnana, and they revealed very similar situations and one of them is the 'truth' that, it is not that easy to get peripheral, often tradition bound, regions to change the 'course'. There is much resentment towards 'new things', and people are looking for 'safe' solutions which leads to the development of those industries and economies that feel safe and familiar. The problem with them is that while they rely on the local economic base, these 'industries' do not bring in new knowledge or information to the region (e.g., Andreoli and Tellarini 1998).

However, at the moment most current theories and ideas of local development stress the importance of local actions that are 'innovative'. There are actually very few theories other than those, which claim that it, is the local or regional that is vital. In this there is, however, a 'built-in' problem, in the sense, that even though local initiatives are looked upon as the 'best', the goals of the development projects are usually coming from outside. In peripheral areas the importance of regional policy and regional development work places the national, or at least sub-national, regional, goals to the forefront. These goals often stress economic performance and competitiveness of a region, which with a traditional industrial structure or mental 'atmosphere' are sometimes very hard to achieve.

The problem in regional development like this is, that there is a need to get contacts and maintain contacts and it is precisely in this that many peripheral regions lack. However, this is not always true and the work on 'pocket development' (see Bond and Tykkyläinen, 1996) shows, that it is possible to get even very peripheral areas to change. The outcome from this approach, however, might become different from the regional development point of view. The process of 'pocket development' might, with the help of networking, turn into a development of small local centres when two similar areas get together and start working together.

Comparison of the regions

Regional development has in all peripheral regions in Western-European countries followed to some extent similar development patterns and the problems of economic development are also common (e.g., Hadjimichalis and Sadler, 1995). The regions and their experiences we discuss and compare here have, however, issues that place them into a similar position, although it is also easy to pick up dissimilarities between the two case areas.

From population density, geographical and climactic points of view the two regions are very dissimilar. According to the 'traditional distance' perspective both Garfagnana and Kuusamo suffer from 'remoteness' in respect with the closest large centre. The distance in Garfagnana from Castelnuovo di Garfagnana to Lucca is not significant in kilometres (only 46 km), but in time it means approximately from 45 minutes to an hour. The distance from Kuusamo to Oulu is much longer (224 km), but in time it is only an hour longer. It is this 'time distance' that places Garfagnana and Kuusamo to a similar level in their aspirations to develop better and faster communications between them and the 'nodes of information'.

Tourism has in both Garfagnana and Kuusamo been part of the economy a long time, but it is only during recent years that a more concentrated effort has been put into this work. Earlier tourism in Garfagnana concentrated on short, usually one or two days, trips from the lowlands to the Apennines or it was second home tourism. In Kuusamo the tourism has become during the last 15 years a major player in the economy of the region. It belongs to those Finnish municipalities that have the most second homes per 1,000 inhabitants (more than 221 per 1,000 inhabitants in 1995).

Tourism as an economy is, however, more important in Kuusamo than in Garfagnana, where the economic structure is more balanced than in Kuusamo, where only agriculture, tourism and public services provide the most of the jobs. The balanced picture in Garfagnana is changing as more industries have been closing down during the last five years and from this point of view the structural economic intervention is becoming more important for the area. This situation resembles that of Koillismaa and Kuusamo, that are heavily relying on the regional policy aids and projects put forward by the help of European Union Regional Development Fund Programs.

Comparison of projects and their aims

The most apparent similarity in the development efforts between the two areas of Garfagnana and Kuusamo is the introduction of telematics and information technology. Information technology and the use of modern communication is nowadays one of the main aims of regional and rural development within the European Community and consequently the LEADER, the Objective-5b, and the Objective-6 programmes emphasise the use of information technology and aim to facilitate the coming of the 'information society' to the rural regions and according to the European Commission (EC 1996a, 1996b):

> The new technologies can potentially contribute towards overcoming social exclusion and regional disparities', but special measures needs to be taken to ensure that the benefits [provided by the information society] are evenly distributed between different parts of the Union and citizens.

This common European 'ethos' on communication and telematics is present in Garfagnana and in Kuusamo. However, the level of project implementation is very different. The Italian project has just started and during interviews one could sense that while expectations are high, there is much uncertainty toward these new methods and tools for development, since they could be very important for helping to change the economic fabric and in providing services for population. The provision of services with the help of information technology was considered as a key issue in both regions and according to interviewees they could contribute in maintaining the population in the more 'remote' areas of the region, that otherwise risk to be totally abandoned.

At the same time, from the draft of the telematic node of Garfagnana and from the interviews one could get an impression, that the information and service part would get less attention. This due to the lacking intervention for spreading know-how and creating a new culture in the area, and consequently, those who are already more entrepreneurial are likely to benefit from these new opportunities. Besides, after the initial first period of about three years, when it is possible to have financial aid, most of the projects are required to become self-sustainable. It was feared, that in this situation the service would be targeted to those, who would most likely to benefit its use, but the majority of potential small business users would stay outside. As a result, from the point of view of civic network and service provision to the local population, there is in Garfagnana, like in Kuusamo, a need get public institutions involved, since in this way it is possible to 'guarantee' a strong willingness and commitment at political level in order to have a chance for obtaining good results.

The project of information technology in Garfagnana is in many aspects similar to that of the Kuusamo project. The main differences with them are the time scale and the initial approach. The Kuusamo project that started eleven years ago in 1987 is only now starting to bring in jobs and new businesses. The initial approach in Kuusamo started with education and building of a culture of business, which could utilise these new tools and from the very beginning the project was closely tied into the major service industry of the area, tourism. Even after 11 years it is difficult to forecast the future, but the strive of Kuusamo towards information society and telematics use will have an influence, since the Finnish approach towards rural and regional development favours these efforts. This is why Kuusamo has been an example for European Union funded Logregis-projects (see http://www.kuntaliitto.fi/locregis), that analyse new types and models of regional development in peripheral areas of the European Union.

The Kuusamo experience of developing the telematics based regional projects that aim to new job creation shows that it takes time before there is enough substance and information within the local area. The first information technology firms started their operation during the second phase in Kuusamo. These firms utilised local needs for tourism and developed a telebooking system for the local tourist operators and hotels. The experience of Kuusamo shows that without a locally developed need for the use of new types of development approaches it is very difficult to launch such projects in a peripheral area.

The current situation in Garfagnana differs that of Kuusamo about ten years ago, when they started the process towards 'information society'. In Garfagnana there are only few that have been even considering the use of modern technologies for rural development and information delivery. The interviews in Garfagnana showed a different picture from Kuusamo, where there is a strong commitment from the side of the municipality, firms operating in the Naturpolis 'techno-park', and the Telecom Finland as well as the ICL that is handling the 'front office', which is the place for getting information about the project and it also gives assistance to new users of the Koillismaa Network (the local LAN).

In Garfagnana at the moment there is no such a centre and the project plans so far seems to be looking at the 'hardware' and 'provider' sides of the system more than the contents and user side of the system. There is also a lack of local involvement in the sense that the current project seems not include local firms or co-operatives as active partners. This is a major difference for the Kuusamo experience, where from the very beginning all those that even 'might' be interested in the new tool were given information and taken as active partners of development. Those responsible for the project interviewed in Kuusamo stressed this aspect very much. The report of the 'First Ten Years' summarises the changes in the culture and concludes that co-operation within the area has intensified between the municipalities and between municipalities and local businesses. This has according to the report 'improved the image' of the region and the region is now attracting educated 'return immigrates', who have valuable know-how for the regional development (Development of Local.... 1997, p. 6).

The plans in Garfagnana have approximately the same aims, but as the project is at its initial status, it is not possible to judge how well it will succeed in the future. The problems encountered in previous regional projects and the results of previous research on the 'nature of the Garfagnino' (see Andreoli and Gouèrec, 1995, 194-198), have been confirmed by the interviews of those responsible for local development. They stressed the problems of local culture, which does not favour fast adoption of innovations, but has a kind of *seeing is believing* attitude towards new development.

Conclusions and future trends

The projects in Garfagnana and Kuusamo are similar in their aims, but especially when it comes to the implementation of the projects Kuusamo seems to be more committed to the project it has started. In Garfagnana there was a kind of 'wait and see' attitude and behaviour towards the new development projects. This mentality means that most of the development input in Garfagnana would be coming from the outside as proposed development projects for the region. It also gives much more room for different agencies to pursue their 'own kind of policies' instead of the locally anchored development efforts. It is thus difficult to say in what respect the projects of tourism and regional co-operation between the LAGs will be a fruitful way to enhance the economic development in the Garfagnana region. The region does have a potential, but if the local development culture stays as it is, it will take more time to spread communication based development methods and practices in the region. The picture of Kuusamo shows that it is possible, but there needs to be a strong local will behind the process.

The use of information technologies and communication telematics is bridging regions with each other. The important aspect in this is, however, that the regions taking the information bandwagon need to be sure that they are themselves in control of the development. At the same time there needs to be a local commitment and local awareness of need for the use of the new tool. This awareness can be 'developed' through education and with an involvement of all those that show an interest towards this type of development. The use of information technology or telematics is not an answer to all problems. It is a tool that when used efficiently may and can lead to new development paths. This 'European' strive towards an information highway means that there will be many projects with the aim to 'enhance local skills in telematics.' However, one needs ask the question: 'For whom and for what purpose?'

This question shows that in the future those responsible for the local development need to be more than ever before aware of the processes and developments taking place in other similar regions. It is very important to understand that you are not alone in the 'world'. There are others in the same situation. This is also a way for building self-confidence within a region.

Notes

1 This paper is the first result of an international collaboration promoted under the project on 'Metodologie e construzione di un osservatorio sull'evoluzione delle necessità del mondo rural toscano e delle attività e degli interventi atti a promuoverne lo sviluppo' (Methodology and experimental implementation of an observatory of the evolution of Tuscany rural society needs and of the activities and interventions able to promote its development), which is having financial support from the ARSIA (Regional Agency on Development and Innovation in Agriculture - Tuscany Region.

2 In this chapter the words 'Europe' or 'European' are refereeing to the European Union unless not stated differently.

3 Between Leader I and Leader II the area in Lucca Province included in the programme had been enlarged and at present this area includes, not only Garfagnana, but also Media Valle and the mountainous part of Versilia.

4 LEADER (Liason Action Development Rurale), Objective-5b and Objective-6 are European Union regional policy programmes for promoting economic development in rural and sparsely populated areas.

5 The 'natural rate' is the same as natural population increase/decrease.

6 The 'social rate' equals that of the in-migration and out-migration balance.

References

Agritec srl (Dic. 1996), *Rapporto di consulenza - Programma Leader - Polo telematico GAL Garfagnana*, draft

Andreoli, M., Gouèrec, N. and Tellarini, V. (1995), 'Percorsi di sviluppo in un'area marginale: fattori locali e non', in M.Miele and Rovai, M. (eds.), *Tendenze globali e tendenze locali nei processi di sviluppo: Modelli interpretativi a confronto*, Ed. Il Borghetto: Pisa.

Andreoli, M. and Gouèrec, N. (1995), 'Tradition and Modernization in Agricultural Development of Tuscan (Central Italy) Marginal Area: The Role of Advisory and Extension Services', in Singh, R.B. and Majoral, Roser (eds.), *Development Issues in Marginal Regions – Processes, technological developments and societal reorganizations*, pp. 179-192, Oxford and IBH Publishers: New Delhi and Calcutta, India.

Andreoli, M. and Tellarini, V. (1998), 'Marginality and development in Italy: a study review', in Jussila, H., Leimgruber, W. and Majoral, R. (eds.), *Perception of Marginality*. Ashgate Publishing: Aldershot.

Bond, D. and Tykkyläinen, M. (1996), 'Northwestern Russia: a case study in 'pocket' development', *European Business Review* 95, 5, pp. 55-61.

Brown, L. A. (1981), *Innovation Diffusion – a new perspective*. Methuen: New York.

'Development of Local Telematics Know-how and Information Society in the municipality of Kuusamo' (1997). Municipality of Kuusamo: Kuusamo.

Di Iacovo, F. and Gouèrec, N. (Dic. 1996), 'Il Leader I in Toscana: un primo laboratorio aperto sulla strada dello sviluppo', in ARSIA, *L'esperienza Leader in Toscana. La rivitalizzazione delle aree rurali per la crescita dell'economia regionale*, (Mimeo)

Di Iacovo, F. and Gouerec, N. (Dic. 1996), 'Leader II: i primi passi di un'esperienza in corso', in ARSIA, *L'esperienza Leader in Toscana. La rivitalizzazione delle aree rurali per la crescita dell'economia regionale*, mimeo.

Elia G., D'Alto, S. and Buonomini, D. (1976), *Il conflitto latente. Aspetti della struttura sociale della Val di Serchio*, E.T.S.: Pisa.

European Commission (1996a), *Green paper living and working in the information society: People first*, COM (96) 389.

European Commission (1996b), 'Communication to the Council, the European Parliament, the Economic and Social Committee and the Committee of the Regions' on *The Implications of the Information Society for European Union Policies – Preparing the next steps'*, Mimeo, European Community: Commission – Internet Services URL: http://www.europa.int/.

European Planning Strategy (1992), *CEMAT: European Conference of Ministers Responsible for Regional Planning*, Council of Europe, European Commission: Strasbourg.

Gouèrec, N. (1995), *La Comunità Montana della Garfagnana, ovvero il fascino discreto della marginalità?*, mimeo.

Gouèrec, N. (1996), 'Rural Development Programs of the EU: An attempt to evaluate their impact in Garfagnana', in Furlani de Civit, M.E., C. Pedone and N. Dario Soria (eds.), *Development Issues in Marginal Regions II: Policies and Strategies*, 93-108. Universidad Nacional de Cuyo: Mendoza, Argentina.

Gouèrec, N. and Tellarini, V. (Apr. 1994), *L'agricoltura in provincia di Lucca: un approccio generale*, Provincia di Lucca - Dip. di Economia dell'Agricoltura, dell'Ambiente Agro-Forestale e del Territorio, mimeo.

Hadjimichalis C. and Sadler, D. (1995), 'Integration, Marginality and the New Europe', in Costis Hadjimichalis and David Sadler (eds.), *Europe at the Margins, New Mosaics of Inequality*, 3-14, John Wiley & Sons Ltd: New York.

IRPET (1994), 'Il reddito disponibile nei comuni di Toscana, Umbria e Marche. Anni 1986/91', in *Economia Toscana. Note di congiuntura*, Anno 9, marzo 1994, n. 3.

ISTAT (1951, 1961, 1971, 1981, 1991), *Censimento generale della popolazione.*

ISTAT (1961, 1991), *Censimento generale dell'industria.*

ISTAT (1992, 1993, 1994, 1995), *Popolazione e movimento anagrafico dei comuni.*

Jussila, H. and Segerståhl, B. (1997), 'Technology Centers as Business Environments in Small Cities', *European Planning Studies* Vol. 5 Number 2.

Jussila, H. (1998), 'The Northern Scandinavian Point of View: On marginality in regional policy research', in Jussila, H., Leimgruber, W. and Majoral, R. (eds.), *Perceptions of Marginality*, Ashgate Publishing: Aldershot.

Nordgreen, R. (1995), 'Regionar, regioninndeling og regionalisering', *Lillehammer College, Working paper no.* 8/1995: Lillehammer.

Statistics Finland (1967, 1992, 1996), *Statistical Yearbook of Finland*, Statistics Finland: Helsinki.

Taxman, P. and Tykkyläinen, M. (1992), 'Finland: restructuring policy in the 1980s', in Neil, C., Tykkyläinen, M. and Bradbury, J. (eds.), *Coping with closure, An international comparison of mine town experiences*, 313-326, Routledge: London and New York.

Tilastokeskus (1997), *Seutukuntakatsaus 1996*: Helsinki.

Tilastokeskus (1997), *Pohjois-Suomen katsaus 1996*: Helsinki.

Tykkyläinen, M. and Jussila, H. (1998), 'Potentials for innovative restructuring of industry in Northwestern Russia', *Fennia* 176:1, pp. 223-245.

Internet sources (URLs as of time of use)

URL http://www.fennica.ascentia.fi/
URL http://www.kuntaliitto.fi/locregis
URL http://www.koillismaa.fi/
URL http://www.regione.toscana.it/
URL http://www.europa.int/

15 Evaluating marginal development:

Local views on modernization in an Indian and Swedish context

LENNART ANDERSSON, KRISTINA LEJONHUD AND BERTIL LUNDBERG

Introduction

We focus on the issue of evaluating development in marginal regions or marginal development, as we prefer to term it. The contribution is a continuation of an earlier contribution with the title 'Evaluating development in marginal regions – Experiences from studies in a Swedish county' (Andersson, Blom and Lundberg 1996) and for background, some of the conclusions from that contribution are referred.

Above all, we stress the vital importance in all evaluation of the perspectives chosen by the evaluators and the viewpoints adopted. It is necessary for the evaluator to be clear in his/her mind about this. The results of evaluations that take just one point of departure and explore only one perspective may differ fundamentally from other approaches.

There are thus obvious discords between a generalist view and a view that takes its stance in the particularities of specific areas, and between a territorial perspective and a functional one. For reasons that are becoming more and more clear, we should be well aware that top-down and bottom-up views, as well as inside and outside perceptions of what is and what should be, are often quite incompatible. These discords must be observed and brought to the surface.

It is obvious that most policies, whether they be national, regional or even local, emanate from and give expression to a top-down and outsider view of development in marginal regions. Evaluation approaches, starting from the goals and values of policies, will most probably fail to detect, acknowledge and measure effects that may be of greater importance from other points of view, for instance, a local one from within.

It was also noted in the 1996 contribution that there are obvious discords between the modernist view of development in marginal regions and local development arrived at through post modernist and local approaches. In the contribution before us we relate to that statement.

Purpose and approach

The purpose is to continue to discuss and successively analyze problems connected with the overriding title 'Evaluating Marginal Development'. We would emphasize even in this contribution the vital importance of the perspective of the evaluator and our interest in highlighting the local perspective. The project may still be considered as being in an exploratory phase. The verbal construct 'Marginal Development' is meant to imply that development in marginal places and areas may also be regarded as occurring at the margin of the global economy and as giving but a marginal contribution to the global economy.

In the next section we penetrate briefly the role of modernization in the dynamics of marginal regions. On the basis of this discussion, we attempt to formulate 'a skeleton model of evaluation' in the section entitled Development – perspectives and strategies. In this model, the combination of development perspectives and strategies define particular forms of policies and plans.

Thereafter the intentions are illustrated in two case studies. Our empirical material is taken from two environments, which we are interested in from a wider research, perspective. The first case deals with the village Chamaon near the city of Varanasi in India. In the second the material is taken from the Finnskogen area in western Sweden, 150 km north of the city of Karlstad. The available empirical material is different in the two cases. To make it possible to discuss the cases together we have chosen, as far as possible, a common basis for the description.

It is very seldom that development issues in such different local environments and situated in such different parts of the world are discussed in one context. The idea is that in the context before us it might be interesting to make some comparative summarizing comments in spite of the differences. We refer to Hettne from whom we cite the following (1995, p. 208):

> One example is the case of the European periphery, since there are obvious structural similarities between the fringe areas of Europe and the global periphery. We shall come back to this. But why not take a further step? Are there perhaps other issues, analysed by development theorists normally concerned with the Third World, that have a bearing upon contemporary

problems in the industrialised countries? Is self-reliance a good strategy for Sweden? To what extent are basic human needs fulfilled in Denmark? Could Poland have an alternative strategy? Can development in Germany be more in tune with the ideals and principles of eco-development? What about the future of modernity in Europe?

Lastly some conclusions are drawn.

On the role of modernization in the dynamics of marginal regions

At the core of our reasoning lies an imaginary battle between opposite futures and opposite modes or views of development. These opposites are associated with dialectic pairs like global and local, general and particular, central and peripheral, mainstream and marginal, order and disorder and several others.

What modernity and modernization might mean, and how the task of defining these meanings has been dealt with by various writers, would take a much more comprehensive essay than this to penetrate. We will simply use these concepts with a quite specific, still rather crude meaning, and the following few paragraphs will have to suffice as definitions.

Modern as the counterpart of traditional, and modernization as the process by which society is infinitely transformed into something else, something supposedly better and more mature, will be our starting point. We must note, of course, that modernity and modernization conceptualized in this way are socially and historically as well as economically constrained notions. Development, another of these annoyingly vague words, adheres too much the same purport and values – in fact, what is commonly meant by development comes very close to being synonymous with 'modernization'. Furthermore, the orthodox view of development renders it a tacit meaning and purpose of westernization. In a very direct account of modernization and development theories and practices, Slater (1995, p. 65) states that

> It was Enlightenment discourse, which originally gave meaning to concepts of the 'modern'. The West became the model, the prototype, and the measure of social progress. It was Western civilization, rationality, and progress that were proclaimed and bestowed with universal relevance.

We should, however, acknowledge that the orthodox theory of development has been contested by scholars, policy makers and popular movements in both the Western and the non-western world. It is also obvious, that the globalization leap that we are witnessing today has a profound effect on the attitudes brought into development policy making as well as on how the world changes, regardless of Western or any other development projects. As Slater (1995, pp. 68-69) observes:

> In a second wave of developmental doctrine, frequently considered as neo-liberal, and customarily couched in the terminology of structural adjustment, privatization, deregulation, free trade and market based development, an apparently new model from the West was prescribed for the Rest, as their model too.

There is yet another concept that has to be taken into consideration along with modernization and development. In a lengthy article in The New Encyclopaedia Britannica (1990, p.255) we come across the following statement:

> Modern society is industrial society. To modernize a society is, first of all, to industrialize it. Historically, the rise of modern society has been inextricably linked with the emergence of industrial society. All the features that are associated with modernity can be shown to be related to the set of changes that, no more than two centuries ago, brought into being the industrial type of society.

In common Western 'language', then, development is intrinsically linked to modernization and to industrialization. However, the glory of modernization and industrialization as the supreme instruments of development by no means stand uncontested. The development policies and projects of the West have, thus, undergone considerable changes during the last decade or so.

Development – perspectives and strategies

Development is basically what is happening, but we usually add a positive value to its meaning: embetterment, a turn for the good, a process leading to a more mature state, etc. This, however, gives rise to several questions and problems. Which values are good and which direction is positive?

In a simple evaluation model (Figure 15.1), we cross-tabulated development perspective and development strategy. By development perspective we refer to the angle, or the point of view, from which development processes or strategies may be regarded and evaluated. We identify, on the one hand, a general or comprehensive perspective, which focuses on matters of the whole, and, on the other, what we have chosen to call a particular or indigenous perspective, which emanates from the local or specific point of view. From a general perspective, places and regions are defined as parts of the whole, and given their values and characteristics accordingly. From the particular perspective, the whole is mainly regarded as an aggregate of autonomous parts.

In Figure 15.1 we also put forward two different development strategies, illustrating strategies of diverse reach: global modernization and local self-reliance. It should be remembered, however, that the specified strategies are merely examples based on economic or providential criteria, and we might just as well identify global and local strategies stressing matters of environment or social cohesion etc. The global modernization strategy assumes that progress and prosperity is best brought to the world and its peoples and places through continued modernization and an industrialization type of production rationality on a global scale. Central to this strategy is presumably the trust in large-scale technological and organizational solutions to development problems. Conversely, the local self-reliance strategy focuses on local needs and local resources. If, although this is not inherent in the genuine local strategy, we should contemplate a global development strategy based on local self-reliance, then we should expect this to be based on an opposite belief (or ideology): a trust in small scale processes within comprehensible contexts and a mistrust in global engineering.

We may consider the two perspectives and the two strategies as opposite extremes on a scale, which, when we use it to 'measure' actual development attitudes, projects or policies, will display various degrees of one and the other. Projects or policies based on a large or a small-scale strategy may embrace regions of an 'elastic' size, and we often discriminate between local, regional, national, supernational and global levels on this scale. The perspectives and the strategies are similar in character, but – and this is an important note – they are not identical. For instance, we may very well imagine local actors or spectators who adopt a general perspective and advocate a global strategy.

There is, however, still another dimension, not visible in the simple layout of the model, which must be taken into account when we estimate the realism, the practicability or the possible success of policies based on different perspectives and strategies. This is a dimension in which configurations like top-down versus bottom-up, centralization versus decentralization, control and regulation versus empowerment and participation, will have a meaning. As a convenient abbreviation we might put power as the prefix of this dimension.

Development attitudes and policies		Development strategy	
		Global Modernisation (M)	Local Self-reliance (S)
Perspective, view	General (comprehensive) (G)	G⇨M / M⇨G	G⇨S / S⇨G
	Particular (indigenous) (P)	P⇨M / M⇨P	P⇨S / S⇨P

Figure 15.1 A skeleton model of evaluation

The interesting part is, of course, what will fall into the resulting cells of the table. What will the two strategies look like when considered from a general and from a particular point of view?

From the general perspective, strategies will be selected on the basis of a general plan or purpose, i.e. strategies favouring overall development by prescribing specific roles for regions and localities. A large-scale strategy, possibly a global one, seems to be best in accord with this perspective. In fact, a general view based on modernity criteria would most certainly result in a global modernization strategy of development. Since the capitalist market economy stands quite uncontested today, and since modernization on an ever larger scale seems to be a vital condition for the continuing prosperity of this kind of economy, bringing the power dimension into the picture would produce a very strong bias towards the global modernization strategy. We will not hesitate to appoint this today's mainstream strategy. In his 'montage' of Sweden, Pred (1995) convincingly argues that the world in which we are living or transiting to is not one of post-modernity but one of hyper-modernity – a speedup version of modernity. As a supposition, we even claim that most governments at all levels support this strategy, through conviction or through fear of losing out. As an illustration to this we refer to studies by Blom (1996) on attitudes to higher education, in which local politicians appear to represent both a local, insider perspective and a central, outsider one. We may interpret this as an adjustment to perspectives and strategies that are believed to harmonize best with the main forces of development. The upper left field of the table, thus, more or less represents the norm (or even dogma) of development thinking. It is, accordingly, hard to imagine local self-reliance as a main development strategy in a general perspective. Still, strategies tending towards the local might very well be advanced as complementary ones. A balanced mix of differently scaled development strategies might be considered to be the most effective development policy even from a purely general point of view – especially if the holder of the view in his or her general experience of the world should include the probability of mistimed and faltering large scale operations.

On the other hand, it is equally hard to imagine global modernization to be the most favoured development strategy from a particular, indigenous point of view, unless a global strategy is regarded as a necessary precondition for the realization of a local strategy. Still, the deeper meaning of the ecologist slogan think globally – act locally implies just that. A global environmental strategy is needed to avoid pollution at a local level and, hence, to maintain a local development potential. Anyhow, an indigenous perspective is probably the one that is most compatible with a local strategy. The lower right field of the table, then, represents the counterpoint of what we have named mainstream development policy.

From the other direction of approach, we realize that different strategies place claims on both general and particular perspectives. A global modernization strategy not only demands general development (regional) policies and measures that are in accordance with this strategy, but it also requires that projects initiated from an indigenous point of view be kept in line with the general, global strategy. Swedish regional policy thinking may be used to stress this point. Until recently, the main attitude towards backward or marginal regions was that they would either gain new development impetus through measures linking them better to the mainstream economy, or be given enough subsidies to maintain reasonable standards of living but with no real hope of development. Recent official reports, however, state that in order to achieve economic growth at the national level, all regions must realize their own resource potential (Arbetsmarknadsdepartementet 1993 and Närings- och handelsdepartemen-tet 1997). Similarly, local self-reliance strategies, although indigenous in character, may need general support in order to protect the local arenas from being disturbed or even exploited by overriding forces or powers.

All in all, it seems necessary that the proposed dimensions – including the implied dimension of power – are born in mind when development strategies, policies and projects are construed and evaluated, since their effectiveness will be measured and valued differently depending on what view is taken.

One final word about the proposed model: we may think of it as a framework in which we place pieces of development activity for consideration. Or, we may place ourselves at various positions within it, and scrutinize existing or feasible policies from each position. Or, we can take a geographical stance and use the model to evaluate what will come out of different strategies and perspectives, or which strategy – or counter strategy – may be employed in order to further the preferred line of development. Whichever way we look at it, we should be careful to use the model in only one way at the time.

Local views on modernization – two case studies

Chamaon Gram Sabha in northern India

Chamaon Gram Sabha is an Indian village situated about seven km northwest of Varanasi City in Uttar Pradesh in North India. The area was studied during the 1970s by a team from Banaras Hindu University, Varanasi (Singh and Singh 1977) and in the 1990s by a team from the department of geography at University of Karlstad, Sweden (Gerhard Gustafsson, Kristina Lejonhud and Karl-Ivar Vålvik) in co-operation with Rana P B Singh, Banaras Hindu University, Varanasi. The description of Chamaon is brief and based mainly on interviews conducted during the field studies in the 1990s.

Chamaon covers an area of 448 acres along the River Varuna. The area lies in the alluvial tract of the river Ganga and the land has been under cultivation from prehistoric time (Singh and Singh 1977, p. 26). In 1996 there were about 2300 people living in the area, belonging to some of the 13 castes that are represented. Most of the land in Chamaon is used for cultivation. Almost every family in Chamaon owns some land. In some cases, farming is a complement to other forms of income e.g. from small businesses or wage earning.

In 1977 the area was perceived as a 'peaceful residence of medium class agricultural communities' (Singh and Singh 1977, p. 26). Twenty years later Chamaon could still be described in some respects as traditional and rural, in other respects Chamaon has changed and become more modernized.

Village development programme. In the traditional Indian villages there were two types of councils, a caste council and a village council. The caste council dealt with issues related to caste rules. The village council was the political organ. Membership of the two councils was inherited within the families (Hettne 1979, p. 27). The traditional Indian village has (interview with Rana P B Singh 1996) been described as an independent unit, where everything was run in its own way. Today the situation seems to be different.

One of the reasons for this change is the new administrative system that the Indian government implemented at the beginning of 1950s after independence in 1947. The main task for the new administrative system was to carry out the government's community development programme (Hettne 1979, p. 27). The purpose of the programme was to improve the living conditions and the agricultural system.

This new administrative system was implemented in Chamaon in 1956. The first election to the village council was held in 1958. Chamaon is a part of Harahua Development Block, which is a part of Varanasi District. It is through the Development Block that the government's village development programmes are canalized down to village level.

The Chamaon village council consists of 15 members and the main role of the council is to form a link between the area and the Harahua Development Block, to ensure that Chamaon gets its part of the government schemes for rural development. According to the chairman of the village council in Chamaon (Interview 1996), the main task for the council is to improve the situation concerning housing, electricity, to install water pumps, land consolidation and to improve the situation for the poorest villagers.

Electricity was seen as one of the most important tasks for the council. Chamaon was partially electrified in 1974 but the poorest part has not yet got access to electricity. The chairman of Chamaon village council underlined the importance of electricity as a prerequisite of economic growth. For example, the water pumps driven by electricity are very important in agriculture for irrigation. Another example of the importance of electricity as a prerequisite for economic growth given by the chairman of the village council was the new power loom that had recently been established in Chamaon. Thanks to electricity, the loom could be run both day and night. The weavers were no longer dependent on only sunlight to see the web. And being able to run the loom 24 hours a day creates job opportunities.

Public service. In Chamaon there is a school and a health centre, run by the government. Before 1995 most of the children in the area went to the public school. In 1995 the situation was changed when a private school started in the area. Both schools provide education from the first to the fifth grade. Nowadays, most of the children in Chamaon go to the new private school. Left in the old public school are only children from poor families who cannot afford to pay the higher school fees in the private school.

According to one of the teachers in the public school (Interview 1996), parents nowadays seem to be more willing than a couple of years ago to send their children to school to get some basic education. One of the reasons for this change in attitudes is that it is supposed to be easier to get a job if you are able read and write.

According to government every village cluster should have a health centre. The health centre in Chamaon was built in the early 1980s. The health centre seems to work sporadically. When people get ill, and the illness is not severe old people use some sort of household remedy based on herbs and spices. Younger people seem no longer to trust this type of traditional medicine, instead they buy some pills in the shops. If the illness is severe, people go and see a private doctor in Tarna if they can afford it. The knowledge of the old traditional household remedy is gradually being forgotten.

Agriculture. Another major change that has occurred in Chamaon is the modernization of agriculture. The visible impact of the changes in agriculture includes the land shift reform, the improved irrigation system, mechanization (more tractors), the increased yield due to new sorts of crops – high yielding varieties (HYV), the use of chemical fertilizers and pesticides etc.

Agricultural production is today more market oriented than before. If they have a surplus, farmers with small land holdings sell their produce in Tarna market. Farmers that have larger holdings with more produce sell their produce in Varanasi to a wholesale market run by the government.

The farmers are very well aware of the market prices and changes in the prices effect their choice of produce. The production of brinjals can be taken as an example of commercialization in agriculture. Formerly Chamaon was very famous for its successful production of brinjals – Chamaon was even called the village of brinjals. The soil in Chamaon was very suitable for this kind of vegetables. Today, with the help of chemical fertilizers, other farmers in the surrounding areas are also able to grow brinjals. As a result of the increased output of brinjals, the market price has fallen and in response to this the farmers in Chamaon changed their production and are replacing the brinjals with, for instance, bananas, which give higher profit.

Some of the changes in agriculture are due to government schemes. There are, for instance, a number of water pumps that are used for irrigation in the area that are government owned. There are special government programmes for improving the lot of low caste people, with government subsidies for planting guava trees for example. Some of the changes are due to personal investment e.g. in tractors. In 1983 the first tractor was bought by one of the farmers and in 1996 there were eight tractors in Chamaon. The tractor is not only used in the owner's own fields but also rented out to other farmers.

Another change in recent years is that farmers now have difficulty in getting farm workers. Low caste people who earlier worked on the farmers' land have recent years started to work in small towns near Chamaon where they earn more and are paid in cash instead of kind.

The Land Consolidation Programme that started in 1994 so far covers 70% of the land in Chamaon. After the shift reform in Chamaon the farmers with large land holdings have three plots. Farmers who have less land have two plots and the smallest have one plot. The land shift reform also has an impact on family structure. In the Consolidation act it is stated that every family should only have ten acres of land. This means that joint families split up to keep their land ownership. In 1977 the higher castes were organized in a joint family system, and the rest of the households in Chamaon were living in nuclear families (Singh and Singh 1977, p. 23). The system with joint families seems to be vanishing rapidly in Chamaon. The restriction on land holding is, of course, not the only reason behind the division of joint families, but could be seen as one of reasons. According to the Harahua Block Development Officer (Interview 1996) the farmers are nowadays more independent as a result of the increased production and more cash income.

There are also examples on how some of the effects of the modernization of agriculture are being questioned. For several years farmers in Chamaon have been aware that the use of chemicals in the fields can be harmful. When asked from where the farmers got this knowledge, the informants say that they have seen the effects of it in their own fields and have got information from the mass media. As a result of this awareness, the farmers used more green fertilizers instead of chemicals. The use of manure has become so popular that the farmer has to book in advance a shepherd who is willing to let his sheep graze on the farmer's fields after harvesting.

Manufacturing. Commercialization is not limited to agriculture, it is also found in manufacturing. Formerly part of the artisans' production was used in the informal exchange system in the village. That informal exchange system seems to have vanished and to have been replaced by money exchange.

In Chamaon there are some handicraft activities going on, for instance, weaving, pottery, carpet making etc. Most of these activities are family businesses but there are also examples of small-scale industries, e.g., a weaving mill with five employees. Some of these activities are traditional and a part of the Indian village like the pottery and ironsmith, some are new to village life like the weaving mill.

In 1996 the first electrified loom, a power-loom was introduced in Chamaon. It is owned by three brothers. The brothers had worked in Jetpura, a centre for the weaving industry and from there got their inspiration to set up their own power loom when their part of Chamaon was electrified in 1994. According to our informants, there will soon be four more power looms working in the area and they think that in ten to twenty years there will probably be no handlooms left in the area. The investments for the weaving mill and for the power loom were financed by the help of government loans.

The local view. The major changes that this part of the contribution has dealt with can be seen as examples of modernization both from a general and from an indigenous perspective. Of course, not all the changes can be classified as examples of modernization. Changes that might be implications of local self-reliance are, however, few and not so easy to spot.

From a general perspective you may say that the changes in the agricultural system in Chamaon are in the form of modernization and mechanization. From an indigenous point of view the modernization of farming has increased the people's dependence on the outside world.

From the general perspective the results are the same for manufacturing as for agriculture, more modernization and industrialization. Manufacturing is mainly for a market outside the area. As in agriculture the development strategy concerning handicraft is more towards modernization than towards local self-reliance.

The changes have effected the community as a whole, the relations between the community and the surrounding areas, but also within the community, the relations between the castes, families and individuals in the village. In short, the dependency relation that previously existed between the members of the village today has gradually been replaced by dependency relations to the outside world. These changed relations are partly due to government policy from above, partly due to the individual engagement from below.

Perhaps these changes signify that Chamaon will in the future be seen not as an agricultural community in its own right, but as a part of the Varanasi City area.

Södra Finnskogen in Western Sweden

Södra Finnskoga is a sparsely populated parish in Torsby, the northernmost municipality in the county of Värmland in the midwestern part of Sweden. Bordering on Norway, Södra Finnskoga lies at the heart of one of the larger Finn Forest areas in western Scandinavia – a region much characterized by the cultural heritage of 17th century immigrant Sweden Finns. The physical conditions of the area, by way of climate, soils and topography, allow for no more than small scale farming of a quite limited range of crops, and, subsequently only limited numbers of livestock.

On the outskirts of industrialization. The forest has long been the main resource, and forestry the basic source of employment and household income. However, the value of the forest resources of northern Värmland were only fully appreciated when the pulp and paper industry established itself as one of the dominant basic industries in the region.

With the growing importance of the forestry industry, employed forestry work became the first and foremost means of sustenance in Södra Finnskoga. Also, more and more of the forestry land became the property of industrial enterprises mainly in the pulp and paper sector – a process commenced in the earlier iron industry era. The mechanization of forestry work, speeded up in the mid 20th century with the introduction of the power-saw, eventually led to rationalizations in both the leaseholding of properties and in the organization of forestry work. From a slow start in the 1960s, the industrialization of forestry work has since presented us with ever larger and ever more effective processing machines and transportation vehicles, turning the forestry business into more or less large-scale wood cropping. Following the bonanza of the time, large sections of the forested area of Södra Finnskoga were clearfelled. The number of workers needed was drastically decreased, and today only a few specially skilled machine operators are what remains of the forestry work force in the area, supplemented by truck drivers for the longhaul transportation of wood and timber to the large industrial complexes further south.

Today, about half of the forestry land in the area is owned by a large forest industry company, with its headquarters outside the county. A substantial part of the remainder is owned from afar, by passive estates and so forth, which means that only a small part of the forest land is controlled locally and available as a resource for indigenous development.

After some three decades of stability, an unchecked process of population decline started in the 1930s accelerated in the 1950s and surged in the 1960s. Since 1965 an exact 50% population decrease has occurred. As a result of the numerous outmigrations due to the failing labour market, Södra Finnskoga is today left with a rapidly ageing population. Still, the unemployment rate is very high by Swedish standards.

An industrial detour. Although Södra Finnskoga has never been industrialized in any real sense through the establishment of manufacturing or servicing plants to any degree, it is obvious that industrialization per se has greatly affected the area and its people, dictating resource use and employment opportunities.

In the 18th and early 19th century there were literally hundreds of small ironworks scattered throughout the part of middle Sweden called Bergslagen – a region surrounding the tradition iron ore mining district to the east of the Finnskogen area. In the late 19th century, and as a consequence of new larger scale technologies and the development of railway transportation, the majority of these ironworks were shut down, predominantly those at a distance from the heart of the iron ore district. Many of these small factory towns practically died.

While the traditional skills of both the forestry workers in Södra Finnskoga and the workers in the closed down manufacturing plants are no longer in demand, there is a subtle difference between the two. In Södra Finnskoga, the local resources – although today generating only little local income – are still valuable and useful. Given an expected further expansion of tourism, the quiet seclusion and beauty of the landscape may well become a valued resource in the near future. Also, the differences between the fairly independent outdoor forestry work and the more routinized, fragmented and controlled lines of work, so often predominant in the lagging traditional industries, may well give rise to slightly different capabilities in dealing with a situation of labour market exclusion.

A last effort? The effects of regional and labour market policies had made it possible for people to remain in the Södra Finnskoga area, in spite of the diminishing employment opportunities. Still, these policies have not meant the establishment of new means of living, to any real extent. In effect, it has at most been a question of keeping this and other similar areas tolerably alive until they are depopulated. However, the Swedish entry into the European Community (EC), as much as it was opposed in these northern parts of Värmland (the feeling of remoteness being even more pronounced), meant a new situation and, just maybe, some new opportunities. Following a series of local information meetings, Ivar Edvardsson – a recently retired forestry worker – initiated a general discussion among representatives from the local societies (the local folklore societies, the game preservation and fishery societies, a local temperance society and others). The impetus was one of 'a last survival effort'. The societies had long minded their own business with as much vigour as they could muster – and with the occasional cross-fertilisation and collisions. Edvardsson felt that, in order to take whatever chance there might be to revitalize the community before it became extinct, these societies and all the locals had to find ways to cooperate. Edvardsson later described his position as follows: We cannot wait for somebody to come to our assistance – since no one will. We have to help ourselves. Thus, the approach was one of local empowerment.

In his capacity as a forestry workers' union representative, Edvardsson had previously been acquainted with the research circle method, as a means of tackling locally defined problems. See Lundberg and Starrin (1990) for an introduction to the research circle as a method for participatory research and action for change. Edvardsson suggested that a group of people, embracing all of these local societies, should form such a circle and attempt to formulate a common revitalization strategy. The circle (or joint work group) was established in April 1996 and met approximately once a month for the following year, with the work in between carried out in smaller settings. One of the authors of this contribution (Lundberg), being experienced in this line of work, was enrolled as a tutor.

By way of introduction, the circle listed all the conceivable problems, difficulties and disadvantages at hand, in order to clear the table for positive thinking. Next, the circle started listing and elaborating all matters of value in the area. Some of the items listed were tried out in a small-scale, tentative way during the summer of 1996.

As the process progressed after the summer, the idea of turning the circle into a more permanent co-operative organization materialized, emanating partly from need for continuity and partly from the realization that the EC context, as well as other instances where local development support was to be found, demanded a local, identifiable and formally responsible partner. Eventually, this idea materialized into the formal establishment of an economic association in the form of a community co-operative.

To these ends, it was stated that the co-operative would:

1 Promote efforts that will strengthen the identity, the self-esteem and the affinity of the people of Södra Finnskoga,
2 Contribute to the creation of a positive image of the area,
3 Contribute to a collective commitment to the community and its development,
4 Promote efforts that will lead to employment opportunities in the area, and

5 Contribute specifically to such united efforts that will strengthen the local tourist trade.

Along the way, the circle has established contact with local and regional authorities and promoting agents, laying ground for future support and partnership ventures. The process has so far had an empowering effect on those participating in the work of the circle, and presumably this effect is spreading.

The local view. From this account of the events, it is clear that the local Södra Finnskoga strategy, as implied by the objectives paragraph of the co-operative's statutes, does not fall unambiguously into any one field of the evaluation model (Figure 15.1). The basis note appears to be one of local self-reliance, in that they feel they are on their own, and in that several sentences are about strengthening the community and the local welfare resources. Still, through this they obviously hope to achieve a better position, also, in their relations with the outer world, which will enable them to be a part of the national and international economy. Thus, we may conceive of this local strategy as a dual one: an economic strategy based mainly on conditions given by the globalized market economy, and a social strategy geared to self-reliance. Borrowing from one of the EC programmes, we may define this as a social economy strategy.

Some comparative reflections

What, then, can be said about the Indian and the Swedish examples? We have, more or less tacitly, represented global modernization as a process where modernity progresses spatially, socially and culturally in much the same way as innovations and ideas gain recognition. The Södra Finnskoga area became involved in the modernization process in the mid20th century, yet some say that modernization has not penetrated fully into the local communities. As for Chamaon, this village seems to be in its early stages of modernization, and its destiny has yet to be seen. From another, more particular and local, point of view, the Swedish example appears to be at the tail end of modernization, on the point of being abandoned. Chamaon is just entering its early modernization phase, where crucial gains and losses are about to be decided. The experiences from and the expectations of the modernization process and modernity seem to produce quite different attitudes to development, varying from pessimistic to optimistic, from dejected to energetic – not necessarily placing Swedes and Indians in separate corners.

The fates of the respective places and areas will depend as much on these attitudes, on the imaginativeness of strategy and policy makers and on the courage and recklessness of anyone involved as on the actual small and large scale turns of (economic) development. Södra Finnskoga still has its forests and the still and running waters, and these can be employed not only as material inputs. Wilderness, silence, seclusion and natural grandeur – the antithesis of urbanism – may well become of such value as to reaffirm an identity within or in relation to the global economy.

The vicinity to the city of Varanasi seems to be the best asset for Chamaon. Unless a firm policy that states otherwise is applied, we anticipate that Chamaon will be engulfed into the urban area and eventually become little more than a residential area. If this occurs, much of what today is Chamaon will cease to exist, as is the case in so many other urbanized areas around the world. With the stepped-up modernity of today, this may well be a rapid process – or it may take a totally different turn, and put us to shame.

Conclusions

The results to be extracted from this contribution may be considered primarily as issues and hypotheses for further research. We emphasize three notes in particular:

1 Different marginal regions have different positions on the 'modernization curve'. The Swedish case suggests that, in some senses and seen from the local standpoint, the generally positive implications of modernization have come to an end. We have identified development work with its base in groups with a strong local perspective and a wish to change the situation by means of a strategy based on self-reliance. In the Indian illustration the modernization period is still in its introductory phase. The implications are mostly seen as positive even when they are considered from the local view. Work based on the self-reliance strategy is weak and probably more of an instinctive character.

2 We get the impression that upgrading the local view and the local perspective even in the Swedish case has only slightly influenced reality and development. Even if it is important to stress self-reliance as the basis of a local development strategy, it is obviously not number one on the agenda today. The number one approach is still to cling to the forces of modernization. Most development strategies, regardless of whether they are implemented from a general or a particular perspective will, however, sooner or later contain elements of both the local and the wider setting.

3 The formulated skeleton model may be a means of analyzing the situation of different local environments. It will be further developed in the coming work. This may make it possible to find ways of illustrating and highlighting the local view of modernization and of contributing to an understanding of the reasons underlying the increasing marginalization and increasing regional disparities.

References

Andersson, L. Blom, T. and Lundberg, B. (1996), *Evaluating development in marginal regions. Experiences from studies in a Swedish county*. Paper presented at the meeting with the IGU Study Group on Development Issues in Marginal Regions, Glasgow, Scotland July 30 – August 4, 1996.

Arbetsmarknadsdepartementet (1993), *Ds* 1993:78, Allmänna Förlaget: Stockholm.

Blom, T, (1996), 'Perspektiv på kunskap och utveckling. Om attityder till högskoleutbildning i några perifera regioner'. *Meddelanden från Göteborgs universitets geografiska institutioner*, Serie B nr 89.

Hettne, B (1979), *Utvecklingsstrategier i Indien och Kina*, Studentlitteratur: Stockholm.

Hettne, B. (1995), *Development theory and the three worlds: Towards an international political economy of development*, Longman Scientific & Technical: London.

Lundberg, B and Starrin, B. (1990), 'Fighting Health Hazards at Work – Experiences from Participatory Research on Workplace Related Health Issues', *Research Report* 1990:1, Centre for Public Health Research: Karlstad.

Närings- och handelsdepartementet (1997), 'Regionpolitik för hela Sverige'. *SOU 1997:13*, Liber: Stockholm.

The New Encyclopaedia Brittanica (1990), vol. 8 (Micropaedia), 15th edition.

Pred, A. (1995), *Recognizing European modernities: a montage of the present*, Routledge: London.

Singh, R.L. and Singh R.P.B. (1977), 'Rural Development in Indian Environment: Assessment and Prospects, A Case Study of Chamaon Gram Sabha near Varanasi City, U.P', *National Geog. Soc. India, Res. Bulletin*, No 29.

Slater, D. (1995), 'Trajectories of Development Theory', In Johnston RJ, Taylor PJ and Watts MJ (eds.), *Geographies of Global Change – Remapping the World in the Late Twentieth Century*, Blackwell: London.

16 Remaining marginal areas in rural Catalonia:
Causes and consequences

ROSER MAJORAL AND DOLORES SÁNCHEZ-AGUILERA

Introduction

The growing regional imbalances in Catalonia in recent decades have created a panorama of marked contrasts throughout the territory. What is immediately apparent are the disparities between inland Catalonia on the one hand, typified by a negative rate of population growth, an ageing population structure, a productive structure of little diversity, and coastal Catalonia on the other, in which the main urban areas are located, coinciding with the most dynamic demographic and economic nodes as it is here, in the coastal strip, that tourism and industry have chosen to establish themselves.

However, this division is overly simplistic and fails to recognize a more complex reality. A more detailed analysis reveals major internal imbalances both on the coast and inland. In inland Catalonia, for example, there are large expanses of irrigated land which have allowed the development of highly profitable farming practices as well as livestock breeding, which in turn have made possible the growth of a specialized agro-industry while, similarly, there are upland areas where tourism has been developed greatly due to the wealth of available resources. Neither is the coastal strip an entirely homogenous space as here, in spite of the widescale development of tourism, the concentration of urban and industrial areas and the presence of good communication networks, there are marked territorial imbalances, with municipalities (territorial subdivisions) and areas which play little part in this development (Sánchez-Aguilera, Majoral and Font 1997).

Aimed at countering the imbalances between areas, aid has been available in Catalonia for more than a decade now for disadvantaged areas, concentrated mainly in mountain regions. These areas have enjoyed comparative benefits and been stimulated by substantial investments, above all, in their infrastructure and services. Government policies of this kind, however, have proven insufficient. Despite recent efforts, some of the areas enjoying these policies have not been able to recover from a situation generated by years of abandonment and a protracted process of emigration which has decimated their population base.

The mountain areas of Catalonia, identified on the whole as marginal areas until the last few years, have found a partial solution to their declining circumstances, primarily, in the exploitation of their resources, though also thanks to increases in state investment in services and infrastructure, applied systematically through detailed plans of regional development (Majoral, Font and Sánchez-Aguilera, 1996). With time a notable change based on the diversification in land use, and in economic activities in general, has occurred in upland Catalonia. These changes, however, have not affected the area equally, but rather have occurred selectively according to the exploitable resources and the specific initiatives undertaken. Thus, at present it is possible to distinguish between an upland area - coinciding with the Upper and Central Pyrenees - which is well developed and which enjoys good services, and which has recovered a good part of the population which had disappeared since the start of the century and another - coinciding with the Lower Pyrenees and the Prepyrennees and the southern Mediterranean mountains - whose resources are few, and which has not witnessed any great changes in its productive base.

In addition to the upland areas which are poor in tourist resources, there exist in Catalonia other areas or, in some cases groups of municipalities, which share with the former the indicators normally used for detecting spatial marginality. Today, marginality is no longer so readily identifiable with specific territorial areas. Initiatives for regional development, as well as the exploitation of new natural resources, which until recently were largely ignored, have brought about notable changes in economic activities, changing traditional habits and improving living conditions and the quality of life. The spatial distribution of marginality is increasingly fragmented in municipalities and small territorial areas throughout the territory, as L.O. Persson (1997) found out in Sweden. These microregions are often separated by considerable distances yet share highly similar characteristics in spite of occupying quite distinct contexts in the region. This said, however, there still exist groups of municipalities which form continuous areas which means we can still talk of fairly large marginal areas.

On the other hand, as illustrated in (Sánchez-Aguilera, Majoral and Font, 1997), marginal areas are not only the product of historical processes, as is the case of upland Catalonia, but also of more recent circumstances. Thus while some traditionally marginal areas are recovering from earlier stagnation or have at least been able to halt the process of decline, other areas that until a few years ago were economically and demographically highly dynamic have fallen into decline as a result of the industrial crisis and have suffered a marked drop in population and income which has converted them, both in absolute and comparative terms, into marginal areas.

The aim of this article is to identify through the application of various indicators, which we believe to be significant, the municipalities and areas – or groups of municipalities – that are marginal within Catalonia. First we discuss our selection of the indicators of marginality, then these are grouped and mapped to illustrate the spatial distribution of marginality.

Selection of variables

As has frequently been seen, in the studies presented at the meetings of this Group (see Tzamarias 1997, for instance), the definition of 'marginal', or the decision to define an area or territory as marginal depends on the indicators which are used, on the regional context of which the area forms a part and, of course, the personal perception of the person who has conducted the study. A systematic analysis using the most appropriate indicators of a specific situation is not easy and can even present certain risks. Following several studies, presented on previous occasions, we feel the time is right to propose a classification and demarcation of the marginal areas in Catalonia.

To do this, we have undertaken a study in two parts. The first step was the selection of those variables which appeared most appropriate. They are without exception socio-economic variables and as such are in line with our proposal at The Hague. A preliminary examination of the available statistics led to the selection of 25 variables which might be said to be significant. The set of variables refers to population, economic activity, infrastructure and accessibility. Following this initial analysis and the application and mapping of the information we found, however that certain indicators were of little significance while others were repetitive or contradictory. In the light of these findings, a second selection of variables was made which appeared to have greater significance and to be more representative (4 demographic indicators, 2 housing, 2 infrastructure and services and 1 referring to income levels) and a classification of the municipalities in Catalonia was drawn up using cluster analysis.

Population variables

Among the available demographic indicators we chose those referring to population density, the accumulative annual rate of variation for the period 1975 to 1991, and population ageing (% of population over 65).

One of the typical features of marginal areas is their low population density. The density map for the Catalan municipalities illustrates the division described above between the coast and the interior (map 1). The contrasts between municipalities with high densities and those with low reflects changes in the settlement of the territory over the last century and a half. In the last third of the XIX century the process of rural exodus began in Catalonia. This consisted of flows which originated in rural Catalonia and which terminated, in the main, in the city of Barcelona. These movements, which contributed substantially to the loss of population in many inland areas, lost strength in the middle of the present century, a moment in which they were replaced by new migratory flows, though now originating in the other Spanish provinces outside Catalonia. This redistribution of population is clearly seen in the concentration of peoples in coastal areas. Inland Catalonia, in contrast, is characterized in general by low densities (Sánchez-Aguilera 1996), which reach higher levels in the Plain of Lleida (irrigation farming), in the municipalities which border the Rivers Llobregat and Ter (industrial colonies) and in some capitals of the *comarcas* (La Seu d'Urgell, Puigcerdà). Secondly, once this stage of large movements was over, it is necessary to examine the demographic evolution undergone by Catalonia in the period 1975-1991. However, these flows have largely conditioned subsequent demographic trends as they modified the age structure and the possibilities for growth by strengthening the fertility rate in certain areas through the arrival of young adults.

In the Catalan municipalities, almost two thirds are suffering population decline and 10% of the municipalities are losing population at rates above 2% per year. The areas which enjoy growth are located principally either in the vicinity of Barcelona, reflecting the processes of suburban growth, or along the coast, reflecting the attractive force of some of the tourist municipalities. Inland population growth is also found in a number of areas including the Plain of Lleida and in some mountain municipalities (High Pyrenees) which boast a dynamic tourist sector (see López-Palomeque 1996). As was mentioned earlier, however the mountain areas are those which suffer the greatest population losses (López-Palomeque and Majoral 1980), due both to the constant migration of young people and their age structure.

This last characteristic and in particular population ageing (% of population over 65) was also included as it is another typical feature of marginal areas. With the exception of the more dynamic areas already mentioned, a large part of Catalonia has a markedly ageing population structure (map 2). More than 80% of the municipalities are above the Catalan average while 55% have age structures in which more than 25% of the population are sixty-five and above. This situation is particularly evident in many areas of the Mediterranean mountains (Priorat, Conca de Barberà, Terra Alta) and the Prepyrenees (Pallars Jussà and Sobirà. Solsonès, etc. In contrast, a relative rejuvenation of high mountain areas has occurred as a result of the arrival of immigrants working in the tourist sector (see López-Palomeque 1996).

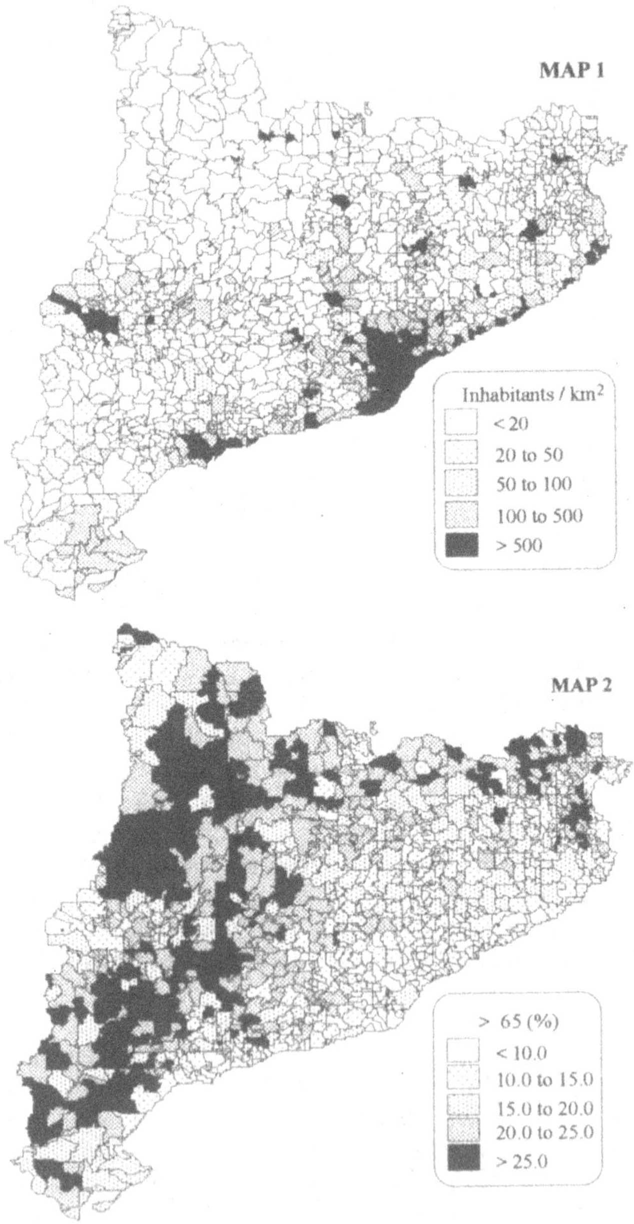

Figure 16.1 Map 1 Population density, 1991
Map 2 Population ageing, 1991

Source: INE: Censo de Población, 1991

Population ageing has, moreover, consequences on the social structure of the territory as in many municipalities the replacement of the generations is by no means guaranteed (García-Coll and Sánchez-Aguilera 1994). This is most clearly evident if we consider that, in 680 of the 941 municipalities analyzed, the number of persons aged 65 and above is greater than that of young people and that in some cases, the number of young people is zero.

Finally, this situation clearly has implications above and beyond the merely demographic, as it is usually associated with the social, and frequently, economic breakdown of these areas.

Economic activity and income levels

Frequently, the marginal areas of Catalonia are identified with agrarian practices. Clearly this does not mean that the areas in which these activities occur are marginal, though in most of the areas considered as being poorly developed or depressed, agriculture is practically the only activity. In 414 municipalities (see map 3), more than 30% of the active population work in the agricultural sector, which in general is typified by dry farming, with little technology and farms with a small turnover, many of them insufficient or non-viable.

One of the most evident symptoms of the lack of dynamism in this sector is the age of the population which works in it and the few possibilities of substitution in the practices. A working population over 65 (theoretically retired) is predominant in many municipalities and affects wide areas of territory. This means few changes are made in production together with little evidence of technical innovation, given the very few possibilities for substituting production. In fact, in just 16 municipalities in Catalonia, the number of young farmers is greater than that for those over 55, a figure that rises to 94 (10% of the municipalities), if compared with the number over 65.

Many of these farms are only maintained thanks to retirement pensions and public subsidies – which they would stop receiving if the activity were to cease. These funds contribute to the maintenance of a fictitious situation as far as production units are concerned, as the number of farms and in turn the actual activity, is considerably less than that suggested by the statistics. The policy of the European Union which gives priority to the extension of land use, moreover, favours this situation.

To complement the economic data, we have used and mapped (see map 4) an indicator of income levels: average earnings per taxpayer in 1992. This index allows the most dynamic economic areas to be identified as it analyses the average income per taxpayer.

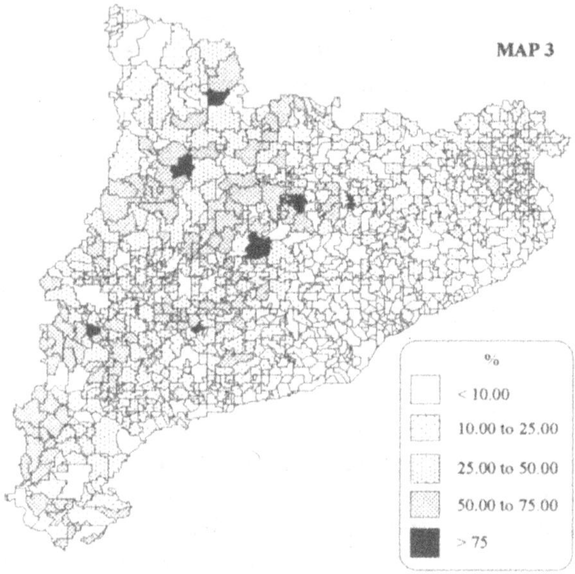

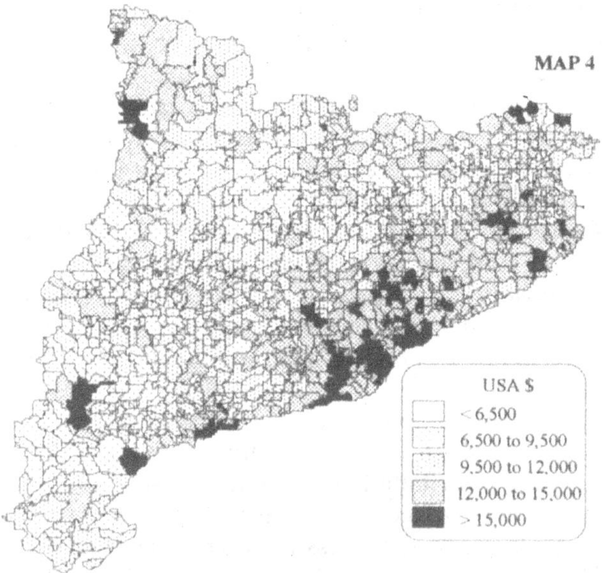

Figure 16.2 Map 3 Population working in the primary sector (%) in Catalonia in Spain, 1991
Map 4 Basic income tax, 1992

Sources: INE: Censo de Población, 1991; IEC: Estadística Municipal 1994-95

The map clearly shows the coastal and precoastal areas, in which the economy is richest and most diversified and a wide area of Catalan territory with declared earnings below an average of 1.9 million pesetas. The cases of high earnings in inland areas are few and far between and where they do exist correspond to the locations of large industrial companies (Erkimia in Flix), energy supply companies (nuclear power stations of Asco and Vandellós) or municipalities specializing in tourist activities (see maps 5 and 6). There are, moreover, two groups of municipalities with earnings lower than a million pesetas: in the southern comarcas (Priorat, Terra Alta and part of the Segrià and les Garrigues and the northern comarcas of la Noguera and part of the Pallars Jussà, Solsonès and Alt Urgell). These meagre earnings are correlated with largely agrarian territories suffering high ageing indices. In fact, in some comarcas such as Priorat, the financial transfers generated by the payment of retirement pensions are the main income for the *comarca.*

Housing, infrastructure and services

Among the variables available for housing we have chosen the date of construction and the state of repair. Although, quite often, the fact that a house was built many years ago does not necessarily mean that the house is in a poor state of repair, as in many cases old houses have been renovated and modernized recently - frequently as second homes - in many other cases, an old house is one in a poor state of repair. This becomes apparent when comparing the maps of houses built before 1920 (map 7) and the map of houses according to their state of repair (map 8). Similarly the map illustrating houses of recent construction (after 1970) coincides with the area of houses in the best condition. Parallel to this, a clear overlap is evident between the state of repair of a house and various services which are described below. In 'houses in a poor state of repair' we include both those considered as being 'deficient' and those which present problems of habitation owing to their state of repair. Houses in this first category are to be found in all the Catalan comarcas, though in very low percentages in some. Houses in the second category are to be found largely in the inland comarcas and those of the Prepyrenees, while they abound also in the *comarca* of Barcelona. Over forty per cent (40.4%) of the housing in Catalonia today has been built after 1970. In many coastal municipalities but also in those away from the coast, in the uplands and central Catalonia, the percentage of housing built after 1970 is often greater than 50% and in some parts even 75%. In other areas, above all in the Prepyrenees and the Central Catalan High Plains, little construction has taken place in recent years. There are groups of municipalities where the proportion of housing built before 1920 is over 75 and, in some extreme cases even more than 90%.

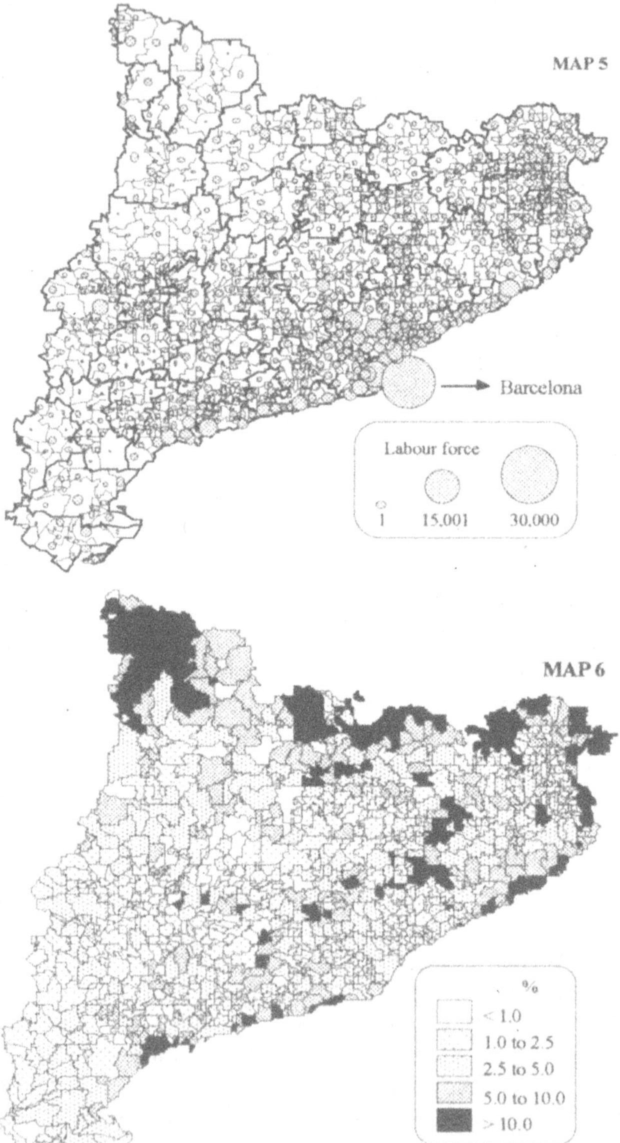

Figure 16.3 Map 5 People working in hotels and restaurants, 1991
Map 6 People working in hotels and restaurants (%), 1991

Source: INE: Censo de Población, 1991

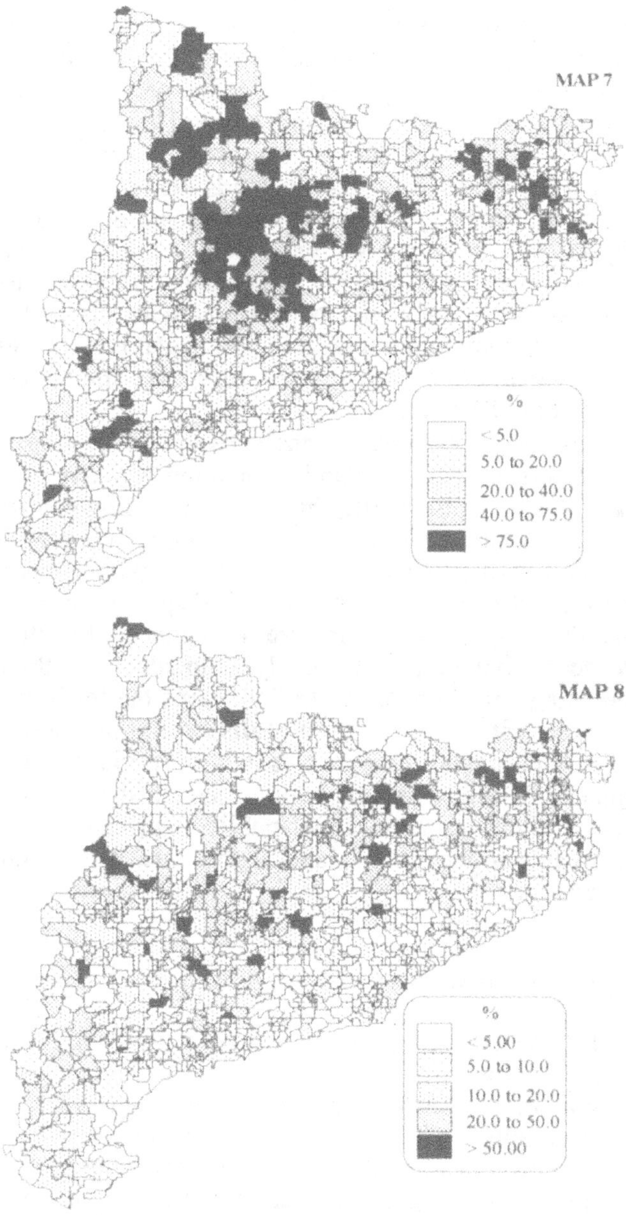

Figure 16.4 Map 7 Buildings constructed before 1920 (%), 1990
Map 8 Houses in a precarious or poor state (%), 1990

Source: INE: Censo de Edificios, 1990

Marginality is closely linked to poor accessibility and the poorest areas in this respect are frequently those with low population densities as their isolation has led in many cases to decline and even the abandonment of many villages, above all in upland areas. The road policy applied in Spain over the last 50 years has always given priority to the main roads over the secondary roads. The current Roads Plan of Catalonia establishes a minimum of 100 inhabitants before the regional authorities will build a road, a figure which compared with that applied in other European countries is too high (Font, 1995; 1996). Isolation has led to decline and even the abandonment of many mountain settlements in Catalonia. The disappearance of some marginal areas in Catalonia means that every inhabited settlement should have its access road maintained in a good condition out of public funds.

In addition to connectivity we analyzed the connection to the general electricity network and the availability of running water in the homes. In the first case (1.88% of the total), the fact of not being connected does not mean a house is without electricity, as this might be supplied locally at small waterfalls or through the installation of solar panels, but rather is indicative of an insufficient supply and inadequacies in the service. The second case (1.36%), houses which are not connected to the public water supply and do not have a private supply, coincides with the area with the highest percentage of old housing. In both cases the territorial distribution clearly coincides with the areas of most dispersed population in Catalonia. The *comarca* with greatest deficiencies in both services is that of Solsonés where a quarter of the houses have no access to the public water supply and 10% are without access to either public or private supplies; the latter being the same proportion of houses that are not connected to the electricity network.

Clustering of the indicators

Following the first stage of selection and the individual evaluation of each variable, an overall analysis of the indicators was carried out. In order to construct a classification which took into consideration the various indicators for all 941 municipalities studied, a multivariate statistical analysis was undertaken, by analyzing the conglomerates or clusters revealed by the SPSS program. Within the multivariate analysis file of this program, we chose to use Quickcluster (analysis of conglomerates based on average distances), as the high number of cases hindered the construction of a dendrogram.

The cluster analysis was carried out on two levels so as to obtain a classification of the municipalities. Firstly a cluster of the groups of indicators was made based on their affinity, that is: population and economic activity, on the one hand, and housing, services and infrastructure, on the other. Secondly, a clustering of the set of variables was made (excluding population density due to large dispersion of values which interfered with the classification); these cluster were then crossed with basic income tax. Finally, a direct clustering based on the 8 variables used was carried out.

After testing various groupings in 5, 7, 10 and even 12 categories, the results obtained with 7 groups seemed, after mapping, to be the clearest and most readily understandable. A smaller number of conglomerations gave rise to an excessively simple map while a larger number produced excessive territorial fragmentation, which became greater as we increased the number of groups. Given that this is just an initial description, the weighting attributed to each of the variables has not been modified.

Analysis of the results

The two first-level clusters gave very different results, both in the size of the groupings as in the size of the territories. Below we analyze the groups separately before looking at the overall results.

Population

The classification of the municipalities based on demographic variables presents somewhat polarized results as a class appears with a high number of cases while others in comparison have very few.

Most of the municipalities fall within the same group, which includes 837 of the 941, that is 89% of the cases. The basic traits of this category are a low population density and an age structure marked by high demographic ageing. These areas are largely located inland, are lacking in demographic dynamism and with tendencies towards decline as in most cases, they are municipalities with a negative balance leading to an overall decline in population.

The transition to healthier demographic situations is found in the second group. This category comprises 32 municipalities, marked by an age structure which shows less ageing than the first group (mature structure), and a tendency to a moderate population decrease.

Two clusters have been identified with only one case each. These are the municipality of Barcelona, and the municipality of Hospitalet de Llobregat (close to Barcelona). Both have points in common: a very high population density due to their urban character and a moderate fall in population. The difference between the two groups is in their age structure, as the municipality of Barcelona shows a higher ageing index.

Finally, three categories of municipalities with more positive demographic features can be identified. A group of three municipalities in the periphery of Barcelona, has very high population densities, moderate demographic growth and a young age structure compared to the Catalan average. In the category P6 there are 6 metropolitan municipalities, with similar characteristics to those described for P5 but with a lower population density. These are cities with between 50 and 100,000 inhabitants, currently undergoing demographic expansion. Finally, group P7, comprising 40 cases, most of them within the metropolitan ring of Barcelona or coastal and tourist towns. This category is the most dynamic in terms of population with a positive growth rate and a young age structure.

One of the most notable aspects of this classification is the effect of population density and demographic ageing as elements in the ordering as, with few exceptions, low density and demographic trends towards stagnation and decline, usually go hand in hand. However, the grouping of municipalities according to demographic variables offers fairly similar results if the use of density is discarded.

Housing

The results concerning housing are much more diffuse. There are three particularly large groups, with more than 150 municipalities and four which are less numerous and which represent extreme cases or municipalities in transition between a variety of situations. The mapping of the results shows areas in which one or other group is predominant but, in general, the map is highly fragmented (map 9). An analysis of the indicators which seem most relevant and from the mapping carried out we are able to define and locate the following seven groups, beginning with a situation of greatest deterioration, that is those municipalities which can be considered as being most marginal and finishing with the group in best conditions.

A centre based largely in the Prepyrenees (Pallars, Alt Urgell, Bergadà), plus other municipalities dispersed throughout other comarcas, form a cluster due to the deficient nature of their infrastructure, that is, the high percentage of houses without connection to the electricity network and the absence of a local infrastructure for the supply of water in most of the houses, and with a high percentage of old houses in a precarious or poor state of repair. This is cluster H1, a group of 40 municipalities. One reason which accounts in part for the deficient nature of their services, is the dispersed nature of the ancient settlement which raises the price of installing electricity lines and means that water has to be obtained on an individual basis without adequate installations.

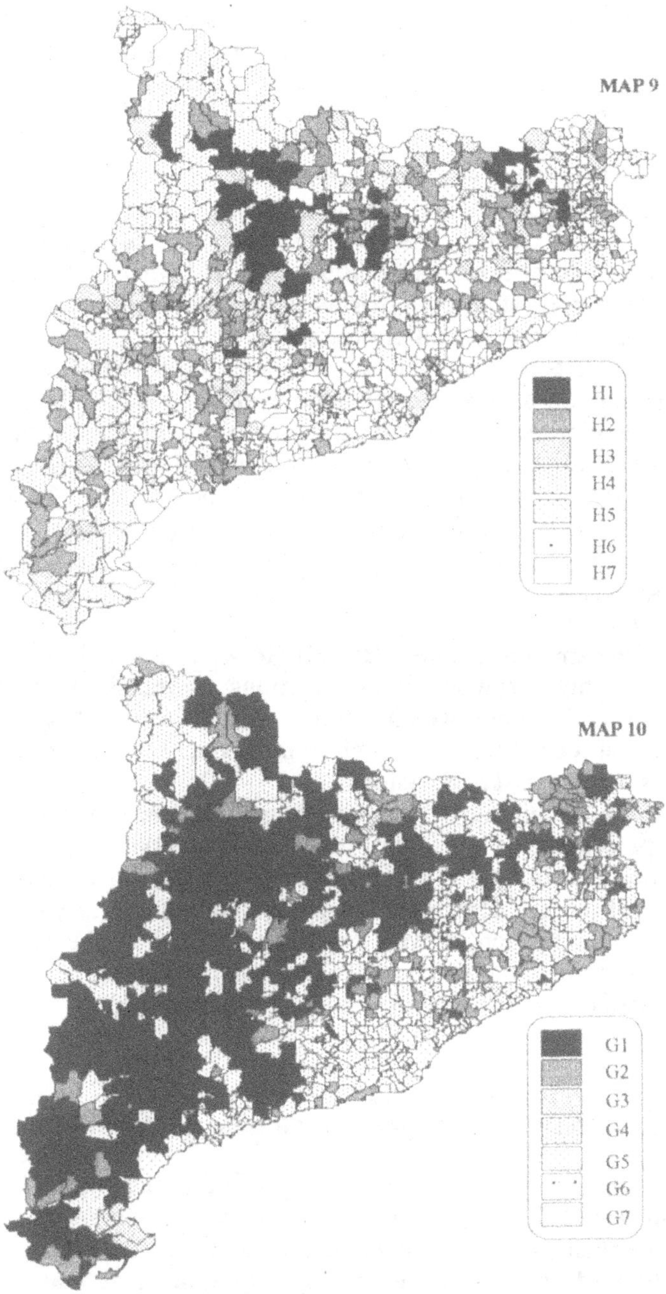

Figure 16.5 Map 9 Clustering of the housing variables
Map 10 Final clustering

The next group (H2), includes a much greater number of municipalities than H1 (152). These are to be found dispersed throughout the territory without forming any major groupings. The houses are also old and their state of repair poor but they have access to the basic services of water and electricity.

Group H3 is comparatively small (84 municipalities). The most numerous group is to be found, as the map illustrates, close to the largest grouping of the H2 cluster. The main distinguishing factor lies in the fact that the percentage of houses built after 1970 is higher and, consequently the houses in a poor state of repair as well as those which do not enjoy basic services constitute a smaller proportion.

The largest group of municipalities belong to H4, which extends basically across the western half of Catalonia in an almost unbroken stretch (with the exception of the most dynamic areas due to tourism in the Pyrenees and the profitable agriculture in the irrigated areas at the bottom of the Central Depression) and dispersed throughout eastern Catalonia. The basic services and infrastructure are generally available, the state of repair of the housing is good though the lack of dynamism in the municipalities of this group is visible in the medium to low percentages of housing constructed after 1970.

Two of the smallest groups (H5 and H6 with 12 and 36 cases respectively), are highly dispersed with situations of transition between the earlier groups and the one which follows. The housing in both cases is of relatively recent construction, though is in a poor state of repair and with deficiencies in the service provision.

Finally the remaining 250 municipalities (H7) are in the best conditions. The percentage of housing of recent construction is high, the state of repair is good and in only a few cases are their gaps in the services analyzed. Most of the municipalities are grouped along a strip which follows the coast up from the frontier with the River Ebro, where the largest tourist offer is concentrated and which widens considerably in the more industrial *comarcas*. Isolated cases appear again in the tourist areas and irrigated areas of the Pyrenees.

A summary of the clustering pattern: an essay of classification

Given that income, an undoubtedly important indicator, had not been included in any of the earlier clusters we carried out an analysis with the results of the clusters of housing, population and income. Thus income was given a third of the overall weighting while the rest was distributed between population and housing. The result illustrates clearly the influence of income, though due this is due to it having been adjudicated a third of the total weight. We believe, however, it to be more correct to use the 8 variables selected at the same level.

The grouping of the 8 variables in 7 groups gives a result which corroborates to a certain extent the division between rich and poor Catalonia which we identified in the introduction. The two groups of municipalities which reflect this situation are G1 and G4. while the other groups are much smaller in number and as in the clusters analyzed above constitute extreme cases or those in transition. The two main groups correspond roughly to the interior and the coast, though there are many exceptions which need to be explained (map 10).

The first group (G1), which comprises almost 400 municipalities, represents Catalonia at its most disadvantaged and marginal according to the indicators analyzed. It extends in an almost unbroken stretch through the western half of the territory with very few exceptions. Population densities are low and ageing indices high. The growth rate is negative or very low when positive. Ageing is particularly marked in agrarian populations, which when we take into consideration that the main activity in this area is agriculture the variable related to the replacement of agrarian production takes on extra significance. The future of most of the farms is highly uncertain and the ratio between young and old people engaged in agriculture is in parts greater than 1000%, in most cases greater than 250% and only in 16 municipalities is positive. Income is, on the other hand, almost always below the average for Catalonia, the construction sector has been particularly depressed in recent years and the state of repair of housing is almost always poor. Similarly, it is here that the services and infrastructure are in their worst state.

The other extreme is represented by the cluster of G4 that provides the other side of the coin in virtually all senses and is representative of Catalonia at its most highly developed, including the coastal and mountain tourist *comarcas* and the industrial areas (335 in total). This is the youngest sector of Catalonia with a positive natural ant total growth. The level of income is in almost all cases above the Catalan average, the dynamism of the construction sector is an example of this positive outlook as most of the housing is of recent construction, are in a good state of repair and enjoy a whole range of services. There are also isolated cases which correspond to this group in inland areas where agriculture based on irrigation produces high income levels, demographic indicators are positive, the continuity of productive activities is assured in most cases and the quality of construction is high and the services adequate.

The group G2, is the transitional group between these two situations (128 municipalities), highly fragmented and distributed throughout the territory or with small centres in which a negative variable is usually to be found. The level of income, is for example lower than in G4 but higher than that in G1; ageing is not quite as marked though population growth is low or equivalent to zero. Housing conditions are adequate and the proportion constructed in recent years is medium to high.

The remaining groups add up to no more than 63 municipalities. G5 (29 municipalities) represents the extreme cases in the best situation and this is seen in their position on the map between the area dominated by the G4 cluster. They are municipalities with a very young population, a very strong demographic growth and a very high level of income. The indicators of housing and services are always positive. They are municipalities with major developments in the tourist or industrial sectors, but they are also municipalities with a residential function in the area around Barcelona.

Finally, in clusters G6 (28 municipalities) and G3 (a mere 6 municipalities) most of the variables coincide with those of groups G2 and 4, though with higher levels of income – generally above the Catalan average. They are distributed randomly in areas where these two latter groups are predominant.

Conclusions

The process of redistribution engendered by the Government, together with local initiatives, are helping to rid the territory of evident imbalances, though this has not been entirely successful. Circumstances arising from their location or those of a structural nature mean that the marginal areas have a certain territorial mobility, that some municipalities can breathe life into their economy with endogenous and external resources and they can escape from the general decline in which they are immersed. However, there are also municipalities or groups of municipalities that given the size and age of their population, and their inaccessibility, have few chances of improving. This is what we have tried to demonstrate throughout this study.

The marginal areas are now not always the old depressed areas, principally in mountain areas (Majoral 1997). Some of the most depressed mountain *comarcas* a few years ago are now among the first in Catalonia in terms of income and quality of life (mainly in Val d'Aran and Cerdanya). However, not even in these *comarcas* is there a uniformity between the municipalities as there is a marked territorial fragmentation, which requires an analysis at the level of the municipality from which we can conclude a classification of growing territorial imbalances.

A prior review of a larger number of variables which have not been included suggests that, with more or with alternative variables, the results would have been very similar.

Note

This article has been prepared as part of the research project entitled *Delimitación y Análisis de las áreas marginales en Cataluña*, funded by the Dirección General de Investigación Científica y Técnica (DGICYT) of the Ministerio de Ecudación y Cultura (research Project PB950905).

References

Font, J. (1995), 'Infrastructura de comunicación y conexión de Catalunya: La red viaria, herencias del pasado y perspectives de futuro', in Majoral R. and SánchezAguilera, D. (eds.), *III Encuentro de Geografia CatalunyaEuscal Herria*, pp. 147164, Àrea d'Anàlisi Geogràfica Regional, Universitat de Barcelona: Barcelona.

Font, J. (1996), 'Marginal zones and road networks in Catalonia (Spain)', in Singh, R.B. (ed.), *Disasters environment and development*, Oxford & IBH Publishing Co. Pvt. Ltd.: Delhi, pp. 415428

GarcíaColl, A. and SánchezAguilera, D. (1994), 'Diferències territorals en l'envelliment de les estructures de població; l'exemple de les comarques de l'interior de Tarragona', in *Treballs de la Societat de Geografia*, vol IX:37, pp. 2941.

LópezPalomeque, P. (1996), 'Rural tourism as a strategy in the development of marginal areas. The case of Catalonia', in Furlani, M.E. et al. (eds.) *Development issues in Marginal Regions II. Policies and Strategies*, Universidad Nacional de Cuyo: Mendoza (Rep. Argentina), pp. 4962.

LópezPalomeque, P. and Majoral, R. (1980), 'Emigración y cambio económico en el Pirineo Catalan', *Supervivencia de la Montaña. Actas del Coloquio HispanoFrancés sobre Áreas de Montaña*, pp. 299332, Ministerio de Agricoltura, Pesca y Alimentación: Madrid.

Majoral, R. (1997), Desarrollo en áreas de montaña, *Geographicalia*, vol. 34, pp. 2350, Universidad de Zaragoza. Zaragoza

Majoral, R., Font, J. and SánchezAguilera, D. (1996), 'Regional development policies and incentives in marginal areas of Catalonia', in Furlani, M.E. et al. (eds.), *Development issues in Marginal Regions II. Policies and Strategies*, Universidad Nacional de Cuyo: Mendoza (Rep. Argentina), pp. 2748.

Persson, L.O. (1997), 'Clusters of marginal microregions', in Jussila, H., Leimgruber, W. and Majoral, R. (eds.) *Perceptions of marginality*, Ashgate: Aldershot, pp. 8199.

SánchezAguilera, D. (1996), 'Evaluating marginality through demographic indicators', in Singh, R.B. and Majoral, R. (eds.), Development issues in Marginal Regions, Oxford & IBH Publishing Co. Pvt. Ltd.: Delhi, pp. 133147.

SánchezAguilera, D., Majoral, R. and Font, J. (1997), 'Marginality migration: A case in the Spanish Pyrenees', in Jones, G. and Morris, A. (eds.), *Issues of environmental, economic and social stability in the development of Marginal Regions: Practices and Evaluation*, pp. 205217, Universities of Strathclyde and Glasgow: Glasgow.

Tzamarias, N. (1997), 'A Socioeconomic Typology for the Scottish Districts and Highlands and Islands', in Jones, G. and Morris, A. (eds.), *Issues of environmental, economic and social stability in the development of Marginal Regions: Practices and Evaluation*, pp. 2547, Universities of Strathclyde and Glasgow: Glasgow.

17 State support and rural dynamics

LARS OLOF PERSSON

Increasing variation

Throughout Europe and North America, there is an increasing variation in growth rates and demographic trends between different rural areas. This is not a simple reflection of differences in peripherality in a geographical sense. More often than before, neighbouring areas with similar resource base and infrastructure perform differently in economic. There is a general finding from empirical studies, that structural factors do not provide a statistically significant explanation of the performance of each region. This leads to the question if there is such a thing as a theory of rural development, which can explain these processes occurring in different countries and regions? Modern explanatory theories consider less tangible development factors like 'innovative milieu' and 'civility' which is defined as the set of relationships occurring within a geographical area which bring unity to the production system, economic actors and an industrial culture. This is supposed to generate dynamic process of collective learning and acting as a way to reduce uncertainty and risk in the innovation process. This explanation is based on theories on endogenous growth. Local factors, local traditions and institutions are supposed to be important.

Since the early 1990s, in Swedish regional policy there is an increasing concern for stimulating growth in each region. This concern for growth is in principle valid both in rural and urban areas. The underlying model is that increased growth should be attained by resource mobilisation and creative co-operation or partnerships between actors – private and public at the central as well as at the local level. At the same time, however, the bulk of public resources especially to rural and marginal areas are still tied to policy programs aiming at compensating for poor economic conditions – i.e., limited growth – by levelling out the socio-economic conditions at the individual level. (SOU 1997:13) This is an important part of the still important welfare state in Sweden. In this paper, we raise the question if this is a restriction for the new policy focusing on the dynamics of rural change.

The first aim of the paper is to describe the emerging variation in growth rates between different regions, especially rural areas, in Sweden and to analyse the current pattern of public transfers to individuals to these areas. The importance of a careful analysis at the lowest territorial level, i.e. the microregional level, is stressed. The aim of the paper is also to give a background to a discussion on a potential shift in the implementation of certain public policy programs in order to more efficiently support the endogenous growth processes. This shift could include a change in focus from subsidies to individuals towards a support to local processes.

Is there a hidden marginality?

In Sweden, marginal regions have been among the regions, which are most protected and compensated by means of transfers within the welfare system. This is valid whether the marginal region is defined as a vast sparsely populated part of the country, a remote county, a set of small peripheral municipalities, a poor housing district in a city or a village in the outback's of a rural region. It is the sum of a range of policy instruments directed to individuals, enterprises, local governments, county councils and county administrative boards, which produces this general support. The short supply of local resources and concentration of low-income households are the underlying rationale for this kind of transfer. In Sweden as in many other countries, marginality has also been strongly associated with poor accessibility, which means that most sparsely populated areas are likely to be considered marginal. It is probably true that – in the thirty years of continuous expansion of the public sector until the mid 80s – several marginal regions became overcompensated in terms of public resources within different sectors. This means, among other things, that the real face of marginality has not always been revealed.

The role of the state in a liberating economy is to facilitate competitiveness of production and services by adjusting the labour force, dealing with the fallout of restructuring, to provide basic services and infrastructure and to encourage sustainability. Stringent fiscal policy to reduce national debts in nations with a fiscal imbalance and the downsizing of government programs are universal prerequisites for the restructuring process to have effects. This constrains the redistribute role of the state which can then be questioned and modified, such that social services, including education and health are downsized and privatisation of government services is encouraged. Modifying the regional redistribution mechanisms, downsizing programs, and privatising others all have implications for marginal areas. The adjustment of the social welfare system and changes to the income redistribution programmes are especially important in Sweden.

Hence, in the present period of cut-backs in the public sector in Sweden, high unemployment, rapid restructuring of the economy as a whole and changing mobility patterns, the spatial distribution of marginality seems to become fragmented (Persson and Wiberg, 1995; Johansson and Persson, 1996). It is not obvious which types of localities and households that are most exposed to changes in material living conditions. Cutbacks in public budgets and structural change are met by socio-economic groups and individuals in different ways. Some profit from the increasing market orientation in all sectors, others are hampered by insufficient compensation within the welfare system. A probable shift in attitudes towards more individualistic life-styles accentuates this fragmentation (cf. Persson *et al.*, 1997).

Modifying the regional redistribution mechanisms

The recession and political shifts in Sweden in the 90s have shown a tendency to an increasing segmentation of the labour market, increasing income differentials and consequently reinforced housing segregation. Tax reforms and revised wage policy contribute to increasing differences in disposable income. Some observers take this as signs of a necessary decomposition of some of the disadvantages of the Swedish welfare model. The spatial outcomes of this process are discussed. Some argue that the net effects will be that a few city regions take the lead in increasing productivity in the Swedish economy as a whole. Marginal and rural areas often considered to become losers and still more dependent on compensatory policy intervention (Fournier and Persson, 1995).

Still, however, at the macroregional level Sweden stands out as a country with a comparatively even distribution of disposable income. This is due to both a relatively even distribution of gross incomes and a redistribution via the tax and transfer system. In the mid 80s, the welfare state was redistributing 53% of the differences in incomes, which is more than in any other country in Europe. Consequently, after redistribution the poverty rate was less than in most other countries in Europe. This has, however, put a heavy burden on the taxpayers and there is a rather broad consensus in Parliament that the tax rate has to be lowered in order to avoid further distortions of the economy. Income transfers to households are worth one fourth of GDP. However, it is not only the size but also the efficiency of the transfer system, which is questioned. According to one estimate the same equalisation could be achieved with transfers worth only 3% of GDP

(Söderström, 1988). Hence, in theory, substantial cutbacks could be done without negative effects on income distribution. In practice, however, it is widely questioned whether this is possible.

There is a continuous debate whether the high taxes is an obstacle to growth in the national and regional economy. It is also a permanent debate whether the still ambitious social security programme is an obstacle or a prerequisite to individual and collective action, e.g., endogenous local processes. Finally, there is currently an intensified debate on whether increasing income differences between socio-economic groups would lead to increased growth and more jobs, particularly in household services. These debates are far from an end, but reveal that there is an increasing concern about the role of the state and the subsidies at one hand side and the dynamics of the economy at the other. This has bearing also on the dynamics of regional and rural change. It seems that there is a general shift from the traditional regional policy objective of equalising the living conditions between regions towards the goal to stimulate growth in as many regions as possible.

Equality at the macroregional level

Administratively, Sweden is subdivided into 24 counties. Most counties contain currently quite expansive regional centres, small towns and rural areas - the latter two types of localities showing an increasing variation in growth and decline. At the county level there is no doubt that the long period of expansion of the public sector and the subsidies to individuals, business firms and municipalities has led to a more or less equal income (Figure 17.1) and employment situation. The geographical pattern in income distribution is relatively stable over this long time period; with three metropolitan regions show the highest per capita figures. The variation in regional employment figures is more ambiguous. Some metropolitan counties have lost a substantial number of jobs (*Malmöhus* and *Göteborg*), while a few predominantly rural counties with expanding SME-sector have gained both in rank and in number of jobs (e.g., *Jönköping, Kronoberg*). Among other things, the decreasing variation in income levels and demand for labour between counties has led to less long distance migration.

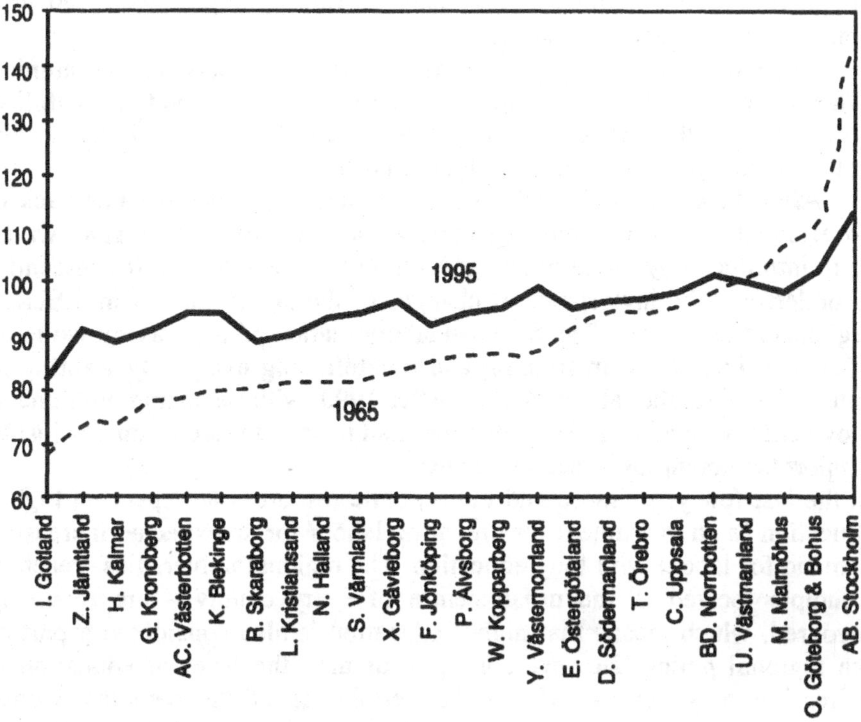

Figure 17.1 Decreasing variation between counties in taxation basis (income/capita) 1965-95. Index of Sweden 1995=100, counties ranked according to 1965 figures

Source: Kullenberg and Persson 1997

More independent municipalities - but shrinking resources

Most social services in Sweden are produced by municipalities and county councils. Previously, central government had strong influence on the allocation of resources in each municipality. There is a trend toward stronger independence, reinforced by the way resources are now transferred to local authorities, i.e., largely in the form of a lump sum. This leaves more room for local priorities.

Local priorities are also decisive for the local income tax rate. There is a tendency for high-income municipalities to keep local taxes low, while low-income municipalities usually have to finance expensive social programmes by increasing the tax level.

Altogether, we anticipate increasing differences between the municipalities due to local policies concerning service subsidies and accessibility. Still, however, the general principle is that there should be a public control of the quality of services and a regulation of fees.

After the elections in 1994, when the Social Democrats came back in government, in practice most of these reforms of the welfare state which were introduced by the previous government are maintained. It is essential to understand the importance of changes of the labour market in different regions in this process. The Swedish labour market policy was known to be offensive, i.e., active in training and rehabilitating everybody wanting to enter or re-enter the labour market. After 1990, with persisting high unemployment, the labour market policy has had to spend more resources just to support the unemployed economically.

In the last few years more and more public resources are spent on higher education as an instrument for preparing labour for an expected increasing demand for labour with long education. The regional universities – each in principle located to the urban centre of every county – are relatively favoured, which means that higher education is also considered a part of the regional policy. However, in spite of that, the level of education is increasing only very slowly in the peripheries of the counties. Correspondingly, the creation of new jobs requiring higher education is limited in these peripheries.

In summary, the following spatial characteristics are expected to emerge from the processes discussed above:

a) A general trend of decentralisation of economic activity and political power with a stronger impact by both individual, commercial and local interests in regional development;
b) A concentration of economic activity, jobs requiring higher education and qualified services to the urban centre of each county;
c) A more uneven distribution of wealth and services between socio-economic regions, discernible primarily at the microregional level;
d) Marginality in terms of unemployment, underemployment, low disposable income level, ethnic and economic segregation, etc. appears in all types of regions, metropolitan as well as rural.
e) This variation is to also reflected by the dependency on state subsidies in different regions.

Increasing variation at the microregional level

This increasing variation in the dependency of public transfers to individuals (Figure 17.2)[1], the education level of the population (Figure 17.3) and the income per capita (Figure 17.4) is evident between the microregions in six municipalities. These municipalities represent different types of regions. The three graphs illustrate – in a compact format – some of the most important dynamics of regional change in contemporary Sweden. In short:

A) Economic performance is poorest in the rural communes and dependency on transfers is highest there.

B) Variation in income level is extremely big in the metropolitan region and increases most there.

C) Variation in public subsidy per capita increases substantially in all types of municipalities.

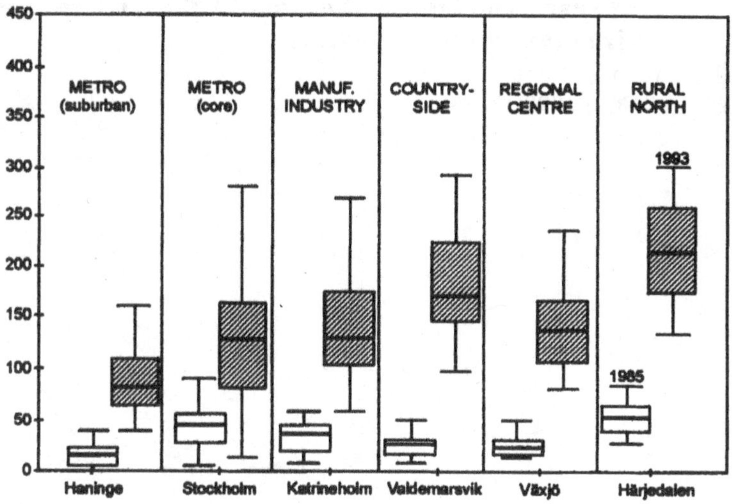

Figure 17.2 Increasing microregional variation in dependency on public transfers to individuals 1985-93, microregions in six municipalities in Sweden, 100 SEK per capita 16-64 years

Source: SOU 1997:13

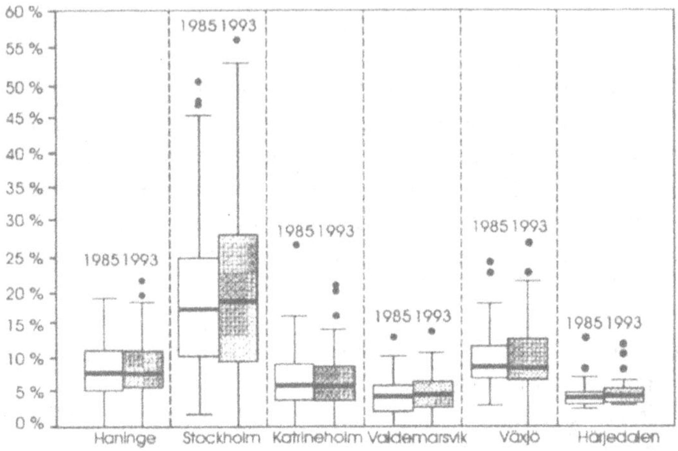

Figure 17.3 Microregional variation in percentage of population 16-64 years with higher education 1990-93, microregions in six municipalities in Sweden

Source: SOU 1997:13

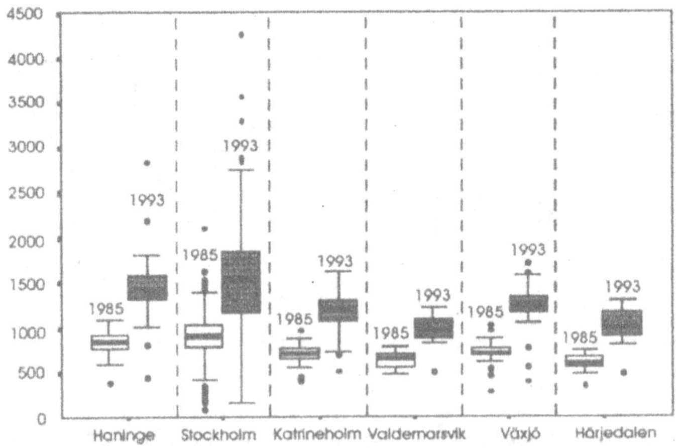

Figure 17.4 Increasing microregional variation in income per capita 1985-93, microregions in six municipalities in Sweden, 100 SEK per capita 16-64 years

Source: SOU 1997:13

Microregional growth and dependency

Hence, there is empirical evidence that economic performance – measured in income per capita – varies increasingly between relatively small geographical areas. We are still in the very beginning of understanding the underlying processes, but we assume that at least two explanations are relevant:

1 Socio-economic segregation processes occur along with increasing disposable income variation, labour market segmentation and less public responsibility for service provision in different areas terms (cf. Berglund and Persson 1997; Bradley 1996).
2 Local endogenous growth processes are initiated unevenly according to different historical, cultural and institutional settings in small localities.

A further analysis of the growth rate – in terms of income per capita – between microregions within or rural commune in northern Sweden (*Härjedalen*) shows that there is a wide variation (Figure 17.5). There are a number of small regions, which show a more than doubled income per capita between 1985 and 1993. During the same period, there are a small number of regions, which do not report any increase in the income level at all. Furthermore, there is no significant relation between different kinds of subsidies to the small regions and their performance in terms of income growth.

In about half of all 39 villages/housing districts in the rural commune of *Härjedalen*, total subsidies to individual are higher that the income per capita. These villages which so strongly depend on subsidies are at the same time the poorest.

Further research issues

There are at least four contradictions involved in this process. These contradictions have to be solved in a political process at both the local and the central level. The also call for new empirical and theoretical studies on the new faces of marginality and the role of the state versus local action.

1 The process of equalisation of socio-economic conditions continues at the county level, while the variation increases at the microregional level. There is not yet a general awareness of this shift in focus of the regional problem. There is a need for empirical research of the spatial pattern of marginality.

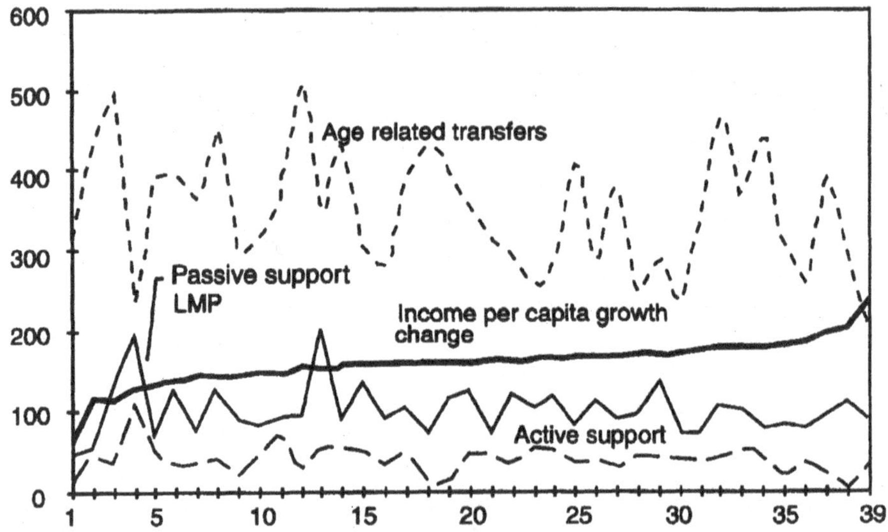

Figure 17.5 Income growth 1985-93 and three kinds of transfers[2] in microregions, Härjedalen, transfers in 100 SEK 1993. Index for income 1985 = 100

Source: FORA and Statistics Sweden

2 There is a tendency to delegate the responsibility for regional and rural development to local and regional actors, but at the same time there is a strong demand for responsibility and intervention from the central government. There is a need for more clear rules both for the limits of the responsibility for each actor and for a rational negotiation process between these actors.

3 The increasing variation in growth rates within rural regions can no longer be explained by structural factors such as density of population, distance to markets and supply of resources. It seems that less tangible development factors play an increasing role in stimulating growth. It is a challenge to rural researchers to develop methods and data to reveal these intangibles and develop the theories for the interlinks between endogenous growth processes and state intervention.

Notes

1 The vertical box for each municipality and each year includes 50% of all microregions (housing districts or villages) which come closest to the average figure for each municipality, the distance between the horizontal marks include all microregions except the extreme outlyers (dots).

2 Age related support: pensions, support to families with children, sickness benefits. Passive support: unemployment benefits in the Labour Market Policy (LMP), welfare grants. Active support; education grants.

References

Berglund, S and Persson, L. O. (1997), 'La restructuration du marché du travail et les processus ségregatifs à Stockholm', in Martens, A, and Vervaeke, M (eds.) *La polarisation sociale des villes européennes*, Antropos-Economica Publishers: Paris.

Bradley, H., (1996), *Fractured Identities. Changing Patterns of Inequality*, Polity Press: Cambridge.

Fournier, S. and Persson, L O (1995), 'The Fall and Revival of the Swedish Welfare Model', in Eskelinen, H and Snickars, F., (eds.), *Competitive European Peripheries*? Springer-Verlag: Berlin.

Johansson, M and Persson, L.O., (1996), *Extending the Reach. Essays on Differing Mobility Patterns in Sweden*, SIR/Fritzes: Stockholm.

Kullenberg, J. and Persson, L.O. (1997), *Tänjbara räckvidder. Lokala arbetsmarknader i förändring*, SIR/Fritzes: Stockholm.

Persson, L O, Westholm, E., and Fuller, T., (1997),'Two Contexts, One Outcome: The Importance of Lifestyle Choice in Creating Rural Jobs in Canada and Sweden', in Bollman, R.D. & Bryden, J (eds.), *Rural Employment: An International Perspective*, CAB International: New York.

Persson, L O. (1998), 'Clusters of Marginal Microregions', in Jussila, H. Leimgruber, W., and Majoral, R. (eds.) *Perceptions of marginality*. Ashgate Publishing: Aldershot.

Persson, L.O. and Wiberg, U., (1995), *Microregional Fragmentation. Contrasts between a Welfare State and a Market Economy*, Physica-Verlag: Heidelberg.

SOU 1997:13 *Regionpolitik för hela Sverige*, Betänkande fran REKO-STAT-utredningen, (Commission Report on Regional Consequences of Restructuring of the Public Sector).

18 Regional development problems of the geographically marginal Binga district in the Zambezi valley of Zimbabwe

JOHAN DAHL AND DANIEL TEVERA

Introduction

The rate of development across geographic space is uneven and the resultant unequal distribution of development is of concern to both planners and policy-makers in the Third World as is reflected in various National Development Plans that indicate concern with issues such as diversified and balanced growth (Mabogunje, 1980; Simon, 1990). It is evident, however, that beyond the rhetorical pronouncements, the development of problem areas is not being given sufficient attention by practitioners of development planning in most Third World countries because the issue is not considered a major political problem. The dualistic economies in the Third World, which are characterised by an underdeveloped traditional sector and a modern/urban sector and growth islands in the rural areas, have contributed to the persistent regional inequalities. The observation made by Seers (1969) that the gap between the rich and poor groups in fact increased during the United Nations' 'Development Decade' of the 1960s is, therefore, not surprising. During the 1990s the situation has become more critical as the number of people living in poverty has increased; unemployment rates are considerably higher; sub-national inequalities have intensified; and north-south cleavages have grown (Sacha, 1993; Hesselberg, 1995).

Zimbabwe, like most developing countries, is characterised by substantial socio-spatial polarization in levels of well-being of the population (Chimhowu and Tevera, 1991). In Zimbabwe, regional differentiation has been associated with physical or natural factors on the basis of which agro-ecological maps indicating areas of greatest and lowest agricultural potential have been developed. Human resource-based development variables such as infrastructural development, or potential human activities also have been developed to indicate existing differentials within administrative regions (Zinyama 1987, Simon 1986, Chimhowu & Tevera 1991). Excluding the national economic core, that comprises the urban areas and the high veld, the Zimbabwean national economic space largely consists of regions experiencing several constraints to development. Within these regions are found most of the spatially marginal areas.

Spatial marginality manifests itself at several levels of spatial resolution, i.e. global, regional, national and sub-national. At the sub-national level, marginal areas are regions that are often peripheral to the rest of the country and invariably have been marginalized compared to other areas in the same state. According to Mehretu (1986, p.31) there is a tendency for 'some classes of people residing in 'central' locations to pre-empt development benefits, while less advantaged masses living in 'marginal' areas continue to lose out in the competition for development resources and access to input and output markets'. In Zimbabwe powerful politicians have often used their influence to channel resources to their constituencies and in the process thereby diverting resources away from the depressed and needy areas.

This paper focuses on marginality at the sub-national level with special reference to one specific marginal area in Zimbabwe, i.e. Binga District that lies in the Zambezi Valley. Of particular interest are the natural conditions and state policies that have caused the underdevelopment of the area. Issues such as the district's long-standing isolation, the fragile physical environment, and a marginal agricultural base, systematic marginalization during the colonial period, and a post-colonial state that is still in search of a regional development policy, help to explain why Binga District is under development. The district remains one of the most impoverished regions in the country as is reflected by socio-economic indicators such as low income levels, high unemployment levels, low levels of investment and high out migration rates.

Location of the study area

Binga District is located in the north-eastern area of Matabeleland North province, and most of it lies in the Zambezi River basin in an area covering 13,200 square kilometres (Figure 18.1). The district shares the Zambezi River boundary with Zambia and a land boundary with four districts: Kariba, Gokwe North, Lupane and Hwange. The remote location, far away from the core areas of the country, makes Binga a peripheral district in the

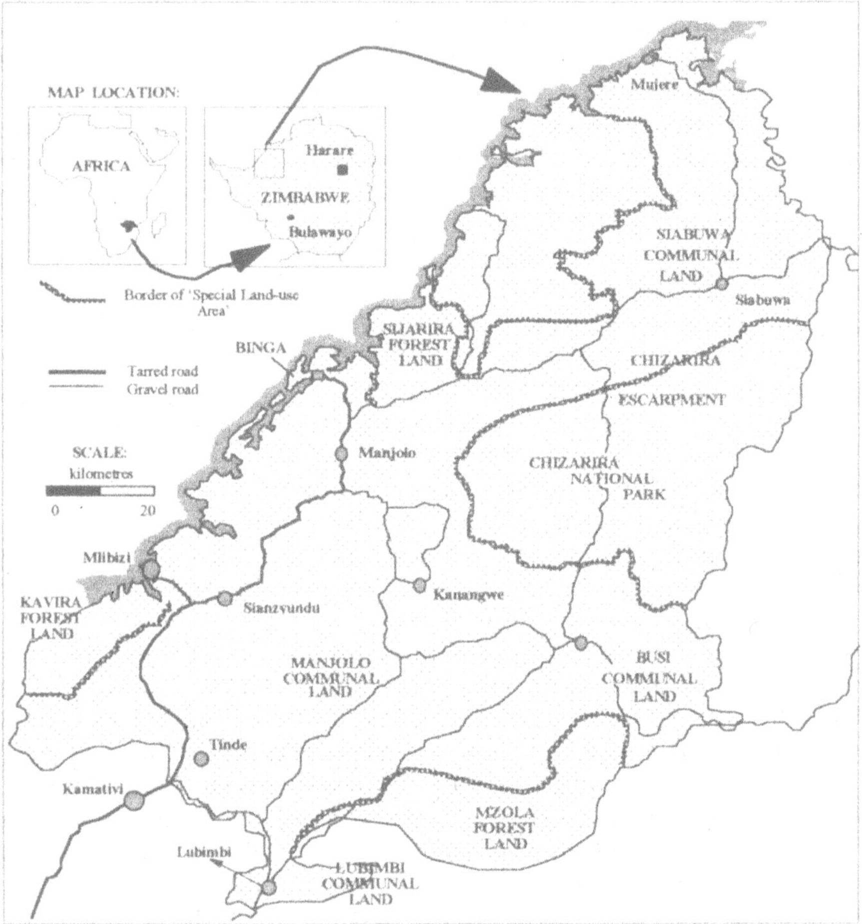

Figure 18.1 The location of the study area

geographical sense although it is also peripheral in the political economy sense as is manifested by infrastructural underdevelopment and low levels of economic performance compared to the majority of other 55 districts in the country.

The district is mostly situated in the low veld where the average altitude is below 600 metres and where, because of the semi-arid environment, agro-ecological potential is lowest. The district is semi-arid and the dry savanna woodland, mainly covered by mopane trees, is the dominant type of vegetation. Geologically the land mostly consists of sedimentaries, sandstone, regosols and lithosols which generally produce soils that are shallow, sandy, highly erodible and have limited agricultural potential (Moyo *et al.*, 1993). Better soils are found in the higher land in the south-east, e.g. the Lusulu area and in the Chizarira plateau, which is a National Park and is not available for agricultural activities.

The district lies in agro-ecological regions III, IV and V and the land area under these regions is 20%, 20% and 60% respectively (Figure 18.2). The agro-ecological regions represent natural regions and farming areas that were delimited largely on the basis of annual rainfall totals and incidence. The relatively high rainfall received in agro-ecological region III makes it possible to cultivate the land semi-intensively while the low rainfall amounts in regions IV and V only permit semi-extensive and extensive cultivation, respectively. The drought prone region V receives less than 450-mm annual rainfall and this makes it only suitable for extensive animal husbandry and cultivation of the drought resistant bulrush-millet. More than 50% of the total area comprises communal areas and is under the jurisdiction of the local authority, Binga Rural District Council, while the remaining area is occupied by National Parks, Safari Areas and government forest-land

The area is characterised by a fragile ecological environment that precludes dense settlement and intensive agriculture. A combination of diseases and erratic rainfall has made it difficult to keep livestock, such as cattle, goats and sheep. Before the implementation of the tsetse fly eradication programme in the 1960s it was difficult to keep cattle in the then frontier region. Outside the agricultural sector employment opportunities are negligible and are confined to fishing. The district lacks resources besides wildlife and this has made it unattractive to both private and public sector investors.

The historical backdrop

Binga District has always been a backward periphery of Zimbabwe since the early colonial days dating as far back as 1890 when the country was formally incorporated as a British colony and later evolved as a settler dominated economy in which the political and economic entitlements of the African people were denied and severely restricted. The colonial state forced the Tonga people into paid labour by the introduction of a hut tax in 1897/98 (Ncube, 1986). The hut tax, which had to be paid in cash, forced Tonga males to temporarily migrate to commercial farms, mines or urban areas in order to raise money for the tax. The manipulation of labour through taxes and land expropriation was not confined to Binga District but practised by the colonial state throughout the country during the early colonial period (Arrighi, 1970; Tevera, 1981). The process of labour migration that was initiated by the hut tax has continued up to the present day although the push forces have changed. During the 1990s young Tonga males in Binga leave their homes in search of money which is required to pay for basic needs such as food, clothing, education and health.

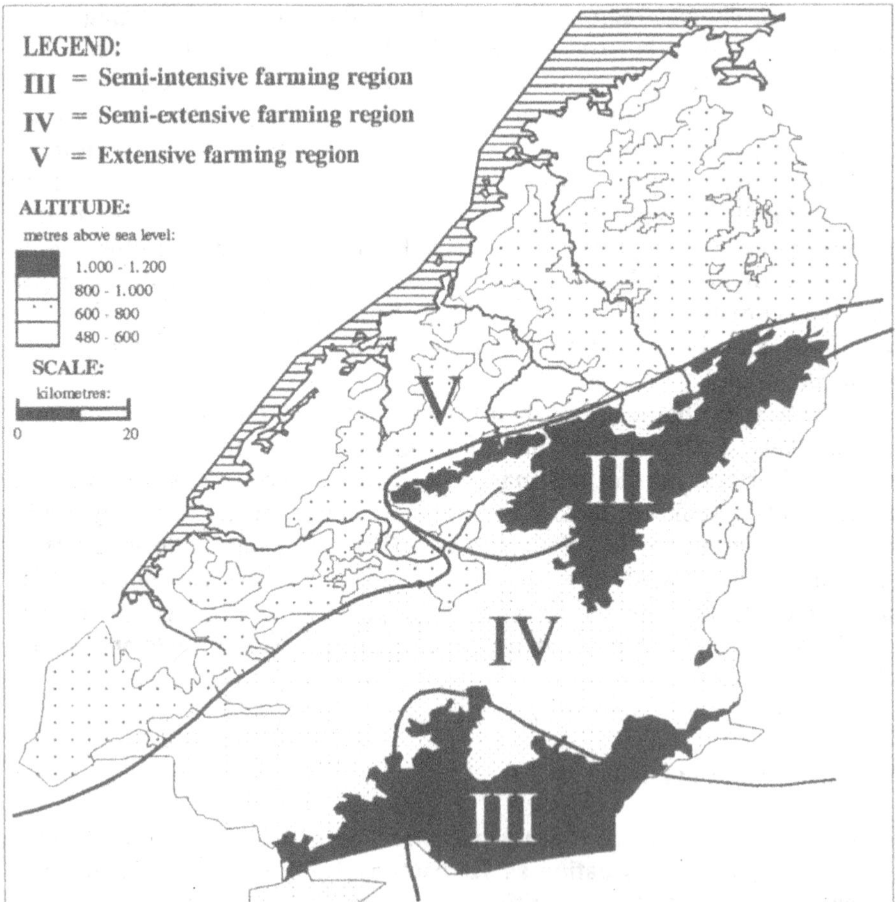

Figure 18.2 The agro-ecological regions of Binga District

The Tonga people living in the area suffered during the 1950s when some of their land was expropriated by the state. They were subsequently resettled to make way for the construction of the huge Kariba Dam project whose goal was to provide industry and the urban areas with cheap electricity. However, the resettlement of communities in order to construct big dams for electricity or irrigation has always been problematic if not planned with considerable care. Wisner (1988) argues that large-scale hydro-electric dams in Africa have caused the resettled rural families a lot of suffering in the form of diseases, famine and social disorientation while the urban based elite have been the beneficiaries of the electricity.

Coercion was used by the colonial state to resettle 23,000 Tonga people inhabiting the area when the Kariba Dam was built during the early 1960s and in the process they lost control over land and water resources which had hitherto been a crucial part of their life. Figure 18.3 shows the 15 Tonga chiefdoms, which were resettled from the Zambezi River lowlands to the uplands further, inland. The Tonga societies that were uprooted from their traditional homes were under severe stress for a long time after resettlement. Although the government distributed free food, such as maize, oil, sugar, salt, beans and game meat, during the first two years after resettlement, most families had not adjusted enough to the new environment to be self-sufficient in food production when the assistance was terminated. Also, the resettled families had to cope with the frequent flooding of their new lands on the Zambezi River banks, which disrupted their dominant economic activities, such as cultivating, fishing and hunting (Cousins and Cousins, 1989). By the mid-1970s food insecurity at the household level had became a real problem and many Tonga families had become more poverty stricken.

The impoverishment of the Tonga was compounded by various regulations that were used to deny them access to the lake water and fish resources previously granted by old traditional common access rights. Dahl (1997, p. 258) notes that through – the commodification of water as a hydro-electrical resource and wildlife as trophies and game viewing resources, the area came to be arranged, shaped and planned in a way that either included or excluded (some) people in the process of modernization'. For instance, regulations such as the issuing of limited licenses, restrictions on fishing net use and fishing points denied the majority of the local peasant families access to fish resources thereby effectively marginalizing them. The new way of living has up-rooted traditional fishing traditions that for long played a necessary complementary role to farming in the local community.

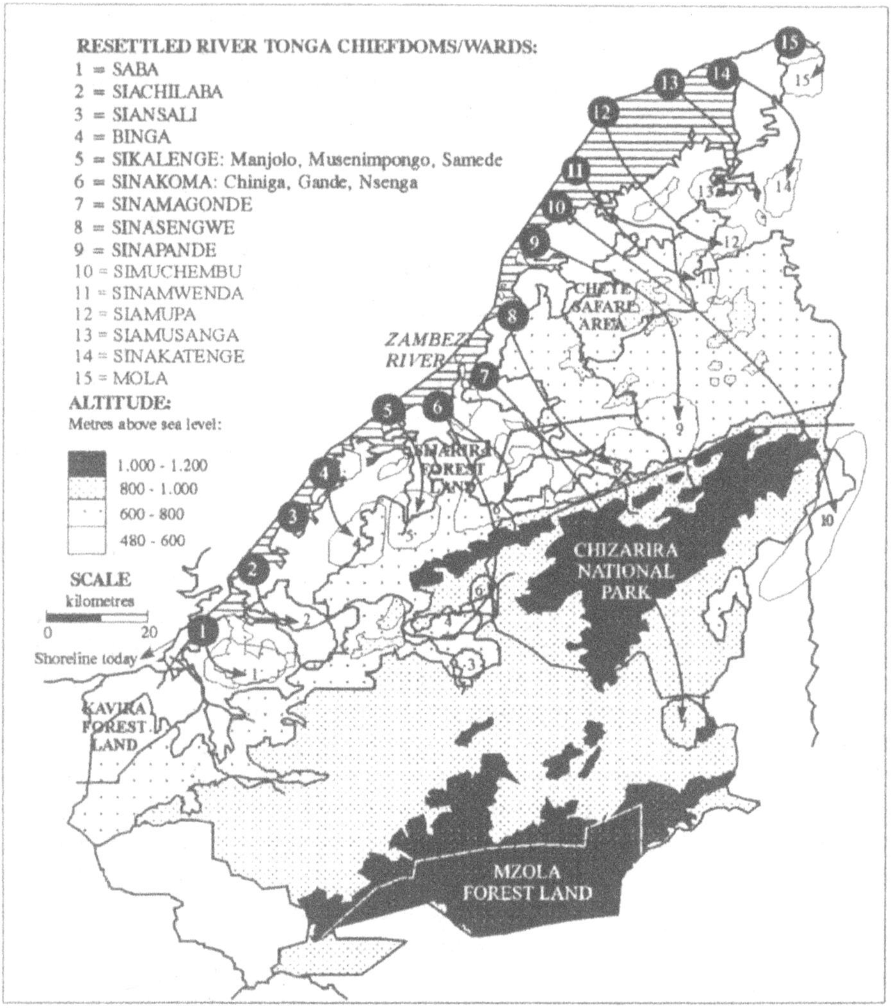

Figure 18.3 Location of the resettled river Tonga Chiefdoms

At the height of the liberation struggle in the 1970s Binga was a 'front-line district' bordering Zambia while Binga Centre was a strategic military point and like all front-line districts, economic and social development was severely curtailed due to the war activities. The problem was compounded by the neglect of roads to a state of disrepair which made access to the district difficult thereby further isolating the area from the rest of the country. After independence in 1980 local politicians from the district sought huge investments to re-dress past imbalances but political upheaval and the tension between the ruling ZANU PF party and the main opposition party, PF ZAPU, from 1982-1987 hampered development throughout the Matabeleland North Province until the signing of the unity accord in 1987.

Population, infrastructure and economic activities

Population

Binga District is mostly inhabited by the Tonga people who are an ethnic minority group that is also found in the neighbouring districts of North and South Gokwe, Hwange, Kariba and Lupane. The Tonga comprises about one per cent of the national population of Zimbabwe. Population in the Binga District increased by 85% from 47,448 in 1982 to 87,802 people in 1992 (CSO, 1994). However, the land under cultivation has not increased much and the pattern of land use and the technology of agricultural production has not changed significantly since independence as has been the case in some of Zimbabwe's rural areas. This has resulted in increased population pressure on the available land and other resources in the district. The population density almost doubled from 3.5 persons per square kilometre to 6.7 persons per square kilometre between 1982 and 1992. However, it remains lower than the 9 persons per square kilometre average for Matabeleland North Province and the 27 persons per square kilometre average for the entire country. The population of Binga District is almost exclusively confined to communal lands and a more accurate population density figure would therefore be about 10 persons per square kilometre, taking into account that more than 40% of the area is designated for other purposes than communal lands.

While 70% of the national population still live in the rural areas in Binga District 97% of the population live in the rural areas with the remaining 3% living in Binga growth point, with a population of 2,700, which is the only urban centre in the district. Natural annual population increase in the district was almost 4% in 1992 compared with the 2.8% average for Zimbabwe. The total fertility rate of above seven births per female in the child bearing age group makes Binga District one of the most fertile districts in the country (CSO, 1994).

Binga growth point reveals both some of the ingredients and limitations of the post independence growth centre strategy whereby a rural business centre is designated a growth point not on the basis of some economic criteria, such as growth potential, but on political considerations using a fairly arbitrary criteria. The growth point has found it difficult to attract investment partly because of its limited market but also because of the general underdevelopment of the district.

Infrastructural provision

During the 1980s the new ZANU-PF government that came into power in 1980 pursued policies aimed to transform the economy in order to redress the legacy of dualistic and unsustainable development mainly by narrowing the gap between rural and urban areas. According to the Growth With Equity policy document published by the government in 1981, the main objectives were to establish a society founded on socialist principles; to achieve economic growth and development; to provide and improve social and economic infrastructure and to resettle some of the peasant families living in the densely populated communal areas and pursuing unsustainable natural resource practices (Government of Zimbabwe, 1981).

The foregoing objectives were to be achieved through several sectoral initiatives such as land redistribution; reduction of rural poverty; employment creation; integration of the commercial and peasant agricultural sectors and development of human resources. Throughout the 1980s the government's rural development strategy involved the provision of bore holes, clinics, schools and tarred roads, especially in the communal areas. By 1986 remarkable social achievements had been made through increased access to education, health, potable water and drought relief. Between 1979 and 1986 enrolment in primary schools in the country increased by 36% and in secondary schools by 812% (CSO, 1989). Most of the new schools were located in the rural areas. Similarly, in the health sector the number of health employees had increased by about 50% during the same period.

The spectacular percentages recorded for the entire country are misleading because the social investments made were not evenly spread throughout the country. Binga District, for example, got less than their fair share of the new investments. In 1989 the district had weak transport linkages with the rest of the country as was reflected by the presence of a single main road which badly needed repair. It was not until 1992 that the road was tarred and hence could provide an all year link from Dete and Binga growth point to Hwange and Bulawayo. The road linking Binga with Harare, via Siabuwa to Gokwe, is still a gravel secondary road up to the district border with Mashonaland West Province and is unreliable during the rain season from November to March, when many of the Zambezi River tributaries overflow and make the road unpassable at several points. Similarly, most of the feeder roads, which are dust tracks, are under-serviced by buses due to the poor condition during the wet season. Consequently, the local population normally spends up to two hours walking long distances in order to catch a bus and often wait for long hours before a bus passes along. The absence of intra-district public transport (e.g., commuter buses, taxis) makes it extremely difficult to travel or transport goods over fairly short distances.

However, the safari areas are well linked with the economic core areas and generally it is much easier and quicker for one to travel from Harare or Bulawayo to the safari area in the district than it is to travel from one part of the district to the other. There are tarred airstrips at Binga growth point, Mlibizi, Kariyangwe and Sengwe mouth as well as in the national park and in Forestry Commission's land. However, no regular services exist as air transport is mostly used by tourists visiting the Safari Area or the National Park.

Over 200 boreholes and 300 wells drilled and dug by the DDF with support from various NGOs, supply many households with potable water (Gunby, 1993; Muir, 1993). Despite the efforts to supply water in the district between 1980 and 1992, only 40% of the households had access to drinking/cooking water from protected boreholes/wells in 1992. Between 1982 and 1992 the number of the households obtaining water from distant surface water sources dropped from 46% to 32% (CSO, 1989). The relatively high percentage of people collecting, drinking and cooking water from rivers, streams and dams suggests that many people are still exposed to diseases associated with contaminated water such as diarrhoea, bilharzia and dysentery.

According to the CSO (1994) in 1992 only 60% of the households were within 1000 metres from water sources while many households obtained water from points several kilometres away. Women in the district commonly spend more than half a day collecting water from distant sources (CSO, 1994). During the 1991/92 drought about 21 wells and 14 boreholes dried up completely and an additional 42 wells could only produce little water (Muir, 1993). Even though the area receives adequate rain during the year many water points still dry up during the late dry season in September-October.

Binga growth point is the only area, which has a reticulated sewage system in the district. About 84% of the households in the district have no toilet facilities and hence use the bush. The remaining population use blair latrines (10%) prevalent at the schools, flush toilets (4%) and shallow pits (2%) (CSO, 1994).

Before independence Binga was poorly served with health facilities but the position has improved considerably during the last 10 years. Binga now has a District hospital at Binga growth point and a small hospital at Binga growth point and a small hospital at Kariyangwe. However, the health clinics at the three rural service centres suffer from the problem of inadequate medicines and nursing staff. For instance, Sianzyundu Clinic, which has about 17,000, persons living in its service area, has a skeletal staff of only two nurses and one nurse-aid although a doctor visits the clinic once a month. Because of remoteness it has been difficult to retain doctors at Binga Hospital and often only one or two full time doctors are based at the hospital to service the entire district. The problem is compounded by the fact that Binga District is effected by malaria and 10 to 30% of the local population are estimated to be infected annually. Bilharzia is also a common disease due to the close proximity to Lake Kariba and other sources with stagnant water.

In 1980 there were 20 primary schools in the district and no secondary schools while in 1994 there were 56 primary schools and 9 secondary schools. In 1982 only 50% of the boys aged 15 to 19 had attained primary school education up to grade 4 or above but the figure increased to 90% in 1994. 76% of all females aged 5+ in the district have not attained (Grade 7) while 24% of the males have not. The above figures show that with respect to the provision of educational facilities, Binga District has done much better than the national average which is a reflection of the objective of the post-independence government to reduce regional inequalities within the country. Between 1980 and 1992 the number of primary schools in the district increased by 360% while the national average was a mere 40% increase. Similarly, during the same year the number of secondary schools increased by 900% and 600% for Binga District and the entire country respectively. Despite these impressive statistics the district still lags behind most of the other districts in the country in terms of access to education. In 1992, for example, only 49% of the people above 15 years of age were literate whereas the national average for the same period was 80%.

Enrolment in secondary schools is low in the district but this reflects a nation-wide tendency whereby only 20 – 30% of the primary school children continue with secondary education. The pass rate in the secondary schools is extremely low and it is not unusual for students to fail all the 'O' level subjects when they write the examinations after four years of secondary school education. Only 11% of the students at Binga Government Secondary School who wrote the 'O' level examinations in 1993 secured the minimum five subjects that are required for a pass. The high failure rates are attributable to the following: (a) the high number of unqualified teachers that are employed in the district. In 1994 less than 25% of the 556 primary school teachers in the district were certified (Dahl, 1997); (b) the poor community which is unable to raise funds to develop the schools; (c) In 1994 only 35% of the 660 teachers in the district were non-Tonga and could not speak the local Chitonga language. According to Dahl (1997) many influential Tonga people in the district lament the erosion of their local culture through domination of their language by Ndebele and English, which are the working languages, and the domination of official jobs by non-Tonga; (d) At several schools students travel long distances to fetch water for the school and the teachers and this makes them too tired to concentrate on their classes; and (e) The high rate of absenteeism during the weeding and harvesting season, between November and March is a contributory factor to the high failure rate.

Economic activity and employment

Despite the many obstacles to development that this area has faced during the pre-independence era the post-independence period has been characterised by socio-economic achievements such as the construction of schools and health facilities and the upgrading of communication networks. Improvements in the health service sector have increased life expectancy. Also, the adoption of ox-drawn implements and hybrid maize varieties as well as the application of artificial fertilizers and pesticides has transformed local agriculture. These innovations have had both positive and negative effects. The overall positive effect has been an increased agricultural production since the 1970s while the major negative effect is that the agricultural system has become more vulnerable due to increased dependence on external inputs. Despite the socio- economic advances recorded since independence the district still lags behind most districts in the country with respect to indicators like standard of living, employment opportunities and access to infrastructual services.

Due to lack of infrastructure the economy of this border district is largely subsistence and there are few commercial activities. The majority of the people live at the subsistence level and have very low purchasing power which limits commerce. Water is scarce despite the fact that Binga is close to Lake Kariba, which is one of Africa's largest fresh water reservoirs. The majority of the peasant farmers produce what they consume, but low yields, land shortage, and in some cases labour shortages as well as droughts compel most households to buy supplementary food. In order to raise the cash required for purchasing food and other items most Tonga families combine food production with other income generating non-agricultural activities, such as beer brewing and fishing, and virtually no households obtain their livelihood exclusively from agriculture.

Binga growth point has been connected to the electric grid since 1991 and Mlibizi and Manjolo service centre were also connected more recently. There is no electricity at the other centres even though the power supply network traverses the area. Lower order centres such as Lusulu, Mwenda, Mlibizi, Tinde, Lubimbi and Mujere are serviced with little infrastructure and have problems coping with the demand for services from the rural population in the district. The rural electrification programme that was halted during the 1992 drought and has not yet been resumed due to lack of funds. In 1992, 98% of the households in the district did not have access to electricity (CSO, 1994).

The rate of unemployment in the district is 28% (including communal farm workers) and 43% (excluding communal farm workers) (CSO, 1994). About 90% of the economically active persons in the district earn a livelihood from peasant farming activities. Peasant households are characterised as those producing mainly for the reproduction of the household. Crops such as bulrush millet and white sorghum dominate but also maize, cotton, cassava and groundnuts and vegetables are cultivated in some areas.

Peasant cultivation has been difficult to develop under these circumstances. Since 1991 agriculture has been in relative decline and peasant farming faces several limitations. Because of the incidence of one drought year in every three years, drought relief is distributed to the local people on an annual basis. During the drought of the 1991-92 there were 65,823 families registered for drought relief. However, during a fairly normal year like 1994 not more than two or three wards out of 21 could produce surplus crops and this has made drought-relief to be a 'regular' way of living for many since 1991. The other serious constraint to agricultural production is not lack of access to arable land; instead it is the general shortage of labour especially during the weeding period. This problem is linked to the problem of selective out-migration from the district whereby the long-term absence of men has cases reduced the efficiency of the food production system.

Non-farm activities, such as fishing, have long been a part of life in the district and in several villages have offered an alternative to both agriculture and long-term migration. Traditional fishing with gill nets under license from the District Council is available for the local people, but the licenses are limited in number. A trading license for selling is also necessary if more than 10 fish are bought for commercial reasons, which makes illegal the activities of many fishermen and traders. This has infuriated the local people because they consider it their traditional common right to use the fishing water without paying fees to the local authority. Approximately 1,000 persons have their income from fishing or crocodile farming, which makes it the most important source of income in the district besides farming and goat/cattle rearing.

Wildlife provides a source of income through Campfire (Communal Areas Management programme for Indigenous Resources) project established in 1989, which generates a substantial income through hunting safari operators, photographic safaris and crocodile eggs. The local communities near the National park and Safari Area further benefit from the wildlife resources for example in 1992 each of the 11 campfire wards earned about Z$38,000 each. However the 10 wards not bordering these wildlife sanctuaries each earned just Z$14,000 yet they also suffer substantially from crop destruction by wild animals such as baboons, elephants, and hippos. The relationship between man and wildlife is still in disharmony despite attempts to solve the problem in a mutual beneficial manner as advocated by campfire.

Campfire is an alternative way of harvesting natural resources and diverting some pressure from agriculture activities. Also, campfire has generated significant amounts of money. The main solution for the development of the district ought to be found in a sustainable solution of the eternal water issue. This issue has yet to be solved within the main conflict between agriculture and wildlife/tourism in order to create both economically and socially acceptable living conditions for the people as well as a guarantee for a sustainable environment. In order to meet this basic need of water for the peasant farmers of Binga District a solution must be found through a combination of dams, boreholes, protected wells and pipelines from the Zambezi River.

It is doubtful that tourism and tourist related projects would generate more than a few employment opportunities for the local people although tourism as the main resource that Binga has and must therefore be used and developed. Several big stands at Binga state land are now designated for hotels and lodges and most of the shoreline is now closed to local people to make way for the new hotels. According to the district development strategy for the 1990s several stands at Binga growth point have been set aside for hotels and lodges (BDC, 1990; BRDC, 1991).

The tourist sector which employed about 200 people in 1993 is expected to grow faster than all the other sectors (excluding farming) due to the priority set by District Council for the coming years. However, there is scepticism about the 'spin-off' effect that it will give to the communal areas although some people are convinced about the employment opportunities that will be created for the local population. Other sources of employment like commerce, service industry, domestic workers, public administration parastatals, Non Governmental Organisation (NGOs), traders and informal sector to employ about 850 jobs (Gunby, 1993).

The present development of the tourism industry related to Binga growth point, Mlibizi, and the National and Safari Parks will only develop 'enclaves' for a few, without any 'sign' or 'trickle-down' effects to the main part of the people in the district and will therefore not be the vehicle of economic development for the majority of the Binga population. Binga District is a marginal area with the overwhelming majority of the population eking an existence as peasant farmers and this has important policy implications.

Migration from the district has involved a complex set of movements carried out over different periods within different households and individual economic and social contexts. Some of the movements are temporary while others are permanent. Similarly, some of the movements are to the urban areas while others were to other rural areas. The movements reflect different responses to the push factors forcing people to migrate. The migration of men from the district to urban areas is considerable and has produced a brain drain from the district. The district mainly functions as a vast labour reservoir for the mines, especially the coal mines at Hwange and the fishing companies operating along the Lake Kariba shore. The population ratio favours females (55%), and this is quite common in most rural areas in Zimbabwe. Selective migration flows by males in search of employment to centres such as Kamativi, Hwange, Victoria Falls, Bulawayo, account for the fact that more than 50% of all rural households in the district are headed by females.

In the absence of appropriate official data it is difficult to estimate how many people have migrated from the district. However, various sources have noted that in recent years better education has encouraged more people to migrate to the urban areas in search for employment in the formal economy. Remittances from the migrant workers are an important source of non-farm income for many families. Remittances and savings bring into most of the villages in the district cash that could not have been earned locally. This strategy allows many households to divide their labour power between domestic food production in the village and cash earning in the urban areas. However, retrenchments due to the effects of the recession and the structural adjustment programme that was introduced in 1991 have resulted in some movement back from the urban areas to the district.

Conclusions

Zimbabwe is still in search of a marginal area policy involving special measures directed towards those areas, which lack the potential for growth. Underdevelopment in Binga District is not a reflection of a short-term aberration but that of almost 100 years of systematic marginalization. Binga remains a marginalized district characterised by low living standards and few employment opportunities. Most males are employed outside the district. Before independence in 1980 the area had limited infrastructure and services (e.g. health facilities, schools, roads, water supplies and agricultural and livestock). However, remarkable expansion of schools, health facilities and boreholes has occurred since 1980. The expansion of the road network in the district has brought mixed blessings: access to consumer supplies in urban areas has improved and this has improved the quality of life of the local population, but increased migration has also resulted from the same developments and has contributed to agricultural stagnation in the district.

It is ironical that the people who once had to sacrifice their ancestral areas and holy shades for the process of progress and modernisation in the form of water and electricity for the urban areas are still using light generated by paraffin or firewood and each day is a struggle for water and food. Lake Kariba is still, almost 40 years after its construction, so near and yet so far away. It remains a mirage for the majority of the people living in Binga District in the sense that it is something they see but have not been able to access.

Given the fact that an increasing number of people in Binga District are finding it difficult to meet their daily basic needs and the fact that the gap (based on macro-economic indicators) between the district and the remainder of the country is widening there is need for a new development strategy that addresses the problem. Many peasant households in the district are caught up in a 'vicious circle', comparable to what Chambers (1983) once called 'the deprivation trap', which is the mutual connection between physical weakness, isolation, vulnerability, poverty and powerlessness that hinders people from self development and empowerment. Lack of employment opportunities within the district is a strong push factor that has triggered migration to various core areas of the country.

The historical condition for the development problems in the district were imprinted during the pre-independence period when the people first were neglected by government and then later-on oppressed through forced resettlement from the fertile river banks up to the dry and sandy soils on the plateau, thereby forcing them to transform their way of living. The predominantly poor peasant population of Binga still needs to break out of the 'vicious circle'. Although after independence the area benefited from government's policy of investing in social programmes, a lot still needs to be done in order to bring about development to the district. A development strategy is required for the district where the basic needs, such as guaranteed safe water for drinking and cooking, for the majority of the rural population in the communal lands are provided. In Binga District the challenge for government is how to promote development in the area so that the income gap between the district and other districts in the country is reduced.

References

Arrighi, G. (1970), 'Labour supplies in historical perspective: a study of the proletarianization of the African peasantry in Rhodesia', *Journal of Development Studies*, 6, pp. 197-234.

BDC (1981), *Binga District Lusumpuko Plan*, Binga District Council.

BDC (1990), *Binga 2000: Binga District Centre Development Plan 1990-2000*, Department of Physical Planning Matabeleland North.

BRDC (1991), *Binga Rural District Council Five year Development Plan*, BRDC.

Chambers, R. (1970), *The Resettlement Experience*, Pall Mall Press: London.

Chambers, R. (1983), *Rural Development: Putting the Last First*, Longman: Hong Kong.

Chimhowu, A and D. Tevera (1991), 'Intra-Provincial Inequalities in the provision of Primary Health Care in Zimbabwe's Midlands Province', *Geographical Journal of Zimbabwe*, 22, pp 33-45.

Cousins R & C. Cousins (1989), *Lwaano Lwanyika: Tonga Book of the Earth*, Baobab Books: Harare.

CSO (1989), 'Main Demographic features of the Population of Matabeland North Province', *1982 Population Census*, Harare.

CSO (1994), *Census 1992. Provincial profile Matabeleland North*, CSO: Harare.

Dahl, J. (1997), 'A Cry for Water. Perceptions of Development in Binga District, Zimbabwe', *Department of Geography, University of Goteborg, Series* B, No 92.

Gunby, D. (1993), 'Binga rural district: a contextual brief, a consultancy report from Planafric for ASV', Harare.

Hesselberg, J. (1995), 'Introduction', in J. Hesselberg (ed.), *Development in the South: Issues and Debates*, Department of Human Geography, University of Oslo, pp. 1-8.

Mabogunje, A. L. (1980), *The Development Process: Aspatial Perspective*, Hutchinson: London.

Mehretu, A. (1986), 'Towards a framework for spatial resolution of structural polarity in African development', *Economic Geography*, 62(1),, pp. 30-51.

Moyo, S. et al (1993), *'Zimbabwe', in the Southern African Environment: profiles of the SADC Countries*, Earthscan: London.

Muir, A. (1993), *Livelihood Strategies and the household Economy in Binga District*, Zimbabwe Save the Children Fund (UK).

Ncube, G. T. (1986), 'Study of the Tonga People of Sebungwe District (Binga District) Under British South Africa Company Rule (1896-1923) and Their Response to Colonisation', University of Zimbabwe, Unpublished Paper.

Sachs, W. (1993), 'Global Ecology and the Shadow of Development', in W. Sachs (ed.) *Global Ecology: A New Arena of Political Conflicts*, Zed Books: London, pp. 3-21.

Seers D. (1969), 'The meaning of development', *International Development Review* 2(6):2-6.

Simon, D. (1986), 'Regional inequality, migration and development: the case of Zimbabwe', *Tijdschrift voor Economische en Sociale Geografie*, 77(1), pp. 7-17.

Simon D (1990), *Third World regional Development. A Reappraisal*, Paul Chapman: London.

Tevera, D.S. (1981), 'The Evolution of a Colonial Space Economy in Zimbabwe; Capitalist Cores and Labour Reserves', Unpublished M.A. Thesis, Queen's University, Kingston, Canada.

Wisner, B. (1988), *Power and Need in Africa: Basic Human Needs and Development Policies*, Earthscan: London.

Zinyama, L.M. (1987), 'Assessing spatial variations in social conditions in the African rural areas of Zimbabwe', *Tijdschrift voor Economische en Sociale Geografie* ,78(1), pp. 30-43.

19 Challenges to the development of a polarized space: The case of Zimbabwe

ASSEFA MEHRETU AND CHRIS C. MUTAMBIRWA

Introduction

The object of his paper is to analyze the nature of marginality in Sub-Saharan Africa (SSA) in general and Zimbabwe in particular and to explore challenges to development that reside primarily in forces of polarization that are corollary to the centre/periphery structure of development. In order to characterize the specific nature of socio-economic marginality in SSA, what is meant by marginality and its principal typologies will be outlined. Generic marginality is a condition of relative deficiency in socio-economic indicators of well-being, which societies and their geography experience when they are adversely, affected either by imperfect markets in laissez-faire processes of modernization or by inequitable hegemonic relations in centre-periphery structures. Socio-economic indicators of well-being generally refer to degrees of political participation and levels of economic performance (see also Mehretu and Sommers, 1994). Two principal typologies of marginality are conceptualized. The first is marginality that is corollary to the laissez-faire modernization process and is referred to as 'contingent marginality'. The second is marginality that is corollary to hegemonic centre/periphery process and is called 'systemic marginality'.

'Contingent marginality' applies to free markets in which a certain degree of 'marginality' is expected as market uncertainties randomly distribute uneven development with some role played by geographic or social vulnerabilities. 'Systemic marginality' applies to hegemonic (dual) markets, which are corollary to an inequitable system of centre/periphery relations. 'Systemic marginality' is often directed at peoples that are characterized by a set of identifiable social and/or spatial factors of vulnerability to marginality. Most cases of SSA marginality fall into the second typology because of the dominant role of hegemonic and inequitable systems that characterize the centre-periphery mode of growth (Galtung,

1971; Rodney, 1972; Amin, 1973b; Mafeje, 1977; Reyna, 1983; Riddell, 1985; Mandaza, 1986; Mehretu, 1989; Blaut, 1993; Aryeetey-Attoh, 1997).

The social and spatial distribution of modern growth in SSA is constrained by the duality that the centre/periphery system imposes in the economy and thus spatial organization is the outcome of man's attempt to use space efficiently. Since the decision process connected with the modern development in SSA has its background in colonial or neo-colonial rationale, the social and spatial impress of the development process has been efficiently organized to meet external rather than internal objectives for progress and development. The space economy, settlement organization, location of modern productive activities, and spatial interaction (local or international) were not developed in response to local markets and needs. They were the result of external (colonial) and internal (post-colonial) hegemonies. When the growth process is governed by the hegemony of the centre, this means that the periphery will be searched and organized for an efficient mode of resource extraction that would maximize benefits that would accrue to the centre, national or international. This often results in the formation of relatively highly developed islands of growth and prosperity in the form of primate cities and commodified 'enclaves' dotting the underdeveloped landscape. The fundamental structure of development polarity in all SSA countries is identical although patterns might vary depending upon historical backgrounds and the degree of incorporation with the international economy (Amin, 1973a; Mafeje, 1977; Shaw, 1982).

Counterposed binaries in centre-periphery systems

Since marginality in SSA mostly results from structural hegemony of inequitable and antagonistic relations, it unfolds itself in a set of counterposed binaries in social and spatial development. Counterposed binaries are contradictory duals or antagonistic tensions that are inherent in core/periphery relations. They are bipolar phenomena which are characterized by win/lose, zero-sum and positive/negative external outcomes in which the core is almost always the beneficiary of positive effects while the periphery sustains systemic adverse effects (Galtung, 1971; Logan, 1972; Amin, 1973a; Mabogunje, 1981; Riddell, 1985; Mehretu, 1989). In this paper, only four of the most important counterposed binaries that afflict SSA peripheries will be defined.

The first counterposed binary lies is the commodification of SSA's economic sectors. In economic sectors, the modern (formal, technological) in the core is counterposed with the non-modern (informal, traditional) in the periphery. One of the most striking bipolarity problems in SSA is found in this area. The degree of bipolarity between counterposed binaries is dependent on the degree of antagonistic dynamics between the modern (commodified) and the traditional (largely subsistence) sectors in these countries as these two domains compete for access to the scarce resources in the nation. Because of the tremendous power that core localities can exercise over the periphery, the latter often loses in the competition and gets increasingly marginalized leaving it at the mercy of central hegemonies which continue to appropriate land resources even if such measures may impoverish rural economies and reduce food securities (Rodney, 1972; Amin, 1973a; Palmer, 1977; Arrighi, 1977; Yapa, 1980; Wallerstein, 1977; Dos Santos, 1984; Ayoade, 1988; Blaut, 1993).

The second counterposed binary is in regional development in which the core, with its advanced infrastructure and integrated space articulated by a hierarchy of urban systems is counterposed with the underdeveloped and disarticulated space of the periphery. The bipolarity in physical and social urbanization in SSA countries is one of the most striking and visible characteristics of the centre/periphery mode of development. Primate cities, ports and resource enclaves enjoy high levels of modern technology, advanced infrastructure, and high levels of living whereas the rest of the country is poor and deficient in basic amenities such as potable water and primary health care that central spaces take for granted. The system enables core domains to enjoy ultra modern conveniences and ostentatious consumption by hegemonic elite whereas rural households lack basic needs (Witthuhn, 1976; Riddell, 1985; Mehretu, 1989; Aryeetey-Attoh, 1997).

The third counterposed binary is characterized by the core's ability to match its economic objectives in raising cash crops with land resources that are suitable for them. This is counterposed by the mismatch between subsistence objectives and constrained access to arable land in the periphery. Generally, colonial and post-colonial economies have produced significant changes in population-land ratios. As vast amounts of rural lands were being commodified for the purpose of export staples, the subsistence sector in SSA, which has always been managed under a communal system, was losing valuable land assets to commercial plantations. Smallholder food producers were relegated to more marginal lands with deficient agricultural potential. Over the years, vast amounts of land with good soils, grasslands, forest, and water have been consolidated and relegated to primary commodities for export or for some other uses such as wild-game reserves, nature reserves, State lands, etc. This meant that less and less land of good quality is available for the increasing numbers of people who needed it for their subsistence. There have also been negative externalities with adverse effects on the periphery including resource degradation, creation of disease ecologies, loss of rural labour due to out-migration, increased pressure on rural women from homemaking, fetching water and firewood, farming, and increased overall communal instability (Heyer, 1975; Yapa, 1979; Mascarenhas, 1983; Chazan, 1988; Cleaver, 1993; Lele and Stone, 1989; Mehretu, 1995; Obia, 1997).

The fourth and final counterposed binary lies in the function of State apparatus. In most SSA countries, government-business compact with aims to integrate the nation with international markets is counterposed with the government's heavy-handed politics in the countryside with outcomes in territorial segmentation and impoverishment (Ayoade, 1988; Azaria, 1988; Chazan, 1988). The State in SSA has done little for territorial integration of its peoples to bring about harmony between their needs and the national economy and its infrastructure (see Friedmann 1988). On the contrary, the State government in SSA countries has been a hegemonic institution, which governed without representation and accountability. Its record in colonial and post-colonial times has been to repress the majority and its territorial demands for democracy, development, and improved standards of living. This was clearly shown to be the recent case in the Congo until the recent overthrow of Mobutu's regime (see also Callaghy, 1979; Mazrui, 1986; Azaria, 1988; Friedmann, 1988; Rothchild and Chazan, 1988; Young, 1988; Mehretu and Sommers, 1990; Gordon and Gordon, 1992; Yeboah, and Aryeetey-Attoh, 1997).

Counterposed binaries and commodification

The pattern and intensity in which the four counterposed binaries unfold in a SSA country depend on the colonial history of the country. Development polarities in SSA varied by colonial and post-colonial experiences and associated commodification. In the first variant are countries, which were historically least, commodified as in the case of Ethiopia and Liberia. In both of these cases significant commodification did not appear until early twentieth century, and it did not involve colonial occupation. As in the other SSA countries, commodification of primary goods gave rise to primate cities and resource enclaves (Mabogunje, 1981; Mehretu, 1989; Aryeetey-Attoh, 1997). In Ethiopia, counterposed binaries are least polarized as the country still manifests relatively weak functional integration with foreign markets. Primate cities like Addis Ababa manifest more indigenous flavour than would be the case in colonial primate cities like Nairobi, Dakar and Harare (Wubneh and Abate, 1988; Mehretu, 1993).

In the second variant are included SSA countries, which experienced colonial occupation with enclave European settlements such as Ghana,

Nigeria and Senegal. In this variant, there have been colonial settlements in selected resource-endowment localities, strategic towns and seaports. The social and spatial organization of the modern economy during occupation was the responsibility of the colonial residents who scanned productive resources and mobilized them for export purposes. Primate cities and selected resource-enclaves were developed with modern technology and infrastructure whose rationale was to efficiently organize the colony for exploitation while making it possible for the colonial elite to live in luxurious surroundings. Polarities between counterposed binaries in economics, geography, resource allocation and government functions were all significant as the core enclave was qualitatively and quantitatively at variance with the peripheral regions. Land appropriation for colonial use meant the loss of good farmland to the indigenous people in the countryside. In the second variant of the postcolonial state, patterns in commodification, regional development, economy/resource match, and the role of the government in territorial integration were all characterized by high degrees of polarity in counterposed binaries (see also Mabogunje, 1981; Shaw, 1982; Mehretu, 1989; Yeboah, 1997).

SSA countries in the third variant of commodification experienced the most extreme degree of polarity in counterposed binaries in development. In countries such as Kenya, Zimbabwe and South Africa, where there were permanent settlements of Europeans, commodification first involved the division of land resources between the natives and the settlers, the latter appropriating the best agricultural lands and those with mineral potentials. The indigenous populations were relegated to residual lands with poor agricultural or mineral potential. Exclusive domains based on racial segregation were written into law by settler populations. Lands with the settler population were heavily commodified and modern industrial establishments along with a hierarchy of urban centres with heavy European flavour were developed in this domain. On the contrary, the African domain was impoverished with high densities of population displaced from appropriated lands and concentrated in marginal areas with little agricultural potential. The African domain eventually became a reserve army of labour from which the commodified domain obtained its cheap work force. In the third variant, patters of commodification, regional development, economy/resource match, and the role of the State in territorial integration were characterized by the highest degree of polarity of counterposed binaries experienced anywhere in SSA (Arrighi, 1970; Kay, 1970; Palmer, 1977; Martin and Johnson, 1981; Ndela, 1981).

The case of Zimbabwe

Historical roots of counterposed binaries

As a former settler colony, Zimbabwe's economy at time of independence in 1980 was characterized by the third variant of advanced commodification associated with a high degree of polarity between counterposed binaries in economic sectors, regional development, economy/resource match, and government role in territorial integration. At the base of the dual economy in Zimbabwe was the colonial division of resources and related demographics into two exclusive and couterposed geographic domains. The first, and by far the most commodifiable space was assembled from lands that contained the best agricultural and mineral resources in the country. This was transformed into commercial land. It contained the most important mines including those associated with the mineral-rich Great Dyke in Southern Africa. Large-scale modern plantation-type farms and manufacturing plants, mostly owned by the settler community, were located in this region (Figure 19.1).

The second, and least commodifiable, space was assembled from the least productive and rugged enclaves of the country and relegated to the African majority population as a communal land. This assemblage of lands and their allocation to exclusive commercial and communal domains produced one of the most polarized sets of counterposed binaries in SSA. What made counterposed binaries in Zimbabwe so pronounced was the fact that lands assigned to Africans were not only poor in resources but also they were dismembered and isolated from each other (Figure 19.1) (Kay, 1970; Surveyor General, 1983). In the communal lands, Africans were not only impoverished by virtue of the poor land resources they had, but they were also restricted by a variety of social, legal and physical barriers from access to development resources in the commodified domain. In the face of increasing population, communal lands began to experience high densities which in turn led to serious degradation of land resources and reduced carrying capacity (Martin and Johnson, 1981; Kay, 1970; Palmer, 1977; Sibanda and Moyana, 1984; Potts and Mutambirwa, 1990).

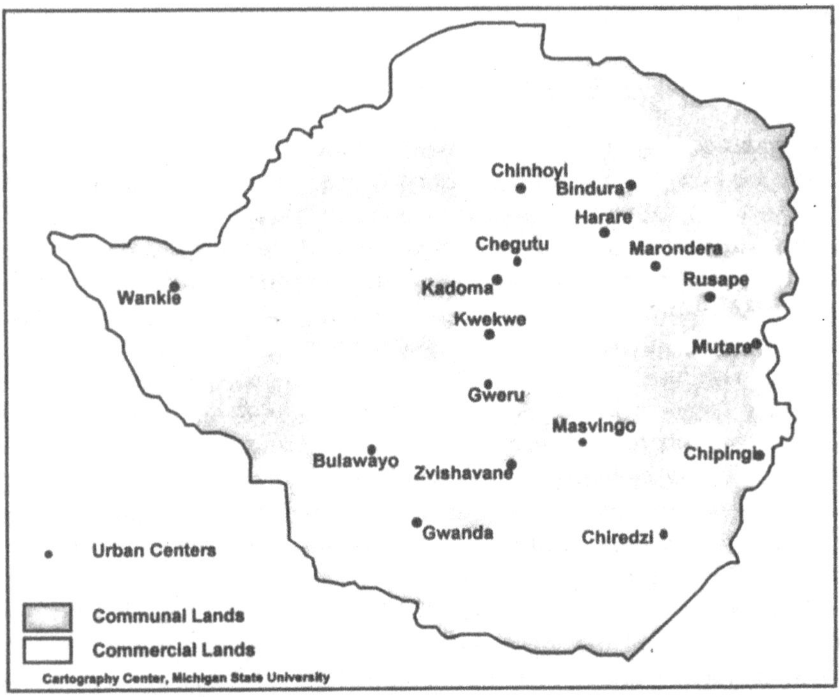

Figure 19.1 Zimbabwe: communal lands and principal urban centres

Counterposed binary in commodification

Current polarities in counterposed binaries in Zimbabwe are the result of the stiff duality that the colonial system put in place. In the colonial system, process and form were spatially dichotomized. The high degree of commodification and modernization on commercial lands had adverse effects on communal lands. As better arable lands became appropriated for commodification, communal lands not only faced unsustainable densities on residual land but also were exposed to severe exploitation of their labour force (Arrighi, 1970; Palmer, 1977; Ndela, 1981; Mandaza, 1986; Mehretu, 1995).

In the communal lands, socio-economic relations of production were very different from those on commercial lands. As there was very little commodifiation of production in the communal lands, few of them were incorporated in the capitalist structure of the commercial-land economy. The communal lands, whose principal economy was subsistence agriculture, served as labour reserves for commercial lands. Because of low-wages on commercial lands, significant processes of differentiation did not happen in communal lands. Development and technological progress in commercial lands were counterposed by almost total lack of technology and modernization in communal lands. This also contributed to demographic and subsistence instabilities in communal lands, as wage-seeking migrants from communal lands, responding to pull-factors in commercial lands, contributed to the constant disruption of the subsistence sector (Arrighi, 1970; Mafeje, 1977; Sibanda and Moyana, 1984; Weiner, 1985; Zinyama, 1986; Potts and Mutambirwa, 1990).

Counterposed binary in regional development

The disparity between the commercial and communal lands in regional development is not only severe but also qualitatively and quantitatively divergent. In the first place, communal lands were spatially disintegrated with many discontiguous patches throughout the country (see Figure 19.1). Communal lands had no urban centres, rail and all-weather road networks, power grids, mining estates, manufacturing and social infrastructure (Sanders, 1989; Scott, 1989). Virtually all the macadamized highways and railway network were restricted to the commercial lands (Figure 19.2) (see Whitsum, 1980; UNDP, 1981; CSO, 1989). Communal lands lacked electricity as electric grid system from the Kariba Dam bypassed the communal lands although the complex has been operating under capacity. Social infrastructure such as schools, hospitals, clinics and other overhead investment are improving since independence but the lagged impact of colonial neglect remains an indomitable challenge.

A profile of poverty in communal lands is exemplified by the case of the amount of time and energy rural households spend to secure basic domestic requirements such as potable water and energy source for cooking. Surveys in communal lands show that domestic chores, especially those that involve trips to water points and sources of firewood, have become heavy burdens especially on women. In the Chiduku and Murehwa communal lands, on the average, each household spent over 30 hours per week on trips to fetch water and firewood (Mehretu and Mutambirwa, 1992; 1996) and most of this burden fell on home-maker females who spend about 20 hours per week on such chores. This becomes critical as female homemakers are also responsible for most of the work in agriculture for food production (GOZ, 1990).

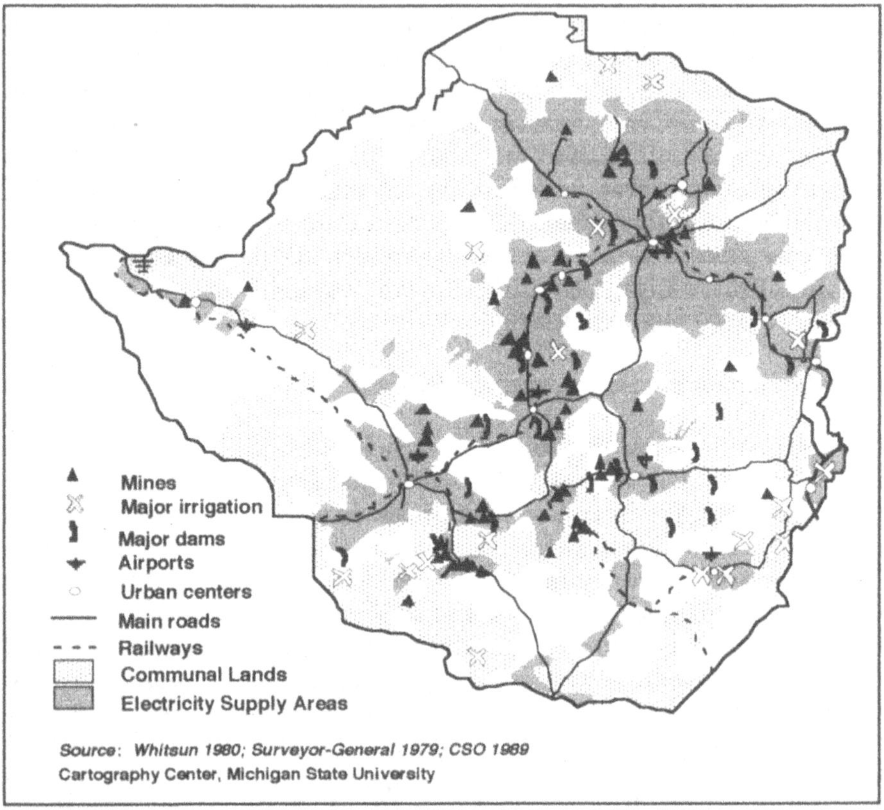

Figure 19.2 Zimbabwe: infrastructure and industrial activity

Counterposed binary in economy/resource match

In Zimbabwe, the match between low-density commercial lands and successful commodification is counterposed with the mismatch of high-density populations on poor land resources in communal lands. The colonial system of land apportionment had introduced a very unfair distribution of the national land. Soon after independence, 73% of the rural population of Zimbabwe resided in communal lands which constituted about half of the rural land surface located in the least fertile areas of the country (Kay, 1970; CSO, 1982; Surveyor General, 1983). None of the rich mineral areas of he Great Dyke are located in the communal lands. More attractive areas which are developed as resorts with lakes and wildlife are all outside the communal lands.

The overall impact of the economy/resource mismatch on communal lands of Zimbabwe meant that not only food security would suffer but that land use will be unsustainable because of the reduced carrying capacity given poor technologies in communal lands. This also led to another serious problem, land degradation. Since communal lands were assembled in fragile, low-quality lands, their use for food production, grazing and provision of domestic fuel meant that degradation was but a certain outcome. Researchers in this area show that most communal lands, especially those with high densities and more proximal to commercial lands, have undergone serious degradation (Elwell, 1985; Whitlow, 1988).

Counterposed binary in territorial integration

The colonial State in Zimbabwe, as in South Africa, was responsible for creating one of the most counterposed binaries in territorial integration (life space). Territorial integration means spatial integration based on commonality in culture, politics and economics (see Friedmann and Weaver, 1980; Friedmann, 1988). The function of the settler state apparatus was to supplant the African mode of life with its own by making the social and physical environments resemble those it left behind in Europe. The settler community was made comfortable with familiar cultural surroundings even though this meant violating the cultural heritage and related human geography of the indigenous populations. The commercial domain was complete with European geographic names for towns and places. Language, clothing, food, entertainment, etc., especially in the commercial sector, were of European influence. The colonial state had achieved a modicum of integrated life space for the settler community in its own exclusive domain completes with a highly successful commercial sector. On the other hand, the historical, cultural and territorial supports of the African life space were destroyed, its land dismembered, and its human power reduced to a labour pool for an alien system. In some cases, Africans were compelled to accept the alien culture or risk losing favours. In the process, the African life space was totally disrupted and relegated to marginal existence in the dismembered communal domain.

This is one of the reasons why, upon independence in 1980, the Zimbabwe Government made it a priority to reintegrate the territorial life space of its citizens by '(supplanting the) socio-economic dualism which characterized the inherited system with an integrated economy' as it launched a plan in 1981 entitled 'development with equity' (GOZ, 1981). The Government's initial plan also indicated that the State would give the 'necessary assistance to regions to attain appropriate degrees of autonomy' (GOZ, 1982; Sibanda, 1985; Wekwete, 1985).

Challenges to resolving counterposed binaries

Redressing polarities in commodification

As has been indicated, the colonial history of Zimbabwe poses a special challenge for planners since it represents one of those rare cases in the continent where there is high degree of counterposed binaries making the communal domain unattractive for large-scale investment. What are the chances then of redressing polarities in commodification?

Due to the fact they had to sustain very high densities of rural population with poor carrying capacity to begin with, communal lands have become degraded of their soils and flora (Riddell, 1978; Whitlow, 1988; Mehretu, 1994a). By virtue of their pedologic and climatic limitations, communal arable lands require considerable investment and reduced population pressure to be viable for commodification. Opportunities for non-agricultural employment in communal lands are constrained by the absence of urban centres and mines. Thus, it would be a major challenge to lessen the current counterposed binary in commodification. There have been many successes especially in introducing agricultural technologies to increase food security and commercial crop production, and improving rural social infrastructure (Weiner, 1985; Rohrbach, 1988; Rukuni and Eicher, 1990). But they are not enough to alter the macro pattern of populations in communal lands looking outside for better opportunities. If communal lands are to be viable economic domains for increased commodification (in food or non-food crops) and retention of their populations, the current mismatch between population density and land with agricultural potential should be resolved (Potts and Mutambirwa, 1990; Mehretu, 1994b, 1995; Potts, 1996).

Redressing polarities in regional development

This is perhaps the most urgent and an area most likely to produce large rewards for investment. The variables that are crucial include investment in basic human needs, food production, housing, health, education, transport, communication and urbanization. The Zimbabwe Government put priority in such redressive projects soon after independence (GOZ, 1982, 1983). In its initial plans the Government has indicated that it would put policy instruments to upgrade housing and provision of other amenities. It has also made specific references to improving the health conditions of the rural population and expanding elementary school facilities in the communal lands. The food sector has been earmarked as a priority area as food security has been a problem in communal lands from time to time (Rukuni

1994). Attention has been given to the development of a settlement and urbanization pattern to articulate the communal lands with a hierarchy of central nodes with commercial and non-farm activity functions (GOZ 1984; Sibanda, 1985, Wekwete 1985).

There have been some significant, if not dramatic, successes in implementing redressive policies in communal lands. Chief among the post-independence accomplishments are the building of rural schools and clinics. The number of elementary schools, and primary health centres has been greatly expanded over the pre-independence levels. The country has also made a significant progress in the agricultural sector for the communal lands. Extension centres are now available to serve communal land farmers by distributing farm inputs. Improved varieties, fertilizers and agricultural machinery have been introduced in communal lands particularly in those areas in which the agricultural potential is better and where the population pressure is significantly higher (Rukuni and Eicher 1994).

However, what has occurred is way below of what is needed to significantly change the regional development of communal lands. The road system in the communal lands is still inadequate and not reliable in the rainy season. Road maintenance in communal areas is poor. Most communal lands are still not electrified. Although the Government is committed to develop urban functions as part and parcel of its rural development program, communal lands remain poor in tertiary functions. There have been some encouraging developments in few communal lands in which a few growth centres have been established with positive results (Sibanda, 1985).

Redressing polarities in economy/resource match

After independence, one of the goals of the Government of Zimbabwe was to bring about improved conditions in communal lands with reduced pressure on the land. It followed this with a two-pronged policy: introducing appropriate technology to small-holder farmers and carry out a land-settlement program without changing the basic dual agrarian structure inherited from the colonial era. Land reform has not been effected and remains a contentious issue (Bratton, 1994; Masoka, 1994; Rukuni, 1994; Mehretu, 1995; Potts, 1996). The mismatch between population density (and its economy) and poor agricultural resources in communal lands continues to be the most important challenge for the Government. The pressure to allocate more high-potential land to communal populations continues to grow. At the same time there is also the concern of destabilizing the highly productive commercial land sector (Roth, 1994). The political, economic and financial implications of significant land reform are daunting. There is also some fear that expanding communal modes of production into land currently 'protected' under commercial management or national reserves would introduce bad resource management habits into the 'protected' areas (Mhlanga, 1982).

The land question remains fundamental to most of the polarities in counterposed binaries in Zimbabwe's economy. The lack of a strong land reform policy will produce a number of problems in the context of high-density communal lands whose resource base is quickly declining with some reaching crisis proportions. The current dual character of land husbandry did not prevent Zimbabwe from becoming an agricultural success story (Rukuni and Eicher, 1994). But this success should not hide the fact that land hungry communal lands, with high rates of population growth, will continue to be poor, and many will continue to lose their people, especially the young and educated, to out-migration heading for the major urban centres in search of better opportunities (Potts and Mutambirwa, 1990; Potts, 1996).

Redressing territorial polarities

After seventeen years of independence, a question may be asked if the Zimbabwe Government has achieved a significant integration of its dual sectors inherited from the colonial economy. This is a question posed not only for Zimbabwe but also for all SSA countries, which operate under post-colonial, centre periphery modes of development. The integration between the dual sectors of SSA economies has not been successfully achieved anywhere to any significant degree. Zimbabwe is no exception. Since inherited polarities have been extreme, structures of division between communal and commercial domains will prevail as economic elite in commercial domains continue to take advantage of structural pawl-effects to enjoy the benefits of the dual system (Mehretu, 1989, pp. 34-35). Thus, the harmonization of culture, politics and economics for territorial integration of the majority population will be a tremendous task. Thus, redressing territorial polarities will be a long agenda, which hopefully will be attained steadily within an orderly path of transition.

The record on SSA governments for achieving orderly transitions from a divided socio-economic structure to an integrated one with free markets and democracy has been disappointing (Mazrui, 1986; Rothchild and Chazan, 1988; Mehretu and Sommers, 1990; Gordon and Gordon, 1992; Yeboah and Aryeetey-Attoh, 1997). Consistent with its stated aims soon after independence to proceed with caution 'to correct the socio-economic ills of the past' (GOZ, 1981) without necessarily making a fresh start, the Zimbabwe Government has made significant gains on its objectives and has made the country one of a few shining examples of stability, economic growth and democratic participation in SSA. Many challenges lie ahead to achieve a higher degree of territorial integration as the State plays critical roles in reducing polarities in counterposed binaries that still characterize the country's socio-economic structure.

Conclusion

The intent of this paper is to introduce an approach to define polarity and marginality for countries with dual economies and explore ways of applying them to cases of SSA in general and Zimbabwe in particular. Because of the structural origins of the SSA economy, polarity and marginality (used synonymously) are corollary and systemic to the centre/periphery mode of growth. They differ significantly from polarities that result from the aberration of free markets in more developed economies where margins are mostly contingent. Polarities corollary to the SSA dual economy have been examined with respect to their impact on four key factors of socio-economic transformation: commodification, regional development, economy/resource match, and government role in territorial integration.

A brief survey of SSA conditions in counterposed binaries with a case study of Zimbabwe demonstrates that contradictory and/or antagonistic tensions between core and peripheral economies, are the root problems of backwardness of majority populations that reside in rural areas. A closer look at the nature of four principal factors of development listed above, produced an outline of baseline conditions at the time of independence and a record of achievements ever since in redressing polarities in counterposed binaries. The study also provided implications for macro-national policies to continue work in the reduction of polarities and bring about a more harmonious national economy without antagonistic tensions. The problem of addressing counterposed binaries that continue to have adverse effects on communal lands in Zimbabwe have especially been emphasized. The structural limitations of the commercial-communal duality and its corollary in counterposed binaries in commodification, regional development, economy-resource match, and government role in territorial integration were outlined. Structural preconditions to significantly redress the polarities to bring harmony between the resource-rich commercial domain, and the resource-poor communal domain were highlighted. The ability of the State in Zimbabwe, and elsewhere in SSA, to launch its people to the challenges of a highly competitive, flexible and globalized economy is predicated on its ability to first and foremost redress polarities at home and make the opportunities of a better life achievable by all its citizens (see also Kristof, 1997).

References

Amin, Samir (1973a), *Le Developpment Inegal*, Les Editions de Minuit: Paris.

Amin, Samir (1973b), 'Underdevelopment and Dependence in Black Africa: Their Historical Origins and Contemporary Forms', *Social and Economic Studies*, 22.

Arrighi, Geovanni (1970), 'Labour Supplies in Historical Perspectives: A Study of the Proletarianization of The African Peasantry in Rhodesia', *Journal of Development Studies*, Vol. 6, No. 3, pp. 197-234.

Arrighi, Geovanni (1977), 'Foreign Investment Patterns', in Peter C. W. Gutkind and Peter Waterman (eds.), *African Social Studies, A Radical Reader*, pp. 168-175,Heinemann: London.

Aryeetey-Attoh, Samuel (1997), 'Geography and Development in Sub-Saharan Africa', in Samuel Aryeetey-Attoh (ed.), *Geography of Sub-Saharan Africa*, pp. 223-261, Simon and Schuster: Upper Saddle River, NJ.

Ayoade, J. A. (1988), 'States without Citizens: An Emerging African Phenomenon', in D. Rothchild and Chazan, D. (eds.), *The Precarious Balance: State and Society in Africa*, pp. 61-82, Westview Press: Boulder, CO.

Blaut, J. M. (1993), *The Colonizer's Model of the World*, The Guilford Press: New York.

Bratton, Michael (1994), 'Land Distribution (in Zimbabwe), 1980-1990', in Mandivamba Rukuni and Carl K. Eicher (ed.), *Zimbabwe's Agricultural Revolution*, pp. 70-86, University of Zimbabwe Publications: Harare.

Callaghy, Thomas M. (1988), 'The State and Development of Capitalism in Africa: Theoretical, Historican and Comparative Reflections', in D. Rothchild and D. Chazan (eds.), *The Precarious Balance: State and Society in Africa*, pp. 67-99, Westview Press: Boulder, CO.

Central Statistical Office (CSO) (1982), *Social Conditions in District Council Areas*, 1982, CSO: Harare.

Central Statistical Office (CSO) (1989), *Zimbabwe in Maps: A Census Atlas*, CSO: Harare.

Chazan, Naomi (1988), 'Patterns of State-Society Incorporation and Disengagement in Africa', in D. Rothchild and N. Chazan (eds.), *The Precarious Balance: State and Society in Africa*, pp. 121-148, Westview Press: Boulder, CO.

Cleaver, Kevin M. (1993), *A Strategy to Develop Agriculture in Sub-Saharan Africa and a Focus for the World Bank*, The World Bank: Washington, DC.

Dos Santos, T. (1984), 'The Structure of Dependence', *American Economic Review*, Vol. 40, No. 2.

Elwell, H. A. (1985), 'An Assessment of Soil Erosion in Zimbabwe', *The Zimbabwe Science News*, 19, pp. 267-268.

Friedmann, John and Clyde Weaver (1980), *Territory and Function: The Evolution of Regional Planning*, University of California Press: Berkeley, CA.

Friedmann, John (1988), *Life Space and Economic Space*, Transaction Books: New Brunswick, NJ.

Galtung, J (1971), 'A Structural Theory of Imperialism', *Journal of Peace Research*, Vol. 21.

Gordon, A. A. and D. L. Gordon (eds.) (1992), *Understanding Contemporary Africa* , Lynne Rienner: Boulder.

Government of Zimbabwe (GOZ) (1990), 'The Nutrition Situation: Current Strategies and Plans', in T. S. Jayne, J. B. Wyckoff and Mandi Rukuni (eds.), *Integrating Food, Nutrition and Agricultural Policy in Zimbabwe*, pp. 8-27, University of Zimbabwe: Harare.

Government of Zimbabwe (GOZ) (1984), *A Program for the Development of Service-Centers in the Rural Areas of Zimbabwe*, Ministry of Local Government and Town Planning: Harare.

Government of Zimbabwe (GOZ) (1981), *Growth with Equity*, Government Printer: Harare.

Government of Zimbabwe (GOZ) Ministry of Finance, Economic Planning and Development (1982), *Transitional National Development Plan*, 1982/83 - 1984/85, Vol. 11, Amalgamated Press (PVT) Ltd: Harare.

Government of Zimbabwe, Ministry of Finance, Economic Planning and Development (1983), *Transitional National Development Plan* 1982/83 - 1984/85, Vol. 2, The Government Printer: Harare.

Heyer, Judith (1975), 'Agricultural Development Policy in Kenya from the Colonial Period to 1975', in Judith Heyer, et.al. (eds.), *Rural Development in Tropical Africa*, pp. 90-120, St. Martin's Press: New York.

Kay, George (1970), *Rhodesia: A Human Geography*, Africana Publishing Corporation: New York.

Kristof, Nicholas D. (1997), 'Tiger Tales: Why Africa Can Thrive Like Asia', *The New York Times*, May 25.

Lele, Uma and Steven. W. Stone (1989), *Population Pressure, the Environment, and Agricultural Intensification: Variations on the Boserup Hypothesis*, The World Bank: Washington DC.

Logan, M. I. (1972), 'The Spatial System and Planning Strategies in Developing Countries', *Geographical Review*, Vol. 62.

Mabogunje, Akin L. (1981), *The Development Process: A Spatial Perspective*, New York: Holmes & Meier Publishers, Inc.

Mafeje, Archie (1977), 'NeoColonialism State Capitalism, or Revolution?' In Peter C.W. Gutkind and Peter Waterman (eds.), *African Social Studies*, pp. 412-422, Heinemann: London.

Mandaza, Ibo (1986), *Zimbabwe: The Political Economy of Transition 1980-1986*, CODESRIA: Dakar, Senegal.

Martin, David and Phyllis Johnson (1981), *The Struggle for Zimbabwe: The Chimurenga War*, Faber and Faber: London.

Mascarenhas, Adolfo (1985), 'Environment, Infrastructure and Rural Development', in John W. Mellor, et.al. (eds.), *Accelerating Food Production Growth in Sub-Saharan Africa*, Forthcoming.

Masoka, Ngoni (1994), 'Land-Reform Policy and Strategy (in Zimbabwe)', in Mandivamba Rukuni and Carl K., Eicher (eds.), *Zimbabwe's Agricultural Revolution*, pp. 304-316, University of Zimbabwe Publications: Harare.

Mazrui, Ali (1986), *The Africans: A Tripple Heritage*, Little Brown and Company: Boston.

Mehretu, Assefa (1993), 'Cities of Sub-Saharan Africa', in Stanley Brunn and Jack F. Williams (eds.), *Cities of the World: World Regional and Urban Development*, pp. 267-303, Harper Collins: New York.

Mehretu, Assefa (1994a), 'Social Poverty Profiles of Communal Areas', in Mandivamba Rukuni and Carl K. Eicher (eds.), *Zimbabwe's Agricultural Revolution*, Harare: University of Zimbabwe Publications, pp. 56-69.

Mehretu, Assefa (1994b), 'Geographic Variations in Producer Decisions on Land Utilization in Communal Lands of Zimbabwe', *Paper presented at the Association of American Geograhers 90th Annual Meeting*, March 29-April 2, San Franciso, California.

Mehretu, Assefa (1995), 'Spatial Mismatch between Population Density and Land Potential: The Case of Zimbabwe', *Africa Development*, Vol. 20, No. 1, pp. 125-146.

Mehretu, Assefa, and Chris Mutambirwa (1992), 'Gender Differences in Time and Energy Costs of Distance for Regular Domestic Chores in Rural Zimbabwe: A Case Study in the Chiduku Communal Area', *World Development*, Vol. 20, No. 11, pp. 1675-1683.

Mehretu, Assefa (1989), *Regional Disparity in Sub-Saharan Africa*, Westview Press: Boulder, CO.

Mehretu, Assefa and Chris Mutambirwa (1996), 'Transport Burdens on Women in Rural Zimbabwe', *Paper presented at the Association of American Geographers 92nd*, Meeting, 9-13 April, Charlotte, North Carolina.

Mehretu, Assefa and Lawrence M. Sommers (1990), 'Towards Modeling National Preference Formation for Regional Development Policy: Lessons from Developed and Less Developed Countries', *Growth and Change*, Vol. 21, No. 3, pp. 32-47.

Mhlanga, L. (1982), 'Development without Destruction in Peasant Agriculture: Past Accomplishments, Present Enlightenment and Future Frustrations', *The Zimbabwe News*, 16, pp. 280-285.

Ndlela, D.B. (1981), 'Dualism in the Rhodesian Colonial Economy', *University of Lund, Department of Economics, Lund Economic Studies*, 22.

Obia, Godson Chintuwa (1997), 'Agricultural Development in Sub-Saharan Africa', in Samuel Aryeetey-Attoh (ed.), *Geography of Sub-Saharan Africa*, pp. 286-324, Simon and Schuster: Upper Saddle River, NJ.

Palmer, R.H. (1977), *Land and Racial Discrimination in Rhodesia*, University of California Press: Berkeley, CA.

Potts, Deborah (1996), 'Migrants must keep their Land', *Zimbabwean Review*, October, pp. 6-8.

Potts, Deborah and Chris Mutambirwa (1990), 'Rural-Urban Linkages in Contemporary Harare: Why Migrants Need Their Land', *Journal of Southern African Studies*, Vol. 16, No. 4, pp. 678-698.

Reyna, S. P. (1983), 'Dual Class Formation and Agrarian Underdevelopment: An Analysis of the Articulation of Production Relations in Upper Volta', *Canadian Journal of African Studies*, Vol. 17, No. 2, pp. 211-233.

Riddell, B. (1985), 'Urban Bias in Underdevelopment', *Tijdschrift Voor Econ. en Soc. Geographie*, 76.

Riddell, Roger (1978), 'The Land Problem in Rhodesia', *Gwelo Socio-Economic Series*, No. 11, Mambo Press: Gwelo.

Rodney, Walter (1972), *How Europe Underdeveloped Africa*, Tanzania Publishing Hourse: Dar es Salaam.

Rohrbach, David (1988), 'The Growth of Smallholder Maize Production in Zimbabwe: Causes and Implications for Food Security', Ph.D. Dissertation, Department of Agricultural Economics, Michigan State University: East Lansing, MI.

Roth, Michael (1944), 'A Critique of Zimbabwe's 1992 Land Act', in Mandivamba Rukuni and Carl K. Eicher (eds.), *Zimbabwe's Agricultural Revolution*, pp. 317-334, University of Zimbabwe Publications: Harare:

Rothchild, D. and N. Chazan (eds.) (1988), *The Precarious Balance: State and Society in Africa*, Westview Press: Boulder, CO.

Rukuni, Mandivamba and Carl K. Eicher (1994), 'Zimbabwe's Agricultural Revolution: Lessons for Southern Africa', in Mandivamba Rukuni and Carl K. Eicher (eds.), *Zimbabwe's Agricultural Revolution*, pp. 393-411, University of Zimbabwe Publications: Harare.

Rukuni, Mandivamba (1994), 'The Evolution of Agricultural Policy 1890-1990', in Mandivamba Rukuni and Carl K. Eicher (eds.), *Zimbabwe's Agricultural Revolution*, pp. 1-39, University of Zimbabwe Publications: Harare.

Sanders, Rickie (1989), 'Rural/Urban Dynamics in Southern Africa: An Agenda for Action', in Andrea Rother (ed.), *Preliminary Discussions on Problems of Urbanization in Southern Africa*, pp. 34-44, Center for Urban Affairs: East Lansing, MI.

Scott, Earl P. (1989), 'Urbanization in Southern Africa: A Discussion Paper', in Andrea Rother (ed.), *Preliminary Discussions on Problems of Urbanization in Southern Africa*, pp.45-51, Center for Urban Affairs: East Lansing, MI.

Shaw, Timothy M. (1982), 'The Political Economy of Africa's Future', in Timothy M. Shaw (ed.), *Alternative Futures for Africa*, Westview Press: Boulder, CO, pp. 1-16.

Sibanda, Backson, M.C. (1985), 'Growth Points--A Focus for Rural Development', *Paper, presented at Workshop on Rural Industries and Growth Point/Service Center Policies*, University of Zimbabwe, Harare, Jan. 29-Feb 1.

Sibanda, M. and H. Moyana (1984), *The African Heritage*, Zimbabwe Educational Books, (Pvt.) Ltd: Harare.

Surveyor-General (1983), *Zimbabwe Land Classification Map*, Department of the Surveyor-General: Harare.

United Nations Development Program (UNDP) (1981), *A Spatial Planning System for Zimbabwe*, UNDP: Salisbury.

Wallerstein, Immanuel (1977), 'Class and Status in Contemporary Africa', in Peter C. Gutkind and Peter Waterman (eds.), *African Social Studies*, pp. 277-283, Heinemann: London.

Weiner, D. (1985), 'Land Use and Agricultural Productivity in Zimbabwe', *The Journal of Modern African Studies*, 23, 251-285.

Wekwete, K.H. (1985), 'Generation of Local Initiative for Growth Center Development in Zimbabwe', *Paper presented at Workshop on Rural Industries and Growth Point/Service Center Policies*, University of Zimbabwe, Harare, Jan. 29 - Feb. 1.

Whitlow, J. R. (1988), *Land Degradation in Zimbabwe: A Geographic Study*, Natural Resource Board: Harare.

Whitsun Foundation (1980), *Rural Service Centers Development Study*, The Whitsun Foundation: Salisbury.

Witthuhn, Burton O. (1976), 'The Impress of Colonialism', in C. Gregory Knight and James L. Newman (eds.), *Contemporary Africa: Geography and Change*, pp. 30-38, Prentice-Hall: Englewood Cliffs, NJ.

Wubneh, Mulatu and Yohannes Abate (1988), *Ethiopia: Transition and Development in the Horn of Africa*, Westview Press: Boulder, CO.

Yapa, Lakshman S. (1979), 'Ecopolitical Economy of the Green Revolution', *The Professional Geographer*, Vol. 31, No. 4, pp. 371-376.

Yeboah, E. A. and Samuel Aryeetey-Attoh (1997), 'Political Landscape of Sub-Saharan Africa', in Samuel Aryeetey-Attoh (ed.), *Geography of Sub-Saharan Africa*, pp. 345-370, Simon and Schuster: Upper Saddle River, NJ.

Yeboah, E. A. (1997), 'Historical Background of Sub-Saharan Africa: Opportunities and Constraints', in Samuel Aryeetey-Attoh (ed.), *Geography of Sub-Saharan Africa*, pp. 61-85, Simon and Schuster: Upper Saddle River, NJ.

Young, C. (1988), 'The African Colonial State and its Political Legacy', in Rothchild, D. and N. Chazan (eds.), *The Precarious Balance: State and Society in Africa*, Westview Press: Boulder, CO.

Zinyama, Lovemore (1986), 'Rural Household Structures, Ansenteeism and Agricultural Labour: A Case Study of Two Subsistence Farming Areas in Zimbabwe', *Singapore Journal of Tropical Geography*, 7, pp. 163-173.

20 São Tomé and Príncipe: The future of a marginal country in the context of its international integration – the role of Portugal

JOÃO LUÍS FERNANDES AND FERNANDA DELGADO CRAVIDÃO

The geography of the African continent in the world context

The Portuguese Discoveries commenced at the beginning of the 15th century with the conquest of Ceuta. They ushered in a new phase of World History, a new step for Humankind as manifested by the broadening of horizons and the dilution of frontiers. Geographical patterns and cultures were then built up.

A group of economic worlds, only superficially in touch with one another, was succeeded by a true world economy. The Portuguese played an active role in a historic period when different territories came closer together. The process of globalisation can be found deep among these roots. The construction of a world-wide geo-economic system coincided with this globalisation. The history of humankind in the 20th century has merely intensified a process begun several centuries ago, aided by the almost merciless imposition of a system known as the 'model of western development', in recent decades. Asymmetry is practically a natural consequence of this. The definition of centres of power and prosperity and the structuring of marginal territories came about as a logical outcome of unequal territorial division and the strengthening of interdependencies.

Africa, despite its geo-human and geo-economic heterogeneity, has emerged as a peripheral continent within this territorial architecture. This positioning of the African continent in the World Economy has made a deep and visible impression on its populations, its geography and its territoriality.

In the past few decades, the almost generalised under-development of Africa, regardless of the subjectivity of the concept, has been accentuated. The end of the Cold War and the opening up of Eastern Europe cast Africa even further into the shadows. With the New International Economic Order, Africa ceased to be a priority for the northern geo-economic powers.

The continent is suffering the consequences of its recent troubled history. The non-recognition of many states, struggling with the shackles of frontiers inherited from colonial days, is just part of a problem consisting of many factors. The continent is weighed down by unmanageable foreign debt; degradation of human resources; insufficient food and the proliferation of infectious diseases. Add to this a chequer-board of armed conflicts that are often difficult to fathom, with all the associated environmental deterioration, augmented by non-sustainable exploitation of resources, and the Continent is now headline news on the front pages of the world's media. The commonest pretext is the need to organise a corridor of humanitarian aid, which can only be done at enormous cost, almost always in response to a survival crisis afflicting defenceless populations. It is at times of increased economic marginalization that ethnic and religious extremists come to the fore and declare themselves, inevitably with the severest effects falling on the most disadvantaged.

Firstly, the destructuring of Africa's human geography has cultural roots. Along with a traditional society showing visible signs of disintegration, we see, in certain social groups, a hasty, poorly consolidated advance towards a Consumer Society. From the wreckage of this process there have emerged demographic masses which, whilst not excluded from the world geo-system, are clearly on its periphery.

It is a continent in turmoil searching for, so far without success, a model for African development. This course must cohabit not only with the manifest potential of these territories, but also with their deep-seated territorial and social inequalities. Pockets of the First World in the midst of the Third World. Modernity walking side by side with the most appalling poverty.

In 1992, according to the United Nations, 18 of the 20 lowest ranked countries on the Human Development Index[1] were in Africa.

Of the 25 countries world-wide which, in 1992, had not achieved an Average Life Expectancy of more than 50 years, 23 are African. Despite some progress (from 1960 to 1992, average life expectancy in sub-Saharan Africa increased from 40.0 to 51.1 years) the gap in relation to the developed world is huge. Industrialised countries enjoyed, on average, a life expectancy of 74.5 years[2] in 1992.

If it is not difficult to analyse these figures, interpretation of other indicators is more complicated. Indicators such as per capita income, illiteracy rate, numbers of televisions per inhabitant, average wages per inhabitant, among others[3], almost always place African countries at the tail end, in the world context. However, they should be viewed with extreme caution.

According to Paulo Freire[4], a Brazilian expert, an illiterate person is one who belongs to a literate society but does not understand the written word. Literacy must be based on a fundamental social need. Reference to illiteracy is only relevant when populations are integrated in a context where command of the written word is crucial to daily survival, and, furthermore, where knowledge of it is sought. This observation is made to illustrate one strategic orientation, which should always be present: the function of seeking a concept of development desired by and appropriate to Africa can only be ascribed to Africans themselves. The imposition of routes that are not desired is not legitimate. The process must be endogenous. Africans must take upon themselves the responsibility for demonstrating that Africa is important in the world system. It is for them alone to decide a strategy for the future: whether to participate in the world system, accepting the rules of globalisation, adapting them to local realities, or to look for another way of fulfilling their peoples' aspirations. To observe and interpret the African reality with focalisations based on non-African values is a sham: the non-acceptance that difference and individuality is legitimate.

Despite the unfavourable image of Africa in the World, the picture cannot be described without the invigoration of some hope for the future. History will not be repeated. Despite their apparent immobility, the continent's territories are not inert and do not have to develop along the same path. The western world need not be the point of reference. The route to follow could be another. Geo-economic marginality is a dynamic concept, not a territorial fatality. Negative connotations could also be turned into comparative advantages. The very notion of marginality is relative. Its conception depends on cultural framework, on geographic references, on the differentiated notion of 'well-being'. This reality will be illustrated with the empirical case of São Tomé and Príncipe.

São Tomé and Príncipe - geographic characterisation of a marginal country in a peripheral continent

São Tomé and Príncipe has been an independent republic since 12 July 1975. It is equatorial, situated in the Gulf of Guinea, between latitude 1°44' north and 0°1' south, and longitude 7°28'and 6°28' east. Its area is around 1000 sq. km. It consists of the two islands that give it its name, São Tomé and Príncipe, and some others nearby, volcanic in origin (Figure 20.1).

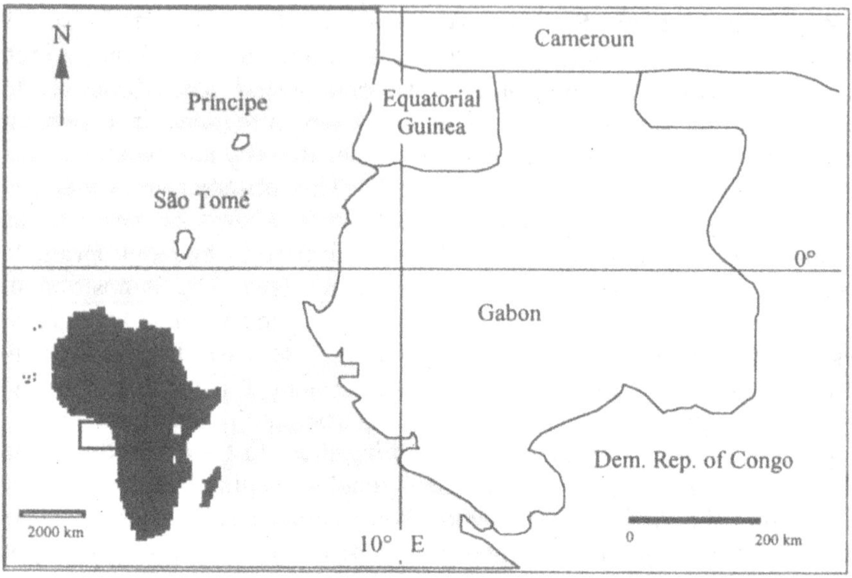

Figure 20.1 Regional context of São Tomé and Príncipe

The population and territory of a marginal country

The structuring of the São Tomé began to reflect, from the very beginning of its settling, the various population waves that were arriving at the island. It occurred in such a way that, even today, the territory occupied by the *Angolares* (those of Angolan origin) is quite distinct from the occupation pattern of the capital, and from other communities of different origins.

A brief look at the demography of São Tomé shows us that its population was around 60 thousand in 1940, had reached 100 thousand by 1981 and, by 1991, stood at almost 120 thousand. In other words, the population of São Tomé and Príncipe doubled in the space of fifty years.

A recent study (Sacramento, 1996) has shown that the growth rate between 1981 and 1991 was 2.2%, largely the result of high birth rates, since, in 1991 it was 43‰, 32‰ in 1994, while the birth rate was 8.3‰ and 8.1‰, respectively. It should be noted that the high mortality rate, still a factor in this equatorial country, prevents the natural growth rate from reaching higher levels. In 1994, in São Tomé and Príncipe, almost 63 children per thousand aged between 0 and 2 years, died. Contrary to the situation in the so-called developed countries, fertility remains high in São

Tomé and Príncipe, with each woman having, on average, 5.4 children. The latest figures, however, show a tendency to decline.

Even though it is a small country, it has huge regional disparities. The history of its settlement, movement towards the capital, São Tomé, the economic failure of sugar cane, coffee and copra encouraged many people from São Tomé to emigrate, particularly to Europe. The average population density is 117.4/sq. km., but some districts have more than 200 people per sq. km. - those closest to the capital – and there is one area having only 30-inhabitants/sq.km. This is Caué, whose population is Angolan in origin.

Population structure

The population structure reflects the above-mentioned phenomena: high birth rate; high infant mortality; life expectancy of around 65 years, and spatial mobility, essentially affecting the young working population.

The 0 to 14 years age group accounts for around 47% of the total populations; the 15 to 64 age group are more or less the same percentage, and the oldest group is not quite 7% of the total.

This age structure in a country with such features as São Tomé and Príncipe has, raises short-, medium- and long-term issues of town and country planning that present considerable problems, not only in respect of anticipation, but also of management. The most worrying domains, in our view, are those of health, education and employment.

Some projections have been made that enable us to construct possible scenarios for São Tomé and Príncipe. Sacramento (1996) says that the population will reach 158 thousand by the year 2000, and stand at around 285 thousand twenty-five years later. Natural growth will tend to decline, but still remain above 2%. Fertility will also decline, since various national and international organisations are running campaigns with this objective, and it is predicted that the average number of children per woman will not be more than 3 by the year 2025. Even though prospects seem good, the structure of the population will not be greatly affected; it will continue to be a young population with education and employment remaining the priority areas, and the most problematic. As regards health, the co-operation arrangements between Portugal, various international organisations, and São Tomé and Príncipe should, we believe, be strengthened since it seems to us that this is one area, which could be assured of success.

In the African context, it should be noted that São Tomé and Príncipe does not appear to be at a disadvantage in terms of health, although malaria is still the leading cause of death (Sacramento, 1996).

Following independence in 1975, São Tomé and Príncipe had to face serious economic and social problems, which were aggravating the deterioration of its economy as well as it, demographic characteristics.

Unemployment is one of the main concerns of the government. According to figures for 1993 issued by the Ministry of Finance and Planning, out of a total active population of 54,260, 14,868 or 27.5%, were unemployed.

Its main products – associated with the major employers of labour – declined rapidly. In addition, the prices of its principal exports (cocoa, coffee and copra) also saw a sharp drop on the international market, rendering the country's economic plight even more acute. An illustration of this is the fact that, in 1986 (after independence) São Tomé exported 4,182 tons of cocoa, whereas in 1994 the figure was less than 3,300 tons. The export of copra similarly fell from 3,133 tons to 872 in the same period. Sacramento (1966) thus says:

> ...losses incurred by cocoa producers and by virtually all the other public enterprises, together with the rapid increase in debt, contributed to worsen the budget deficit, creating extremely difficult economic conditions for the people of São Tomé. Dependence on other countries for food (90%), consumer goods, machines and components, just as much as for external transport and communications aggravated the difficulties.

We do not find in São Tomé and Príncipe many of the main structural problems experienced by most sub-Saharan African states. There is no history of civil war; the transition to democracy was relatively quiet; there are no disputes about borders; conflicts among the various national groups are unknown; the islands have never experienced a dramatic refugee problem. Yet São Tomé and Príncipe is not immune to other constraints common to the African continent. The weakness of the State, with its consequent political instability has, for instance, led to successive changes of government. This has restricted prospects for a coherent, long-term development project.

Which development model(s) for São Tomé and Príncipe?

The answer to this question is not straightforward, nor does it have one single emphasis. On the contrary, the routes leading to development, according to the relativity, which we have thus far defended, are many. Furthermore, it is important to re-emphasise that the initiatives must come from the Africans themselves, and so it is legitimate to search for a specific development model. The transposition of models and systems, it has been proved, is not the most effective way to integrate the nations of Africa. São Tomé and Príncipe is no exception. Our opinions, therefore, should be taken in this context. They are suggestions only, not directives to be imposed.

Survival of the State of São Tomé and Príncipe in the context of the World Economy is bound up with integration: in the continent of Africa and in the World. The development model for São Tomé and Príncipe should not be separate from the African reality. On the other hand, under GATT and World Trade Organisation agreements, countries, no matter how insignificant in the world hierarchy, have become hostages to the world development model, which would seem to make liaison inevitable. In spite of all the relativity that analysis of these problems requires, isolating territories is not a viable path, in the long term. The tendency towards internationalisation is, because of its driving force, unavoidable.

Within the globalisation process, it is of the utmost importance to question the functionality of spaces. What is the function of São Tomé and Príncipe in the world geo-economic context and the international division of work?

São Tomé and Príncipe has no energy and mineral resources. It differs from other African countries in that it has no resources whose ownership has proved to be crucial for development model(s) in the 20th century (such as gold, diamonds, oil and other minerals). On a first and immediate reading, its territorial characteristics constitute, for this and for other reasons, an obstacle to the country's future. Its small size and insular character could be marginalizing factors. Island territories have problems with transport, accentuating their isolation. The demands for construction and maintenance of infrastructure, like airports, seaports are beyond the technical and financial capacities of a small country with a modest economy. But fatalism should not be a barrier to objective intervention in marginal areas.

A country can make an impression internationally without having a vast area or unlimited resources. São Tomé and Príncipe must make the most of its assets. In the context of globalisation, territories should be valorised by demonstrating their specific importance; '…a sovereignty of recognized service indispensable to the global order...' (Adriano Moreira, 1996, p. 18).

The specificity of São Tomé and Príncipe begins with its geographic position and is reinforced by its insularity. The Atlantic Ocean has been a barrier to contact among peoples. With the Portuguese Discoveries it became a stage for communication, and so it will be in the future. The model(s) for development is (are) dependent on the sea. Movement within the continent is difficulty. Access to the sea is not easy, with few natural ports and a coastline that is small in relation to the total area of the African continent. Control of the sea is thus a strategic imperative for Africa (Sacchetti, 1990, p. 198).

The 21st century will be the century of the oceans, and so the geographic location and insularity of São Tomé and Príncipe could be exploited in a variety of ways.

The archipelago could regain its function as a distribution centre, one course previously exploited. In the 17th century, and those following, São Tomé and Príncipe was the trading centre for slaves captured in West Africa, whose destination was Brazil.

One attractive option for São Tomé and Príncipe would be to establish itself as an interface for goods and transportation, and also for information. This is why the development of telecommunications, and assistance in creating an Information Company is an avenue worth exploring.

Some authors (Martins, 1991, p. 145) also advocate the setting up of a 'fiscal paradise'. This is an eternal functional alternative for territories on the periphery of major capital flows. The exploitation of maritime resources in its Exclusive Economic Zone is another possibility.

Tourism is viewed as another alternative for peripheral territories. Marginality, through conservation of the countryside, can thus be regarded as a comparative advantage. São Tomé and Príncipe has mesologic charms which give it good reason to dream of an active future in this field. Idyllic scenery could be the focus of international affirmation of the island group. Fundamental to this is the provision of equipment.

Tourism, besides, is an area which São Tomé intends to encourage, and for which it is seeking foreign investment. Quite recently, for instancc, European businessmen with interests in Portugal (Algarve) have renovated a hotel employing 100 local people. As regards the higher qualified cadres, workers come from South Africa, England and Germany.

According to Ernâni Lopes[5] development in Africa will only be achieved after a long process of conciliation and reconstruction restructuring. In the case of São Tomé and Príncipe, the conciliation problem does not arise. This republic was not one of the theatres of war during the colonial conflicts that preceded independence (after 25 April 1974). Nor did it subsequently suffer the evils of civil war. As a relatively peaceful society, it is at a considerable advantage. But what this archipelago needs more urgently than reconstruction is infrastructure, as soon as possible, it needs a seaport and airport, of international standards. Along with this, proper utilisation of human resources is indispensable to any affirmative strategy plan.

Difficult tasks to accomplish in a situation of territorial isolation. The end of the bipolar arrangement of the World System has made the [re]integration of countries in geo-economic blocs very pressing. South-South integration is, in these cases, very difficult. Yet interdependency is unavoidable.

At any rate, one line to explore, should the African populations see it that way, would be association with Portugal in a strengthening of the interrelationships within the Lusophone world.

São Tomé and Príncipe and the Lusophone space

Portugal can see much of its past in Africa and, as such, much of its identity. For example, the Portuguese were the first to set eyes on these islands in the 15th century. The Portuguese peopled them, at first with slaves from the coast of West Africa, deportees and Castilian Jews.

To a greater extent than other ex-colonisers, Portugal was the first to arrive at, and the last European country to abandon Africa. A constant presence for several centuries, interrupted by colonial war, destructive to both sides, but without hatred. A country with historical responsibilities and a tradition of easy dialogue with African cultures.

The Portuguese feel a mixture of attraction and longing for Africa. The geography of African territory is dotted with vestiges of the Lusitanian presence. The greatest bequest was the spread of the language of Camões. As economies become increasingly internationalised, a language in common must be valued as a cultural dimension of economic relations and the integration of spaces.

Lusophonia could be a line of affirmation for the world's Portuguese-speaking nations. A means of drawing closer to the principal centres of decision in the World, by way of its integration. A strategy for attenuating the marginality of some of these countries.

Among the nations of the recently created 'Comunidade dos Países de Língua Portuguesa' (CPLP), i.e., (Community of Portuguese Speaking Countries), officially constituted Lisbon on 17 July 1996, Portugal is the only one linked to an economic bloc within the world economy. Portugal is located on the fringes of a geo-economically wealthy bloc; it is a country situated on the 'periphery of the centre' (Barreto, 1995, p. 841). However, although, in the context of world geo-economics, they occupy different relative positions, the relationship of Portugal with its African partners is characterised by easy dialogue. The territories are different, but not irreconcilable. Portugal, through its History, has a special vocation for articulation and could be a suitable mediator, bringing the African countries nearer to the European Union, and even to the United States.

Economic integration in the Lusophone area is still fragile. Even so, the advantage of strengthening these ties is unarguable, not only for the countries of Africa, but also for Portugal. Indeed, the country's position in Europe will be enhanced by the valorisation of its interdependency with Africa. The project of European integration is not incompatible with the strengthening of the CPLP.

In these conditions, co-operation without paternalism, without complexes, based on a common past and close cultural identity, should be given its full potential. The presence of Portugal in Africa should not become a reductive North-South relationship. The historic and cultural circumstances of the countries concerned are incompatible with such a simplification.

In this sphere Portugal has a multiple role to play. On the one hand, consolidation of the Portuguese language in these territories, giving force to instruments such as RDP Africa (Portuguese Radio Service for Africa) and RTP Africa (Portuguese Television Service for Africa). Co-operation could equally take the form of training local technicians. Portugal could also participate in the process of restructuring and [re]construction of local geo-economies.

In addition, African countries with Portuguese as their Official Language (PALOP) suffer from being surrounded by other areas of influence, like Spanish and French, the latter being very obvious in the case of São Tomé and Príncipe. Even so, these other spheres are not incompatible with a Portuguese presence. The tripartite co-operation option could be well worth exploring. As regards the relations between São Tomé and Príncipe and the Lusophone world, its position is coming to have a strategic importance. Indeed, it is significant that one can draw a triangle in the South Atlantic with Portuguese-speaking sites at each vertex (Portugal, Africa and South America) (Figure 20.2). This is not the same historical Atlantic trade triangle of the 17th and 18th centuries, with the African coast connecting with Brazil and Portugal, but rather the affirmation of a space encompassing affinity and communication. Such interdependence does not conflict with Portugal as a member of the EU, nor with Brazil's place in Mercosul and the 'PALOPs' in other organisations. The key words are articulation, complementarity and inter-regional solidarity.

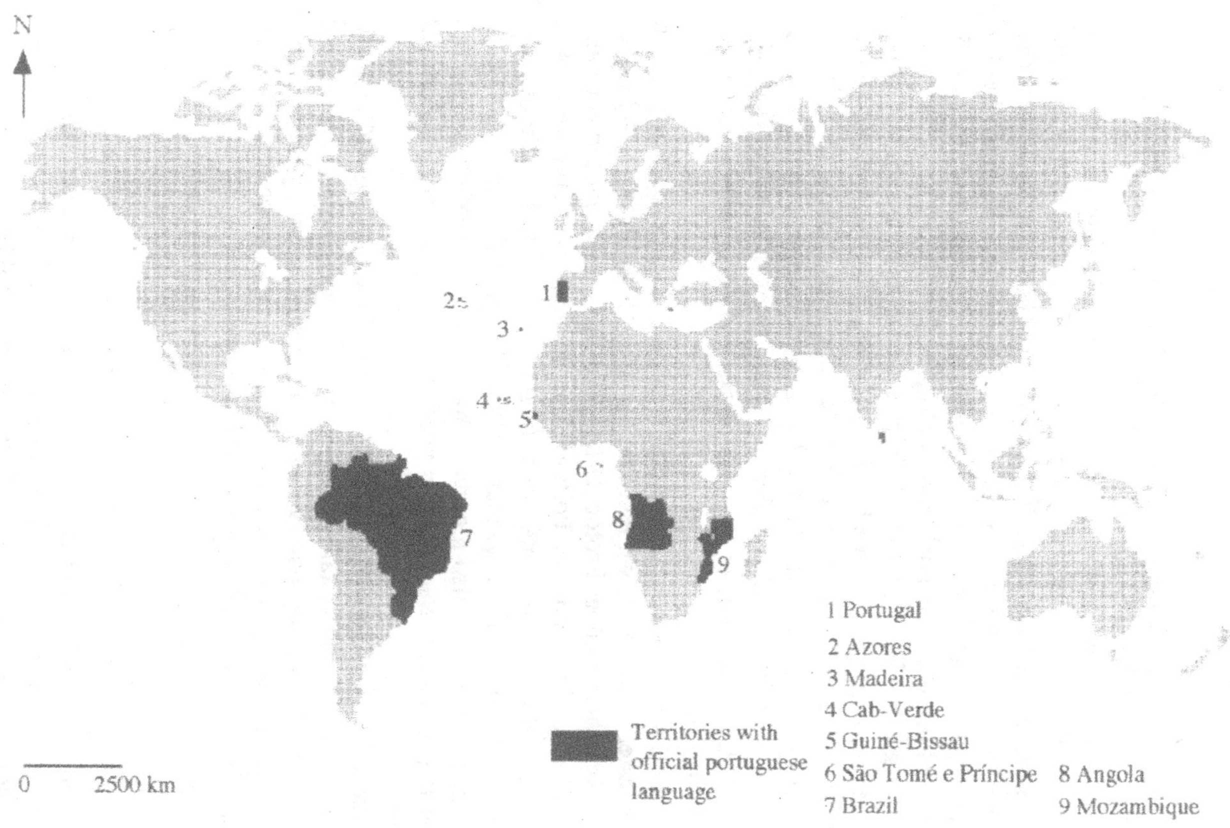

Figure 20.2 Territories with Portuguese as official language

Conclusion

Solving the problems of the Democratic Republic of São Tomé and Príncipe is not easy, and is unlikely to be quick. What does seem certain, as we have said, is that some of the key words concern Equatorial Africa and involve its political stability. Having a favourable location in the Atlantic, São Tomé can profit from its strategic position. There are, however, other difficulties of a domestic nature. Help could and should be given help to overcome them. By efforts of world solidarity in general and, in specific domains, by Portugal. Education and Health, far from being neo-colonialist models, are greatly deprived and this is where co-operation should develop forms that constantly respect the local population. It is essential not only to understand but also to put into effect development models that do not originate from models adopted by the so-called developed countries. Local cultures, ways of living and the physical fragility of these territories have to be respected. The right of peoples to be, and to organise themselves must to be respected.

Portugal, for historical and cultural reasons is in an excellent position to collaborate. At any rate, we feel that the area of health is a good example of what is being done. Protocols between this equatorial territory and the finest health care units in Portugal ensure that, whenever necessary, patients are sent from São Tomé to Portugal for treatment. In addition, several teams of health workers go there to work temporarily. As regards education, although there is also a certain amount of co-operation, we do not feel that it yet matches São Tomé's needs, nor is it as much as Portugal could give.

In the words of Sacramento (1996), 'we believe that, [given] consolidation of the recently-installed democratic process, with internal and external credibility in the country increasing through growing privatisation of the public sector by stimulating investment, the economic and social situation of the country will know' a better future.

Notes

1. Development indicator calculated on the basis of life expectancy, adult illiteracy, average number of years schooling and per capita income (see 'Report on Human Development 1994', United Nations Development Programme, p. 108).
2. 'Report on Human Development 1994', United Nations Development Programme.
3. 'Report on Human Development 1994', United Nations Development Programme.
4. According to an interview published by the 'Público' newspaper, 4 May 1997.
5. Conference held at the 'Instituto de Altos Estudos Militares', Lisbon, November 1996.

References

Amaral, Ilídio do (1995), 'A África no Limiar do Século XXI: um Continente em Crise', *Verbo-Enciclopédia Luso-Brasileira de Cultura* XXIII: Lisboa.

Barreto, António (1995), 'Portugal na periferia do centro: mudança social, 1960 a 1995', *Análise Social* XXX: 134, Revista do Gabinete de Investigações Sociais: Lisboa.

Barke, Michael and Greg, O'Hare (1991), *The Third World, Conceptual Frameworks in Geography*, Oliver & Boyd: London.

Bessa, António Marques (1990), 'O Problema Africano: a Questão do Atraso', *Africana* 7, Centro de Estudos Africanos da Universidade Portucalense: Porto.

Carvalho, Virgílio de (1992), 'África, Parente Pobre da 'Nova Ordem Internacional', *Africana* 10, Centro de Estudos Africanos da Universidade Portucalense: Porto.

Chapman, P. Graham and Kathleen M. Baker (1992), *The Changing Geography of Africa and the Middle East*, Routledge: London and New York.

Charrie, Jean-Paul (1990), 'Les Relations entre la Communauté Économique Européenne et les Pays Afrique-Caraibes-Pacifique', *Revue de Géographie de Bordeaux – Les Cahiers d'Outre-Mer* 169: Bordeaux.

Cole, John (1996), *Geography of the World's Major Regions*, Routledge: London and New York.

Cunha, Joaquim da Silva (1988), 'Subdesenvolvimento em África. Quem é o Responsável?', *Africana* 2, Centro de Estudos Africanos da Universidade Portucalense: Porto.

Dollfus, Olivier (1990), 'Le Système Monde', *L' Information Geographique* 54: Nov./Dez., J. B. Baillière et Fils: Paris.

Fontoura, Luís (1990), 'O Cooperação Luso-Africana', *Africana* 7, Centro de Estudos Africanos da Universidade Portucalense: Porto.

Gonçalves, Paulo Frederico (1994), 'Leste Europeu ou África – Que Prioridade para a Europa Ocidental', *Africana* 14, Centro de Estudos Africanos da Universidade Portucalense: Porto.

Lourenço, Eduardo (1996), 'Tempo Português', *Janus 97 – Anuário de Relações Exteriores*, Público & Universidade Autónoma de Lisboa: Lisboa.

Martins, José Abílio Lomba (1991), 'Portugal Tropical e Lusofonia (Cenário dos Pequenos Países Africanos de Língua Oficial Portuguesa)', *Africana* 8, Centro de Estudos Africanos da Universidade Portucalense: Porto.

Martins, Manuel Gonçalves (1991), 'A Comunidade Europeia e o Desenvolvimento dos Países ACP', *Africana* 8, Centro de Estudos Africanos da Universidade Portucalense: Porto.

Monteiro, Fernando Amaro (1990), 'Em Torno do Pan-Africanismo', *Africana* 6, Centro de Estudos Africanos da Universidade Portucalense: Porto.

Moreira, Adriano (1996), 'Soberania de Serviço', *Janus 97 – Anuário de Relações Exteriores*, Público & Universidade Autónoma de Lisboa: Lisboa.

Mouafo, Dieudonné (1991), 'Les Difficultés de L'Intégration Économique Inter-Régionale en Afrique Noire: L'Exemple de la Zone UDEAC', *Revue de Géographie de Bordeaux – Les Cahiers d'Outre-Mer*, 174: Bordeaux.

Sacchetti, António (1990), 'A Europa, a África e o Atlântico no Quadro da Cooperação – Aspectos Estratégicos', *Africana* 6, Centro de Estudos Africanos da Universidade Portucalense: Porto.

Sacramento, A., Francisco (1996), 'A Problemática do Crescimento Demográfico no Processo de Planeamento do Território em S.Tomé e Príncipe; análise no sector de educação, saúde e emprego': Coimbra.

Van Schoor, Marthinus Oliveira (1992), 'Myths and Realities', *Africana* 10, Centro de Estudos Africanos da Universidade Portucalense: Porto.

21 Australian microeconomic reform and Tasmania:
An economic and social appraisal

PETER SCOTT

Introduction

Since 1983 Australia's export-oriented economy has not only expanded by more than one-third but improved its growth performance relative to other OECD countries. This achievement stems from a program of economic reform begun in 1983 when Australia's economic growth was threatened by its declining competitiveness in export markets (Scott, 1994). In the 1980s reform focused primarily on financial deregulation and latterly trade liberalization but in the 1990s, while financial and trade reforms continue, the focus has shifted primarily to microeconomic measures. Microeconomic reform aims to boost the labour productivity of individual enterprises, both public and private, largely by measures facilitating competition, reducing protection, and imposing more flexible and efficient workplace practices. The resultant structural change has brought major changes to the composition of exports, primary products falling from three-quarters in the mid-1980s to three-fifths a decade later and manufactured goods rising from one-fifth to one-third; high value-added elaborately transformed manufactures, which comprise instruments, scientific equipment, telecommunications technology, transport equipment, and industrial machinery, even rose from one-tenth to one-fifth. Meanwhile, inflation fell below that of Australia's main trading partners and in early 1997 was lower than at any time since the Depression of the 1930s. Wage restraint was also historically outstanding.

Yet despite an improved economy Australia's reform process at both Federal and State levels lacked coherence and latterly has progressed too slowly. Although Australia has more than doubled exports to East Asia, the world's fastest growing region, its share of East Asian imports has steadily declined. Underlying the decline are two major persistent problems: a high current account deficit (CAD) in the balance of payments; and a high level of unemployment (8.7% of the April 1997 workforce). The CAD problem persists because of low levels of saving: Australians save about 16% of gross domestic product (GDP), invest about 21%, and bridge the gap with foreign capital. To address the problem requires major changes to taxation and social welfare policy. The unemployment problem persists because of the slow rate of labour market reform, and a more radical approach requires changes in attitude by both employers and employees. But without such change Australia is unlikely to achieve the high growth rates needed to reduce unemployment significantly.

Porter (1990), a leading world authority on international competitiveness and a former adviser to the Victorian and New Zealand governments on economic reform, contends that Australia has yet to make an irrevocable commitment to competition (The Australian, 11 April 1997, p. 23). Victoria has pursued with marked success the most rapid and vigorous program of microeconomic reform so far undertaken by an Australian State but its progress has been hampered by the slow pace of Federal Government reform and specific regions have suffered substantial social dislocation. New Zealand's spectacular economic success, the most outstanding on the world scene, was achieved at a high social cost that would be unacceptable to Australians. Already alienation exists within parts of the Australian community brought about by globalization, economic restructuring, and social change. This article reviews briefly Australian microeconomic reform, and against this background the economic and social impact of economic reform in the slowest growing and traditionally lagging island State of Tasmania.

Microeconomic reform in Australia

Australian microeconomic reform comprises mainly the national competition policy, labour market reform, and trade liberalization. In sharp contrast to New Zealand, where reform was implemented swiftly and comprehensively, Australian competition policy was not adopted until 1995, industrial relations reform has been incremental throughout the reform period but the most important changes were not enacted until 1996, and tariff barriers have been lowered progressively since 1983 or removed. Before the mid-1990s, various reforms to increase competition had also been initiated by individual State Governments. One reason for the contrasting rates of reform between New Zealand and Australia is that New Zealand has a unitary system of government whereas most microeconomic reform in Australia requires action by up to nine governments: six State, two Territory, and the Federal Government. Only in financial deregulation, trade liberalization, and labour market reform-covering workers under federal awards has the Federal Government acted unilaterally. This section outlines the salient features of the three main microeconomic reform areas, and summarizes their relevance to Tasmania.

Competition policy

Australian competition policy has long been embodied not only in the Trade Practices Act 1974 but also in voluminous legislation covering inter alia the competitive behaviour of firms. In the late 1980s it became increasingly evident that despite this legislation and the reforms already made by all levels of government to enhance competition, much of the economy remained effectively sheltered from domestic and international competition. Moreover, a growing need was widely felt for a consistent set of business rules, which transcend State boundaries. In 1992 a committee was appointed to develop a national competition policy based on principles established by the Council of Australian Governments (COAG).

The Hilmer Report (Australia, 1993) recommended reform in six areas: competitive conduct rules, anti-competitive legislation, public monopolies, access to essential facilities, restricting monopoly pricing, and competitive neutrality (government business competing with private business). Four sectors were highlighted for reform: public utilities, the building industry, transport and communication, and the professions. Although COAG endorsed the Report, the States demanded compensation, since four-fifths of the reforms would be their responsibility but two-thirds of the extra revenue would accrue to the Commonwealth. After protracted negotiation, COAG agreed in 1995 to reform electricity, gas (not relevant to Tasmania), and road transport industries by 1997-98, water supply by 1999-2000, and to have completed all reforms by 2001-02. At each stage, if the reforms are delivered, the States receive financial compensation on terms already agreed, but if they fail in their undertakings, they will be penalized financially. In 1995 the Industry Commission estimated that within eight years the reforms should increase GDP by 5.5%, employment by 30,000, real wages by 3%, and save the average household A$1,500 a year. Spread over eight years these improvements are likely to be obscured by growth trends and cyclical factors. No mention was made of short-term social costs.

Implementation of the reforms in Tasmania, where structural change lags behind other States by about two or three years, should bring considerable economic benefit. A Report by the University of Tasmania Centre for Regional Economic Analysis (CREA), commissioned jointly by ten national employer groups for the COAG deliberations, reveals that Tasmanian productivity is likely to increase by about 75% of the improvement estimated to occur nationally (Madden, 1995). The lower outcome is attributed to greater efficiency in electricity generation, rail transport, the ports, and communication. On the other hand, Tasmanian service industries are generally less efficient than those in other States and have more to gain from reform. Over the reform period the workforce participation rate is estimated to increase more or less similarly across all States owing to interstate migration, a questionable assumption, and the reduction in Tasmanian unemployment to be about 1.15%.

Labour market reform

From 1983 to 1996 the Labour Government maintained the welfarist and centralist approach that had characterized Australian industrial relations throughout most of this century. At the outset it established an Accord with the trade unions and business, which failed to produce the flexible labour market necessary to maximize productivity growth and competitiveness. Even the misnamed Industrial Relations Reform Act 1993, which aimed to facilitate a rapid shift to flexible enterprise bargaining that had begun a year earlier, maintained a comprehensive award system and the basic monopoly rights of unions. Its unfair dismissal provisions overly favoured employees, and deterred many employers from hiring permanent staff. The Act almost doubled the size of existing industrial relations legislation, in itself a far cry from deregulation. Consequently, many Australian companies, including subsidiaries of multinationals such as Gillette, Heinz, Kraft, and Unilever, relocated production to New Zealand where the labour market had under-gone radical reform in 1988.

The Liberal Government's Workplace Relations Act 1996, despite introducing only incremental changes, constitutes the first break with paternalistic industrial relations this century and the first radical move toward genuine workplace relations. It furnishes a statutory procedure for non-union agreements, and recognizes employment contracts made at common law. Companies remain free to continue negotiating collectively with unions, which in 1997 numbered among their members only one-quarter of the private sector workforce. The Act also provides for an award safety net of fair minimum wages, important for low-paid workers in such industries as textile, clothing, and footwear (TCF). In 1997 only about one-third of employees were still covered by industrial awards, a sharp fall from the two-thirds coverage in 1993. For the changes to have universal application in Australia, the States must either cede their industrial relations power to the Commonwealth, as Victoria did in 1997, or enact State legislation containing the new provisions. The new industrial relations agreements would seem especially attractive to small business, which aside from a few large, mainly metal and paper industries predominate in Tasmania.

Trade liberalization

Since 1983, when Australian manufacturing was protected not only by high tariffs but also by quantitative restrictions on highly sensitive categories of imports, protection has been progressively reduced, so that by 1997 almost all industry had tariffs of only 5 or less, giving Australia one of the lowest tariff levels in the OECD. While the manufacturing sector has contracted as factories close or reduce their workforce to remain competitive, most manufacturing now displays innovation, technological development, increasing productivity, improving quality of product, and export growth. These features typify manufacturing in all States, including Tasmania.

Two highly sensitive industries in which protection remains high but steadily declines are motor vehicle manufacture and the TCF industry. Import quotas for cars have been abolished, and tariffs reduced from 57.5% in 1983 to 22.5% in 1997; the rate is set to fall to 15 per cent in 2000. A car industry export facilitation scheme, which allows manufacturers to import goods duty-free in return for exports, underpins the growth in exports, of which about half is automotive components. Assembly plants are confined to Adelaide and Melbourne, three plants having been forced to close, but automotive component factories are widespread in south-eastern Australia, including Tasmania. The TCF industry is a diversified, labour-intensive industry that employs one-tenth of the manufacturing workforce. Since 1989 protection has been phased down by more than one-half, and many firms have not survived, especially those located in the poorest neighbourhoods of metropolitan areas. But the industry includes a growing number of efficient firms exporting high-quality products worldwide. Tasmania has examples of both types of manufacturers.

Economic reform in Tasmania

Tasmania, the smallest (68,330 sq. kms) and least populous (470,000 inhabitants) of the Australian States, is a forested mountainous island where settlement is almost wholly confined to an arcuate belt through the north and east, isolated mining centres are scattered through the superhumid western ranges, and the south-west comprises uninhabited temperate wilderness (see Figure 21.1). Although economic reform has brought much benefit to the island, it has also, as in various other regions of Australia, accentuated social disadvantage. The State continues to display the lowest productivity per worker, amounting to little more than three-quarters of the national average, the highest unemployment (10.8% of the April 1997 workforce), the highest net State debt relative to gross state product (GSP), the worst credit rating, and paradoxically, when the State seeks to attract investment, the greatest reliance on business taxes. Its industrial structure is made up of a few large industries together with numerous small and some medium businesses, many family owned, and among the smaller many operating below capacity. Real unemployment, particularly having regard to the high incidence of self-employment, hidden unemployment, and persistent out-migration, is probably much higher than suggested by official statistics. The industrial structure also has a bearing on Tasmania's insolvency rate, the lowest of the States.

Microeconomic reform has had its greatest impact to date on the public sector. Tasmania has long been grossly overgoverned, and in 1993 local government areas (LGAs) were belatedly reduced from 46 to 29 (Scott, 1996a). State Government plans a further reduction from 29 to 15 for the near future, and holding a referendum on whether the Legislative Council, an independent upper house of State parliament without party representation, should be abolished. Long before the adoption of a national competition policy, State Government had begun to reform public monopolies, separating policy functions from commercial operations. The Hydro-Electric Commission (HEC) was restructured with independent business units, the publicly owned TT Line operating the Bass Strait ferry was corporatized, a Forestry Corporation established, and the Tasmanian Government Insurance Office privatized. Non-core functions of government departments and major service provision were outsourced. All these and other changes contributed to downsizing of the public administration sector throughout the 1990s. Yet so large had been the sector at its peak that in 1995-96 it still accounted for a bigger share (4.5%) of GSP than it had in 1983-84 (4.4%), whereas the sector's average share in other States had fallen from 3.7 per cent in 1983-84 to 3.3% in 1995-96. Downsizing has been most marked in major service centres, notably Hobart, Launceston, Devonport, and Burnie.

Over the reform period, manufacturing, which in Tasmania as well as nationally is the leading sector in output and exports, has probably been foremost in upgrading its efficiency, quality of product, and competitiveness. Modernization of long-established plants has led to retrenchments, notably at the Hobart electrolytic zinc refinery in 1993, then Tasmania's largest industry, where the workforce was reduced by one-third. Other large industries forced to downsize include the Burnie paper mill, the George Town manganese smelter, and the New Norfolk newsprint mill.

The George Town aluminium smelter has regularly upgraded its plant but in the 1990s greater efficiency was achieved through the introduction of individual staff contracts offering high salaries in return for more flexible working conditions. Their introduction prompted a prolonged fight with the unions, which the company eventually won. Tariff reductions combined with high business taxes forced the closure of numerous factories, including the State's largest textile factory in Launceston, which relocated to Dunedin, another textile plant in Devonport, tool manufacturing in Hobart, and a Hobart glassware factory that had supplied 70% of the Australian drinkware market. From 1983-84 to 1995-96 manufacturing's share of Tasmania's GSP fell from 18.2 to 14.8 per cent, a trend common to all States.

In general, manufacturers who export are more innovative, more productive, invest more capital, and pay higher wages than their non-exporting counterparts. Among numerous Tasmanian examples are the high-tech companies located in the Hobart and Launceston technoparks. These include a Hobart firm founded in the early 1980s that expanded production fivefold in five years (1992-96) exporting lightning conductors to thirty countries. Long-established examples are a Hobart marine engineering company, also exporting to thirty countries, and a boot manufacturer with escalating exports to the high-fashion British, continental European, and American markets. Since 1993 the latter company has freighted leather to Auckland for manufacture into uppers which are returned to the Hobart factory, a procedure less costly than making the uppers in Hobart and paying 50% government imposts on the considerably higher wages incurred (Behrens, 1995). But the most spectacular growth of an innovative export industry is the manufacture in Hobart of large ocean-going aluminium catamaran ferries for export to East Asia, Europe, and the Americas, an industry founded in the 1980s and now the State's biggest employer. Its growth has been assisted by a federal shipbuilding bounty of 5%, which enables the company to compete with foreign shipbuilders receiving subsidies ranging from 9 to 25%. However, the bounty is scheduled to end before 2000.

In both Tasmania and nationally transport is the sector expected to gain most from microeconomic reform (Madden, 1995, p. 17). Intrastate transport has been shackled by regulations introduced before the Second World War to protect public railway and tramway services from road transport competition. In 1997 legislation to reform road transport in Tasmania was blocked by the Legislative Council on the grounds that inter alia deregulation would enable interstate firms to operate in Tasmania and adversely affect about 100 businesses. Failure to pass the legislation put the State in breach of the national competition policy guidelines and risked non-receipt of federal compensation but the legislation was eventually passed. The Tasmanian Government had also planned to privatize the Metropolitan Transport Trust (MTT) bus services but owing to strong opposition from employees, unions, social welfare agencies, and the wider community gave the Trust three years to cut costs, maintain services, and attract more passengers. Meanwhile the MTT is to be corporatized. In 1997 Tasrail, which the Australian National Railways Commission had operated solely as a freight service between Hobart, Launceston, and the north-west coast, was corporatized and privatized, Australia's first railway to be sold to a private company. The State Government will receive financial compensation over two years to offset job losses. The Federal Government, which has already privatized Qantas, plans to privatize the Hobart and Launceston Airports. It also partially deregulated telecommunieations in 1988, established a duopoly, and fully deregulated the industry in 1997. There remains to be overhauled postal services, port administration (a State matter), and the waterfront.

Public utilities present much less scope for improving productivity than transport but the potential gains are substantial. Since Tasmania's economic development throughout much of this century stemmed from hydro-industrialization, the proposed privatization of the HEC, which operates the most efficient State electricity system in Australia, has provoked widespread controversy. Early in 1997 the Tasmanian Government announced that the State would retain control of the dams and generating system but privatize the transmission and retail assets. The proceeds would be used to facilitate the construction of a Bass Strait link between the Tasmanian and Victorian grids, to retire State debt, to reduce payroll tax, and to stimulate new enterprise in information technology and advanced telecommunications. No State has yet begun to reform its water supply utilities. CREA calculated that reforming utilities to best practice through competitive pressures would improve labour productivity in electricity and urban water supply by 32 and 26% respectively (Madden, 1995, pp. 5-6). Clearly jobs would be lost.

No other sector offers major benefits from microeconomic reform. In general, the export-oriented primary sector already has highly competitive arrangements, and the main benefits to be realized would flow from transport, utilities, and labour market reforms. In the building industry productivity would increase with the removal of unnecessary building regulations and approval delays, while in the professions the removal of monopolies and restrictions would confer community-wide benefits.

Social marginality in Tasmania

While economic reform has brought considerable benefits to the Australian economy, it has also impacted adversely on specific local communities, many of which were already disadvantaged by high unemployment, low incomes, and poor environmental and social conditions. To gain a preliminary perspective on their regional significance in Tasmania, an index was constructed from five variables: the percentage of the workforce unemployed, the workforce participation rate, the proportion of families with one parent and dependent children, the proportion of families with incomes below A$12,000 (the poverty line for one-parent families), and the ratio of rented public housing to total dwellings. Workforce participation rates are especially significant, because the closure of industries with largely female employment affects participation more than unemployment. On ranking the indices the first two quintiles were deemed to have very high and high social marginality.

Figure 21.1 portrays the resultant pattern. Since LGA data are available only for census years and in mid-1997 the 1996 census had yet to be published, the map depicts the 1991 results. It has the merit that it shows the broad distribution of social marginality following economic reform in the 1980s and prior to the predominantly microeconomic reforms of the 1990s. It furnishes a backdrop against which may be viewed recent retrenchments and the closure of major industries discussed above. Where LGA boundaries coincide with higher uninhabited land the boundaries are smoothed and no boundary was extended beyond the limit of settlement.

Although the method employed masks the complex mosaic of micro-regional marginality, it nevertheless reveals a meaningful macro-regional contrast between the north and the south. The rich agricultural lowlands of the central north are bounded by extensive upland and mountain regions where rates of social marginality are generally high. The western highland belt extends from Bothwell on the central plateau through Deloraine to encompass much of the north-western basalt plateau, which rises from the coast inland beyond the limit of settlement. Significantly, social marginality is not pronounced in the highly productive, large-scale farming region of the far north-west around Smithton, nor in the north-eastern basalt basin around Scottsdale where intensive innovative farming prospers. By contrast, southern marginalized regions are confined to five comparatively small but distinctive coastal environments, while farming areas near Hobart and the extensive grazing country of the upper Derwent valley

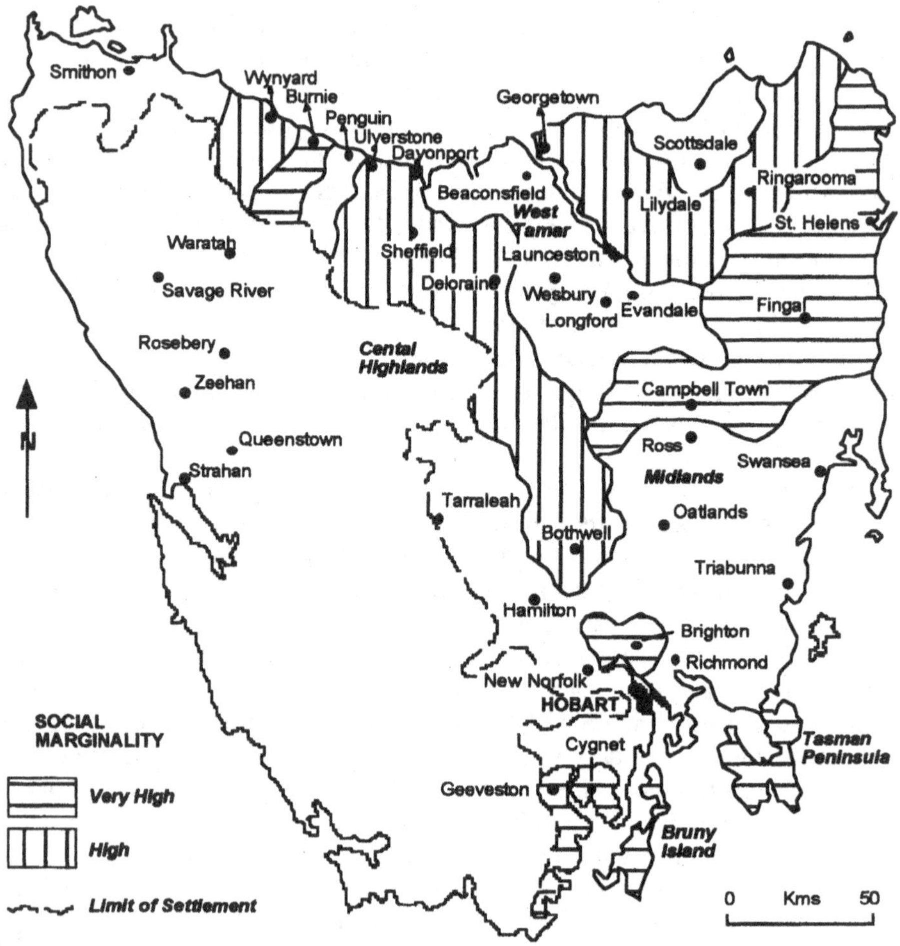

Figure 21.1 Macroregions of social marginality in Tasmania, 1991

Source: Australian Bureau of Statistics, 1991 Census: Local Government Areas: Tasmania, Catalogue No. 2790.6

north-west of Hamilton, the Midlands, and the east coast display more favourable social conditions. The western mining centres, despite population decline and out-migration, have scant social marginality.

Four types of socially marginal communities may be distinguished, though within a given locality two or more may be present and small pockets of marginality are scattered through much of the high country, especially on its western margins. Firstly, casualties from economic reform tend to be located not only within the stricken industrial centres but also in nearby rural areas of small farms from which so many industrial workers commute. Foremost among these areas are the north-western basalt plateau tributary to the industrial port towns of Burnie and Devonport, the former orcharding hill country around Lilydale tributary to George Town and Launceston, Tasmania's second city, and another former orcharding hill region around Cygnet. Secondly, traditional marginality, evident from persistent unemployment, out-migration, and poor farming, typifies most remote peripheral areas, notably the higher inland margins of the settled land in the north-west, the far north-east, the Fingal valley, the central Midlands around Campbell Town, and the far southern coastlands south of Geeveston. Thirdly, public housing policy has created urban communities with very high rates of social marginality, most notable being the Bridgewater and Gagebrook estates located north of the Hobart metropolitan area in the Brighton Municipality. They house large numbers of low-income commuters and their families, and by almost any social measure have the worst performance of any region in the State. Fourthly, former urban residents who have opted for a rural lifestyle, including many from mainland cities, tend to occupy smallholdings within commuting distance of the major towns and cities but are also to be found throughout the periphery including the southern coastal regions of Cygnet, Bruny Island, and the Tasman peninsula. While most would seem to be fairly affluent, others eke out a precarious existence little better than subsistence.

Community dislocation resulting from closures and downsizing cause much intrastate and interstate migration. Each year from 1991 to 1996 Tasmania experienced a net out-migration, and in 1996 the population growth rate fell to zero. Although Tasmania performs the worst of any State on almost all-economic and demographic criteria, it has the highest expenditure per capita on education, and graduates are prominent among job seekers leaving the island. The State also has the highest proportion of its population receiving social welfare payments, no less than 27 per cent in June 1996. Over the decade 1986-96 the number of recipients grew by one-third, attributable only in part to rising unemployment. Other factors were an increased range of family programs and an ageing population. In early 1997 the Tasmanian Council of Social Service stated that more than one-tenth of the State's population lived below the poverty line (The Mercury, Hobart, 4 February 1997, p. 3).

Conclusion

Tasmania, which has lagged behind other Australian States in economic growth throughout this century, is currently suffering acutely from industrial restructuring and increased competition, accentuating an already high incidence of social marginality. The suffering has been aggravated not only by the generally slow pace of reform, which contrasts sharply with New Zealand's highly successful, rapid transformation, but also by uncoordinated deregulation and the lack of a coherent national industry policy. Trade liberalization in advance of labour market reform, which is only just starting, and of transport and port reform, still yet to come, has placed much of the island's – and the nation's – industrial base at risk. The reformers have assumed that undesirable consequences of reform would be offset through the tax/transfer system, which is a more efficient and effective social mechanism than regulation. But the drive for greater efficiency through corporatization and privatization has led to smaller government, shrinking public sectors, reduced budget deficits, and low inflation at the expense of employment growth and social justice. Australia urgently needs not only to accelerate and co-ordinate economic reform but also to overhaul its Federal-State financial relations and taxation system (Scott, 1996b, pp. 215-218), so that Federal and State Governments are enabled more effectively to facilitate economic growth and to provide essential social infrastructure and welfare support. Meanwhile, more insight needs to be gleaned on the microregional patterns of communities disadvantaged and in some cases disaffected by the reform process.

References

Australia (1993), *National Competition Policy: Report by the Independent Committee of Inquiry*, Australian Government Publishing Service: Canberra.

Behrens, N. (1995), *The True Cost of Employment*, Tasmania Chamber of Commerce and Industry: Hobart.

Madden, J.R. (1995), *The Impact of Implementing the Hilmer Report on the National and State Economies*, The University of Tasmania Centre for Regional Economic Analysis: Hobart.

Porter, M.E. (1990), *The Competitive Advantage of Nations*, Macmillan: London.

Scott, P. (1994), 'Global Economic Restructuring, National Economic Reform, and Regional Marginalisation: A Tasmanian Perspective', in Chang, C.D., Jou, S., and Lu, Y. (eds.), *Marginality and Development Issues in Marginal Regions*, pp. 163-177, .National Taiwan University: Taipei.

Scott, P. (1996a), 'Local Government Restructuring in Tasmania: Community Response and Attitudes to Development', in Singh, R.B. and Majoral, R. (eds.), *Development Issues in Marginal Regions: Processes, Technological Developments and Societal Reorganizations*, pp. 265-275, Oxford and IBH Publishing: New Dehli.

Scott, P. (1996b), 'Development Strategy and Economic Growth in Tasmania', in Furlani de Civit, E., Pedone, C., and Soria, N.D. (eds.), *Development Issues in Marginal Regions II: Policies and Strategies*, pp. 207-221, Universidad Nacional de Cuyo: Mendoza.

Part four

Conclusions

22 Synthesis and conclusions

HEIKKI JUSSILA, ROSER MAJORAL AND
CHRIS C. MUTAMBIRWA

This book about 'Marginality in space – past, present and future' has discussed and elaborated on the theme corresponding to the first year of the research program of the IGU Commission on Dynamics in Marginal and Critical Regions. The book is ordered in three main parts. Each of which concentrates on a special aspect of the theme.

The first part of the book elaborates the theoretical and methodological approaches towards the issue of marginalization in space, and the five chapters are based on research that has been going on in previous years. While the chapters included in this first part contain mainly theoretical and methodological aspects, other chapters of the book do take up models and techniques for measuring and describing different kinds of marginality.

The chapter written by Sommers *et al.* aims to typify socio-economic marginality. This work compares the images of marginalization in the North and the South. According to their research socio-economic marginality is a condition of socio-spatial structure and process in which components of society and space in a territorial unit are observed to lag behind an expected level of performance in economic well-being compared with the average condition of the territory as a whole.

In the 'southern' context, the spatial models are more explanatory than applicable by nature, but the discussion reveals that they can be used at least to predicting potential future scenarios or routes of development if local conditions are known. The discussion regarding land use systems, however, shows that these systems are significantly different in the 'southern' context and consequently differ markedly from those of the developed 'world' and from the 'classical' models. In the chapter by Grossman *et al.*, a clear deviation from the 'normal' von Thünen models is observed. The familiar von Thünen 'rings' are not clearly defined and agriculture can be encountered even in the city centre.

When moving to the 'northern' areas the approach towards the issue of 'how to define marginality' takes a different path. The discussion put forward by Pelc in his chapter aims to look at marginality within a nation state by using some very general and at the same time typical parameters to 'measure' the extent of marginality. His approach via the 'illiteracy in Slovenia', however, places marginality spatially on the edges of the country. The approach according to him, does not confirm the real existence of marginal regions, but it does indicate that marginality – if defined as social – does exist in the country, which in economical and political contexts may not be regarded as marginal.

The approach taken by Tykkyläinen is to assess the spatio-economic development in Russia, which is and will be a spatially uneven, selective process. The findings of this research suggest that economic growth takes place in only a few enterprises, which are located in conducive pockets of development linked to advanced technology, capital, business practices and markets. One of the conclusions in the chapter by Tykkyläinen is that Russian industrial communities are on the way to social fragmentation rather than moving towards increasing cohesion. Due to this fragmentation process, it is evident that current development will lead to socio-spatial marginalization.

The qualitative approaches taken up by, e.g., Furlani *et al.* and Capella and Font and the socio-economic point of view taken up by others (e.g., Andersson *et al*., Lonsdale and Archer, Muilu *et al.*, and Potts and Mutambirwa) give attention to the globalization effects of economic development that, not only alter marginality situations, either by stressing or weakening them, but by also inducing a tendency to uniformity not inconsistent with local diversity. Thus, an occasion is perceived for the alleviation of marginality without loss of cultural identity, all of which makes a plurality of viewpoints for its understanding not only possible but also necessary. The definitions of these marginality situations result from the coincidences found in the perceptions of historians, sociologists, economists, and geographers on the incidence of such processes upon a country's territory and society.

The qualitative theoretical approach proposed by Furlani *et al.* is a refreshing one. They have chosen to analyze marginality through literature searches. Consequently, the authors they have chosen for this purpose are writers of essays concerned with Latin-American and national reality. The choice of this literary genre, very common in Spanish-America, and especially in Argentina during the nineteenth and twentieth century, is not fortuitous. Indeed, it is a current form for the interpretation of the political and social problems that have afflicted the Spanish-American scene. In them, the appeal to history as a tool to find the key to the problem in question is very common. Finally, the essay exerts, either in an intended or in a suggestive way, a strong evaluative and persuasive pressure upon the reader.

In the second part, we can distinguish between papers that approach marginality from a cultural, social and/or economic point of view. Capella and Font analyze how cultural links play an important role in the development dynamics of an area south of Catalonia (Spain). On the other hand Meir, in his studies on nomads in Israel speaks about the tension between the modern society represented by the state and the cultural and land tenure problems existing currently. The conflicts have also a political dimension in Israel since the Bedouins now use their cultural heritage for developing their own 'marginal political power', as Meir calls it.

The discussion by Mehretu and Mutambirwa about the effects of the colonial time on Sub-Saharan Africa and Zimbabwe in particular shows that there is a 'rocky road' ahead. In Zimbabwe, for instance, the communal lands were very different from those of commercial lands in respect to the socio-economic relations of production. There was very little commodifiation of production in the communal lands; few of them were incorporated in the commercial-land economy. At present, the disparity between the commercial and communal lands in regional development is not only severe but also qualitatively and quantitatively divergent. Communal lands are spatially disintegrated with many discontinuous patches throughout the country and without any significant infrastructure.

In connection with land property and tenure problems, Petagna analyses the social polarization represented by the extremes of the social spectrum in the Argentinean Pampa following the colonization. The analysis is based on the case of the rich landed aristocracy and the working class depending on sharecropping and on the case of the process when most of the tenants became owners.

Lonsdale and Archer taking the example from the United States approach marginality by using various demographic features, like net migration or natural rate of growth, common to most marginal regions, which directly reflect the social and economic 'health' of an area and thus the degree of marginality. In their conclusion, they show clearly that, there should be little doubt about the utility of demographic data. Measures such as population loss, migration rates, people in poverty, etc., tell us a great deal about these places and provide valuable insights into the problems that exist there. However, they do 'warn' that when it comes to delimiting marginal areas, one must proceed with considerable caution. The same demographic aspects underlie the chapter by Majoral and Sánchez-Aguilera about Catalonia.

Potts and Mutambirwa look at migration from the point of view of an individual, when discussing the rural-based migrants who have recently come to live in Harare. In their discussion about the changes in economic and social policy, the underlying fact is that without the 'safety-net' provided by the rural areas the economic hardships could be much worse. Zanamwe further takes the case of the elderly in Zimbabwe as an indicator of social marginality.

Muilu *et al.* present in their chapter the extent of unemployment as a sign of social exclusion in Finland. They stress that especially long-term unemployment leads to degeneration in skills and knowledge of the human resources. From the point of view of the society this leads to a 'wasting' of resources as part of the labour-force is not used. Their approach is to some extent similar to that of Pelc as they also aim at developing a 'measure' for marginality. Illiteracy is also one of the indices that Fernandes and Delgado Cravidão use for the ex-Portuguese colony Sao Tomé and Príncipe, when they discuss the possibilities of its economic and social development.

The third part of the book looks at the 'regional development and policies applied'. This part concentrates on the issues for alleviating marginality, be it cultural, social or economic by nature. The chapter starts with two comparative studies, i.e., Jussila and Andreoli and Andersson *et al.*, and continues towards more general aspects of regional development and policy.

The chapter by Andreoli and Jussila is a comparison between two developed European countries, Finland and Italy, and the marginal regions within them. They use the current regional policy approaches that European Union countries emphasize of self-reliance and self-help. They show that in the European peripheries, the use of information technology is becoming one tool for overcoming peripherality problems. Peripheral European regions are also looking for 'regional and local difference' for surviving in the increased competition between regions and firms and, for this reason, the development projects that aim at building connections and networks between different areas have become quite popular.

The chapter by Andersson *et al.* takes a different route for comparison. They use two areas that have a completely different culture and position in the continuum of modernization. Their examples are from India and Sweden. In their conclusion they stress that the fates of the respective places and areas will depend much on the attitudes, on the imaginativeness and strategy of policy makers and on the courage and recklessness of anyone involved in the actual small and large scale turns of (economic) development. This puts the role of the surrounding society (the state) and indeed also currently globalization (world economy) into the picture.

The role of state in regional and socio-economic development is put forward in the chapter by Persson. He looks at the ways state intervention in Sweden is used to counteract both 'marcromarginality' and 'micro-marginality'. He concludes that while the process of equalization of socio-economic conditions continues at the county level, the variation increases at the microregional level. The processes of economic liberalization lead to new paths of development. Consequently, there is an increasing variation in growth rates within rural regions, which can no longer be explained by structural factors alone such as density of population, distance to markets and supply of resources. It seems that less tangible development factors play an increasing role in stimulating growth.

These same processes of development and growth imbalances are also present in the study by Majoral and Sánchez-Aguilera. The process of redistribution engendered by the Catalan Government, together with local initiatives, are helping to rid the territory of evident imbalances, though it has not been entirely successful. In contrast to Tykkyläinen who speaks about the 'pockets of development', Majoral and Sánchez-Aguilera discuss the 'pockets of marginality', i.e., small areas that have been 'forgotten' and consequently left behind. This study shows that marginality is not a 'static' phenomenon, but is 'moving' in time and space.

The discussion dealing with the general economic disparities and polarities in Zimbabwe is taken up by Mehretu and Mutambirwa, when they discuss the development occurring in a polarized space. Dahl and Tevera contribute with an example of this polarized development pattern, by presenting the case of Binga District in the Zambezi Valley. In this region, the challenge for government is to promote development so that the existing labour reservoir can be transformed into a vibrant region that is linked positively with the rest of the national economy.

The most general aspect of regional development is taken up by Fernandes and Delgado Cravidão who look at the economic integration taking place in the world economy and place the former Portuguese colony São Tome and Príncipe into this context. According to them, the development model for São Tomé and Príncipe should be considered within the African reality, but under the general World economic context (GATT and World Trade Organization agreements). Countries are interconnected in the world development model and, consequently, isolating territories is not a viable path for development in the long term. The tendency towards internationalization is currently the driving force and is unavoidable.

The chapter by Scott looks at the effects of changes in economic and regional policy in Australia and uses the State of Tasmania as an example. Currently, in sharp contrast to the macro-policy, that disregard differential regional impacts, national competition policy, the cornerstone of microeconomic reform along with reforming the workplace, takes account the varying impacts among the States and Territories. The policy of economic liberalization has brought about significant changes in the public sector economy of Tasmania. In order to 'measure' the effects of the economic reform of Australia Scott has developed an index for this purpose. However, more insight needs to be gleaned into the microregional patterns of disadvantaged communities as well as those disaffected by the reform process.

All the different chapters of this book reflect the common concern about globalization and its effects on the 'small communities' of the world which, inspite of cultural and social differences, are the cornerstones of our civilization. This globalization is in some ways, an assimilation process, which makes it more difficult to understand marginality in a macro sense. This is the reason for the increasing interest in 'micromarginality' or 'pockets of marginality' as well as the 'pockets of development' in various peripheries of the world.